A Wilderness of Miseries

JOHN E.
FERLING

A Wilderness of Miseries

WAR and WARRIORS in EARLY AMERICA

Contributions in Military History, Number 22

GP

GREENWOOD PRESS
WESTPORT, CONNECTICUT • LONDON, ENGLAND

Library of Congress Cataloging in Publication Data

Ferling, John E
  A wilderness of miseries.

(Contributions in military history; no. 22 ISSN 0084-9251)
  Bibliography: p.
  Includes index.
  1. United States—History, Military—To 1900.
2. Indians of North America—Wars—1600-1750.
I. Title. II. Series.
E181.F44   301.16'334'0973   79-8951
ISBN 0-313-22093-X

E
181
.F44

Library of Congress Catalog Card Number: 79-8951
ISBN: 0-313-22093-X
ISSN: 0084-9251

First published in 1980

Greenwood Press
A division of Congressional Information Service, Inc.
88 Post Road West, Westport, Connecticut 06881

Printed in the United States of America

10 9 8 7 6 5 4 3 2 1

To
Elizabeth Cometti and William D. Barns
Teachers and Friends

Contents

Illustrations

Acknowledgments

I am indebted to several persons who have assisted in the completion of this study. The Learning Resources Committee of West Georgia College, chaired by E. M. Blue, generously provided a research grant. Albert S. Hanser offered helpful suggestions for investigating the warfare of eighteenth-century Europe, and, when possible, he endeavored to provide a teaching schedule conducive to research and writing activities. Robert Calhoon offered encouragement for the study, as well as insightful suggestions for exploring the partisan warfare during the War for Independence.

A small portion of Chapter 6 originally was published in a substantially similar manner in *The Historian,* vol. 50 (May 1978). I am grateful to the editors of that journal for their kind permission to reuse portions of that article.

Several members of the library at West Georgia College responded unflaggingly to my requests for assistance and for the procurement of research materials. In particular, I am grateful for the help I received from Susan Smith, Jean Cooksey, Jan Ruskell, Sally Rigg, Kathleen Hunt, Betty Jobson, Anne Chowns, and Jackie Davis.

Introduction

Research for this study began six years ago, in the aftermath of the turbulent 1960s. It seemed manifest then—and equally true today, though perhaps more veiled—that America's recurrent experience with war had made a significant imprint on this country. Yet, historians had seemed to take little notice of warfare in the early, formative years of Anglo-American society. With a few notable exceptions, when early military history was treated at all, the studies were, as Walter Millis once complained, "overwhelmingly concerned with battle tactics and strategy."[1] Too often, moreover, novelist James Jones' complaint about scholarly accounts of World War II could have been applied to the studies of earlier wars. Historians had seen war "from the viewpoint of the upper class commanders," Jones exclaimed, and too often history appeared to have been "written by the upper class for the upper class."[2]

Fortunately, scholarly interests seem to be changing. What Professor Richard Kohn has called a "new military history" recently has begun to appear. Although yet in its "professional adolescence," according to Kohn, this new approach is concerned with how war shapes society and, in turn, how war is shaped by society. It is an attempt by historians to show that "there is an intimate, sometimes direct and sometimes subtle, relationship between military affairs and the complex web of a nation's history."[3]

What follows, I hope, will be seen as an example of "the new history" of warfare. No attempt has been made to write a definitive or encyclopedic history of America's early warfare. Rather, the study is designed to bring together some of the perceptive new lines of inquiry and conclusions of historians in this field and, in addition, to suggest alterations and emendations to these insights when appropriate. Moreover, through original research, the study endeavors to break new ground. The end result, hopefully, will show how early Americans, collectively and individually, experienced war, what they thought of war, and what impact war had on the world in which they lived.

The study is divided into two parts. The first part deals with the nature of war in early America. It endeavors to compare conflict in America with contemporary European warfare, to investigate native American fighting methods and compare them to those of the settlers and the European professional armies, and to

---

1. Walter Millis, *Arms and Men* (New York, 1956), pp. 5–6.

2. James Jones, *WWII* (New York, 1975), pp. 70–71.

3. Richard H. Kohn, "War as Revolution and Social Process," *Reviews in American History* 5 (March 1977), p. 57.

compare the nature of fighting between Europeans with that between Europeans and Indians.

The second part scrutinizes the colonial experience of warfare. The study attempts to show how the conflict that had become endemic to the colonists affected their attitudes toward war and warriors. Chapter 3 treats the colonists' attitudes concerning the justification of war and their views toward soldierly virtues. Two chapters investigate how men experienced war. Chapter 4 treats the soldiers themselves; an attempt is made to show why some men wanted to become soldiers, what they regarded as their proper roles as warriors, how they lived, and how they might have felt and acted under combat conditions. Chapter 5, unlike the other chapters, is a microcosmic study of two leaders who played a significant role in helping to produce a war, and seeks to show how each man reacted to the bloodshed for which he felt somewhat responsible. The final chapter attempts to show how this violent heritage, and the intellectual baggage of such a milieu, played a role in the seminal events of late eighteenth-century America.

By way of explanation, perhaps this is the appropriate place to indicate why I have ignored naval warfare in early America. First, relatively few Americans experienced naval encounters until the American Revolutionary era, and I hoped to draw some conclusions about war in the nearly two centuries preceding that rebellion. In addition, only a small portion of the civilian population—principally the few Americans who lived in coastal villages and cities, as well as the families of the sailors—directly experienced any reverberations of naval warfare.

Abbreviations

Following the initial citation, these abbreviations are used in the footnotes and bibliography:

Adams D&A	—	Adams Diary and Autobiography
Adams FC	—	Adams Family Correspondence
AHR	—	American Historical Review
AJIL	—	American Journal of International Law
AQ	—	American Quarterly
CHR	—	Canadian Historical Review
CHS	—	Connecticut Historical Society
CSM	—	Colonial Society of Massachusetts
GHQ	—	Georgia Historical Quarterly
HSD	—	Historical Society of Delaware
MA	—	Military Affairs
MHS	—	Massachusetts Historical Society
MVHR	—	Mississippi Valley Historical Review
NEQ	—	New England Quarterly
NYHS	—	New York Historical Society
PMHB	—	Pennsylvania Magazine of History and Biography
PP	—	Past & Present
VMHB	—	Virginia Magazine of History and Biography
WMQ	—	William and Mary Quarterly

Part One

The Nature of American War

This Country was from the Beginning a Colony of Soldiers. (Governor Thomas Pownall, 1757)

When the sword is once drawn, the passions of men observe no bounds of moderation. (Alexander Hamilton, 1788)

It is the object only of war that makes it honorable. (Thomas Paine, 1776)

We are reluctant to admit that essentially war is the business of killing, though that is the simplest truth in the book. (S.L.A. Marshall, 1964)

Warfare was neither unanticipated by nor uncommon to the Europeans who settled in seventeenth-century America. "Your enemies can be but of two sortes, strangers and natives," the earliest planters of Virginia were warned by those who bankrolled the venture from London.

They were correct, of course. By late in the century a series of conflicts betweeen Europeans and their colonial allies were recurring spasmodically. Often simultaneously, but sometimes sandwiched between these Old World wars, there was a savage ebullition of bloodletting between native Americans and the European settlers.

Although warfare was anticipated by the settlers, and though hostilities were common in America, in many ways conflict was unlike the war that stalked Europe. Indeed, just as the London "adventurers" predicted that there could be but two enemies, they might have forecast that there could be two kinds of warfare in colonial America: European war, transported to America and altered subsequently by the New World environment; and the mercilessly unrestrained conflict with the natives, a strain of combat for which only the professional soldier of the age had any preparation.

Chapter 1

War and Society

To get our bread with the perill of our lives

The small fleet of three ships slowly drifted northward. A warm mid-spring breeze nudged the vessels forward, the glistening sun bouncing myriad patterns off the calm waters. About one hundred men and boys, the prospective settlers of the London Company's first colony in Virginia, strained to see the shorelines and the forests of this land that would be their new home.

Although apprehensive of what awaited them ashore, most were jubilant that the long voyage finally was ending. The expedition had departed England four months earlier, in December 1606, pursuing a route quite familiar to English mariners. Before England was even out of sight, however, stormy seas marooned the voyagers off the coast of Kent for nearly thirty days. By early February Captain Christopher Newport, a former privateer and the commander of the fleet, ordered the vessels to cast off. The crafts sped to the Canaries, where they paused shortly for repairs and replenishment of supplies.

The Atlantic crossing took six weeks and was marred by one violent storm. The fleet stopped at several points in the West Indies late in March to secure additional provisions. The natives encountered in these isles were peaceful, and bargains were struck for vegetables and fruit. The men relaxed, too, plunging into warm springs, though the baths had to be enjoyed in shifts, since, "fearing wee should be assaulted by the *Indians*," some men were always posted as sentinels. After two idyllic weeks the fleet sailed again, but the water acquired in the Indies was so sulphurous that still another stop was required. This final pause came at Mona, an island between Puerto Rico and Hispanola, where, in addition to water, search parties secured fresh meat and eggs. On April 10, Newport ordered the voyagers to raise anchor for the final leg of the journey.

The trip generally was uneventful for experienced mariners, but it had not been terribly pleasant for those men unaccustomed to the sea. Some had been overcome instantly by sea sickness; being removed from the sight of land for weeks unnerved many of the heartiest landlubbers. All were uneasy during the severe storm. Even the occasional choppy seas and minor turbulence provoked anxiety among some of the planters. At times the boiling sun of near equatorial waters scorched and parched the migrants. The diet of biscuit, salt pork, codfish, and ale, though adequate, quickly had become monotonous. As the journey lengthened, anxious, cramped, impatient men found their nerves frayed. Minor incidents easily flared into bitter quarrels.

At first, the voyage north from Mona was tranquil. Then still another storm arose, pushing the ships more rapidly than even Captain Newport had reckoned. Again the sea was calm. Most believed land was still a few days away when, suddenly, men were roused from their sleep at four in the morning on April 21 by shouts announcing the sighting of land. Cries of "the Land of Virginia" reverberated through the three vessels. As dawn broke, the Chesapeake Bay stood yawning before the sailing craft.

Captain Newport wasted little time. He directed the fleet to a point just west of Cape Henry, where the anchors splashed down. By late morning Newport and about twenty others, each garbed in the bulky armor of European soldiery and each carrying a flintlock musket and a sword, descended into small boats and rowed ashore. The party landed unmolested, but Newport ordered them to stay together. None knew what to expect of the Indians who undoubtedly were nearby. None trusted the natives.

The reconnaissance party clamored ashore, the armor and shields clanking in a great racket, the men panting as they floundered through the silt. Cautiously, they disappeared into the foliage. They inspected the trees and grasslands, and made mental notes of the variety of game spotted. When a freshwater creek was discovered, each man, sweaty and thirsty from apprehension and exertion, plunged forward for great gulps of water. The party had labored for nearly eight hours without event and had found "nothing worth the speaking of."

Emboldened, Newport continued to probe, into the early evening hours. By now most of the men were relaxed. No Indians had been encountered; no difficulties were anticipated now in this region. About sunset the men paused to eat and rest. It felt good to be on land again, and there was something tantalizing about searching a wilderness region on which no other European had set foot. Following the meal the men explored again, until Newport, aware that his commanders on the ship would fear some ill event had befallen them, ordered the reconnoiterers to prepare to return to their vessel. Equipment was gathered and the men trudged back toward their landing craft.

Suddenly, with a whoop, Indians sprang from the brush firing arrows into the party. A few of the natives, wielding tomahawks, charged. Some of the startled men discharged their muskets, but the Indians were not frightened. They continued to fire until their arrows were spent. Then they retreated. One solider had been hit twice and had to be carried. Another was wounded in both hands; his baggage had to be carried by others. Newport hurriedly moved his men to the shore, directing a portion of the party to set up a defensive perimeter while the remainder loaded the craft. Then all clamored aboard and hurriedly rowed for safety.

In their first hours ashore, in England's first permanent colony, warfare had begun.[1]

The Europeans whom the Indians attacked that balmy evening on the Chesapeake were not strangers to war. Indeed, some were skilled warriors trained in the contemporary manner of European war. Their understanding of war had evolved from centuries of western martial experiences. It is essential to understand this in order to grasp the tactics and ideals that prevailed at the time America was setted by Englishmen.

The Greeks of antiquity were the earliest major western culture to be plagued by frequent wars. The natural frontiers of Greece which afforded some protection from foreign foes also divided these peoples into small states that warred with willful truculence. In their initial phases these Greek states attempted to settle their differences by designating limited numbers of strongmen to duel individually. Later, formal armies, almost solely comprised of infantrymen, emerged. Service was restricted to society's elite. Accompanied by their slaves, the infantrymen, or hoplites, of the contending armies marched toward one another in phalanx formations. The ensuing battle was swift and confused, and generalship ceased once the chaos of the battle commenced. The war normally terminated with that one engagement, the encounter ending when one infantry broke and fled the field.

The Asiatic invasions of Greece that began in the fifth century B.C. altered Greek military tactics. Learning from their new foes, the Greeks introduced slingers, archers, dart throwers, charioteers, and cavalry to their armies. Greek armies sometimes used chemical fire bombs, made of sulphur, pitch, niter, oil, and quicklime, as well as a powerful gas derived from sulphur fumes. This transformation of the armies, as well as the increasing utilization of lighter weapons and armor, introduced an element of mobility that had not existed previously in Western warfare. By the following century the Greeks had become aggressive warriors. In 334 B.C. Alexander invaded Asia Minor with an army of forty thousand, a force that included, in addition to these innovations, an artillery and engineering corps, as well as medical personnel.[2]

1. The best general accounts of the voyage and the earliest exploration can be found in George Percy, *Observations gathered out of a Discourse* . . . in Edward Arber, ed., *Travels and Works of Captain John Smith* . . . , 2 vols. (New York, n.d.), vol. I, p. 5. See also Philip L. Barbour, *The Three Worlds of Captain John Smith* (Boston, 1964), pp. 109–23.

2. Lynn Montross, *War Through the Ages* (New York, 1960), pp. 3–42; David H. Zook and Robin Higham, *A Short History of Warfare* (New York, 1966), pp. 33–43; Hans Delbrück, *History of the Art of War, Antiquity* (Westport, Conn., 1975), pp. 123–237; Bernard and Fawn Brodie, *From Crossbow to H-Bomb* (Bloomington, Ind., 1973), pp. 14–22; F. E. Adcock, *The Greek and Macedonian Art of War* (Berkeley, Calif., 1967), pp. 1–28, 47–63, 82–97; Eugene S. McCarney, *Warfare by Land and Sea* (New York, 1963), pp. 25–86.

While Alexander was snatching the territories of his eastern neighbors, the Romans were making their earliest overtures to expansion. Initially, the Romans were less than fully successful. A humiliating defeat at the hands of the Samnites two years after Alexander's death prompted Rome to alter its tactics. The Roman legion, perhaps the most formidable army in antiquity, was formed. Typically, the legion entered battle in a formation consisting of three parallel lines, the *hastati,* was composed of young veterans, the *principes,* highly experienced veterans, and *triarii* and *velites,* were half older veterans and half younger recruits. All men between the ages of seventeen and sixty years who held Roman citizenship were eligible for service, although only the most fit were inducted; those selected served for the greater part of their adult lives. Persistent domestic turbulence in the second century B.C. occasioned a restructuring of the legion. Conscription was instituted to allow the proletariat and even slaves and aliens to serve. Because so much booty was available for the usually victorious legionnaires, most recruits chose to serve for life; officers were frequently politicians who utilized conquest as a steppingstone to power. After more than a century of expansion, however, Rome again reformed its army. Emperor Augustus proclaimed the fulfillment of the empire. Henceforth, Rome utilized a volunteer army as a defensive force to implement the *Pax Romana,* the maintenance of the natural frontiers of the vast empire. The composition of the army likewise changed. Since additional mobility was required to resist the repeated influx of mounted barbarian invaders, the cavalry eventually grew to nearly one-quarter of the legion.[3]

Warfare, like most other aspects of society in the West, underwent considerable change following the demise of the Roman Empire. War now affected the daily lives of the inhabitants almost to the same degree as religion and agriculture. Combat returned to the primitive methods that had predominated centuries earlier. With the deterioration of commerce and the unavailability of money, troops increasingly were compelled to provide their own equipment. Charlemagne, for instance, made military service mandatory for property owners; those who owned small tracts of land were required to act in concert to provide a quota of armed men when the ruler so ordered. The decline of Roman roads led to the replacement of the foot soldier by the armored knight. Equipped primarily with lances and axes, and adorned with heavy armor or mailed garments, these mounted troops became the backbone of the medieval military forces. Tactical maneuvers and concerted generalship often were nonexistent once an engagement had commenced; an exception was the new science of siege warfare that developed following the increased fortification of vulnerable cities and properties in the ninth century.

    3. Montross, *War,* pp. 43–88; Zook and Higham, *History of Warfare,* pp. 45–56; G. R. Watson, *The Roman Soldier* (Ithaca, N.Y., 1969), pp. 31–125; Graham Webster, *The Roman Imperial Army* (New York, 1969), pp. 107–65; Delbrück, *History of the Art of War,* pp. 393–428, 508–14.

By the thirteenth century, largely because of an absence of capital, European warfare consisted primarily of private encounters waged by barons. Often battles were prearranged, since the feudal warrior could be compelled to serve only forty days a year, and English vassals could not be made to serve abroad. The cavalry, generally composed of feudal knights weighted down with body armor and equipped with the sword and the crossbow—a cumbersome weapon that discharged metal bolts capable of piercing armor—became even more important in the scheme of war. The foot soldier still existed, but he was almost certainly a peasant and he was utilized primarily in siegecraft operations or as an orderly.[4]

In the fourteenth and fifteenth centuries there were considerable military changes. Strategists were amazed when British cavalry and infantry, the latter equipped with the longbow, won several shocking victories over the French cavalry. The Swiss, meanwhile, achieved equal success over cavalry forces by resurrecting the infantry and the tactics of antiquity. Swiss footmen, armed with pikes, missile weapons, and the halberd, an eighteen-foot iron pike, attacked their enemy with the ancient phalanx formation.

The longbow was the first serious threat to the supremacy of the mounted knight. This new weapon, which could be fired five times as frequently as the crossbow, discharged a thirty-seven-inch arrow capable of penetrating chain mail and armor; it could kill a horse at two hundred yards.

The appearance of gunpowder completed the transition. By the late fifteenth century both artillery pieces and handguns were commonplace accoutrements of the soldier; professional infantry had replaced cavalry as the preeminent component of armed forces; and, as weapons that could pierce armor were developed, protective tactics were replaced by the strategy of mobility. Changes in warfare were also related to the changed economic face of Europe. The rising bourgeoisie, which dominated the new urban areas, frequently hired mercenaries to increase or protect commerce. Eventually many cities created professional armies to rid themselves of these mercenaries.[5]

During the sixteenth and early seventeenth centuries the use of crossbows and massed columns of pike gave way to balanced forces of cavalry, infantry, and artillery. The cavalry survived by discarding its armor and adding pistols to its normal complement of lances and sabers. Infantrymen, armed with muskets and later with flintlocks, formed into several ranks, the forward lines firing while

---

4. C. W. C. Oman, *The Art of War in the Middle Ages* (Ithaca, N.Y., 1953), pp. v, 57–72, 130; Montross, *War*, pp. 91–103, 132–43, 158–72; Zook and Higham, *History of Warfare*, pp. 57–73.

5. Oman, *Art of War*, pp. 116–20; Montross, *War*, pp. 158–214; M. G. A. Vail, "New Techniques and Old Ideals: The Impact of Artillery on War and Chivalry at the End of the Hundred Years War," in C. T. Almands, ed., *War, Literature and Politics in the Late Middle Ages* (New York, 1976), pp. 57–72; Brodie and Brodie, *Crossbow to H-Bomb*, pp. 37–8, 44–61; Tom Wintringham, *The Story of Weapons and Tactics* (Boston, 1943), pp. 127–34; Alfred Vagts, *A History of Militarism* (New York, 1959), pp. 41–48.

the rear lines reloaded their spent weapons. The pikeman began to disappear, one historian noted, when it was realized that "he needed the protection of the musketeer more than the musketeer needed his." Field artillery was used both in the open field and in sieges, although it was neither terribly reliable nor efficient; most such guns could fire orange-size missiles more than twenty-five hundred yards, but each weapon could be fired only about one hundred times per day.

During this era soldiers were first trained with war games, horsemen routinely used firearms, and troops were equipped with telescopes, time-fuse weapons, bayonets, and hand grenades. According to Andre Corvisier, this was the era of the "warrior mentality," a time when soldiers were correctly perceived as more brutish and remorseless than courageous. Soldiers were characterized by "wild and ruffianly conduct, and . . . violent impulsiveness." Whereas gentlemen were popularly thought to be seeking personal glory, soldiers were believed to be interested only in personal profit.

This was also an era in which war remained commonplace. In the seventeenth century there were only seven years during which no war existed between European states, and many major powers were at war nearly half the century. What did not change was the brutal nature of warfare. During the Thirty Years' War perhaps twenty thousand Swiss towns and villages were destroyed, and 7,500,000 Germans—one-third of the population—perished. In this and other wars, entire cities were besieged as castles had once been attacked. The new weaponry and tactics, the destruction of food supplies, and a high incidence of disease, exacerbated by the primitive state of medicine, combined to accelerate war-related suffering to its greatest intensity since the last days of the western Roman Empire.[6]

As war in Europe was transformed and grew even more grisly, the English prepared for the colonization of America with the expectation of hostilities. No one was certain what course relations with the aborigines might take, but most planners cautioned that the settlers should be prepared for conflict. Richard Hakluyt, the prolific chronicler of exploratory ventures and an intriguer in Queen Elizabeth's court, thought the native Americans would be "gentle and tractable," but if they resisted English preemption the colonists must be prepared to "proceed with extremitie, conquer, fortifie" the new settlements. Although no one

6. J. R. Hale, "Armies, Navies, and the Art of War," in G. R. Elton, ed., *The Reformation, 1520–1559*, 2 vols. (Cambridge, 1958), vol. II, pp. 481–503; J. R. Hale, "Sixteenth Century Explanations of War and Violence," *Past & Present* 51 (May 1971), pp. 3–4; Theodore Rapp, *War in the Modern World* (Durham, N.C., 1959), pp. 9–28; Montross, *War*, pp. 262–346; Zook and Higham, *History of Warfare*, pp. 89–100; Andre Corvisier, *Armies and Societies in Europe, 1474–1789* (Bloomington, Ind., 1979), pp. 183–84; G. N. Clark, *War and Society in the Seventeenth Century* (Cambridge, 1958), pp. 98–113.

knew what to expect of the Indians, difficulties were anticipated with Spain. Sir Humphrey Gilbert revealingly entitled his 1577 memorandum which advocated colonization, "How Her Majesty may annoy the King of Spain." Richard Hakluyt, nephew of the colonial promoter, addressed the same topic in 1584, and told the Queen that Spain's American settlements were too small to jeopardize English plantings; moreover, Hakluyt anticipated an English-Indian alliance in the face of any Spanish threat.[7]

The orders communicated to the colonial settlers leave little doubt as to England's expectations. The first charter authorizing colonization in America, Queen Elizabeth's license to the ill-fated Gilbert, directed the expedition to explore, settle, and fortify "heathen and barbarous lands." Gilbert, in addition, was to "encounter, expulse, repell and resist," by whatever means he deemed necessary, the colonists of any other power that attempted to settle within two hundred leagues of his settlements.[8]

Later, when Virginia was settled, the London Company's instructions echoed the earlier directives of the Crown. Opened by the planters while crossing the Atlantic on the *Susan Constant,* the orders instructed the leaders to establish the colony in a secure, cleared enclave up river from the Chesapeake entrance. In addition, the colony was to fortify the entrance to the river, and to take precautions that no Indians be permitted to dwell between the fort and the colony and that no natives be allowed access to English weapons; after fulfilling these orders, the colony was to be divided, with one-third of the colonists immediately set to constructing a fortification at the principal settlement. "Above all things," the adventurers in London advised, "do not advertize the killing of your own men," for if the natives "perceive that you are but common men, and that with the loss of many of theirs they diminish any part of yours, they will make many adventures upon you. . . ." If "you neglect this," the settlers of England's first permanent colony were told, "you neglect your safety."[9]

The inhabitants of most other colonies were given similar instructions. Immigrants to Maryland were warned to expect "incursions" by Indians, pirates, robbers, and the armed forces of foreign powers. Lord Baltimore authorized reprisals "even without the limits" of Maryland to extirpate any attackers. The initial charter of the Massachusetts Bay colony instructed the governor to prepare for the "special defense and safety" of the colony and to repulse by force all its foes. Later, Massachusetts, New York, and New Jersey were ordered to assist one another in the event of an attack. Still later, the governor of Massachusetts

7. Gerald Nash, "The Image of the Indian in the Southern Colonial Mind," *William and Mary Quarterly,* 3d Ser. 29 (April 1972), pp. 202–3; George B. Parks, *Richard Hakluyt and the English Voyages* (New York, 1961), p. 89.

8. *Sir Humphrey Gilberte and his enterprises of Colonization in America* (New York, 1967), pp. 95–98.

9. Arber, *Works of Smith,* vol. I, pp. xxxv–xxxvi.

for a short period was made commander-in-chief of the militia forces of Rhode Island, New Hampshire, and Connecticut.[10]

Before sending any colonists to Virginia, the London Company fretted over the number of soldiers the new colony would require, eventually deciding that a force of five hundred could fortify the colony within one month sufficiently to withstand up to three thousand invaders. A few years later, the future inhabitants of Plymouth were advised, prior to disembarking, to settle in compact areas so they might "be in a capassite . . . to defend themselves from the assault of an enimie. . . ."[11]

In 1630, John Cotton, a young Puritan minister of Boston in Lincolnshire, journeyed to Southampton to preach the farewell sermon to John Winthrop and his fellow immigrants. Cotton's sermon was a revealing mixture of the emigrants' attitudes. About to invade a strange continent, they believed that God not only countenanced but directed the venture. Cotton's sermon was based on II Samuel 7:10. "Moreover I will appoint a place for my people Israell," Cotton read, "and I will plant them, and they may dwell in a place of their owne, and move no more." Indians would be encountered, he advised. Conversion of these heathens was desirable, but Cotton counseled the colonists to "Neglect not walls, and bulwarks, and fortifications, for your owne defence. . . ." Likewise, Edward Johnson, who later migrated to Woburn in Massachusetts, instructed the emigrants who were about to sail to "store yourselves with all sorts of weapons for war, [and to] furbish up your Swords, Rapiers, and all other piercing weapons."[12]

Thus, the English migration took the form of an armed invasion of the New World, a tactical approach that persisted until near the end of the colonial era. When Britain contemplated extending its hegemony into the transmontane region on the eve of the French and Indian War, it toyed with the notion of moving "at Once by One large Step over the Mountains with a numerous Military Colony." The earliest colonists were accompanied, and sometimes led by, professional soldiers. John Smith in Virginia and Miles Standish in Plymouth are the best remembered soldier-colonists, but many early settlements hired men of similar ilk. Usually veterans of England's wars on the continent or in Ireland,

---

10. Patrick M. Malone, "Indian and English Military Systems in New England in the Seventeenth Century" (Ph.D. diss., Brown University, 1971), p. 152; Leonard Woods Labaree, ed., *Royal Instructions to British Colonial Governors, 1607–1776*, 2 vols. (New York, 1935), vol. I, pp. 427–28; Philip S. Haffenden, *New England in the English Nation, 1689–1713* (Oxford, Eng., 1974), pp. 102–3.

11. Darrett Rutman, "A Militant New World" (Ph.D. diss., University of Virginia, 1959), p. 486; Morison Sharp, "Leadership and Democracy in the Early New England System of Defense," *American Historical Review* 50 (January 1945), pp. 244–60.

12. John Cotton, "God's Promise to His Plantation," in *Old South Leaflets,* 8 vols. (New York, n.d.), vol. III, no. 53; Louis K. Brown, *A Revolutionary Town* (Canaan, N.H., 1975), p. 3.

these warriors were employed to train the colonists in the martial arts and to fortify their settlements.

Military men were also often given the governor's post in some of the early colonies. John Smith was president of the Virginia colonists for nearly a year after September 1608; a succession of soldiers, all with considerable experience in the Netherlands campaigns, ruled the colony after Smith until the Crown seized control in 1624. Sir Thomas Dale, on leave from his regiment on the continent, was commissioned knight marshall of Virginia; acting under Governor Sir Thomas Gates, Dale imposed martial law on many aspects of life in the colony. Under "Dale's Laws," the settlers were called to duty—farming, hunting, soldiering—at 6:00 A.M. and toiled until late in the day. Those colonist-soldiers who disobeyed, robbed the company store, or trafficked with the Indians were subjected to the most barbaric military and civil punishments of the day, including being broken on the wheel, burned at the stake, or even starved to death.[13]

The earliest settlers of Massachusetts were accompanied by five artillery pieces and skilled craftsmen who were to build gun carriages, mine for the necessary materials for ammunition, and construct fortifications. Additionally, Massachusetts Bay selected a governor with a military background less than a decade after its establishment. Captain Thomas Dudley, a former commander of English volunteers under Henry of Navarre, was chosen governor in 1634. In fact, 20 percent of the known leaders of early Massachusetts had been military commanders before their immigration. Within a few years, such governance was commonplace. Between 1660 and 1727, 87 percent of the governors in Britain's American colonies were English army officers. Each carried at least the rank of colonel in the Royal army and general in the provincial forces. The average commander of this background had served for more than ten years as an officer in the English army before his arrival in the colonies.[14]

Those Englishmen who emigrated to the colonies were expected to go as armed settlers. The earliest laws of the New England colonies included statutes that required most males to possess dependable firearms. Europeans coming to the southern colonies were told to bring one musket and several pounds of

13. Stephen Saunders Webb, "Army and Empire: English Garrison Government in Britain and America, 1569–1763," *WMQ*, 3d Ser. 34 (January 1977), p. 6; Timothy H. Breen, "English Origins and New World Development: The Case of the Covenanted Militia in Seventeenth-Century Massachusetts, *PP* 57 (November 1972), p. 81; Darrett B. Rutman, "The Virginia Company and Its Military Regime," in Darrett B. Rutman, ed., *The Old Dominion* (Charlottesville, Va., 1964), pp. 5–10; Richard L. Morton, *Colonial Virginia*, 2 vols. (Chapel Hill, N.C., 1960), vol. I, pp. 29–31; Wesley F. Craven, *The Southern Colonies in the Seventeenth Century, 1607–1689* (Baton Rouge, La., 1949), pp. 104–7.

14. Rutman, "A Militant New World," pp. 457–58; Samuel E. Morison, *Builders of the Bay Colony* (Cambridge, Mass., 1930), pp. 65, 87; Douglas Leach, *Arms for Empire* (New York, 1973), pp. 9–11; Webb, "Army and Empire," pp. 14–19.

powder and lead. South Carolina promised one hundred acres to each immigrant who complied, and inhabitants of early Georgia could own land only if they swore to bear arms in defense of the province.[15]

In addition to their muskets, the first settlers came armed with pikes and swords and garbed in helmets and restrictive body armor. Indian tactics, as well as the heavily wooded, swampy terrain, quickly rendered such paraphernalia useless. Colonial soldiers were soon wearing heavy, padded coats. Knives, hatchets, and, of course, the flintlock musket, became the standard gear. The flintlock musket remained the basic weapon of colonial and European armies until after the American Revolution. A smooth bore gun weighing about fifteen pounds, the musket had an effective range of approximately sixty yards; the soft-lead bullet it discharged tended to spread upon impact, to produce massive wounds. The weapon was not terribly efficient; it could be fired only about four times a minute, and it tended to misfire frequently. Moreover, it was inefficient in damp weather and useless in the rain. The primeval forests of America rendered the weapon less useful than in the Old World.

A mounted soldier in this era might carry one of several guns. He could be armed with a flintlock pistol, a "bastard musket," a gun that was smaller than an ordinary musket but larger than a pistol, or a "caliver," a shoulder weapon. During the first half-century of settlement many in New England preferred the matchlock musket, a twenty-pound monstrosity that could be fired only from a forked rest. In the eighteenth century some regiments substituted the bayonet for the sword, and late in the colonial era the rifle—a Pennsylvania invention—became popular in the middle colonies and the upper South. While the flintlock rifle had a greater range than the musket, it was slower to load and was used principally as a sniper's tool.

Infantry and cavalry in early America also were assisted by mortars and artillery; the latter included behemoths capable of hurling more than forty-pound iron projectiles against an entrenched enemy, and mortars could lob two-hundred-pound missiles into a fortification. Some foot soldiers even used dogs to ferret out the enemy and to provide an early warning of a foe's presence.[16]

These weapons were useless in the hands of the unskilled. Therefore, the laws requiring training in the use of arms were among the earliest enacted in British

---

15. Malone, "Indian and English," p. 75; William Hilton, *A Relation of a Discovery lately made* . . . [1644] in Peter Force, comp., *Tracts & Other Papers* . . . , 4 vols. (Washington, D. C., 1836), vol. II, pp. 2, 24; *A Relation of Maryland,* in Clayton C. Hall, ed., *Narratives of Early Maryland, 1633–1684* (New York, 1910), p. 94; Thomas Cooper and O. J. McCord, eds., *Statutes at Large of South Carolina,* 10 vols. (Columbia, S.C., 1836–1841), vol. IX, p. 618.

16. Leach, *Arms for Empire,* pp. 4–8; Edward P. Hamilton, *The French and Indian Wars* (Garden City, N.Y., 1962), pp. 81–93; Edward P. Hamilton, "Colonial Warfare in North America," in Massachusetts Historical Society, *Proceedings* 80 (1969), pp. 8–12; Malone, "Indian and English," pp. 75–77; Haffenden, *New England,* pp. 79–80.

America. Prompted by the example of the Virginia Massacre of 1622, a sudden, daring Indian raid that resulted in the death of nearly one-third of the settlers, the New England Company ordered the governor of Massachusetts to see that "both our servants and other planters and their servants, be exercised in the use of arms, and certain times be appointed to muster them." By the mid-1630s Massachusetts and Plymouth had adopted laws encompassing this spirit, the latter colony merely institutionalizing what it had done for more than a decade. Also, in the wake of Virginia's tragedy, George Wyatt, that colony's former governor, recommended that his successor create a militia force of 120 companies; Lord Baltimore, meanwhile, instructed that "all sorts of men . . . be mustered and trained in military discipline." Eventually, London ordered each governor to see that all freemen be armed and trained, but it warned against unreasonable "REMOTE marches, musters, AND trainings." The Crown also directed each governor to prepare inventories every six months of the arms, ammunition, and fortifications within his province, to survey coastal areas for possible invasion sites, to erect military installations where needed, and to ascertain that existing structures were maintained.[17]

Soon a formal militia system, based on the system that had existed for generations in the parent state, was instituted in each colony. Professional soldiers such as Miles Standish immediately created militia companies. Plymouth, for instance, had four functioning companies within a few months of the landing of the *Mayflower*; a decade later a company existed in each of seven new settlements in that colony. Massachusetts created two companies in 1631, and within only five years fourteen companies, comprising three regiments, had been created.[18]

Militia forces were not created without some apprehension, however. Fear lingered that a militia force might be corrupted and eradicate a people's liberty. The English immigrants transported to America their anxiety that a professional officer class would destroy rule by law and that vice-ridden soldiers inevitably would be obsequious to their tyrannical masters. The Puritans quickly discharged some of the professionals who had accompanied them across the Atlantic, though less from fear of tyranny than from anxiety that their licentious, earthy behavior and their "vain and unsettled" dispositions might corrupt the saintly. Yet even after the bloody Pequot War of 1637 Massachusetts refused a petition of Bostonians to form a private artillery company on the grounds that it was "dangerous . . . to create a standing authority of military men, which might easily, in time, overthrow the civil power." Still later, several members of that colony's

17. Leach, *Arms for Empire*, pp. 10–11; Malone, "Indian and English," pp. 152–53; J. Frederick Fausz and Jan Kukla, eds., "A Letter of Advice to the Governor of Virginia, 1624," *WMQ*, 3d Ser. 34 (January 1977), p. 107; Hall, *Narratives*, p. 23; Labaree, *Royal Instructions*, vol. I, pp. 392–93, 398–402, 410, 441.

18. Leach, *Arms for Empire*, pp. 10–11; Malone, "Indian and English," pp. 153–58.

general court voted against the establishment of new companies because they regarded them as "very unfit, and not so safe in time of peace."[19]

Nevertheless, the exigencies of the era required some sort of military organization, and a militia force generally was thought to be safe if properly disciplined and composed of "men of fortunes, of education and virtue" who were "excited to the most vigorous action . . . to . . . fight for their fathers and mothers,—for their wives and children,—for their private property,—for their liberty,—their religion. . . ." Plymouth's militia law of 1658, hence, was not untypical. It called for each village—in the sparsely populated South the onus usually was placed on each county—to create a company for use in "case of any sudden and unexpected approach of an enemy or insurrection within yourselves. . . ." Public monies, customarily raised by taxes and special fines, were used to procure weapons, powder, food, clothing, and hardware; during actual war, salaries were paid from these funds. But the greatest burden was placed on the militiaman, who was to arm himself. In Massachusetts, for example, the soldier who owned a musket was required to provide himself with a pound of powder, twenty bullets, and two fathoms of match.[20]

Those "men of fortunes, of education and virtue" who were called upon to serve actually represented a cross section of the general male population. The New England colonies originally required free men between the ages of sixteen and sixty years to serve; exemptions were granted to public officials, the clergy, teachers, physicians, tradesmen, some skilled artisans, one man from each farm with twenty acres and twenty cattle, and the unhealthy. In addition, the wealthy could hire substitutes.

Not all men were overjoyed at the prospect of military service. In order to maintain morale and secure soldiers during King Philip's War, Massachusetts felt compelled to issue a special proclamation explaining the reasons for the conflict and offering veterans land and cash bounties. During the initial days of the American Revolution, in Concord, nearly every able-bodied male over forty served in the village militia; within a few weeks less than half of these men were still willing to serve. Occassionally gimmicks were initiated to procure troops. Benjamin Franklin, for instance, suggested cash payments for each scalp garnered by an enlisted man when warfare ravaged the Pennsylvania frontier. But the more common procedures included requiring those other than white freemen—principally indentured servants and recent immigrants—to enroll, or

19. Simeon Howard, *A Sermon Preached to the Ancient and Honorable Artillery-Company* . . . (Boston, 1773), pp. 26–27; John Lathrop, *A Sermon Preached to the Ancient and Honorable Artillery Company* . . . (Boston, 1774), pp. 37–39; Breen, "English Origins," pp. 81–82, 88.

20. Lathrop, *A Sermon*, p. 37; Rutman, "A Militant New World," p. 25; Jack S. Radabaugh, "The Militia of Colonial Massachusetts," *Military Affairs* 18 (Spring 1954), pp. 2, 11–13; Louis Morton, "The Origins of American Military Policy," *MA* 22 (Summer 1958), pp. 81–82.

to institute conscription. As a result, vagrants and unemployed single males were inducted.

Still, problems occurred, such as draft-dodging and urban riots in opposition to impressment gangs. Sometimes "mutinies" were sparked. The troops of Ipswich once went on strike against further peacetime training. During the Revolution, the First Company of the Philadelphia Militia Artillery, a contingent consisting mostly of artisans, protested that while they had suffered and their comrades had died, many of the affluent had not only "artfully evaded" service but had "enormously advanced the prices on every necessary and convenience of life." These militiamen formed a "Committee of Privates," a vigilante band, to control prices and to demand that "every able bodied man" be conscripted. Twenty-seven of the militiamen were arrested.[21]

Considerable care was taken to maintain civilian control of the militia. Everywhere, a commander-in-chief—usually called the "sergeant-major-general" in New England and the "muster master general" in the South—reported to the civil authorities. In Massachusetts this could be a lucrative post, for this officer stayed at home during wartime, but shared in the spoils of victory; moreover, his family was exempt from drills. Each company was commanded by a captain, an ensign, three sergeants, and three corporals. It was not uncommon for the officers to be elected, although in Massachusetts only the highest office remained elective after 1668.[22]

In the first years of colonization the trainbands often assembled each week for exercises and drill. In less than a decade Massachusetts cut its company drill sessions to eight days a year, and subsequently the militia was required to assemble as infrequently as three or four times annually. Regimental drills were usually conducted just once a year, though in wartime, they were held several times a week.

The troops that gathered for the training exercises consisted mostly of foot soldiers, although the more affluent colonists—those capable of providing a horse, saddle, bridle, halter, pistol, and sword—were frequently assigned to the cavalry. The drill usually was conducted in or near the village of the militiamen, and the actual training generally lasted six or seven hours. During this time, the soldiers practiced close order drill, various formations, and the manual of arms, fought a mock battle, took target practice, and stood review and inspection. This

21. Malone, "Indian and English," pp. 153–55; Radabaugh, "Militia of Colonial Massachusetts," pp. 10–11, 14; Douglas E. Leach, *Flintlock and Tomahawk* (New York, 1958), pp. 123–24; Benjamin Franklin to ——, nd, and Benjamin Franklin, "The Organization of John Van Etten's Company," in Leonard W. Labaree et al., eds., *The Papers of Benjamin Franklin* (New Haven, Conn., 1959), vol. VI, pp. 349–50, 353–54; John Shy, *Toward Lexington* (Princeton, N.J., 1965), pp. 6–7; Pauline Maier, "Popular Uprisings and Civil Authority in Eighteenth-Century America," *WMQ*, 3d Ser. 27 (January 1970), pp. 8–9; Breen, "English Origins," p. 90; Philip S. Foner, *Labor and the American Revolution* (New York, 1976), pp. 190–96.

22. Radabaugh, "Militia of Colonial Mass.," pp. 2, 5; Breen, "English Origins," pp. 82, 91, 93.

regimen was of doubtful usefulness in the engagements with the Indians, and, since the militia companies usually could not be sent beyond their colonial borders, of little practical value in the event of an intercolonial war. By mid-afternoon the exercises concluded with a prayer, and the remainder of the daylight hours were consumed, as one young soldier put it, by "Hallowing [and] carousing," that is, picnics, games, visits with neighbors, and much swilling of rum and ale.[23]

The militia primarily was designed as a defensive unit. The charter of the confederation of New England, the short-lived union of the mid-seventeenth century, permitted militia troops to be sent outside their respective colonies for short periods, and militia companies were utilized on occasion in offensive operations against both Indian and European foes. But this activity was detested by colonists, who wished to remain at home, to protect their own families from sudden assault and tend their agrarian enterprises. Most colonial expeditions, therefore, were composed of free and bonded conscriptees or volunteers, men who enlisted for plunder, adventure, prestige, or as an escape from boredom or bondage. Increasingly, Professor John Shy has noted, fighting "ceased to be a function of the community as such."[24]

Inadequately trained and infrequently utilized militia forces had acquired an appalling reputation by the eighteenth century. Governor Alexander Spotswood was convinced that Virginia's militia was "the worst in the King's Dominions." Cadwallader Colden, Lt. Governor of New York, surely would have disagreed and claimed that his units were the worst in the New World. On the eve of the French and Indian War, Colden complained to London that his forces not only were devoid of engineers and adequate equipment, but that "Our militia is under no kind of discipline" and the "Officers themselves [can] not be brought to observe discipline. . . . There is a licentiousness, under the notion of liberty, [that] so generally prevails, that they are impatient under all kind of superiority and authority."[25]

The disgraceful reputation was probably deserved. It prompted Great Britian to send regulars to the colonies for occasional operations and, after 1730, to consider creating a standing army for America; the discreditability of the militia forces even led Governor James Oglethorpe in Georgia to recommend that a battalion of five hundred British soldiers be stationed in each colony.

The colonists not only were armed and underwent some training, but each colony fortified itself for the anticipated hostilities. The idea was to be "enclos'd

23. Radabaugh, "Militia of Colonial Mass.," pp. 4, 13–4; Morton, "Origins of American Military Policy," p. 79; Shy, *Toward Lexington,* pp. 6–9; R. G. Albion and L. Dodson, eds., *Journal of Philip Vickers Fithian, 1775–1776* (Princeton, N. J., 1924), p. 158.

24. Daniel Boorstin, *The Americans: The Colonial Experience* (New York, 1958), pp. 345–52; Shy, *Toward Lexington,* pp. 13, 15–6, 19–32, 183.

25. Cadwallader Colden to Halifax, 3 August 1774, in Stanley Pargellis, ed., *Military Affairs in North America, 1748–1765* (New York, 1975), pp. 88–89.

by *Military Lines,* impregnable against the *Savages,* and which will make our whole Plantation one continued Fortress.'' When a new settlement, such as Henrico in Virginia, was founded, the initial chore facing the settlers was to fence in the hamlet, ''building at each corner of the towne, very strong and high commanders or watchtowers . . . and storehouses.'' Only thereafter were the lodgings and the church constructed. Although these fortifications were constructed primarily to afford protection from the Indians, the native Americans were not always disturbed by such installations. The Indians sometimes requested that a fort be erected in order to intimidate their enemies. In 1756, for instance, the Cherokees ceded seven hundred acres to England for the construction of Fort Loudoun so that the Shawnees might be frightened.[26]

Military realities were seldom absent from the thoughts of the new village planners. Lodgings were situated close to one another so that ''upon anie *All-arme* they can second and succor the other.'' Within a year of its founding, Plymouth was enclosed by a pallisade twenty-seven hundred feet in length, and artillery pieces had been placed on the high ground in the vicinity of the settlement. Massachusetts similarly fortified the elevated regions about Boston, as well as the harbor islands. Virginia was careful to install artillery pieces quickly at strategic points along its important rivers.

Several varieties of forts were constructed. The simplest and quickest to erect was a stockade, an edifice consisting of merely a wall of logs that abutted a trench around the circumference of the planned fort; these installations were not sturdy and could be demolished by the lightest artillery. The earliest fort at Jamestown may have resembled this kind of installation. At any rate, a Spanish spy notified his government that the fort had been built ''without skill. . .by unskilled men'' and that its ramparts were ''so weak that a kick would break them down.'' More resilient forts could be built of logs packed with earth, although the timber eventually rotted. The best combination of impregnability and durability were bastions made of stone. Some forts were spherical, others triangular, and still others were pentagonal or hexagonal. North Carolina even built a frontier fort in the 1750s that was three stories tall and constructed of oak logs nearly one and a half feet thick; the installation could accommodate one hundred men firing muskets from each of the three floors.[27]

The Indians often built forts too. In New England the native Americans usually enclosed an area of forty to fifty square feet with logs approximately one foot

26. Sir Robert Montgomery, *A Discourse* . . . in Force, *Tracts,* vol. I, pp. 7–8; Ralph Hamor, Richard B. Harwell, ed., *A True Discourse* (Richmond, 1957), pp. 29–30; Wilcomb E. Washburn, *The Indians in America* (New York, 1975), pp. 88–89.

27. John Rolfe, *A True Relation of the State of Virginia* (Charlottesville, Va., 1971), p. 9; Douglas E. Leach, ''The Military System of Plymouth Colony,'' *New England Quarterly* 24 (September 1951), pp. 347–48; Malone, ''Indian and English,'' pp. 220–21; Webb, ''Army and Empire,'' p. 6; Lyon Gardiner Tyler, ed., *Narratives of Early Virginia, 1606–1625* (New York, 1907), p. 416; Don Diego de Molina to Don Alonzo de Velasco, 1613, in Tyler, ed., ibid., p. 221; Hamilton, ''Colonial Warfare,'' pp. 3–4; Hugh T. Lefler and William S. Powell, *Colonial North Carolina: A History* (New York, 1973), p. 142.

thick. One end of each log was buried in three feet of earth, but the other end rose to a height of ten to twelve feet. Loopholes were notched, through which the Indians fired on their enemies.[28]

Despite the cold-war, and all too often the hot-war, atmosphere that existed in America, the colonists guarded their provincial independence so jealously that they were reluctant even to consider the creation of formal military alliances. Aside from the New England confederation in the 1640s, wartime cooperation between the colonies was uncommon. It was often more profitable, in fact, to stay out of wars than to join the fight; a "neutral" colony could become the supplier for its fellow countrymen while it continued to trade with the foreign belligerent. Several calls emanated from New England for joint expeditions to seize Canada, that "unhappy fountain from which issue all our miseries." In the wake of King William's War, some even called for establishment of a modified version of the dominion of New England; in 1701 Robert Livingston of New York proposed that for military purposes the colonies be consolidated into three entities, and in the same year an anonymous Virginian, probably Robert Beverly, suggested a national union that would act through a national congress. Other variations of these formulations occasionally were promoted before 1754 when Benjamin Franklin formally proffered the most famous scheme, the Albany Plan of Union. This plan would have created a national congress and an executive official whose duty it would be to "make Peace or Declare War" with the Indians, to "raise and pay Soldiers, and build Forts for the Defense of any of the Colonies," to issue military commissions, and to fortify the continent's rivers and coast. These formal plans were greeted with disinterest or hostility throughout the colonies. Typically, only one colony responded with troops when New York, whose northern frontier was ravaged by French and Indian invaders, appealed for assistance in 1694. Virginia once refused to send assistance for an invasion of Canada, then its council adopted a resolution expressing gratitude that God kept the "Dominion in peace, when all the Neighboring Colonies have been in great disturbance and Dangers. . . ." When intercolonial wars flared in America, the Crown directed the requisition of men and supplies, and when the colonies did cooperate during these conflicts, it was usually the result of British inspiration or direction.[29]

The colonists' reluctance to cooperate was not due to any lack of war. Throughout the colonial era there was seldom a moment when a war was not in progress, or in the planning stage, in some part of England's American Empire. Most

28. Phillip Vincent, "A true relation of the late Battle fought in New England between the English and the savages," MHS, *Collections,* 3d Ser. 6 (1837), pp. 38–39.

29. Haffenden, *New England,* pp. 115–17; Colden to Halifax, 3 August 1754, Pargellis, *Military Affairs,* p. 21; "Albany Congress: Representation of the Parent State of the Colonies," (9–14 July 1754); Labaree, *Papers of Franklin,* vol. V, pp. 389–90; Harry Ward, *Unite or Die* (Pt. Washington, N.Y., 1971), pp. 3–22, 116, 256–57; Winfred T. Root, *The Relations of Pennsylvania with the British Government* (New York, 1912), pp. 262–65.

colonies were plagued with wars with the native Americans for the first two or three generations. Normally, each war was waged on a more remote western frontier than its predecessor. Unlike Virginia or Massachusetts, the more fortunate colonies experienced almost all of these conflicts in their sparsely settled frontier zones.

But other wars occurred, too. In the midst of its first colonizing venture, England went to war with Spain; later, in the seventeenth century, England fought three wars with the Dutch. And some of these troubles, like most European conflicts, spread to the New World. In the century preceding the American Revolution, Britain was at war almost as frequently as it was at peace. Each of the parent state's conflicts triggered hostilities in the colonies.

The wars in America in some ways were not unlike those in Europe. Like European conflicts, hostilities normally commenced in the spring and ceased with the onset of cold, wet weather. Nor was the action diminished in the New World. Of one typical encounter, a British lieutenant wrote home that "the oldest soldiers here say that it was the hottest fire they ever saw." Moreover, even though campaigns frequently were waged in wilderness regions, the European armies quickly adapted to the new conditions, learning to cut roads through the dense forests for advancing armies and generally surmounting the engineering obstacles posed by a primitive continent so as to avoid ambush. This meant that war in America was often so similar to European warfare that the belligerents could send regulars, professional troops, to the colonies—hence, the famous confrontation of Montcalm and Wolfe on the Plains of Abraham, a battle largely fought along eighteenth-century European lines.[30]

In these contests European professionals bore the brunt of New World fighting. The colonists contributed to intercolonial conflicts and undertook most of the engagements with the native Americans, but English regulars usually directed professional armies against other European armies. Early on, in fact, regulars were sent to the colonies. Oliver Cromwell assigned regulars to Virginia in 1651, and they returned during the next decade in the struggle with the Dutch for New York. Thereafter, British regulars were garrisoned on the New York and South Carolina frontiers and in Canada and in the West Indies; in addition, regulars were dispatched in small numbers to assist Sir Edmund Andros's control of the Indians during the Dominion of New England experiment, and they accompanied Governor Oglethorpe in his invasion of Spanish Florida in 1740. When the French and Indian War erupted, there were four thousand English regulars in America. At its peak commitment during the war, Britain had more than thirty thousand troops in the colonies. Although American troops at times served with the regulars, it was usually in the capacity of auxiliaries; frequently, for instance, frontiersmen screened the flanks of advancing regulars. The result

30. Lt. William Fielding to Basil Fielding, 18 July 1775, in Marion Balderston and David Syrett, eds., *The Lost War* (New York, 1975), p. 33.

was a higher casualty rate among British units. During the Battle of Ticonderoga in the French and Indian War, for example, British casualties amounted to about 20 percent of their total force, whereas the colonial casualties came to about 1 percent of their troops.[31]

But the wars the colonists waged with the Europeans, and with the British during the Revolution, also differed substantially from the wars fought in Europe. Sieges occurred less frequently in America, and campaigns were more likely to be waged in an aboriginal wilderness. The civilian population in the colonies experienced more of the agonies of war than their counterparts in Europe. European tactics and equipment were quickly modified to suit the new environment and the new kind of fighting. In some instances, English commanders learned new approaches to guerrilla tactics before they ever saw America. By the 1740s some military men had encountered similar tactics during the suppression of the Jacobite rebellion, when they had faced an enemy "without order, and without discipline." Soon manuals appeared to teach how to prepare for such an enemy, and there is evidence that by 1750 Generals Forbes, Bouquet, and Wolfe had familiarized themselves with such literature. Similarly, European equipment was Americanized. Invading armies used Indian birch canoes, English whaleboats, and the North American bateau; the latter, a flat-bottomed craft capable of carrying about three tons of cargo, including more than twenty soldiers, became the most widely used vessel. Of course, the heavier, more cumbersome weapons—halberds and swords, for instance—were replaced with lighter, more practical weapons, such as muskets. New environs and a strange enemy demanded that troops learn to fire their traditional weapons in new ways, such as from the prone position. Armor and encumbering uniforms, as well as less useful contingents such as the cavalry, likewise were discarded or modified. Indian allies, for instance, frequently were used to fulfill the role of cavalry. Some thought it essential to scuttle much of the European art of war and to adopt Indian fighting methods. General John Forbes thought "wee must comply and learn the Art of Warr, from the Enemy Indians or anything else who have seen the Country and War carried on in it." Forbes, General Bouquet, and Benjamin Franklin recommended "equipping Numbers of our men like the Savages" with bows and arrows, but the suggestion does not seem to have been implemented. The Puritans used dogs against the Indians in the seventeenth century, and Franklin called for similar tactics during Pennsylvania's border warfare a hundred years later. Franklin thought the dogs should be "large, strong, and fierce." The canine corps could be used to detect foes lurking in ambush, and they could be turned against the enemy for physical attacks.[32]

31. Hamilton, "Colonial Warfare," pp. 5–8; Shy, *Toward Lexington,* pp. 4, 19–35.

32. Peter E. Russell, "Redcoats in the Wilderness: British Officers and Irregular Warfare in Europe and America, 1740 to 1760," *WMQ,* 3d Ser. 35 (October 1978), pp. 630–31, 635, 641, 647; Leach, *Arms for Empire,* p. 440; Lynn Montross, *Rag, Tag, and Bobtail* (New York, 1952), p. 42; Carl Van Doren, *Benjamin Franklin* (New York, 1938), p. 247.

Wars in America were also waged on a smaller scale than those in Europe. The largest armies fielded in the eighteenth-century conflicts were only one-quarter the size of France's standing army in the seventeenth century. Nevertheless, the wars of America were frequently more brutal than those waged in Europe. The Indian allies who usually accompanied or assisted the colonial or European armies were unfamiliar with the rules of continental war; the colonists who learned of war at first-hand from Indians often were indifferent or hostile to European forms. All forces resorted to terrorist tactics at one time or another, but in American warfare terrorism was commonplace. A favorite tactic was to starve an opponent—civilians as well as soldiers—into submission. Wherever "we march we keep our Horses in the Fields among *Corn & Oats,* So that the *Enemy* if they gain the Ground may have poor Fare for them & their Horses," a private in a frontier regiment noted. British troops stripped Philadelphia before abandoning it in 1778, and the British command was prepared to put the torch to Boston in 1776 if General Washington attacked during their evacuation.[33] Wars in Europe were serious business, but they seldom could be thought of as "total war" after the late seventeenth century; monarchies lost wars, negotiated peace terms, and remained in power to fight, and perhaps to be defeated, once again. However, wars in America were life-and-death struggles. If a colonial power suffered defeat, as France learned in 1763, the blow could mean the inability to remain active as a colonial entity in North America. Colonists who lost a struggle could lose their homeland, as well as their cultural and economic ties abroad.

Those Americans who participated in major encounters as part of a colonial army were less likely than Europe's soldiers to be adequately led and provisioned. The colonial expedition against Louisbourg in 1745 was planned by Governor William Shirley, a lawyer without military experience, and commanded by William Pepperell, a rich merchant who had served without particular distinction in the Massachusetts militia. Shirley also commanded the unsuccessful Niagara campaign a few years later. In the wake of that campaign's failure, he was accused of improperly training his troops—"my children," he called them—and of a most amateurish construction of his fortifications at Oswego;[34] British military engineers who inspected his installation reported that the

flanks of the half bastions do not defend the opposite faces, the wings are enfiladed from end to end, the terreplain [is] seen almost throughout, the north wing towards the Lake [is] quite open, with only a small cliff of earth and rock where anybody may run up and down.[35]

33. Howard Peckham, *The Colonial Wars, 1689–1762* (Chicago, 1964), p. 2; Lt. Fielding to Basil Fielding, 18 July 1775, and 28 April 1776, in Balderston and Syrett, *Lost War,* pp. 33, 77.

34. Louis E. de Forest, ed., *Louisbourg Journals, 1745* (New York, 1932), pp. xv, 5; John Schutz, *William Shirley* (Chapel Hill, N.C., 1961), pp. 208, 213.

35. Hamilton, *French and Indian Wars,* p. 113.

The troops were often even less prepared for war than their leaders. Enroute to Canada in 1745, ill-prepared New Hampshire soldiers "were Ordered Ashore . . . and Taught How to Use the firelock. . . ." One participant found the expedition to be a "scene of confusion and frolic." Increase Mather, commenting on earlier wars, acknowledged that unprepared Puritans "sometimes unhappily shoot *English-men* instead of *Indians*."[36]

Conditions had not changed much when the Revolution began. In the first encounter of that war Concord militiamen ran amok. Some went home, many were without leaders. One of the men noted that "Every man was his own commander." The American armies frequently were sent to the field with meager provisions. It was not uncommon for poorly constructed boats to capsize, causing the destruction of provisions and the drowning of troops. During the utterly disastrous invasion of Cartegena the colonists were furnished with inedible meat, biscuits "which like a piece of clockwork moved by its own internal impulse, occasioned by the myriads of insects that dwelt within it, and butter . . . that tasted like train oil thickened with salt." In campaign after campaign pay seemed invariably late, an affront which often occasioned "Great Uneasiness" or "A Great tendency to a General Mutiny." Medical facilities were primitive, if they existed at all. Captain John Underhill, one of the professional militarists hired by the early Puritan settlers, complained of an expedition during which "our chirgeon, not accustomed to war, durst not hazard himself where we ventured our lives." Some of Underhill's soldiers "were brought to a great strait" and others perished "for want of speedy help." When field hospitals were erected, they seldom had sufficient supplies of food, medicine, liquor, or beds. During the Revolution, Benjamin Rush, for a time a surgeon general in Washington's army, complained that soldiers with a chance to survive nevertheless succumbed due to their incarceration in poorly equipped hospitals.[37]

The wars fought in the colonies, even if one does not consider the struggles with the Indians, were waged with a macabre intensity not seen in Europe for generations after the mid-seventeenth century. One aspect of these wars that contributed to their wanton character was the unavoidable involvement of the civilian population. Whereas the more streamlined transportation facilities in Europe had mitigated pillage by linking military forces to their quartermaster corps, most armies in America routinely engaged in execrable plundering. Many men enlisted in expeditionary forces solely in the hope of securing plunder. The New England enlistees in the attack on Louisbourg in 1745 stole cows, fowl, horses, sheep, wine, cider, and molasses from the French farmers who lived along the attack route. The troops "had no particular orders," one diarist noted,

36. Increase Mather, *A Brief History of the Warre with the Indians in New England* . . . (Boston, 1676), p. 5.

37. Robert Gross, *The Minutemen and their World* (New York, 1976), p. 126; *The Journals of Lieut. William Feltman* . . . (Philadelphia, 1853), p. 3; John Tate Lanning, "The American Colonies in the Preliminaries of the War of Jenkins' Ear," *Georgia Historical Quarterly* 11 (June 1927), p. 155; John Underhill, "News from America," MHS, *Collections*, 3d Ser. 6 (1837), p. 26; George W. Corner, ed., *The Autobiography of Benjamin Rush* (New York, 1948), pp. 131–33.

and therefore "everyone did what was right in his own eyes." There was considerable spoilage during the Revolution. General Washington usually attempted to prevent plundering, except for the acquisition of straw and grain in sheath. In desperate times, however, he authorized house-to-house searches for clothing, blankets, shoes, and food. He acknowledged after one campaign in 1780 that "every ounce of Forage . . . and a good deal of the Provision, has been taken at the point of the Bayonet."[38]

The Tories in the path of the Continental Army were always in danger of pillage. But the British reciprocated, plundering Connecticut villages during William Tryon's invasion in 1779. In addition, Tory guerrillas in Virginia seized necessities in daring coastal and backcountry raids throughout the conflict. After 1779 the British army assisted the Tories in the old dominion, eventually producing property losses estimated at more that £2,000,000. During the occupation of Philadelphia, the British preyed on both the urban and the suburban residents, frequently paying little heed to the loyalties of their victims. Upon arriving in Philadelphia the British and the Loyalist allies commenced arresting those suspected of patriot activities. They also seized food, livestock, poultry, wagons, clothing, and even houses. They acted in "an ungenteel manner," one resident remarked, "abus[ing] many old, inoffensive men." Charles Willson Peale, the young painter who had moved to Philadelphia in 1776, saw a neighbor lose "every shirt he had, except the one on his back." Even the possessions of children were stolen. The "abuse of the inhabitants is beyond description," Peale remarked, and he thought the worst offenders were the female camp followers of the Hessians, Britain's hired allies. The losses in Philadelphia alone perhaps exceeded £180,000. Even the Loyalists were alarmed at the conduct of the redcoats and their allies. One Tory predicted during the occupation that the "ravages and wanton destruction of the soldiery will . . . soon become irksome to the inhabitants, as many . . . are now entirely and effectually ruined by the soldiers being permitted, under the command of their officers, to ravage and destroy their property." When the British withdrew from Philadelphia, they not only carried off as many provisions as possible, but they also put the torch to a number of private dwellings.[39]

38. Hamilton, *French and Indian Wars,* p. 113; George Washington to Gouverneur Morris, 10 December 1780, in John C. Fitzpatrick, ed., *The Writings of George Washington,* 39 vols. (Washington, D.C., 1931–1944), vol. XX, p. 458; Charles K. Bolton, *The Private Soldier under Washington* (New York, 1902), pp. 208–15; Journals of John Henry, in Kenneth Roberts, ed., *March to Quebec* (New York, 1938), p. 367; *Memoirs of Col. Benjamin Talmadge . . .* (New York, 1858), p. 30.

39. Elizabeth Cometti, "Depredations in Virginia during the Revolution," in Rutman, ed., *Old Dominion,* pp. 136–38, 140, 145–47; "The Diary of Robert Morton," *The Pennsylvania Magazine of History & Biography* 1, no. 1 (1877), pp. 10, 20, 30, 37; "Extracts from the Journals of Mrs. Henry Drinker, of Philadelphia, from September 25, 1777, to July 4, 1778," *PMHB* 13, no. 3 (1889), pp. 298–300; "Diary of James Allen, Esq., of Philadelphia, Counsellor-at-Law, 1770–1778," *PMHB* 8, no. 3 (1884), p. 296; "Journal of Sergeant William Young, Written during the Jersey Campaign in the Winter of 1776–77," *PHMB* 8, no. 3 (1884), p. 277; Page Smith, *A New Age Now Begins,* 2 vols. (New York, 1976), vol II, pp. 1031–41.

This wanton destruction and terrorism was common in most American wars. The role of the civilian population, indeed, was frequently a predetermined aspect of an army's strategy. Compte de Frontenac, the iron ruler of French Canada, hurled war parties against English border settlements late in the seventeenth century in an effort to break the British resistance to French settlement and expansion in the New World. Professor Shy has noted, moreover, that civilians "came to be the major factor in planning" during the last phase of Britain's Revolutionary strategy. By shifting the center of the conflict southward after 1778, Whitehall clearly hoped to reap a harvest of Tories. Congress noted even earlier that while civilians were often indiscriminately victimized, there were numerous instances of planned "rage and vengeance"; Congress believed the non-Anglican clergy were the most frequent victims. The clergy were not the only victims, however, and wartime atrocities were not always carried out by the armies. Fearing that the approaching British army might seek assistance from the Quakers, who were generally neutral, not Loyalists, the Revolutionary government in Pennsylvania arrested twenty Friends in the fall of 1777 and relocated them in Virginia; some died during captivity. Women were often the easiest marks for an armed soldiery. Rapes occurred in most conflicts, and during the Revolution Tory raiders allegedly entered the bedrooms of women living on plantations in Virginia and stripped the ladies "almost to nakedness." In the South white women were terrified of the blacks who often accompanied British or Loyalist contingents, although there is no evidence of depredations by the freedmen. Troops normally entered civilian abodes "uttering the most abusive language imaginable and making as if to hew us to pieces with their swords." To beseech the attacker to be merciful often drew "a hearty curse." Eliza Wilkinson, who lived outside Charleston, told of British soldiers storming her family's plantation, "bellowing out the most horrid curses . . . oaths and imprecations." They seized everything from garments to wedding rings. One "inhuman monster" spotted her shoes and demanded "them buckles," whereupon his companion, "a brother villian, whose enormous mouth extended from ear to ear, bawled out, 'Shares there, I say; Shares.' So they divided my buckles between them."[40]

Those who could escape the path of an army took every opportunity to do so. Besieged by Iroquois during King William's War, the inhabitants of Montreal stripped the lead eaves-troughs and window moldings from their homes to melt down for bullets in a desperate attempt to preserve their bastion. When British forces plunged into New Jersey in 1776, civilians fled to remote corners of the

---

40. John Shy, *A People Numerous and Armed* (New York, 1976), p. 209; Worthington C. Ford, ed., *Journals of the Continental Congress, 1774–1789*, 34 vols. (Washington, D.C., 1904–1937) vol. VII, pp. 277–78; Hamilton, *French and Indian Wars,* p. 113; Cometti, "Depredations," p. 138; Smith, *New Age,* vol. II, p. 1394; Caroline Gilman, ed., *Letters of Eliza Wilkinson* (New York, 1969), pp. 28–30.

province, hiding in barns, dwelling in makeshift huts, or crammed into "common smoky quarters" of river craft in the course of flight. Later in the Revolution, Admiral Thomas Graves gave the inhabitants of Falmouth (now Portland), Maine, two hours to evacuate the town; once cleared, he levied a "horrible shower of balls" upon the village, destroying three-fourths of the dwellings and virtually every store and warehouses.[41]

Many were not so fortunate. British troops apparently broke into the homes of Concord residents on the first day of the War for Independence and "most barbarously and inhumanely murdered" unarmed civilians. When Britain shelled Savannah in 1779 the civilians took to cellars, but many were "mangled in that supposed place of security." The "poor women and children have suffered beyond description," a contemporary noted. Indeed, as a woman at Yorktown reflected in the course of the battle fought there: "What an alarming crisis is this. War in itself, however distant, is indeed terrible, but when brought to our very doors . . . the reflection is indeed overwhelming." An American soldier in Norwalk, Connecticut, in 1779 reported seeing civilians driven from their burning homes with redcoats in pursuit. Colonel Banastre Tarleton, the leader of Tory contingents in the southern fighting, attempted to extract information from a luckless female captive by having her flogged; when she still refused to talk, the colonel allegedly ordered the body of her late husband exhumed and exhibited before her eyes, and when that too failed, he ordered her house looted and burned.[42]

Not all civilians met such a fate. Lund Washington, in charge of the general's estate, bribed the British contingent that visited Mount Vernon "with a view to prevent a conflagration." Obviously, bribery worked in this instance, although ironically the caretaker lost his own dwelling to British torches. Civilians hundreds of miles from the nearest military action might still be victimized. Women left to tend farms in the absence of soldier-husbands often witnessed the precipitate decline of the estate. Soldiers' pay often was too meager to assist their families left behind. Of course, war also produced widows and orphans. The depredations were not committed by only one side, but since the English colonists were most frequently engaged in sparsely settled Canada, they had fewer opportunities to prey on the civilian population. Nevertheless, colonial armies sometimes summarily executed English civilians who were apprehended

41. W. J. Eccles, "Frontenac's Military Policies, 1689–1698: A Reassessment," *Canadian Historical Review 37* (September 1956), p. 207; "Journal of Sgt. Young," pp. 255–56.

42. Peter Force, comp., *American Archives,* 4th Ser., 4 vols. (Washington, D.C., 1837–1846), vol. II, p. 674; Mary Beth Norton," 'What an Alarming Crisis Is This': Southern Women and the American Revolution," in Jeffrey J. Crow and Larry E. Tise, *The Southern Experience in the American Revolution* (Chapel Hill, N.C., 1978), p. 215; John Jones to Polly Jones, 7 October 1779, in Benjamin Kennedy, ed., *Muskets, Cannon Balls & Bombs* (Savannah, 1974), p. 132; *Memoirs of Col. Talmadge,* p. 30; Hugh Rankin, *Francis Marion: The Swamp Fox* (New York, 1973), p. 144.

among the enemy; in addition, New Englanders at war occasionally dressed as Indians as a cover for the atrocities they planned.[43]

Perhaps the worst victims of the European struggle for America were the frontiersmen in every war and the Loyalists in the American Revolution. Children on the frontier sometimes were forced to shuttle to and from school—if, indeed, they could attend at all—for fear the enemy might be skulking in the adjacent wilderness. Their parents were often forced "to get our bread with the perill of our Lives," anxiously tilling and sowing, while keeping one eye on the nearby forest for telltale signs of the enemy's presence. Cotton Mather spoke of frontiersmen whose corn "Fields [were] watered with their Blood" and who themselves became *"Sheep for the Slaughter."* Professor Howard Peckham has estimated that as much as 25 percent of the population in New England frontier counties perished in King William's War in the 1690s. In one war half the settlements in the entire province of Maine disappeared, while sixteen towns in Massachusetts and four in Rhode Island were obliterated. Some hamlets were hit repeatedly. Deerfield, Massachusetts, was totally annihilated in 1676, badly damaged in a furious battle in 1694, and sustained the loss of nearly half the population in still another assault in 1704. But no other depredation quite compares to the British removal of the Acadians from Nova Scotia in 1755. Having decided that those unfortunates were a fifth-column support for the French, Great Britain transported more than six thousand people from their homeland to the alien culture of English colonies, another six thousand or more Acadians were also dispersed, including those who fled into "voluntary" exile.[44]

The Loyalists were the losers in the American Revolution, and they paid dearly for their defeat. Suspected Tories were often stripped of their civil rights—voting and officeholding rights, the right to sit on juries—even before independence was declared. The activities of some were circumscribed by zealous local patriotic committees. Some were placed under house arrest. Others were incarcerated, at times in the most loathsome confines; the most infamous jail was the subterranean copper mine in Simsbury, Connecticut, a dark, vermin-infested hole that broke the health of many captives; those jailed at West Point had hardly more luxurious surroundings, since their facility lacked a complete roof and "all the rain which fell upon it passed through . . . and the water, with the mud and filth collected, was commonly ankle deep." Some Tories were abused physically by mobs, while still others suffered daily social ostracism or

43. Cometti, "Depredations," pp. 145–46; Elizabeth Cometti, "Women in the American Revolution," *NEQ* 20 (December 1947), pp. 329–32; Morris Talpaler, *The Sociology of the Bay Colony* (New York, 1976), p. 345; Mather, *Brief History of the Warre,* p. 22.

44. James Axtell, *The School Upon a Hill* (New Haven, Conn., 1974), p. 173; Leach, *Arms for Empire,* p. 129; Cotton Mather, *Frontiers Well-Defended . . .* (Boston, 1707), p. 4; Peckham, *Colonial Wars,* pp. 53, 63; Lois Kemball Matthews, *The Expansion of New England* (New York, 1909), pp. 57–63; Lawrence Henry Gipson, *The British Before the American Revolution,* 14 vols. (New York, 1958–1968), vol. VI, pp. 282, 286–344.

economic boycott. By the late 1770s, most states had begun to confiscate Loyalist property, eventually seizing millions of acres and property whose total value probably exceeded £6,000,000.[45]

Civilians, however, were not always adversely affected by war. Many civilians played important roles in these conflicts. During the Revolution, women made uniforms for the Continental Army in their leisure time. They also organized drives to collect scarce items, or even donated their own household articles to the cause. Other women served as nurses, and those who followed the army—a group that irritated General Washington, except, of course, for his own wife and the mates of other high-ranking officers—frequently served as cooks, laundresses, and medical auxiliaries. By helping to provide better prepared food and a more sanitary environment, their presence, John Shy has contended, may have helped forestall camp diseases which so often decimated armies in this period.[46]

Countless civilians served on local committees that handled wartime details; during the Revolution, for instance, village committees sprang up to ensure that economic boycott laws were enforced and to curtail the activities of suspected Tory spies. Some civilians were hired to assist armies. Local labor often was employed to transport heavy artillery for a siege operation, and expert wagoners were frequently hired to haul the bulky provisions for an expeditionary force. A labor force capable of manufacturing arms and other supplies was essential in every war.

Almost from the beginning of colonization some workers were excused from wartime service. Several colonies exempted fishermen, carpenters, iron workers, and millers. On the other hand, several colonies impressed laborers and artificers for nonmilitary, but related services during the various intercolonial wars. Some were conscripted to build fortifications, others to repair firearms or to make shoes for the troops. During the Revolution some states offered tempting bounties as inducements for the production of firearms, ammunition, and iron, and most states, on the recommendation of Congress, exempted workers in powder mills and munitions installations from military service. Women and children, apprenticed and enslaved laborers, convicts, and even enemy deserters were employed in some industrial establishments.[47]

45. Wallace Brown, *The Good Americans* (New York, 1969), pp. 126–42, 189; Alexander C. Flick, *Loyalism in New York During the American Revolution* (New York, 1901), pp. 62–3, 67, 81–82, 84–85, 138–39; Catherine Crary, ed., *The Price of Loyalty* (New York, 1973), pp. 203, 208, 211; Robert O. de Mond, *The Loyalists in North Carolina during the American Revolution* (Durham, N.C., 1926), pp. 47–59; Thomas Jones, *History of New York* (New York, 1879), p. 75; Harold B. Hancock, *The Delaware Loyalists* (Boston, 1972), p. 41; Otis G. Hammond, *Tories of New Hampshire in the War of the Revolution* (Boston, 1972), pp. 6, 17–18, 26–27.

46. Cometti, "Women," pp. 33–45; Hamilton, "Colonial Warfare," p. 3.

47. Richard B. Morris, *Government and Labor in Early America* (New York, 1946), pp. 279–80, 295; Elizabeth Cometti, "The Labor Front During the Revolution," in John E. Ferling, ed., *The American Revolution: The Home Front,* West Georgia College *Studies in the Social Sciences,* vol. XV (1976), pp. 80–81; Foner, *Labor and the Revolution,* p. 181.

Occasionally, civilians were offered a more direct opportunity to participate in a war. From time to time inhabitants of both French and British colonies were given cash bonuses for every enemy scalp—women and children included—that they could secure. Moreover, Indian captives were frequently offered to civilians as the bounty of war, prisoners who could be used as bonded laborers.[48]

England launched its colonial experiment with the certainty that force would be required to win a foothold in America. Over the next century and a half, the English secured the eastern half of North America by means of armed conflict. The English adventure in America frequently took on the characteristics of an armed invasion.

The earliest settlers were accompanied by professional soldiers who armed, trained, disciplined, and fortified the inhabitants. At almost every moment in the seventeenth and eighteenth centuries, English colonists somewhere were either engaged in war, on the verge of entering a war, or just concluding hostilities.

The American environment altered the nature of European warfare. The colonists often continued to use the same weapons as their contemporaries in Europe, but warfare retreated to a degree of savagery not seen in Europe for generations. War became a life-and-death struggle, not just for the soldiers in the field but for the civilian population who often found itself living in a war zone. At stake in these conflicts was the very survival of England's American Empire and the maintenance of the colonists' homeland. With such stakes the wars waged between the colonists and the Europeans on American soil descended to a level of almost indescribable terrorism and malevolence. Woeful as these conflicts were, however, the wars between the settlers and the Indians (the subject of the next chapter) took on a tone of barbarism perhaps not witnessed in the Western world since antiquity.

48. *Pennsylvania Archives*, 4th Ser., 8 vols. (Harrisburg, Pa., 1935), vol. II, pp. 596–97; Hamilton, *French and Indian Wars*, p. 38.

Chapter Two
The Indian Wars

the way of conquering them

In the early evening hours of February 9, 1676, throughout the small hamlets in which most people in the Western world lived, yeomen snuffed out their candles and retired to the warmth of a winter's bed. For most, the day had been uneventful. Nor was anything extraordinary anticipated when they arose with the next sunrise. The pace of life slowed during these winter months. Planting was still a few weeks in the future. Time was now occupied by a repetitive round of chores: tending the livestock, repairing the farm tools, mending fences, maintaining the house, caring for the children. Tomorrow would bring only more of the same.

In earlier Februaries, life had been like this in Lancaster, Massachusetts, a frontier village of 250 inhabitants about twenty-five miles northwest of Boston. Aside from the Puritan clergyman and a blacksmith, and perhaps one or two additional skilled artisans, all the settlers were farmers. The town was not quite a quarter-century old. In 1653 a few founders, mostly younger sons and their new brides from other, older Massachusetts villages, had acquired the land from the colony's general court and had moved to the virgin soil. They lived in sparsely furnished, tiny clapboard cottages, and for most of the year they toiled with the fickle weather and the forbidding soil to produce ten or twelve acres of wheat, oats, and corn.

But in the early days of the year 1676 no one in Lancaster could sleep with equanimity. Since the previous June war between the colonists and the Wampanoags, the Narragansetts and the Nipmucks had swept across parts of the northern colonies. For months the militia forces of New England had engaged in inconclusive firefights with the Indians. Repeatedly, the natives had struck at remote villages, despoiling the hamlets in a matter of hours, then retreating to the vast wilderness with their plunder and hostages. Only six weeks earlier the tide seemed to have turned. A large force of colonists, accompanied by Indian allies, surprised an important Narragansett village in Rhode Island. Moving swiftly, the well-coordinated attackers decimated the Indians; more than five hundred natives perished in a few hours in what soon became known as the Great Swamp Fight. Ironically, the colony's victory meant only additional problems for the inhabitants of the frontier hamlets. The Indian survivors, now more desperate than ever, began in late January to prey even more systematically on remote villages, seeking revenge as well as food and other provisions.

The residents of Lancaster prayed that their village might be spared, but they knew an attack was possible. A few days earlier, in fact, a Christian Indian of the Nashaway tribe had warned the governor of Massachusetts that an attack on Lancaster was being planned, but the government ignored the warning. Even the troops who had won the Great Swamp Fight decided, after a bitter argument with the high command, to withdraw rather than pursue the native remnants in the wilderness. The villagers, however, had not been inactive. They had written the colony's leaders requesting assistance. When that failed, the community sent its minister, Joseph Rowlandson, and a lieutenant of the local militia to plea personally for aid. That ploy failed, too. The residents also constructed five log garrison houses at strategic points in the township. The Rowlandson house, likewise, was being converted into a garrison house. Although work on the structure was not yet finished, the mistress of the dwelling, Mary Rowlandson, her sister, and thirty-five additional villagers crowded into these quarters on the evening of February 9 as they had for the past several nights.

Outside the palisaded house, the afternoon sun ebbed, and a dark, cold New England winter night settled in. In the warm garrison, the inhabitants hurriedly gulped a light evening meal. No one cleaned the dishes; that could await morning. The familiar Puritan prayers were uttered, and then the children were put to bed. Later, most of the adults retired, many to spend a restless, anxious night. Outside, a bitter wind stirred to irregularly punctuate the silence. Otherwise, only the familiar rousings of the livestock and the occasional bleatings of the night beasts of the forest, the animals that the Indians customarily imitated to relay signals to one another, disturbed the quiet. Inside the Rowlandson garrison, some men stood watch, not prepared to relax until relieved by a compatriot on the next shift. Once again this night, as they had each night for the past two weeks, the sentries squinted into the blackness, straining to see any unusual movement, hoping they would hear no strange sounds, and wondering which sounds were uncommon.

The night dragged in the atmosphere of tension. Men shifted occasionally to relieve a sentry. Children stirred in bed. Once or twice infants cried out, their mothers feverishly trying to quiet them so the guards could listen unhindered. Even as the night chill descended on the rude house, the inhabitants sensed the claminess of their own skin and breathed the odor of anxiety about them.

Finally, after what seemed an eternity, a time when the night dawdled and lagged and every sound wrenched the garrison dwellers, another Stygian evening was nearing its end. In minutes the first beams of the morning sun would illuminate the forest, and the Indians would probably not attack in the daylight hours. Some in the Rowlandson house were stirring already, preparing for another day's chores. A sensation of elation and euphoria, mingled with fatigue, set in. The potential danger had passed for a few more hours.

Suddenly, gunshots were heard in the distance. Several inhabitants raced to the windows, calling back in a moment that Indians were attacking. The natives, they said, had struck first at some of the outlying garrison houses. Fires now could be seen, and smoke was discerned to the west.

Momentarily, the settlers saw the Indians pierce one garrison and drag five villagers from their compound. They were too far away to be identified, but to the horror of the onlookers, they could clearly see the Indians tomahawking a man, then a woman and a child. Helpless, the garrison watched two children being dragged into the forest. Soon two other villagers were captured. One was quickly murdered, but the other, after a brief struggle, fled into the woods. Involuntarily, the members of the garrison cheered at the escape. A moment later a man dashed for safety from an adjacent compound. He did not make it. He was brought down by a single gunshot; the inhabitants of the Rowlandson house, peering out of their windows, saw the wounded man plead for his life, but a moment later a native split his head with a hatchet. Other natives stripped off his clothing and mutilated his remains, holding his entrails aloft for the mortified residents to see. Seconds later an imprudent farmer raced from his garrison house to save his barn; he was easily shot. Shortly, three other neighbors were seen to fall from gunshot wounds. In the meantime, homes, some belonging to those in the Rowlandson garrison house, were set afire. The torch was also being set to barns and sheds, and in the eerie light cast by the flames and the early rays of the sun, the inhabitants could see their livestock being herded into the forest. The acrid smell of charred timber drifted to the Rowlandson house to mingle with the feral screams of the attackers and the terrified whimperings of some of the inhabitants.

Slowly, methodically, inexorably the Indians completed their grisly chores at each of the garrisons. The grim work of flushing the occupants from their posts and apprehending and subduing, or killing, those who attempted to flee took about thirty minutes at each shelter. The Rowlandson garrison watched all this without being molested. Now, almost two hours after the initial attack, they saw Indian warriors start for their pallisade. Positioned behind mounds and lodged inside barns, the natives opened fire. Bullets smashed the windows. In only seconds three men fell wounded. The steady thud of bullets against the heavy oak logs added to the shock and panic. Sentries from within got off an occasional ineffective shot. The pungent odor of spent gunpowder permeated the cramped quarters. Someone shouted that the Indians were about to set fire to the garrison. They were observed gathering flax and hemp from a nearby barn; soon a native raced forward with a torch and ignited one corner of the house. An intrepid inmate struggled out and doused the flames, but it was quickly fired again. A stifling pall of smoke seeped into the lodging. Each person knew he must either flee or certainly perish in the burning garrison. As men unbolted the heavy door, some said final prayers; others grappled with the wounded, hoping to drag them to safety. Some men reloaded their muskets. Perhaps one good shot as they dashed for concealment in the forest might save their lives. Some did nothing; immobilized by fear, they stared into space.

The door swung open, but a salvo of bullets so thick that it sounded as if several handsful of stones had been thrown against the garrison slammed into the portal. Momentarily, instinctively, the inhabitants were driven back into the suffocating atmosphere. The garrison brought forward its six large dogs, beasts who had been trained to react viciously when an Indian approached. Perhaps the dogs would fend off the Indians until the settlers could escape. But the dogs, too, were paralyzed with fear. Finally, the first of the garrison, Mrs. Rowlandson's brother-in-law, stepped out. He advanced only a step beyond the door before a bullet tore through his throat. Others darted out. Mrs. Rowlandson, carrying her infant child, clambered through the door. A few steps out of the inferno, she was grazed by a bullet in the side; though she was not badly wounded, the projectile cut into her child. She continued to run, but the Indians overtook her and dragged her back. She had only a second to examine her wound and that of her child. Both were covered with blood, but beyond that she could not assess the damage. She looked up in time to see her eldest sister and her nephew gunned down. Most of the men were caught and tomahawked. Some, mortally wounded, were left to crawl about in agony before their families. The sight reminded her of a flock of sheep torn by wolves. Her eyes searched for her other children. She did not know whether they, too, had been shot or captured or had even escaped the burning house. Now the Indians began to drive their captives and plundered livestock away from Lancaster. Almost three hours after the attack had commenced, Mary Rowlandson, dazed by the suddenness and the savagery of the assault, was a prisoner of the Indians.[1]

The military nature of the English migration to America indicates that the settlers suspected war was more than a mere possibility. The well-documented Spanish experiences, as well as some unpleasant occurrences during the early explorations, particularly during Martin Frobisher's first voyage in 1576, indicate that conflict with the native Americans was virtually certain. If nothing else, the English rationale for laying claim to territory in America put the settlers and the Indians on a collision course.

The colonists claimed to legitimately possess New World territory because of the doctrine of "first discovery." Queen Elizabeth authorized the first colonist, Sir Humphrey Gilbert, to settle all "territories not actually possessed of any Christian prince or people." Though Indians might inhabit the region, the Crown regarded the lands as belonging to England because they were unoccupied by Christians. This notion was later voiced principally by New England settlers; American land was seen as *vacuum domicilium,* that is, legally wasteland. John

---

1. The preceding account is based on Mary Rowlandson, *The Sovereignty and Goodness of GOD . . . Being a Narrative of the Captivity and Restauration of Mrs. Mary Rowlandson* (Cambridge, Mass., 1682). The account has been reprinted in Charles H. Lincoln, ed., *Narratives of the Indian Wars, 1675–1699* (New York, 1913), pp. 107–67, and in Richard Van Der Beets, ed., *Held Captive by Indians: Selected Narratives, 1642–1836* (Knoxville, Tenn., 1973), pp. 41–90.

Cotton, for instance, told the passengers on the *Arbella,* who were about to embark for Massachusetts Bay, that America was a "convenient . . . vacancy." The land need not be purchased, he added, for in "a vacant soyle, hee that taketh possession of it, and bestoweth culture and husbandry upon it, his Right it is." John Winthrop, the early governor of that colony, believed that God originally gave men possession of the land for purposes of "soweing, and feeding where he pleased"; as civilization grew more complex, God gave men the civil right to own "certaine cells of ground by enclosing," that is, to possess private property and to plow that earth and profit from that soil. But the "Natives in New England they inclose noe land neither have any settled habitation nor any tame cattle to improve the land. . . ." Property "Wch [sic] lies comon & hath never been replinished or subdued," he added, "is free to any that will possesse and improve it," according to God's admonition to mankind in Genesis 1:28.[2]

This concept persisted for generations. Even during the Revolution, troops were sent to conquer the Indian lands of western New York with the understanding, stated by the troops' chaplain, that it would be a "just and complete conquest" because the unimproved lands were "so fertile a part of the western world." Others claimed Indian lands because the natives were thought to be "savages." Robert Gray contended that God had not intended that any land be "usurped by wild beasts, and unreasonable creatures, or by brutish savages," particularly those who, because of their "godless ignorance and blasphemous Idolatrie," were worse than beasts. England additionally justified territorial possession through either sustained possession, seizing and holding land, or by the voluntary obsequience of the natives.[3]

On the eve of colonization the English view of the Indians consisted of conflicting images. At times the English regarded the Indians as bellicose, unmalleable savages who were certain to "practice violence either in repelling the Christians from theyr Portes and safe Landings or in withstanding afterwardes. . . ."[4] On the other hand, the Indians were sometimes thought to be friendly and tractable if treated cordially; this was the Indian the English hoped to meet, not only for the obvious reasons but also because the English believed trade between England and the natives was essential for colonial development.[5]

2. Samuel E. Morison, *The European Discovery of America,* 2 vols. (New York, 1971–1974), vol. I, p. 566; John Cotton, "God's Promise," *Old South Leaflets,* vol. III, no. 53 (n.d.); Chester E. Eisenger, "The Puritan's Justification for Taking the Land," *Essex Institute Historical Collections* 84 (April 1948), pp. 131, 135, 138, 140.

3. Alfred Hazen Wright, comp., *The Sullivan Expedition of 1779* (Ithaca, N.Y., 1943), p. 2; Francis Jennings, *The Invasion of America* (Chapel Hill, N.C., 1975), pp. 105–6, 110, 117, 135; Francis Jennings, "Virgin Land and Savage People," *American Quarterly* 23 (October 1971), pp. 521–22.

4. George Peckham, *A True Report . . . of the Newfound Landes,* quoted in Gerald Nash, "Image of the Indians," *WMQ* 29 (April 1972), p. 204.

5. Nash, "Image of the Indians," p. 204.

This dual image of the Indians hardly vanished with colonization. Throughout America during the initial generations of coexistence, many colonists discerned positive facets of the Indians' character and society. From the outset, colonists like John Smith marveled at the natives' feats of courage, strength, speed, and endurance. Many colonists were astonished at the level of Indian civilization. As late as the American Revolution, some soldiers who were sent to the wilderness found, according to one historian, that the Indians were living in a state of civilization "equal to, and often better than, that of the frontier whites." Although the colonists disdained the natives' religious practices, the Europeans were impressed that they did worship and were confident that conversion to Christianity was not impossible. The English were likewise impressed that the Indians had a structural form of government, and, additionally, some considered it commendable that the native rulers, unlike those of the parent state, did not come "creeping from a Country Farm, into a Courtly Gallantry" but achieved preeminence by being the "most cruelly Valorous."[6]

Precolonial suspicions, English ethnocentrism, and frequent clashes with the natives, however, led most colonists to a less charitable impression. At least until the Indian warfare ceased or was waged only on some remote frontier, most settlers regarded the natives as superstitious, ruthless, and vengeful. Many colonists simply dismissed the Indians as savages. Articulate colonists believed the natives were "inhumanely cruel," "without mercy," "blood-thirsty heathens," "barbarions," "savage villians," "exceedingly dirty," "more than devils," "the Devil," "Children of the Devil," "hellish fiends, and brutish men that Devils worshiped," "the devil's instruments," "like carnivorous beasts of the forests," "Ravenous howling wolves," and "as greedy after their prey as a wolf, and to whom the woods [are] equally natural and familiar." The colonists, moreover, were convinced that the Indians were masters of deceit. Many a settler was warned not to "bee too confident of the fidellitie of the savages." Even when the Indians offered assistance—such as Powhatan's gifts of corn and pleas for peace—the settlers merely regarded such behavior as typical of the "cunning tricks" and "slippery designs" of the "perfidious Savages."[7]

---

6. John Smith, *A Map of Virginia* . . . [1612], in Arber, *Works of Smith,* 2 vols. (Birmingham, Eng., 1884), vol. I, p. 65; Barbara Graymont, *The Iroquois in the American Revolution* (Syracuse, N.Y., 1972), p. 220; J. H. Elliot, *The Old World and the New, 1492–1650* (London, 1970), pp. 41–49; George Alsop, *A Character of the Province of Maryland, by George Alsop* (London, 1666), in Clayton C. Hall, ed., *Narratives of Maryland* (New York, 1910), p. 367.

7. William Douglass, *A Summary, Historical and Political, of the British Settlements in North America,* 2 vols. (Boston, 1755), vol. I, p. 549; Wright, *Sullivan Expedition,* no. 6, pp. 2, 32, 107; Frederick Cook, ed., *Journals of the Military Expedition of Major General Sullivan against the Six Nations* . . . (Auburn, N.Y., 1877), pp. 45, 60, 91; Samuel G. Drake, ed., *The History of the Indian Wars in New England* . . . *From the Originial Work by the Rev. William Hubbard,* 2 vols. (Roxbury, Mass., 1865), vol. I, pp. 42, 53; Peter Carroll, *Puritanism and the Wilderness* . . . (New York, 1969), pp. 77, 136; Cotton Mather, *Souldiers Counselled and Comforted* . . . (Boston, 1689), p. 110; "Thomas Hutchinson," in Lawrence S. Mayo, ed., *The History of the Colony and Province*

Indian warriors sometimes won grudging accolades from the colonists. Captain John Smith was impressed by their bravery, agility, and stamina. John Underhill characterized most of his Indian adversaries as "courageous fellows." A contemporary historian, William Douglass, admired the Indians' "great fortitude in enduring torture and death." Some soldiers believed Indians were a stronger and more deadly enemy than European professional troops. One colonial warrior estimated that a normal battle with the natives would "do us more harm" than an engagement with ten times as many European soldiers. Those who experienced combat alongside Indian allies were almost always impressed. General Horatio Gates, who was assisted by Indians when he resisted General John Burgoyne's invasion of the United States in 1777, regarded his allies as "Brave men [who] fought like Bull dogs." Nor was it uncommon to laud the Indians' abilities as foragers and scouts."[8]

The more common view of Indian warfare, however, was less favorable. Accustomed to the European manner of combat, most colonists were appalled by Indian tactics. The deliberate killing of women and children was unconscionable to many settlers. So, too, was the natives' guerrilla style of fighting. Sacking villages, kidnapping the defenseless, or shooting "down, from behind a fence, the ploughman in his furrow," were denounced as the methods of cowards and savages. This manner of warfare was so exasperating that the chief justice of South Carolina probably spoke for many when he lamented that "we may as well goe to War with Wolfs and Bears." Increase Mather echoed this attitude toward the Indians when he claimed that "they act like wolves." The colonists often labeled the Indians "unmanly" and characterized their conduct as "skulking" and "creeping." Indian trickery—ambushes, surprise attacks on the heels of "peaceful professions"—was denounced as immoral behavior.[9]

Many colonists ridiculed the nature of the warfare among Indians. These conflicts, a settler noted, were "farre lesse bloudy and devouring than the cruell Warres of *Europe*. . . ." Seldom more than twenty Indians perished in these encounters, and the colonists believed the Indians "reckon it a bloody battle" if as many as a dozen were killed. Roger Williams, the stubborn Puritan clergyman, observed that the Indians fought with such "leaping and dancing, that seldom an Arrow hits"; even when an enemy was wounded, he added, he was

of Massachusetts-Bay, 3 vols. (Cambridge, Mass., 1936), vol. II, p. 75; Nash, "Image of the Indians," p. 213.

8. Smith, *Map of Virginia*, p. 65; John Underhill, *News from America*, MHS, *Coll.*, vol. VI, pp. 24–25; Douglass, *A Summary*, vol. I, p. 549; Hiram Bingham, *Five Straws Gathered from Revolutionary Fields* (Cambridge, Mass., 1901), p. 15; Graymont, *Iroquois*, p. 155.

9. Hugh T. Lefler and William S. Powell, *Colonial North Carolina*, (New York, 1973), p. 143; Richard Sherman, *Robert Johnson . . . Proprietary & Royal Governor of South Carolina* (Columbia, S.C., 1966), p. 19; Douglass, *A Summary*, vol. I, p. 549; Douglas Leach, *Flintlock and Tomahawk* (New York, 1958), pp. 92–93; Wright, *Sullivan Expedition*, no. 6, p. 6; Carroll, *Puritanism*, pp. 76–79, 136.

frequently not captured. One professional European officer believed the Indians "might fight seven years and not kill seven men." The Indians, he insisted, fought one another from great distances. When they discharged their missile "they gaze up in the sky to see where the arrow fall, and not until it is fallen do they shoot again. This fight is more for pastime, than to conquer and subdue. . . ." The Indians, in fact, complained to the New Englanders that European warfare was "too furious, and slays too many men." Some considered the Indians cowards because they frequently fled in the face of colonial soldiers, leaving "their wigwams, or houses, and possessions to the use of our soldiers." Many believed the Indians would flee when the first firearm was discharged in a battle. Regardless of the odds, another colonial leader suggested, the natives would "durst not look an *Englishman* in the Face in the open Field"; instead, they allegedly would resort to some manner of skullduggery. Early on, perhaps even before settlement, colonists concluded that the Indians could never defeat a trained European army.[10]

Warfare among the native Americans, of course, was unlike the seventeenth- and eighteenth-century continental wars with which the European settlers were familiar. Conflicts between tribes traditionally were small in scope. Indian weaponry was inaccurate and lacked sustained firepower. The forest provided a natural defensive bulwark for the warriors, and it virtually precluded the concept of cavalry tactics. Furthermore, unlike European troops, the Indians had no tradition of making a death-defying stand against another tribe. When pressed, the native warriors simply fled, prompting a New England chronicler to note that "he that hath no armes to fight, findes legges to run away." As a result, it was unusual for a tribe to lose more than a score of its warriors in an engagement.[11]

If tribal warfare was limited, however, it was not infrequent. War, in fact, was nearly constant among the natives of the Atlantic seaboard. Conflicts arose over boundary disputes, to avenge insults, to gain prestige, to assure hegemony over weaker neighbors, and to strike down a burgeoning enemy. The Iroquois technically were at war with those tribes with whom they were not allied, and their male warriors were always free to form a war party without the consent of their superiors; indeed, the younger men were frequently difficult to restrain, for military heroics afforded the most rapid route to glory and power. Among

10. Roger Williams, *A Key into the Language of America,* in *The Complete Writings of Roger Williams,* 7 vols. (New York, 1963), vol. I, p. 204; Douglass, *A Summary,* vol. I, p. 550; Underhill, *News from America,* MHS, *Coll.,* vol. VI, pp. 6, 26; Graymont, *Iroquois,* p. 155; James Axtell, "The Scholastic Philosophy of the Wilderness," *WMQ,* 3d Ser. 29 (July 1972), p. 351; Leach, *Flintlock and Tomahawk,* pp. 92–93.

11. Alden Vaughn, *The New England Frontier . . .* (Boston, 1965), p. 39; John K. Mahon, "Anglo-American Methods of Indian Warfare, 1676–1794," *Mississippi Valley Historical Review* 45 (September 1958), pp. 254–61; William Wood, *Wood's New England Prospect* (Boston, 1865), p. 95.

other tribes, war could commence only if called for by the sachem, the chieftain, and approved by his council and military leaders. Some southern tribes entered war upon the exhortation of the "war captain" or the "Big Warrior."[12]

Having decided, as a Chickasaw chief once declared, that "their tomahawks were thirsty to drink the blood of their enemy," the warriors plunged into battle. With their skin painted, their hair oiled with bear grease, and garbed in feathers and beads but only lightly clad, the tribesmen danced off to conflict, perhaps singing of the wartime exploits of their ancestors. These men had been trained since adolescence for this moment. As boys they had played with hatchets and bows; later they were trained in marksmanship. They had played violent tribal games, akin to modern rugby or football, and more dangerous games, such as learning to dodge, "with swift conveighance," an arrow shot in their direction by a playmate. Folk tales, hunting, and running (Roger Williams claimed some Indian youths could run a hundred miles in two hours) had been part of their preparation.[13] Participation in the torture of some luckless captive from a previous battle perhaps capped the training.

In all likelihood the ensuing battle would be fought in a densely wooded environment, but some tribes were besieged in their palisaded fortifications. Before the arrival of the Europeans, the primary weapon was the bow, a five- or six-foot long, painted mechanism shaped from witch hazel or hickory; the accompanying arrows were six- to eight-inch lengths of elder wood, tipped with stone, copper, bone, antlers, or eagle talons. Arrows could be shot nearly two hundred yards, but they were accurate for only about a quarter of that distance. They struck with great force. A Frenchman in America reported seeing an arrow pass cleanly through a dog and then strike a soldier with such force that the warrior died instantly. Lieutenant Lion Gardener, another professional warrior hired by the Puritans, seeing one of his soldiers perish when a Pequot arrow smashed through his right rib cage and lodged in his left side, removed and "cleansed it, and presumed to send [it] to Massachusetts Bay, because they said that the arrows of the Indians were of no force."[14]

Other Indian warriors were equipped with tomahawks, clubs, knives, or spears. The Indians occasionally devised weaponry dictated by the logistics of their situation. As they gained more expertise in storming fortifications, the Wampanoags, in King Philip's War, constructed a rolling incendiary device. They fitted long poles to a barrel, then affixed this mechanism to truckle wheels.

12. Malone, "Indian and English," (Ph.D. diss., Brown University, 1971), pp. 25–41; Graymont, *Iroquois*, p. 21; James Adair, *The History of the American Indians* . . . (London, 1775), p. 380; Ruth Murray Underhill, *Red Man's America* (Chicago, 1953), pp. 37–94; David Cockran, *The Creek Frontier, 1540–1783* (Norman, Okla., 1962), pp. 25–27.

13. Underhill, *Red Man's America*, pp. 37–38; Alsop, *A Character*, p. 367; Wood, *Wood's New England*, pp. 95–98; Malone, "Indian and English," pp. 18–19.

14. Malone, "Indian and English," pp. 8–15; Lion Gardener, "Gardener's Pequot Warres," MHS *Coll.*, 3d Ser. 3 (1833), pp. 139–40, 144.

The front was loaded with combustibles, such as flax or hay, ignited, and sped toward the entrenched foe. After Europeans arrived, the Indians possessed fire-arms. While they did not learn the technology of constructing these pieces, the Indians quickly developed blacksmithing skills essential for the repair of the arms; in addition, the Indians rapidly learned to make gunpowder, molds for the production of ammunition, and new forms of armor that afforded some protection from the musket.[15]

Indian warfare was largely undisciplined and based on individual encounters. One English settler was aghast at the sight of Indians proceeding toward their enemies "in a disordered manner, without any souldier like marching or warlike postures, being deafe to any word of command, ignorant . . . of double ranks or files. . . ." There was a plan, of course, to most Indian battles. Surprise attack was the desired objective. Moreover, while the fighting was often chaotic, each side hoped to surround its foe. Having completed their foray, the Indians withdrew. They "approach like foxes, fight like lions and disappear like birds," a French adversary marvelled. The Europeans castigated such tactics as the tactics of cowards, but the Indians thought the English methods foolish. It was "better [to] ly somewhere, and Shoot a man, and hee no see! That the best Soldier," an Indian remarked. If the element of surprise was lost, the Indians often simply charged pell-mell into their opponents, "running to and fro, and shooting their Arrows at Random."[16]

Warfare between the Indians was also characterized by curious inconsisten-cies. On the one hand, their encounters were small-scale affairs, resulting in relatively few casualties. The warriors, in fact, had little desire to destroy large numbers of the enemy. These conflicts were waged with limited objectives in mind. The procurement of territorial rights or the redressing of some alleged grievance did not always require total war. In addition, the conflicts were often a manifestation of a tribal rite, a symbol of the coming of age of the young male generation, a collective endeavor designed to exalt the values and ethos of the people's culture. Hence, it was not uncommon for the combatants to agree upon guidelines for the war before the first arrow was unsheathed. The belligerents, for example, frequently consented to spare women and children in the ensuing conflict. On the other hand, those unfortunate souls who fell captive to the enemy were treated with a barbarism that would have taxed the sadistic ingenuity of Europe's most ruthless despots.

The colonists were divided over how to treat the native Americans. The settlers knew that Indian assistance might be beneficial, even essential, in en-

15. Patrick Malone, "Changing Military Technology Among the Indians of Southern New Eng-land, 1600–1677," *AQ* 25 (March 1973), pp. 57–58.

16. Wood, *Wood's New England,* pp. 94–95; Malone, "Indian and English," pp. 254–61; Underhill, *Red Man's America,* p. 96; Axtell, "Scholastic Philosophy," p. 343; John Mason, *A Brief History of the Pequot War,* MHS, *Coll.,* 2nd Ser. 8 (1819), p. 142.

hancing or saving the quality of life in the provinces. Frequently the settlers were left to their own devices by their compatriots in the homeland, and, despite European technology, they were helpless to cope with the American wilderness.[17] Additionally, the colonists soon learned that trade with the natives could be lucrative, and, despite the most hideous punishments for such practices, some of the earliest settlers in each colony engaged in this clandestine activity. So many Indians bartered for English weapons that Plymouth's Governor William Bradford was moved to versify that

> Thus like madmen we put them in a way,
> With our own weapons us to kill and slay.[18]

Furthermore, many settlers came to America with a sense of mission to convert the natives to Christianity. The Puritans quickly commenced proselytizing in the wilderness; even the Virginia Company planned a college for the Indians, though they never sent a single missionary to America. Whatever their intent, the settlers fatalistically assumed that some conflict was likely, and they soon realized that there were wide differences between Indian warfare, real or fancied, and wars in England and on the continent. The colonists' varied interests and desires, coupled with their experiences, divided the settlers.

From the outset some colonists counseled for the most moderate treatment of the Indians. The younger Hakluyt suggested restraint, adding that if relations soured the colonists should endeavor merely to "scourge" the natives rather than resort to violence. George Peckham, an Elizabethan colonial publicist and planner, admonished the immigrants to act in a "good and fayre" manner toward the Indians. The colonists also were advised that the natives were capable only of inflicting "sleights," but that real damage was unlikely. Indian depredations, therefore, should not be feared. The colonists were urged to "shew mercie to them and theirs," and they were warned that to resort to war "shall make your names odious to all . . . posteritie. Instead of Iron and steele you must have patience and humanitie to manage their crooked nature to your form of civilitie. . . ." Even after the surprise Indian attack on Virginia settlers in 1622, some called for moderation. Former Governor George Wyatt still believed that only "mildnes" and an "easie hand" could bring "those Barbarians to Civilitie."[19]

In time, the Indians were driven to ever more remote frontiers and the problem seemed to wane. The colonists perceived more positive aspects of native Amer-

---

17. Jennings, *Invasion of America*, pp. 32–37.

18. William Bradford, "Bradford's Verse History of New England," MHS *Coll.*, 1st Ser. 3 (1794), p. 82.

19. Wesley Frank Craven, "Indian Policy in Early Virginia," *WMQ*, 3d Ser. 1 (January 1944), pp. 66–67; William Welby, *The New Life of Virginia* . . . , in Foner, *Tracts*, vol. I, pp. 18–19; S. Frederick Fausz and Jan Kukla, eds., "Letter of Advice," *WMQ* 34 (January, 1977), pp. 112–3.

ican culture; intermarriage between Indians and the white settlers occurred with greater frequency, and, while not encouraged, such practices rarely resulted in ostracism. Much later, some attempts were made to transform white attitudes toward the natives. After white vigilantes, known as the Paxton Boys, murdered several innocent Indians in Pennsylvania during 1764 in reprisal for the depredations of Indians on the frontier, Benjamin Franklin counseled his fellow colonists that all Indians were not alike any more than all whites were similiar. The "poor Wretches" who were victims of the mob, he suggested, "would have been safer, if they had submitted to the Turks." Franklin called for better understanding and appreciation of native American culture, and, by implication, a greater degree of assimilation of Indians into the white culture of Pennsylvania.[20]

Few colonists ever countenanced such views. From the outset most colonists seem to have regarded conflict as unavoidable, and steeled themselves against that eventuality, differing only over the manner of coping with the inevitable. The Puritans who arrived in Plymouth were prepared to treat recalcitrant natives with the same severity that Israel had used against its foes in the Old Testament narratives. These Puritans even believed that a plague which eliminated large numbers of the natives on the eve of the European migration to New England was of providential origin.[21]

In the early years of the Virginia settlement, a rapidly unfolding series of incidents culminated in full-scale war. The English were bitter and anxious in the aftermath of the ambush of Captain Newport and his reconnaissance party in their first hours on Virginia soil. Shortly thereafter, some Indians tried to steal weapons from the English garrison at Jamestown. From time to time, moreover, settlers who unwisely strayed from the compound were murdered by Indians. The Jamestown leaders also learned from native informants that some other settlers, a mysterious Europeanlike group who had lived and mined near Jamestown, had been killed at the orders of Powhatan, the confederation chieftain, shortly after the arrival of the *Susan Constant;* the sketchy information was accepted at face value, and, in fact, many presumed the murdered foreigners were the remnants from England's long-lost colony at Roanoke Island. All doubts concerning the inclination of the Indians probably vanished when Powhatan himself, after an initial period of testing, bluntly told the settlers that war was inevitable if "your comming is not for trade, but to . . . possesse my Country." Moreover, the sachem boasted that if the English did not confine themselves to Jamestown, "he would give a command to his people to kill us, and do unto us all that mischief which they at their pleasure could." The Virginians, by now led by Captain John Smith, and fearing that "those bravadoes would but encourage the Savages," took the offensive. Indians were killed,

20. Benjamin Franklin, *A Narrative of the late Massacres . . . of a number of Indians . . .* (1764), in Labaree, *Papers of Franklin* (New Haven, 1959) vol. XI, pp. 55, 58, 66, 68.
21. Vaughn, *New England Frontier,* pp. 19–25.

their villages were plundered and burned, their fishing weirs were demolished, they were captured and "went by the heels"—that is, they were put in irons or flogged and tortured.[22]

It was Smith's hope to bring the natives to such a point of "feare and obedience, as his very name would sufficiently affright them." Peace was purchased for a time, especially when Pocahontas, the sachem's favorite daughter, was kidnapped and threatened with execution if the natives did not lay aside their arms and furnish foodstuffs for the settlers. The ploy worked for a time, and an uneasy peace settled over Virginia for a decade. But grievances arising from petty sleights, as well as from the earlier turbulence, accumulated among the Indians.

After 1618 the natives in the Jamestown region were led by Opechancanough, the brother of Powhatan, a sachem who may have harbored bitterness from a humiliating experience he suffered years before at the hands of Captain Smith. In 1608, while on a reconnaissance mission, Smith, with only fifteen compatriots, suddenly found himself surrounded by hundreds of natives led by Opechancanough. Smith told his squad to "fight like men, and not die like sheep" if the Indians attacked. To forestall a full-scale battle, however, Smith challenged the native leader to a personal duel to the death, the victor to be "Lord and Master" over the other side. Opechancanough balked at the challenge, whereupon Smith grasped his adversary by the hair, thrust a pistol against his chest, and "led the trembling King, neare dead with feare, amongst all his people." The Indians dropped their weapons, and Smith and his party made their escape. The sachem had been humiliated before his own people.[23] Less than four years after he came to power, in 1622, Opechancanough sought his revenge in the stunning surprise attack on Virginia.

Following the massacre, Virginia's authorities acted in a manner that made Smith appear angelic by contrast. With "much grief" the Virginia Company called for a "sharp revenge uppon the bloody miscreants," even to the degree of "rooting them out for being longer a people upon the face of the Earth." Christopher Brooke of London was moved to draft a poem in which he called the Indians "Errors of Nature" and the "very dregs, garbage and spawne of Earth." He proposed their annihilation, "leaving not a Creature." Another London writer proposed that the natives be captured alive if possible and used as galley slaves. Sir Edwin Sandys, formerly the treasurer of the company, advised the settlers to lull the tribesmen into a sense of false security, then "followe their example in destroying them." John Smith, by this time a middle-aged historian in England, advised the company to "endeavor to inforce the Savages to leave their Country"; he offered to return to America and take the

---

22. Barbour, *Three Worlds of John Smith* (Boston, 1964), pp. 78, 192–95; David Beers Quinn, *England and the Discovery of America, 1481–1620* (New York, 1974), pp. 432–88; John Smith, *The Generall Historie of Virginia . . .* (1624), in Arber, *Works of Smith*, vol. II, p. 451; Smith, *Map of Virginia*, in ibid., vol. I, pp. 151–53.

23. Smith, *Map of Virginia*, in Arber, *Works of Smith*, vol. I, pp. 107, 142.

lead in "tormenting the Savages." The most vituperous response came from
Edward Waterhouse, a secretary of the Virginia Company. He rejoiced that
"our hands which before were tied with gentlenesse and faire usage, are now
set at liberty. . . ." The English, he argued, at last were free to seize Indian
lands "by right of Warre, and law of Nations." Moreover, because "the way
of conquering them is much more easie than of civilizing them," Waterhouse
proposed nothing less than the systematic extermination of the natives of Virginia, these "deformed Savages [who were] no other than wild beasts."[24]

The company heeded much of this advice. It sent over scores of barrels of
powder and hundreds of additional arms, which the company candidly identified
as "Murtheringe peaces." It even sent over money to be posted as a reward for
the capture of Opechancanough. The next few months produced the first total
war in English America. In less than a year, more Indians were killed than had
perished at the hands of Englishmen in the previous fifteen years. Some natives
were killed in open combat; others were ambushed or tracked down by dogs
and murdered when captured. As many as 250 natives were deliberately poisoned
at what were supposed to be peace parleys. Countless hundreds, perhaps thousands, died of starvation as the English destroyed their crops, their hunting
grounds, and their fishing equipment.[25]

Virginia's misfortune of 1622 was like a beacon for settlers elsewhere in
America. Other settlers were determined to avoid the woes that had struck the
Old Dominion. The primary question among these earliest settlers was not how
to avoid war, but how best to face the anticipated conflict. Some believed a
defensive strategy was the wisest course and the policy most consistent with the
colonists' militia training. These individuals suggested that each colony heavily
fortify itself. Virginia only at this time commenced the systematic construction
of forts at strategic sites throughout the countryside. A half-century later, when
the Virginia frontier again festered, a portion of Governor William Berkeley's
domestic problems with Nathaniel Bacon stemmed from the executive's plan
to deal with the Indian depredations by constructing a series of wilderness
fortifications. Bacon and his western followers sneered at these "immobile
garrisons." Elsewhere, the fortification scheme was more popular, its desira-
bility hinging on the Indians' lack of cannon and effective rams.[26]

24. Council of Virginia to Governor, Sir Francis Wyatt, 1 August 1622, in Susan Myra Kingsbury,
ed., *The Records of the Virginia Company of London*, 4 vols. (Washington, D.C., 1906–1935),
vol. III, pp. 672–73; Fausz and Kukla, "Letter of Advice," p. 108n; William S. Powell, "Aftermath
of the Massacre: The First Indian War, 1622–1632," *Virginia Magazine of History and Biography*
66 (January 1958), pp. 48, 59; Smith, *Generall Historie*, in Arber, *Works of Smith*, vol. II, p. 588;
Edward Waterhouse, *A Declaration of the State of the Colony and Affairs in Virginia* (London,
1622), pp. 22–24.

25. Powell, "Aftermath of the Massacre," pp. 51–59, 68.

26. Ibid., p. 51; Wilcomb E. Washburn, *The Governor and the Rebel* . . . (Chapel Hill, N.C.,
1957), p. 32; *The Autobiography of Benjamin Franklin* (New York, 1944), p. 167; Wood, *Wood's
New England*, pp. 94–95.

Generally, however, the colonists rejected a defensive strategy in favor of more aggressive tactics planned for, and dictated by, the realities of the American environment. The colonists learned quickly that their knowledge of European warfare would bring them little success against a formidable enemy that had no knowledge of, or use for, continental conventions of battle. Some even came to think it best not to burden the colonists with British professionals in fighting the natives. Their tactics were thought to be so unsuited for these unconventional wars that they were like "a bird ready for the snare." Furthermore, some colonists thought the professionals, realizing their experience counted for little, would be "frightened out of their wits at the sight of Indians." Until the colonists learned the nuances of wilderness warfare, they too suffered humiliating set-backs. Even as late as the eighteenth century a South Carolina force in pursuit of Cherokees permitted itself to be lured deep into Indian territory, where, the Indians later boasted, the troops were "shot down . . . like turkeys." Some colonists urged the adoption of winter warfare, a style uncommon to both Indians and Europeans. Many advocated the use of Indian-like attacks, claiming that the only way to fight the natives was to be "light and naked, as they come Against Us, creeping near. . . ." During King Philip's War, Benjamin Church ordered his troops to "creep . . . on their bellies, until they came as near as they could; and that as soon as the Enemy discovered them they would cry out; and that was the word for his Men to fire and fall on."[27]

The colonists learned quickly from the natives. They soon wore mocassins and snowshoes into combat, banned smoking and other behavior that might reveal their location, divided their forces into smaller units to prevent ambushes in narrow defiles, and avoided ambushes by never "return[ing] the same way that [they] came." In addition, the colonists began to use Indians as guides, and they abandoned the European practice of all men firing simultaneously in volleys "lest the Enemy should take the advantage of such an Opportunity to run upon them with their Hatche [t]s" while all the troopers were reloading their weapons.[28]

Not all colonists agreed with the adoption of Indian tactics, however. William Hubbard, clergyman and historian of Indian warfare, continued to express faith in the more traditional continental methods, believing that the natives would not fight a large force of armed Europeans. Most thought differently. Surprise attacks on Indian villages—a native American tactic which the colonists originally had denounced as cowardly—became a favorite stratagem. The tactic compelled the

27. Lefler and Powell, *Colonial North Carolina*, pp. 141–42; Robert Meriwether, *The Expansion of South Carolina, 1729–1765* (Kingsport, Tenn., 1940), p. 231; Drake, *Hubbard's History of the Indian Wars*, vol. I, pp. 28, 32–33, 47, 121; Powell, "Aftermath of the Massacre," p. 48; Stanley Pargellis, "Braddock's Defeat," *AHR* 41 (January 1936), p. 256.

28. James Axtell, *School on a Hill* (New Haven, Conn., 1974), pp. 259–60; Douglas Leach, *Arms for Empire* (New York, 1973), p. 153; Mahon, "Anglo-American Methods of Indian Warfare," p. 266; Malone, "Changing Military Technology," p. 58.

Indians to fight and it afforded the colonists an opportunity to destroy both the enemy's food supplies and his technology, since native American blacksmiths were always ruthlessly killed and the Indians' forges and tools systematically destroyed.[29]

After the debacle of 1622, the colonists' warfare against the natives can best be characterized as the tactics of remorseless terrorism. Increasingly, the colonists spoke of "exterminating all Indians," as the frontiersmen often put it, or of "the design of Providence" that the settlers "extirpate the savages," as some among the elite suggested. Even Thomas Jefferson spoke of eliminating those "wretches" by "pushing into the heart of their [Indian] country. But I would not stop there," he continued. "I would never cease pursuing them while one of them remained on this side [of] the Misisippi." When Quaker hegemony waned in Pennsylvania, the provincial commissioners recommended to the governor that the colony's armed forces "hunt them in all their Fishing, Hunting, Planting and dwelling places" so that "the Enemy [be] kept in Continual Allarm. . . ." The aims of warfare against the Indians in the eighteenth century hardly differed from those of the early New England Puritans who dreamed of making "those brutes their servants, their slaves, either willingly or of necessity, and docile enough if not obsequious."[30] Only the means to those ends were altered as the colonists learned what was required to realize their goal.

War with the Indians, therefore, was total war. It was far more savage and brutal than the intercolonial conflicts, which, for all their inhumanity, were nevertheless tempered by the fact that the combatants came from similar backgrounds and embraced a common faith. Moreover, the European armies that grappled on American soil were composed of professional troops, men who had undergone prolonged and expensive training. Their commanders were loathe to sustain heavy casualties among such costly troops. The Western world had not seen contests waged with the ruthless intensity that characterized encounters between the settlers and the natives since perhaps the medieval era. Even then, although the warfare might have caused greater suffering among a larger percentage of the civilian population, it is doubtful that the warriors systematically practiced such demonic depredations on their foes, and especially upon civilians, as they regularly did in these primitive American encounters.

The instructions to the colonists who marched to war with the natives were monotonously similar in the early years of colonization and during the Revolution. The troops were ordered, as the Massachusetts Bay contingent had been

29. Drake, *Hubbard's History of the Indian Wars*, vol. I, pp. 133, 145; Mahon, "Anglo-American Methods of Indian Warfare," p. 266; Malone, "Changing Military Technology," p. 58.

30. Washburn, *Governor and the Rebel*, p. 32; *Autobiography of Franklin*, p. 137; Thomas Jefferson to John Page, 5 August 1776, in Julian P. Boyd et al., eds., *The Papers of Thomas Jefferson* (Princeton, N.J., 1950 —), vol. I, pp. 485–86; "Provincial Commissioners to Robert Hunter Morris," 13 June 1756, in Labaree, *Papers of Franklin*, vol. VI, p. 455; Malone, "Indian and English," pp. 261–62.

during King Philip's War, "to seeke out for the enemy . . . and if you meet the enimy you are to use your best skill & force to surprise . . . kill and destroy the enimy. . . ." Those colonists who remained at home were told by official proclamation that the Indians were responsible for the war's commencement and they "must not expect to have [the Indians'] lives spared. . . ." About one hundred years later, General Jeffery Amherst decided the Cherokees, a "vile and fickle people," had to be severely punished. The colonel placed in charge of the ensuing operation was to "destroy every [Cherokee] house, every corn-field, every orchard, and every vegetable plot."[31]

The colonists repeatedly used a few proven tactics against the natives. One tribe was played off against another with the expected results. Colonial leaders used favors to solidify an alliance with one tribe if war against another tribe seemed imminent. Indians were frequently used as military allies in these strug-gles; in fact, the Indians sometimes leapt at the opportunity to ally themselves with the whites, as a means of settling some old score with an ancient foe. At times Indians marauded other natives in order to curry favor with the English. Sensing that the Pequots were doomed, for instance, rival tribes seized fleeing warriors and sachems of the vanquished natives and murdered them, sending their severed heads to the English because, according to Lion Gardener, "they all feared us." The divide and conquer ploy worked miraculously time and again, permitting the settlers to humble isolated tribes either by warfare or by negotiation at sword's point.[32]

But the favored strategy was unbridled terror. In fact, in fighting the Indians the colonists not only abandoned much of the ritual of European warfare, they embraced some of the tactics of their native American foes. The colonists justified their actions by claiming, as Increase Mather suggested, that the Indians "act like wolves & are to be dealt withall as wolves." Solomon Stoddard, a New England clergyman of Mather's generation, argued in the same vein, claiming that if the "Indians were as other people are, & did manage their warr fairly," they would be dealt with humanely. With these rationalizations, the tactics of terrorism went unchallenged. If the foe was believed hiding in the underbrush, the torch was applied to the dry grass and the Indians were massacred as they raced out. The torch was also set to native villages. When the Puritan invaders decided to burn out the Pequot's settlement at Mystic, Connecticut, scores of inhabitants died in the conflagration. Others tried to flee, but the "soldiers received and entertained [them] with the point of the sword." Still others attempted to fight, but they were "deprived of their arms," for the "fire burnt their very bowstrings—and so [they] perished valiantly." Some even "crept under their Beds," where they perished of suffocation or by the sword.

31. George Madison Bodge, *Soldiers in King Philip's War* . . . (Boston, 1906), pp. 267, 305, 312; David Corkran, *The Cherokee Frontier* (Norman, Okla., 1962), pp. 245, 251–52.
32. Gardener, "Gardener's Pequot Warres," p. 151; Jennings, *Invasion of America*, pp. 212–13.

At the battle's conclusion, one warrior reported, "so many souls lie gasping on the ground, so thick, in some places, that you could hardly pass along." Governor Bradford noted that the Indians were "frying in the fire" and their blood quenched the inferno; how "horrible was the stink and stench," he complained. Following another encounter, an Indian survivor stated that he had "seen the most Dead Bodies all . . . over that I never Did see." The blood was "a Stream Running down on the Descending ground. . . ." Some of the wounded were "crying for help. But [there was] no mercy for them."[33]

Nor were such tactics employed solely by the British. About five years after the destruction of the Pequots, the governor of the New Netherlands, William Kieft, ordered a similar fate for unfriendly natives near New Amsterdam. In a surprise attack Kieft's forces slaughtered scores of the natives; his men threw children into a nearby river, and when the parents swam out to save the youngsters, "the souldiers would not suffer them to come ashore but caused both old and young to be drowned." Children who escaped into the forest were "murdered in cold blood" the following morning when they appeared to beg for food. The natives were beheaded and their "gory heads were laid in the streets of New Amsterdam, where the governor's mother kicked them like footballs."[34]

During the wars with Europeans in America, starvation tactics were normally used only in siege operations, and, in those instances, food resources were usually made available upon surrender to those troops who had been besieged. But the attempt to starve the enemy to death, not merely into submission, was common in the engagements with the Indians. The English often preferred such tactics because they were less likely to produce casualties among their own troops. When the Puritans attacked the Pequots at Mystic, Captain John Mason admonished his soldiers, who were about to charge the settlement with swords unsheathed, that "We should never kill them after that manner. . . . WE MUST BURN THEM. . . ." In the reprisal that followed the 1622 massacre, Virginians destroyed enough Indian corn in two days to feed four thousand natives for one year. The Puritans followed suit during the Pequot War. A soldier-diarist noted that "We burnt above 500 houses, left but 9, burnt all their corn." The following day's entry claimed that the soldiers "burnt 200 wigwams more. . . . We fetch in their corn daily and that undoes them." Captain Underhill even ordered his troops to slaughter the Indians' dogs, so that they might not be eaten to prevent starvation.[35]

33. Axtell, *School on a Hill,* p. 255; Gardener, "Gardener's Pequot Warres," p. 143; Underhill, *News from America,* p. 139; Underhill, *Red Man's America,* pp. 73, 75; Graymont, *Iroquois,* p. 139.

34. Allen W. Trelease, *Indian Affairs in Colonial New York* (Pt. Washington, N.Y., 1971), pp. 68–80.

35. Mason, *History of the Pequot War,* p. 139; Jennings, *Invasion of America,* pp. 212–13, 220–21; Powell, "Aftermath of the Massacre," p. 68; Bodge, *Soldiers,* pp. 174–75; Underhill, *News from America,* p. 7.

The policy of wanton property destruction was effective during the Revolution when General John Sullivan led an expedition through Pennsylvania and western New York in an effort to destory Great Britain's Indian allies. General Washington regarded Sullivan's terrorist measures as "just & necessary," and he was delighted to learn that the countryside had been "overrun & laid waste." Henry Dearborn, a soldier in the expedition, noted that his company came upon forty acres of corn "fit to roast, which we cut down & destroy'd." Six days later an entire village was leveled, and the following day still another town "was made a bon fire of." In the next two weeks three more villages were destroyed, another two weeks later, and in the remaining three weeks five additional hamlets and their fields were burned. A lieutenant on the foray saw the "largest [field of corn] that ever I saw grow" set ablaze. In all, the expedition obliterated forty Indian villages. The army estimated that 160,000 bushels of corn and countless quantities of other commodities were pillaged. One regiment claimed to have seized thirty thousand dollars worth of plunder.[36]

Other common tactics in warfare between Indians were introduced. A colonel in the Sullivan expedition acknowledged that he ordered some of his squads to dress and paint themselves as Indians before retaliating. Some soldiers apparently delighted in using Indian weapons—particularly the tomahawk—against their foes. Women who were left behind were seized and forced to endure long marches, and though it was not typical of Indian behavior toward their white captives, white soldiers sometimes raped their prisoners. Indeed, such conduct prompted one disgusted officer to remark that "Bad as the savages are, they never violate the chastity of any women, their prisoners."[37]

Most of the European powers condoned scalping. Count Frontenac offered bounties for the scalps of Indians who allied themselves with the English. Great Britain granted the Iroquois eight dollars per scalp during the War for Independence, a strategy that produced "such cruelties," according to one redcoat, that service was made "very disagreeable to the King's Troops." Likewise, the colonists, who always seemed to lack revenue for essential services, proffered handsome subsidies for Indian scalps. During Queen Anne's War, the going rate per scalp in Massachusetts was £40. During the next war the colony offered up to £105 to any settler who would, at his own expense, "go out and kill a Male Indian of the Age of twelve Years or upwards"; women and children under twelve years of age fetched a mere £50. If the colony furnished the bounty hunter with his weapons, the reward was reduced to £75 for males killed and £78, 15s for those captured; under these conditions, one could net £35 for each

36. R. W. G. Vail, ed., *The Revolutionary Diary of Lieut. Obadiah Gore, Jr.* (New York, 1929), pp. 29, 31; Wright, *Sullivan Expedition,* no. 6, p. 15, and no. 7, p. 28; Howard Peckham and Lloyd A. Brown, eds., *Revolutionary War Journals of Henry Dearborn, 1775–1783* (Chicago, 1939), pp. 172–90.

37. Wright, *Sullivan Expedition,* no. 6, p. 11; Peckham and Brown, *Dearborn Journals,* pp. 178, 191; Graymont, *Iroquois,* pp. 123, 196, 231–32.

woman or child killed. Militia troops were paid a maximum of £30 for each male corpse or scalp. Even Pennsylvania in 1756 offered to pay 150 Spanish dollars for the scalp of each adult male Indian, and 90 percent of that amount for each Indian taken prisoner. The clergy and the militia officers assured the colonists that God ordained such grisly conduct. "When a people is grown to such a height of blood, and sin against God," the Reverend Stoddard argued, He "puts them to the sword, and the most terriblest death that may be. Sometimes the Scripture declareth women and children must perish. . . . We had sufficient light from the word of God for our proceedings." In fact, victory for the settlers was indicative that "God was above them [and] laughed at his Enemies and the Enemies of his People. . . . "[38]

The troops quickly became inured to the savagery of the warfare. Accounts from officers frequently noted that the troops were "enraged at [the natives'] former cruelties" or "bereaved of pity" because of the Indians' barbarous conduct, and, in such a state of mind, "fell upon the work without compassion" or "shewed the utmost ardor to engage" the enemy. Sometimes the troops even quarreled over who should have the opportunity to scalp a foe. At times the soldiers were so aroused that they went beyond scalping. Some soldiers on the Sullivan expedition "skinned two of them [Indians] from their hips down," and fashioned "boot-legs" for their major and their lieutenant from the membrane.[39]

Though warfare among the Indians was limited in scope and tinged with ceremonial overtones, their conflicts with the Europeans were wars of survival. The colonials, amused by the diffidence with which the Indians fought one another, soon discovered that their wars with the native Americans were not occasions for levity. The earliest lesson the settlers learned was that the Indians could fight with "hellish spite & rage . . . from which we are taught the necessity of fighting those more than devils to the last moment rather than fall into their hands alive."[40]

The Indians could inflict frightful damage on the European settlements in America and arouse enormous anxiety among the settlers; but, because of their technological limitations, the natives could not jeopardize the existence of the colonies. In reality, as Professor Francis Jennings has observed, the "greatest human obstacles to European colonization existed in Europe itself," and those obstacles could be minimized if the ocean communications with the parent state were kept open.[41]

38. Hamilton, *French and Indian Wars*, p. 38; Samuel Penhallow, *The History of the Wars of New England* . . . (Boston, 1726), p. 10; Spencer Phips, *A Proclamation for . . . Volunteers* . . . , Broadside (Boston, 23 August 1745), *Pa. Archives*, 4th Ser., vol. II, pp. 596–97; Roy Harvey Pearce, *Savagism and Civilization* (Baltimore, 1953), p. 23; Underhill, *News from America*, p. 25; Mason, *History of the Pequot War*, pp. 140–41, 148.

39. Cook, *Journals of the Sullivan Expedition*, p. 11; Bolton, *Private Soldier* (New York, 1902), p. 199.

40. Peckham and Brown, *Dearborn Journals*, p. 188.

41. Jennings, *Invasion of America*, pp. 32–37.

The natives were also aware of the odds against them and perhaps this knowledge, as well as the vast cultural differences that separated the combatants, reduced the warfare to a primitive, savage struggle. The natives fought the Europeans by combining surprise attack with psychological warfare. The devastation wreaked on Virginia's inhabitants in 1622, and again in 1644, could not have been attained through any means other than sneak attacks. Surprise raids on northern frontier villages produced havoc and destruction—and, in several instances, the demise of the settlement—well into the eighteenth century. So effective was the strategy that a larger proportion of the population died in King Philip's War in 1675 to 1676 than in any war in American history. Because the Indians lacked the ability to hold regions they had overrun, they were unable to plunder as successfully as the English. If they succeeded in a surprise attack, as at Schenectady in 1690 or at Deerfield in 1704, the natives burned as many houses and confiscated whatever valuable goods—principally firearms and livestock—they could manage and retreated hastily, for they were likely to be pursued by a militia force from a nearby hamlet. Crops were sometimes destroyed, but this tactic was not always possible. The settlers, consequently, were less often faced with the likelihood of starvation than was the enemy, although the attrition of livestock was liable to produce severe deprivation. Ironically, other than the famous "starving time" faced by the first generation of settlers in Virginia, the only times during the early period of settlement that large numbers of colonists were in danger of starvation they were rescued by foodstuffs offered by the Indians; in one instance, the terroristic tactics of John Smith and his successors in Virginia netted supplies, but in Plymouth and Massachusetts the settlers were assisted by the generosity of the Indians.

Although limited technologically, the Indians were masters of psychological warfare—probably the most adroit practitioners of the art that Europeans had encountered since their sixteenth-century battles with the Turks in eastern Europe. Considerable anxiety, arising from the colonists' innate fear of the unknown, was aroused by the natives' alien culture. Painted bodies, masked faces, either virtually naked loins or limbs and trunk adorned with animal pelts added to the colonists' terror. The Indians waged war in a brutal manner calculated to test the nerve of the most battle-hardened veteran. In one campaign a company came upon the corpses of sixteen of their comrades; the victims had been positioned in a ring, clubbed to death, then grimly propped back into a seating position to await the arrival of the relief party. As mounted colonial troops plunged into Indian strongholds, they would intermittently encounter abominable reminders of Indian depredations—bloodied uniforms of their colleagues tacked to trees, blood-smeared stakes, scalps nailed to boards, heads pinioned atop pikes, dismembered hands, feet or sexual organs strewn about the pathways, even pugnacious notes, as a Massachusetts company discovered in King Philip's War, which indicated that the natives would fight for twenty years if necessary, "adding also, that they had nothing to lose, whereas we had Houses, Barnes and Corn. . . ." Occasionally, Indians were seen wearing apparel fashioned from flayed skin, or hatbands constructed of severed fingers and toes. The Indians went out of their way to circulate stories of cannibalistic natives who gnawed "their [captives'] flesh piece-meales off their Bones." Such encounters and rumors "much daunted" the soldiers, Increase Mather acknowledged.[42]

Even worse was the detection of the victims. Some of those discovered were maimed in such a manner that they would slowly bleed to death. One company of soldiers during the Revolution came upon an entire family, all severely wounded but not dead, "gasping & expiring & the Hogs rooting their Body's." A Pennsylvania soldier came upon a mortally wounded trooper with a tomahawk "sticking in his private parts." Shallow graves containing scores of soldiers were discovered. The most agonizing discoveries were of the mutilated bodies of comrades—the skin stripped from the body "leaving the ribs bare," the "eyes punched out," finger and toe nails extracted, the "Privates . . . nearly cut off & hanging down," multiple stab wounds, decapitation, even roasted flesh. At times the Indians engaged in psychological warfare to lure troops into a trap. They might desecrate a Bible in full view of the soldiers. More 'effective, of course, was the deliberate murder or torture of captives while in sight of pursuing troops.[43]

The Indians' treatment of captives reflected ceremonial, even religious, practices, but, as employed against the European invaders, it was partially a psychological gambit designed to arouse fear among the colonists and, perhaps, even cause the settlers to eschew war. Without a doubt, Indian practices provoked considerable uneasiness among the settlers. Even professional militarists, who claimed to feel little anxiety at dying "like a soldier in the field, with honor," acknowledged that they trembled at the prospect of captivity and torture. But the Indians' strategy backfired. It tended, if anything, to induce the colonists to fight more frantically to avoid the often terrible fate of captivity, and it only confirmed the colonists' opinion that the natives were truly demoniacal.[44]

The Indians seized captives for several reasons. Some were held for ransom, a practice that steadily grew as English inflation and Indian bartering acumen increased. Other prisoners were adopted into the tribe, as surrogate spouses or children to replace those tribesmen lost in battle. A majority of the captives in the Pennsylvania region, and perhaps elsewhere, were probably treated in this manner. At times the relationship which emerged between captive and conqueror was warm and genuinely familial; for some, however, the relationship never evolved beyond the state of bondage. Among the former, including adults as well as children raised from infancy by the natives, such close ties often developed that the "captives" had no desire to be repatriated among the English.

    42. Peckham and Brown, *Dearborn Journals*, pp. 158–59; Wright, *Sullivan Expedition*, no. 5, p. 13; Drake, *Hubbard's History of the Indian Wars*, pp. 19, 63; J. Franklin Jameson, ed., *Johnson's Wonder-Working Providence, 1628–1651* (New York, 1910), p. 78.
    43. Wright, *Sullivan Expedition*, no. 5, pp. 11, 32; no. 6, p. 6; no. 7, p. 28.
    44. Gardener, "Gardener's Pequot Warres," pp. 152–53.

Some who were "liberated" by colonial armies fled back to their Indian brothers at the earliest chance. The phenomenon concerned many colonists, including Franklin, who could not explain why the natives taken captive by whites would return to their tribe if permitted "one Indian Ramble with them," whereas whites captured by the Indians would, upon their release, "in a Short time . . . become disgusted with our manner of life . . . and take the first good Opportunity of escaping again into the Woods. . . ."[45]

Many luckless prisoners, however, were neither adopted nor bartered, but were subjected to a barbarism perhaps unparalleled even in the most fiendish dungeons of Europe. The more fortunate among them were quickly dispatched. Documented accounts abound of troublesome small children dashed against trees as the raiding party made its arduous trek to the homeland. Others perished of fatigue and exposure during the march. Once at a safe distance from their pursuers, some captives were compelled to run the gauntlet and were clubbed to death. Some captives were slowly starved to death. Those who were dragged in "slave straps" back to the tribal village and tortured suffered unimaginable agonies. In many tribes the women and children were the chief practitioners of the gruesome act, but the entire tribe was on hand to "jeer, taunt, laugh, whoop, and rejoice" at the spectacle. The ordeal was regarded as especially successful if it lasted for hours or days. To that end, water often was offered to or poured over the victims to prevent fainting and to prolong the suffering. The ceremony culminated in the dismemberment of the captive, and, on occasion, even the consumption of his cooked remains.[46]

The Indians were not unique in committing atrocities on prisoners. The Europeans in America frequently proved themselves equally debased, although they pursued a double standard, generally treating the prisoners of conventional war according to the traditions of Europe, but resorting to depredations against their Indian captives which rivaled in indecency the practices of the natives. Thomas Jefferson, for instance, drew a distinction between "civilized" and "savage" warfare. He lauded the practice of modern states which fought limited wars and treated "captive enemies with politeness and generosity." But as governor of Virginia he denounced the "cruel and cowardly warfare" of the natives, conflict which was designed "to extinguish human nature," and he treated white captives who had consorted with the Indians in military affairs as

45. Axtell, "Scholastic Philosophy," pp. 55–56; Franklin to Peter Collinson, 9 May 1753, in Labaree, *Papers of Franklin*, vol. IV, pp. 481–82.

46. Rowlandson, *Sovereignty and Goodness of GOD*, in Richard Van Der Beets, ed., *Held Captive* (Knoxville, Tenn.) pp. 48–49; Graymont, *Iroquois*, p. 139; Cotton Mather, *Decennium Luctuosum* . . . in Charles Lincoln, ed., *Narratives of the Indian Wars* (New York, 1913), p. 275; Adair, *History of the American Indian*, pp. 147–51, 390–91; Underhill, *News from America*, pp. 94–96; Charles P. Whittemore, *A General of the Revolution* (New York, 1961), p. 145; "Intelligence from Col. Peter Schuyler," in Isabel M. Calder, ed., *Colonial Captives, Marches and Journeys* (Pt. Washington, N.Y., 1967), p. 141.

criminals, not as prisoners of war; furthermore, he ordered his commanders to secure the "extirmination" or "removal" of the natives, yet he treated captured British officers with considerable charm, even fraternizing with them at Monticello.[47]

The instructions sent to colonial authorities prescribed harsh treatment for prisoners of war. The governors of proprietary Maryland were told by Lord Baltimore either to execute captives "by the Law of warre, or to save them at their pleasure. . . . " The King sent similar instructions to Sir Edmund Andros, governor of the Dominion of New England. Depredations inevitably occurred. In one of the earliest international encounters in North America, Samuel Argall, acting under a commission granted by the governor of Virginia, attacked and overran a French settlement near the Bay of Penobscot, flogged some of the captives, and set the remainder adrift in the open sea without adequate supplies or equipment. There were unfortunate instances, too, when European forces were unable or unwilling to keep their Indian allies from committing atrocities against their prisoners. But these were uncommon occurrences. During the intercolonial wars, colonial authorities normally interned, relocated, or exchanged their colonial and European prisoners. The temptation to lash out at captives was often present but, as at Louisbourg in 1745, when several Americans contemplated reprisals against their seven hundred French prisoners, the urge was usually suppressed. Such abysmal conduct, one trooper explained, "t'was below the respect of an Englishman." The well-documented frequency with which prisoners attempted to escape indicates that prison conditions were not always homey, but discomforts customarily arose from inadequate provisions and the outbreak of disease rather than from policies of systematic brutality. For instance, English colonists confined in Quebec during the French and Indian War suffered food shortages, but the civilian population experienced similar deprivation. The prisoners' daily allotment of food consisted of just four ounces of bread and "a little salted fish."[48] Formal peace settlements normally called for the repatriation of all European and colonial captives.

The misconduct that occasionally characterized American treatment of European captives pales by comparison to the colonists' routine treatment of Indian prisoners. During the Pequot War, with Captain Underhill looking on, one unfortunate native prisoner had one leg tied to a post and a rope looped about his other leg, then twenty of his captors "pulled him to pieces." Underhill shot

---

47. Reginald Charles Stuart, "Encounter with Mars: Thomas Jefferson's View of War" (Ph.D. diss., University of Florida, 1974), pp. 48–51.

48. Lord Baltimore's Instructions to the Colonists, 1633, in Hall, *Narratives of Maryland*, p. 107; Commission of King James the Second to Sir Edmond Andros, 3 June 1686, in Force, *Tracts*, vol. IV, no. 8, pp. 8–9; Francis Parkman, *Pioneers of France in the New World*, in *The Works of Francis Parkman*, 20 vols. (Boston, 1897–1898), vol. II, pp. 133–35; Hamilton, *French and Indian Wars*, p. 36; "Journal of Roger Wolcott at the Siege of Louisbourg, 1745," CHS, *Coll.* 1 (Hartford, Conn., 1860), p. 134; "Intelligence from Schuyler," in Calder, *Colonial Captives*, p. 141.

"a pistol through him to dispatch him." Some captives, including women, were "torn in peeces by Doggs," others either shot or marched long distances to captivity. Some boasted of "fattening their dogs on Indian carcasses." One old man at Mystic, so decrepit he could not walk, was captured; one eyewitness recalled that "sum wold have had him devoured by doges but the tenderness of sum of them prevailed to Cut ofe his head" instead. During King Philip's War some of the troops begged Colonel Church to permit them to kill a captive; the commander at first demurred, then relented, but as he took "no delight in the Sport, [he] fram'd an arrant [errand] at some distance" from the murder. The colonists frequently handed their Indian captives over to their native allies for ritualistic massacre or enslavement. Normally, however, the settlers kept their prisoners as slaves, selling some of them within the colonies, but dispatching most to the West Indies for a lifetime of bonded labor. Governor Winthrop ordered one expedition against the Narragansetts and the Pequots to "put to death the men . . . but to spare the women and children, and to bring them away . . . as hostages. . . ." Some of the captives were destined to remain personal booty of the soliders. A Puritan captain sent about fifty native prisoners to Winthrop, but he noted that "there is one, that is the fairest and the largest that I saw amongst them, to whom I have given a coat to clothe her. It is my desire to have her." He added that there "is a little squaw that steward Calicut desireth."[49]

Some native American leaders were executed by the hangman or by firing squad following ritual trials in colonial courts. In some instances, the death sentence followed days of interrogration and torture, either physical or psychological. Even Indians who were at peace with the colonists—in some instances even those who were nominal allies of the settlers—were sometimes treated harshly in the orgiastic milieu of these wars. The so-called "Praying Indians," natives who had been converted to Christianity and who, in peacetime, lived within the confines of the Purtian state, were, in effect, arrested and relocated in a bleak concentration camp on Deer Island in Boston Harbor during King Philip's War; they remained imprisoned for two years following the conflict. Inadequately fed on a monotonous diet of shellfish and poorly housed and clothed by their Massachusetts friends, a considerable number of these captives perished while in custody.

England's colonial experiment commenced with the knowledge that war was likely, and the colonists and imperial planners quickly found their worst fears confirmed. War occurred and recurred. Most important, perhaps, was the fact

---

49. Phillip Vincent, *A true relation,* MHS, *Coll.* 6 (1837), p. 36; Richard M. Brown, *Strain of Violence* (New York, 1975), p. 71; Bodge, *Soldiers,* pp. 17, 69; Peckham and Brown, *Dearborn's Journals,* p. 191; Corkran, *Cherokee Frontier,* pp. 195, 209, 253; Axtell, *School on a Hill,* p. 262; William Hubbard, *The Present State of New England* . . . (London, 1677), p. 127; John Winthrop, in James Savage, ed., *The History of New England from 1630–1649* [1690], 2 vols. (Boston, 1853), vol. I, pp. 192–93.

that warfare was total, a savage struggle for the survival not just of individuals but of entire cultures.

These terrible struggles affected the colonists' attitude toward war and warriors, and soon, as the next part will demonstrate, led to an American perception of war that channeled the flow of early American history.

Part Two

The Experience of War

The Welfare of a State does therefore call for Valor as well as Policy; and the Soldier is as Necessary to a Community as the Magistrate. (Rev. Samuel Cooper, 1759)

A military man is not to inquire whether a war be just or unjust; he is to execute his orders (Benjamin Franklin, 1785)

The fatigues of war are much less destructive to health than the painful, laborious attention to debates and to writing, which drink up the spirit and consumes the strength. (John Adams, 1776)

A Soldier's Life is such that no one can have a true Idea of without the Trial. (Sgt. Hiram Bingham, 1777)

The deluded American people are made to believe they are invincible. (Major John Pitcairn, 1775)

War occurred, or threatened to occur, with enough frequency in the world of the English colonists that they were concerned, if not preoccupied, with the prospect of conflict. War in colonial America erupted spasmodically, although most wars bore some tenuous relationship to the conflict that preceded it. In the early decades, a major Indian war occurred about once each generation. While each war originated from separate and distinct causes, the hatreds and biases that arose in these conflicts helped prepare the ground for future turmoil. These wars, and the jostling in the interim between full-scale wars, were usually confined to the remote frontier. Likewise, the intercolonial struggles, in full bloom by the late seventeenth century, were waged intermittently. Two wars were conducted between Britain and its continental rivals in the space of a quarter century (1691-1713), followed by a full generation of peace, and then two additional wars in the next quarter century (1739-1763). Some historians regard the American Revolution, particularly after Britain declared war on France and Spain in 1778 to 1779, as still another intercolonial war. Much of the fighting in these wars, as in the Indian conflicts, was confined to the frontier areas of America. Even so, these various wars had an impact on large numbers of people. Perhaps 25 percent or more of the inhabitants of a colony might reside in the frontier sector and experience war—or the dread of impending conflict—at firsthand. Moreover, militia and conscriptees from throughout a colony might be dispatched to a far corner of the settlement to engage in hostiliu... . And even wars that did not touch a colony's soil could produce political, social, and economic ramifications.

These wars, whether traumatic or liberating, sorrowful or joyous, were pervasive realities for much of the population in early America. As such, the bloodletting shaped American thought. Conflicts impinged on the lives of the colonists, even on those who never bore a weapon. The era culminated in a great struggle for independence, a conflict that, in part, germinated in this violent, amorphous experience and, in turn, was fashioned in indeterminate ways by the convulsive force, rage, and idealism it unleashed.

Chapter Three

"Just Wars" and "Truly Valient Soldiers"

*homo homini lupus**

The colonists' knowledge of war was garnered from numerous sources. For many, rumor and hearsay or the braggadocio and reminiscences of acquaintances who had soldiered served as the medium for wisdom. Some had lived, as militiamen or civilians, in a battle zone. The clergy, especially in New England, preached an astonishing number of sermons that fulminated against foreign enemies, philosophied on war, or lectured the citizenry on the proper virtues for soldiering. The educated and the articulate—the leaders in the deferential societies of the colonial era—could reflect on the ideas expressed by the best minds through the centuries concerning struggle. The experience of war, in league with an accumulated baggage of ideas concerning the nature of war and warriors, shaped the colonists' outlook. Experience and ideas interacted, until eventually the two forged a peculiar American way of war, as well as a native view of conflict and its ramifications.

One source of perceptions concerning the nature of war for the articulate colonist was a vast literature that had accumulated since antiquity. There is considerable evidence that many articulate colonists consumed this literature, or that, if these ideas were not read directly, they were transmitted through the classics that youngsters read in the Latin schools, sermons, pamphlets, newspaper essays, and word of mouth.

There were few pacifists among the renowed writers of antiquity. Before technological advances cheapened the cost of weapons, leading to the enlargement of armies and the transition from war by the elite to war of the masses, combat generally was glorified. In early Greece, cowardice in battle was excoriated. Homer wrote of the joy in conflict, of his "lust for the spear-handle." Most writers lamented that war was inevitable, but admonished their readers that only "just wars" should be pursued. The Greeks were hardly more unan-

*Man is wolf to man (old German proverb).

imous than their successors in determining what constituted a "just" endeavor. Plato, for instance, thought that war with the barbarians, whom he regarded as inferior to the Greeks, was justified, and he considered racial warfare to be legitimate; the philosophical utopian state he concocted was capable of waging war and was required to create a trained army for external defense. Aristotle believed war was a legitimate means of settling disputes, but in general he argued that war should be waged only for the purpose of securing peace, that is, he asserted the doctrine of warfare to prevent additional war. Like Plato, however, he perceived racial differences and concluded that wars waged "against men who, though intended by nature to be governed, will not submit," were "just" wars.[1]

The Greeks were also the earliest Western theorists to contemplate the legal ramifications of war. At one time or another, the Greeks legitimized neutral behavior during wars and prohibited battles at certain times and in particular locales. Greek legalists also believed the barbarians were beyond the pale of the laws governing warfare.[2]

The early republican wars of Rome were frequently greeted by antiwar resistance movements, but the later wars for imperial expansion were normally applauded. It was believed that the subjugation of nearby peoples fostered both domestic and foreign peace, and it was commonly presumed that order, peace, and prosperity were the logical accompaniments of the *Pax Romana*. Roman thinkers generally distinguished between wars that were an element of the natural world order and select wars. The former were unavoidable; a select war was regarded as *justum bellum*, a legally justifiable conflict when one nation attacked a perpetrator of injuries who refused to make amends. Only marginal movements arose to denounce the wars of the empire, and even then only "unjust" wars—instances of clear-cut Roman aggression—were criticized; violations of a treaty, truce, or armistice, as well as offenses committed against an ally, violations against Rome's neutrality, violations of its territorial rights, or the refusal of another country to surrender an individual who had allegedly committed a crime against Rome were considered legitimate reasons for the precipitation of war.[3]

Neither the Greeks nor the Romans had as great an intellectual impact on the settlers of early America as did the Hebrew and early Christian thinkers. The

---

1. Wallace E. Caldwell, *Hellenic Conceptions of Peace* (New York, 1967), pp. 9–43, 53–63, 85–86, 91–101, 127–32; Gerardo Zampaglione, *The Idea of Peace in Antiquity* (South Bend, Ind., 1973), pp. 18–37, 42, 71, 82–94.

2. Joachim von Elbe, "The Evolution of the Concept of the Just War in International Law," *American Journal of International Law* 33 (October 1939), p. 666; William Ballis, *The Legal Position of War* (New York, 1973), pp. 12–17; W. Kendrick Pritchett, *Ancient Greek Military Practices* (Berkeley, Calif., 1971), pp. 109–26.

3. Zampaglione, *Idea of Peace*, pp. 131–37, 140–50, 166–68; von Elbe, "Concept of Just War," pp. 666–67; Ballis, *Legal Position of War*, pp. 20–27.

Hebrew Scriptures depicted man, in the aftermath of Adam's sin, as doomed to dwell in a violent world inhabited by imperfect sinners. The early Hebrews envisioned themselves as the "chosen people" whom God protected. They also believed their god, Yahweh, to be vengeful and prone to use His people for divinely inspired wars. In fact, they engaged in crusades or holy wars designed to secure Yahweh's favor. The Hebrews believed that "the Lord your God is He that goeth with you, to fight for you against your enemies, to save you." But they also developed large standing armies to be on the safe side; Solomon, for instance, maintained a force of 1,400 charioteers and 12,000 cavalry. The early Hebrew wars were brutal and cruel conflicts typical of those waged by nomadic peoples, although the wars were sanctioned as raids to acquire booty to "put into the treasury of the house of the Lord." As Hebrew society gradually grew more settled and pastoral, the sect's prophets increasingly longed for a Messiah who, through impartial and perfect rule, would first subdue the wicked and eventually render warfare obsolete.[4]

The early Christians perceived Jesus as the Messiah promised to the Hebrews. Jesus' message amounted to a ringing denunciation of war. He admonished men to forgive their enemies and to behave meekly and charitably. When all men acted in such a manner, the world would be purged of conflict. He taught that "they that take the sword shall perish with the sword," and in the Sermon on the Mount he taught that the peacemakers were blessed "for they shall be called the children of God." In the same sermon, he admonished his followers to resist one who is evil, turn the other cheek, go the second mile, love your enemies. The early Christian leaders were pacifists who emphasized love and deplored killing, but within a few generations of Jesus' crucifixion the early Christians learned the value of working within the Roman Empire. This vast polity covered an enormous geographical area in which diverse peoples lived under a common political order. Attempts were made to improve relations with the imperial government by abandoning the rebellious overtones of Christian dogma. Even the traditional Christian opposition to military service in the Roman Legion was soft-peddled. From the days of the apostolic communities onward, the early Christians had criticized soldierly pursuits as inimical to Jesus's strictures against violent behavior. Armies were criticized because soldiers were compelled to engage in activities that clashed with Christian concepts of morality, such as assisting in the execution of death sentences. Moreover, soldiers had to participate in ceremonies that glorified earthly rulers; some thought soldiers wore emblems that smacked of paganism, and others believed the camp life of soldiers engendered behavior incompatible with Christian precepts of purity and moderation. Nevertheless, Christian cells sprang up in the Roman army, perhaps

4. Zampaglione, *Idea of Peace*, pp. 185–206; The quotations are from Deuteronomy 7:17–18; 20:4; and Joshua 6:24. See also Roland H. Bainton, *Christian Attitudes Toward War and Peace* (New York, 1960), pp. 44–45.

because soldiers drew sustenance from the Christian teachings of eternal life and a forgiving deity, and perhaps because such a compact organization as a military force was relatively easy to organize.[5]

By the fourth century A.D., with the promulgation of the Edict of Constantine, the church was recognized and afforded protection by the government. Henceforth, moderate theologians who wished to avoid a clash with the state predominated. State policy increasingly became church policy, and the wars of the Roman state were perceived by the church hierarchy as divinely sanctioned. Church councils in the West even went so far as to deprecate soldiers who deserted their posts. Ambrose, the Bishop of Milan late in the fourth century, was the first divine to articulate a Christian ethic of war. He believed non-Romans were barbarians and concluded that the defense of the Empire was synonymous with the defense of the faith. He insisted, however, that only defensive wars were "just wars."

The change in church policy was most clearly evident in the writings of Augustine, who amplified Ambrose's embryonic tracts. In *De civitate Dei* he contended that wars not only were ordered or authorized by God as part of His cryptic design, but that He also determined who would win these wars. The purpose of war, he added, must always be to secure peace. Therefore, military service is a Christian duty and, if in the course of battle one should kill an enemy, the act should be seen as meritorious. War became objectionable only when it was launched by a "desire for domination," or when the warriors were motivated by "the desire to hurt, the cruelty of revenge, the violence of uncontrolled rage. . . ."[6]

Following the collapse of the Roman Empire in the West and the emergence of the persistent warfare that characterized the middle ages, the church, Europe's leading intellectual and moral authority, grappled for the means to control the turmoil. Church leaders attempted to circumscribe the warfare by limiting conflict to prescribed days of the week and designated seasons; the church also hoped to prevent relatives of belligerents from entering a conflict until the war had been in progress for forty days, and it exempted clerics, peasants, and merchants from the obligation to fight. The church frequently mediated disputes in this era; on an average, every other year a conflict was submitted to clerical arbitration during the thirteenth to fifteenth centuries. In *Decretum Gratiani* (c. 1140), the church recognized a war as "just" if it was waged to avenge an injustice or restore territory, or if the struggle was a conflict between equals. Generally, the church considered only defensive wars to be "just" unless, as with the Crusades, an offensive war was waged in the interest of the church. In all instances, the church insisted that wars could be properly waged only if declared by the legitimate ruler of the state.[7]

5. Zampaglione, *Idea of Peace*, pp. 207–59; Bainton, *Christian Attitudes*, pp. 61–62, 81.

6. Zampaglione, *Ideas of Peace*, pp. 259–315; Bainton, *Christian Attitudes*, pp. 89–100.

7. Ballis, *Legal Position of War*, pp. 32–49; von Elbe, "Concept of Just War," pp. 669–73; Bainton, *Christian Attitudes*, pp. 105, 110, 116.

Although marked changes in warfare occurred in the sixteenth and seventeenth centuries, traditional attitudes toward conflict barely changed. Some attempts were made to legitimize neutrality for those states not wishing to take an active role in a war. In addition, efforts persisted, without notable success, to outlaw warfare in certain geographic areas and to curtail the plundering of the countryside and the looting of cities that had capitulated. Plans were even formulated, likewise without success, proposing arbitration of all conflicts by a papal-appointed council.

Otherwise, few Christian pacifists emerged to denounce war. Conflict was thought to be inevitable. It was noted that men differed from animals by their practice of organized war; some philosophers believed that war arose from man's corrupt nature—perhaps because of Adam's sin or, some speculated, because of some hidden quality in man's being—while others attributed repetitive conflict to the vagaries of climate and geography or to economic and societal defects.

Whatever the cause, warfare not only was thought likely to be immutable but was viewed as having certain positive features. Rabelais, the French humorist, believed that "in war every kind of beauty and virtue shines out, every kind of evil and ugliness is abolished." Other writers frankly stated that warfare diverted the discontented masses from problems at home. Some believed that violence was an inevitable aspect of man's nature and that it was best to channel man's aggressiveness against foreign peoples. Still, most writers distinguished between "just" wars and the "unjust" variety. Machiavelli, for instance, simply stated that those wars that were necessary were just. Martin Luther defended wars of self-defense, as well as conflicts that arose when one antagonist refused to settle the quarrel "by legal procedures, discussion, or agreement." Sir Thomas More discovered what he called a "juster cause": a country could legitimately invade another region to enhance its commerce. In the late seventeenth century, John Locke, who defended wars of defense against aggressors, also considered as "just conquerors" those armies that overran primitive civilizations where "the grass of [the] enclosure rotted on the ground, or the fruit of [the] planting perished without gathering, and laying up. . . ."[8]

Despite the general absence of new concepts concerning war and peace in this era, some important ideas emerged. In the early seventeenth century, Hugo Grotius conceived a system of international law that included a definition of "just war," as well as a plan for the avoidance of warfare. In *De Jure Belli ac Pacis,* first published in 1625, Grotius, a Dutch businessman and diplomat,

---

8. Hale, "Armies, Navies and the Art of War," in G.R. Elton, ed., *Reformation* 2 vols. (Cambridge, Eng., 1958), pp. 501–2; Elizabeth V. Souleyman, *The Vision of World Peace in Seventeenth and Eighteenth Century France* (Pt. Washington, N.Y., 1965), p. 13; J. R. Hale, "Sixteenth-Century Explanations of War," *PP* 51, pp. 11–26; Ballis, *Legal Position of War,* p. 66–74; von Elbe, "Concept of Just War," pp. 673–76; Paul Jorgensen, "Elizabethan Religious Literature for Time of War," *Huntington Library Quarterly* 37 (November 1973), p. 7; M. Seliger, *The Liberal Politics of John Locke* (New York, 1969), pp. 91–92, 109–18; John Dunn, *The Political Thought of John Locke* (Cambridge, Eng., 1969), pp. 168–76.

argued that as men in society required law to preserve domestic order, so men required a law of nations to maintain international order. Grotius recognized that at times order was disrupted and war occurred. He recognized three kinds of "just wars": wars of self-defense; wars to recover lost property or territory; and wars of revenge. But he also believed that even "just wars" might be prevented if an international organization to enforce international law existed, and he further contended that a code to govern the conduct of men and nations at war was not unrealistic. Later in the century, several French writers surfaced to denounce war as "folly," to attribute all warfare to glory-seeking monarchs, and to contend that grandeur could be attained only through peaceful contributions to humanity.[9]

The most significant seventeenth-century movement concerning war was the emergence of the English Quaker pacifists. George Fox, the movement's founder, based his defense of noncombatancy on intuition, claiming to act in imitation of Jesus rather than to refer to particular Scriptures. He claimed that "he that killeth with the sword, must perish with the sword," and he reminded his followers that the "peacemaker hath the kingdom." After Fox, the best known of the early Quakers was William Penn, who, though the son of an English admiral, accepted Quakerism after hearing the sect's founder preach. He, too, preached pacifism, arguing that if judged by traditional Christian behavior, one might think Jesus had taught that "Blessed are the contentious, backbiters, talebearers, fighters, and makers of war." Believing that "Our present condition in Europe needs an olive branch," Penn, in 1693, published a plan to secure lasting peace on the continent. He urged the creation of an international congress of states—including the major nations of Europe, as well as England and Turkey—that would adjudicate disputes among potential combatants. Quaker pacifism spread to the continent, but the sect remained small. Even in England, not more than 50,000 inhabitants of a population of 5,500,000 had joined the movement by the end of the century.[10]

With the exception of the notions promulgated by the avowed pacifist sects, the early colonists made no attempt to refute Europe's basic conceptions of war. Many European attitudes were embraced openly in the colonies, though perhaps modified somewhat by environmental factors or provincial religious mores. The articulate colonists commonly perceived war as a "teeming womb of mischief" that legitimized every imaginable terror. "When the sword is drawn," one colonist noted, "the passions of men observe no bounds of moderation." Some

9. Hugo Grotius, *The Law of War and Peace* (Indianapolis, Ind., 1925), pp. xxxiii–xxxvii; Ballis, *Legal Position of War*, pp. 66–74; von Elbe, "Concept of Just War," pp. 678–80; Souleyman, *Vision of World Peace*, pp. 31–52.

10. Peter Brock, *Pacifism in Europe to 1914* (Princeton, N.J., 1972), pp. 262–63, 274–76, 300–303.

were troubled and mystified by the seeming ease with which the initiation of war could transform rational men into monsters. A perplexed clergyman, for instance, anguished at the reports of horrors in the new colony of Virginia, wondered, "Why is there no remedie, but as soone as we come on land, like Wolves, and Lyons, and Tygres, long famished, we must teare in peeces, murther, and torment the naturall inhabitants, with cruelties never read, nor heard of before?"[11]

But few colonists believed that war could be averted. Many writers, perhaps not suprisingly considering the milieu, attributed the scourge of warfare to a divine plan to punish mankind. When men strayed from God, the Lord was certain to raise up some foreign peoples to smite the "Degenerate Estate." Other writers, however, believed that at times "it pleased God so to stir up the Hearts of . . . Men" that war might be waged for some providential design. Some Puritans, for example, believed that God directed the Pequots to attack the settlers so that the English might overwhelm the natives and extend Christianity. One New England commentator concluded that God frequently provoked internecine conflict among the Indians, and he ascertained that the Puritans "made advantage of some of these Warres." The Deity, in fact, was not uncommonly spoken of as "the Lord of Hosts, the Man of Warr. . . ."[12]

The largest group of early American writers concluded that war grew from the breasts of wicked, greedy men. Some commentators believed that all men were irredeemably corrupt; collectively, therefore, nations simply unleashed those unruly passions and lusts that swept the rulers to war. More typically, early American writers dumped the responsibility for war on the leadership elite of their enemies. Those who "breake the Peace of the World," Cotton Mather charged, were "the Jeroboams of the world." He and Thomas Bridges, another New England clergyman, believed such rulers used the tactics of deception, flattery, and guile to "corrupt and poison their Subjects" into belligerent behavior. The goal of some rulers was the riches of neighbors, whereas vanity led others to seek conquest for self-gratification. Still other writers believed the rulers were the victims of a cruel cycle. Nathaniel Appleton, a Boston pastor, concluded that strong princes were compelled to surround themselves with an armed force to remain in power, but inevitably the "insatiable Avarice, Cruelty and Blood-thirstiness of their Officers and Soldiers" dictated aggressive policies.

11. Anthony Benezet, *Thoughts on the Nature of War* . . . (Philadelphia, 1766), p. 7; Thomas Barnard, *A Sermon Preached* . . . (Boston, 1758), pp. 15–17; Samuel Mather, *War is Lawful, and Arms are to be proved* (Boston, 1739), p. 9; James Madison, Alexander Hamilton, John Jay, *The Federalist* 16 (New York, 1941), p. 96; William Symonds, *Virginia. A Sermon Preached at White-Chapel* [1609] (New York, 1968), p. 14.

12. John Mason, *History of the Pequot War*, MHS, *Coll.*, vol. VIII, p. 132; John Underhill, *News from America*, MHS, *Coll.*, vol. VI, pp. 10–11; [Anon.], *The Planter's Plea* . . . [1630], in Force, *Tracts*, vol. II, pp. 5–6; John Richardson, *The Necessity of a well experienced Souldiery* . . . (Cambridge, Mass., 1679), p. 15.

Later, Anthony Benezet of Philadelphia, an avowed pacifist, envisioned a deadly cycle of war for trade, followed by an era of peaceful commerce that inevitably ended when the marketplace enhanced the "sensual and malignant passions" which "naturally tend to generate another War."[13]

The colonists were troubled by the brutality of warfare, of course, but they were also anxious over other aspects of conflict. War was uncertain. Even the Puritans acknowledged that God, in His mysterious way, occasionally permitted those of "mean and contemptible appearance [to] do wonders." But some feared, with Benjamin Franklin, that even "successful Wars at length become Misfortunes." These colonists were apprehensive that wars would brutalize and corrupt the citizenry, provoking a loss of virtue that would result in social pathology, not the least dangerous manifestation of which was a tendency toward bellicose behavior. Some, for instance, thought executive tyranny was certain to rise, even where standing armies did not exist, from the barrack-state atmosphere that accompanied warfare.[14]

Since they were not optimistic that war might soon vanish, the colonists expended considerable intellectual energy seeking means of assuring success in battle. One wag noted that the best means to victory was for a people to "end their Wars, before their Wars begin." Other colonists made more concrete suggestions, generally centering on the concept of military preparedness. Few would have taken issue with the New England clergyman's admonition that the colonists must "cultivate the regular art of war." Franklin phrased the same sentiment more earthily. The force with the most "fierce fighting animals," he wrote, would normally triumph.[15]

The preferred remedy for success was a vigilant defensive posture. Colonial writers usually attributed the collapse of earlier civilizations to the failure to

---

13. David Osgood, *A Sermon preached . . .* (Boston, 1788), pp. 14–15; Arthur A. Buffinton, "The Puritan View of War," Colonial Society of Massachusetts, *Publications* 28 (Trans. 1930–1933), p. 74; Thomas Bridge, *The Knowledge of God . . .* (Boston, 1705), pp. 10–11; Mather, *War is Lawful,* pp. 8–9; Amos Adams, *The Experience and Utility of War . . .* (Boston, 1759), p. 15; Gerald Stourzh, *Benjamin Franklin and American Foreign Policy* (Chicago, 1969), p. 241; Zabdiel Adams, *The Grounds of Confidence and Success in War, represented* (Boston, 1755), p. 5; Nathaniel Appleton, *The Origin of War examin'd and applied . . .* (Boston, 1733), p. 14; Benezet, *Thoughts on the Nature of War,* pp. 5–6.

14. Henry Gibbs, *The Right Method of Safety . . .* (Boston, 1704), pp. 17–18; James Lockwood, *The Worth and Excellence of Civil Freedom and Liberty Illustrated . . .* (New London, Conn., 1759), p. 33; Franklin to Richard Price, 6 February 1780, in Albert H. Smyth, ed., *The Writings of Benjamin Franklin,* 8 vols. (New York, 1905–1907), vol. VIII, p. 9; Benezet, *Thoughts on the Nature of War,* pp. 7–8; James Burgh, *Political Disquisitions . . . ,* 2 vols. (Philadelphia, 1755), vol. II, p. 429.

15. [Nathanial Ward], *The Simple Cobbler of Aggawan,* in Force, *American Archives,* vol. IV, no. 8, p. 32; Jason Haven, *A Sermon Preached . . .* (Boston, 1761), p. 32; Benjamin Franklin, *Plain Truth . . .* (1747), in Leonard Woods Labaree, ed., *Papers of Franklin,* (New Haven, Conn., 1959), vol. III, p. 202.

prepare for war. Lion Gardener, the soldier hired by the early settlers of Mas-sachusetts, believed that a false sense of security produced by arrogance had crippled many former states. A contemporary drill manual also suggested that a "Victory that intoxicates the conqueror is more dangerous than a defeat." The fall of Rome was easily the most carefully scrutinized collapse of a civilization. John Smith, Virginia's soldier-governor, reflected common sentiment when he attributed Rome's demise to the sloth and corruption that eroded its military vigilance. In a similar vein, Cotton Mather warned that Massachusetts would be safe unless its people grew "lazy, feeble, effeminate and pusillanimous." The early European immigrants to America were admonished to trust no one in the New World. In "a strange Countrey, we must looke for enemies," a clergyman insisted. Such advice, according to another minister, followed the dictum that the "likeliest way to prevent an evill, is to be prepared for it, *fore-warned, fore-armed.* . . ." Franklin concurred. "One Sword," he suggested, "often keeps another in the Scabbard." When Virginia was stunned by the surprise Indian attack in 1622, John Smith explained the catastrophe as a result of inadequate preparedness. "The cause of the Massacre," he told an investi-gating panel in London, "was the want of marshall discipline; and because they . . . were not provided to defend themselves against any enemy."[16]

Only a tiny fraction of colonists, mostly Quakers, denounced warfare as unconscionable. Members of the Society of Friends lived in most colonies in the eighteenth century, and by mid-century more Quakers lived in the Western Hemisphere than in England. Quakers interpreted the biblical admonition to "Resist not one who is evil" in the most literal terms. Some, like John Woolman of New Jersey, believed God had created a universe in which all forms of life were to exist in natural harmony. War would destroy the order that God had created. Their aim was "to overcome our enemies with courteous and friendly offices and kindness, and to assuage their wrath by mildness and persuasion."[17]

In peacetime, the Quakers normally got along satisfactorily with their neigh-bors. When they were persecuted, as in Massachusetts in the 1650s and 1660s, the issue did not involve Quaker pacifism but religious dissidence. In wartime, however, the Quakers often faced considerable hardships. Massachusetts forced some Quakers who refused to serve in King Philip's War to run the gauntlet as punishment, while those who refused to pay war taxes could be compelled to work off fines at a military fortification or have their property distrained; the

16. Thomas Simes, *The Military Guide for Young Officers* (Philadelphia, 1776), p. 191; Gardener, "Gardener's Pequot Warres," MHS, *Coll.,* vol. III, pp. 137–40; Smith, *Description of New England,* in Edward Arber, ed., *Works of Smith,* 2 vols. (Birmingham, Eng., 1884), vol. I, p. 209; Mather, *War is Lawful,* p. 27; Symonds, *Virginia,* p. 42; Richardson, *Necessity,* p. 1; Franklin, *Plain Truth,* in Labaree, *Papers of Franklin,* vol. III, p. 203; Smith, *Generall Historie,* in Arber, *Works of Smith,* vol. II, p. 616.
17. Peter Brock, *Pacifism in the United States* (Princeton, N.J., 1968), p. 26.

same colony unsuccessfully attempted to sell defiant pacifists into temporary bondage. Fines and jail terms were also inflicted upon Quakers during various colonial wars in New York, Maryland, and Virginia. Several additional pacifist sects immigrated to America in the eighteenth century. Most, like the Mennonites, were willing to pay fines in lieu of military service, and, consequently, they avoided much of the domestic persecution that hounded the Friends.[18]

In Pennsylvania the Friends became the ruling order following the Crown's grant of this territory to William Penn. These Quakers had no reservations regarding the exercise of power, believing that enforcing the law against a domestic lawbreaker was proper but that warring with an external foe was improper. Once the intercolonial wars commenced in the late seventeenth century, pressures built against Quaker hegemony both within the colony and in London. The Friends withstood their attackers for nearly three-quarters of a century, however, largely by appropriating funds for nonmilitary expenditures during the imperial wars, as well as by permitting the creation of volunteer militia forces by the nonpacifist elements. Time ran out on the Friends during the French and Indian War. Faced with the real prospect of the loss of their charter, most Quakers resigned their Assembly seats so that the non-Quaker majority could govern during the emergency.[19]

Pacifism was espoused by only a few colonists. Most writers denounced the philosophy and maintained that war, within certain limitations, was justified. Samuel Chew of Philadelphia went to the heart of the matter. When attacked by a foreign power, he wrote, a people could exercise two options, reliance "upon prayers or tears," or resistance by the use of force. Chew added that if the first alternative was pursued, government should be abolished as useless; of course, he believed governments necessary, and he deemed it legitimate "to repel force . . . by force." Several writers attempted to demonstrate that God sanctioned self-defense. One argument noted that Jesus instructed his disciples to arm themselves with swords even if they were required to sell their clothes to purchase their weapons; another demonstrated that Jesus was a taxpayer to a war-making Roman government. Several writers advanced the notion that since God had granted man whatever bounty he possessed, defense of these material elements was required. Daniel Shute told a Boston congregation that men were "under moral obligations" to protect God's gifts. Cotton Mather taught that the "Light of Nature" compelled men to protect their "Lives, Liberties, Properties." Christianity, Mather added, "never instructed men to lay down that Natural Principle of Self-Preservation." Some writers equated pacifism with suicide, a sin in the eyes of God. Others stressed that pacifism

18. *Ibid.*, pp. 21–80; Winfred T. Root, *Relations of Pennsylvania* (New York, 1912), pp. 257–58.
19. Brock, *Pacifism in the U.S.*, pp. 81–158.

only increased warfare. The tyrant's vices of "Ambition and Avarice" would be whetted if there was no resistance to his depravities. Only if tyrants were given "Blood to drink in their Turn" could injustice be stopped.[20]

The colonists, however, did not justify all wars; some conflicts were denounced as unjust. Most writers admitted that it was extraordinarily difficult to determine the precise cause of wars. These writers usually admonished soldiers simply to fight and not to think about the morality of the conflict, for its causes were likely to be "so complicated and perplexed" that the average warrior could not fathom them. Cotton Mather was an exception. When the cause of a war was so unjust as to be "notoriously Evident and Apparent," he instructed the citizenry to refuse to bear arms. Most colonial writers denounced offensive wars to gain property and enlarge the national domain. Governments engaged in such aggression were labeled national highwaymen by one writer. These nations were not engaged in war but in "open Violence, Robbery and Murther." Similarly, many writers denigrated wars waged to enhance the pride of the ruler. These vainglorious leaders—Alexander the Great probably was the most commonly displayed ruler—had "prostituted the art of war" and were morally responsible for the blood they spilled. Even defensive wars were considered unjust if the nation became engaged for transient reasons. Recourse to the "devouring Sword" was legitimate only in "a desperate case."[21]

Despite the condemnation of certain kinds of wars, most writers found many reasons to justify the occurrence of war. One of the alleged virtues of warfare was that mankind was improved by struggle. Courage, intelligence, magnanimity, and "a masterly command of the passions and actions of men" resulted from combat. Society, was also improved through the stimulation of new discoveries and inventions and the opening of new avenues of commerce and industry. It also was suggested that long periods of peace tarnished the manly virtues. Following a prolonged peace, Hamilton noted on the eve of the Revolution, the officer corps would inevitably be reduced to "effiminate striplings . . . better calculated to marshal the forces of *Venus,* than to conduct the sturdy sons of *Mars."* William Williams, a New England clergyman, believed

20. Samuel Chew, *The Speech of Samuel Chew* . . . (Philadelphia, 1775), p. 4; James Cogswell, *God, the pious Soldier's Strength* . . . (Boston, 1757), pp. 9–10; John Carmichael, *A Self-Defensive War Lawful* . . . (Lancaster, Pa., 1775), p. 13; Daniel Shute, *A Sermon* . . . (Boston, 1767), p. 21; Buffinton, "Puritan View of War," p. 75; John Lathrop, *A Sermon Preached* . . . (Boston, 1774), pp. 6, 8, 10–12, 23; Gilbert Tennent, *The late Association for Defense, encouraged* . . . (Philadelphia, 1748), p. 12; Samuel Davies, *The Curse of Cowardice* . . . (London, 1759), p. 5.

21. William Williams, *A Sermon Preached* . . . (Boston, 1737), p. 16; Buffinton, "Puritan View of War," p. 79; Lathrop, *A Sermon,* pp. 8–9; Appleton, *Origin of War,* pp. 19–20; Peter Clark, *Christian Bravery* (Boston, 1756), p. 29; Nathan Perkins, *A Sermon preached to the Soldiers* . . . (Hartford, Conn., 1775), pp. 7–8; Gibbs, *Right Method of Safety,* pp. 9–10.

the virtues men should seek were "a warlike Genius, dextrous Skill and un-
daunted Courage."[22]

New England Puritans added a special wrinkle to their support of war. They
believed the blood spilled in warfare washed away the transgressions of society.
War, in their cosmology, served as atonement, the means by which a people
expatiated the errors of its ways. The Puritans reached this conclusion logically,
though a labyrinth of dogma first had to be traversed. At the heart of Puritan
doctrine was the presumption that God regenerated sinners; these newborn, or
elect, were transformed—often in a shattering, emotional experience—into per-
ceptibly saved persons, sometimes called "visible saints." The elect, who, not
without coincidence, were the elite in Puritan society, covenanted or contracted
the society they represented with God. This society, these people, consequently
became the "chosen people" in the eyes of God. But men remained sinners,
and God visited His wrath upon those, including the "chosen," who sundered
the covenant. Famine, floods, and, of course, the pestilence wrought by war
were the most obvious signs of God's displeasure. By the 1670s, that is by the
eve of King Philip's War, articulate Puritans discerned abundant signals that
they were the "worst of men." In everything from its dress to its lust after
material gain, the Puritans found frequent diversions from the "pure and perfect
truths of Christ." "Is it a wonder that we find war at our gates?" a contemporary
asked. It was not a wonder to the Puritans, and, though hardly welcome, the
impending war would have its saving grace. It was a sign of God's attention
that the "Little Flock of Christ, is hem'd round with devouring Wolves";
besides, as Increase Mather reminded them, "the Lord's people are subject unto
great troubles." The presence of difficulties, John Hull suggested, indicated
that God was keeping His "rein upon them, chastening and trying, nurturing,
lopping and pruning his poor children . . . for their good." Of greater moment,
however, was the effect of war. On the eve of conflict, Mather gave the sign:
through the "Calamity of War," which he described as a "Wilderness of Miseries," God's chosen, garbed in "garments rolled in blood," would "arrive at
the heavenly *Canaan*," a period of "glourious times, wherein Peace and Prosperity shall run down like a River." At war's end Mather was confident that
a reformation had occurred. "Health [has been] restored unto us," he noted in

22. Barnard, *A Sermon*, pp. 15, 17; John Thornton Kirkland, *A Sermon* . . . (Boston, 1795), pp.
17, 19–20; Tristam Burges, *War, Necessary, Just and Beneficial* . . . (Providence, R.I., 1799), p.
7; Thomas Ruggles, *The Usefulness and Expedience of Souldiers* . . . (New London, Conn., 1737),
p. 12; Alexander Hamilton, *The Farmer Refuted* [1775], in Harold C. Syrett and Jacob E. Cooke,
eds., *The Papers of Alexander Hamilton*, 26 vols. (New York, 1961–1979), vol. I, pp. 158–59;
Williams, *A Sermon*, p. 6.

his contemporary history of the conflict, but the price exacted by the Divine was that "Blood be first taken from us."[23]

Colonial writers usually justified any war that could be labeled defensive. By offensive war most colonists meant the molestation of others, or as Gilbert Tennent, the Presbyterian leader in New Jersey and Pennsylvania, put it, war to satisfy "the corrupt *Lusts* of Men, their *Ambition* and *Avarice*"; defensive wars were commonly regarded as those conflicts waged for the preservation of life, liberty, and property. Most colonial writers believed God looked favorably upon such wars, pointing to His admonition to Abraham to make certain wars and to the recurrent conflicts of the Israelites which they believed He had sanctioned. Although Jesus had exhorted his followers not to resist evil men, according to one writer, He merely meant not to resist "small injuries." Jesus thus forbade wars "unless they are necessary." According to Roger Williams, Jesus legitimized two kinds of warfare: the suppression by force of domestic turbulence, and wars fought for the "preserving of life or lives." Most colonial clergymen agreed that no passage could be found in the Scriptures that would "interdict the Use of Arms" in a defensive posture. Even one as secular as Benjamin Franklin pointed to biblical references that allegedly justified defensive wars. Such wars, therefore, were routinely defended as no more immoral than the legal execution of a murderer.[24]

In spite of the rhetoric, when several New England colonies combined in 1643 in a military alliance called the Confederation of New England, its charter spoke of the confederates waging "just warrs whether offensive or defensive." Much of the cant regarding battle, in fact, openly defended discernably offensive war. The legitimacy of making encroachments upon the Indian homelands was seldom denied by the English. The tone was set for later writers by the earliest imperial planners in London, men, like Hakluyt, who presumed that much of the New World territory rightly belonged to England because the Indians were non-Christian. The English usually insisted that it was not their intent to destroy the Indians but to civilize and convert the heathens. Then the native Americans

23. Timothy Breen, *The Character of the Good Ruler* (New Haven, Conn., 1970), p. 87; Jameson, *Johnson's Wonder-Working Providence*, p. 58; William Hubbard, *The Happiness of a People in the Wisdom of their Rulers* (Boston, 1676), pp. 58–59; Gibbs, *Right Method of Safety*, p. 7; Increase Mather, *The Day of Trouble is Near . . .* (Cambridge, Mass., 1674), pp. 3, 5–10, 20, 23; Mather, *History of the Warre*, p. 5. The John Hull quotation is from Perry Miller, *The New England Mind* (Cambridge, Mass, 1953), p. 27.

24. Tennent, *The late Association*, pp. 3, 9; Samuel Nowell, *Abraham in Arms . . .* (Boston, 1678), p. 2; Simeon Howard, *A Sermon preached . . .* (Boston, 1773), pp. 17–18, 20; Edmund S. Morgan, *Roger Williams* (New York, 1967), pp. 120–23; Samuel Phillips, *Souldiers Counselled and Encouraged . . .* (Boston, 1741), p. 15; Gibbs, *Right Method of Safety*, p. 10; David Jones, *Defensive War in a Just Cause Sinless* (Philadelphia, 1755), p. 16; Benjamin Franklin, *The Absolute and Obvious Necessity of Self-Defense* (Philadelphia, 1748), p. 1. Franklin cited Mark 14:47; Luke 20:49–51; John 8:10; and Matthew 26: 51–54.

and the European immigrants would live side by side in harmony. "Our intrusion into their possessions shall tend to their great good, and no way to their hurt," Robert Johnson maintained, "unlesse as unbridled beasts, they procure it to themselves."[25]

Later, when war with the Indians flared in Virginia, Edward Waterhouse defended English policy because the "way of conquering them is much more easie than of civilizing them . . . for they are a rude, barbarous and naked people." William Symonds, an English clergyman, and Robert Gray most fully developed the argument rationalizing the offensive expropriation of Indian possessions. Symonds argued that God instructed his followers to fill every corner of the earth, even if the pagans were exploited in the process. But how, Symonds wondered, could the English in "equitie . . . offer to thrust them, by violence, out of their inheritance?" His answer was ingenious and revealing. The colonists should enter the "waste country" and simply wait "till they be constrained by injustice, to stand upon their defence." In other words, a "peaceable" invasion would precipitate an Indian reprisal, which, in turn, could be enjoined by a "defensive" response! Gray, likewise, thought it axiomatic that "a Christian king may lawfullie make warre upon barbarous and Savage people." Yet, he advised moderation toward the Indians. There was enough land to go around; moreover, he strongly believed that the colonists must try to convert the Indians. But he defended the genocide of those who resisted conversion. Destruction of the native pagans was "warranted . . . rather than to let them live, if by no other means they can be reclaimed."[26]

Many early American writers attempted to sanctify battle by linking God and war. Some believed that being unprepared for war was a certain sign that the people had fallen from God's favor. One writer suggested that God expected parents to properly train and discipline their children so they might endure the spartan life. "A tender, softly, effeminate People is a curse and misery" in the Deity's eyes, he added. God not only sanctioned pugnacious behavior, He basked in it, according to another writer; to learn the art of war "gives much glory to him who is author of every commendable art." Many writers noted that God was a vengeful and truculent ruler. "The Lord is a Man of War, the Lord is His Name," more than one pastor reminded his flock. Other writers went a step further and counseled that God was on the side of Englishmen. God, they suggested, sent the English abroad as His chosen people. Although this mission into the wilderness inevitably meant war, the settlers were instructed that God

25. Harry Ward, *The United Colonies of New England, 1643–90* (New York, 1961), pp. 389–90; Richard Hakluyt, *Divers Voyages Touching the Discoverie of America* [1582] (Ann Arbor, Mich., 1966), n.p.; Robert Johnson, *Nova Britannia* . . . , in Force, *Tracts*, vol. I, p. 30.

26. Ralph Hamor, *A True Discourse,* Richard B. Harwell, ed. (Richmond, 1957), p. 48; Edward Waterhouse, *Declaration* (London, 1622), p. 23; Symonds, *Virginia*, pp. 6, 9, 11–15; Robert Gray, *A Good Speed to Virginia* [1609] (New York, 1970), n.p.

would protect and guide His people and intervene to terrify England's enemies.
Both Virginians and New Englanders were convinced that God caused large
numbers of Indians to die of English diseases so that the colonists might be
safe.[27]

The most commonly sanctioned conflicts were those fought to protect the
"innocent" from attacks by alien forces. The operative words in these "just"
wars connoted defense: "preserve," "maintain," "defend," and "secure" the
"public good" when the colonists' welfare was threatened by the "proud," the
"envious," the "fraudulent," the "oppressive," the "lustful," the "despotic,"
and the "vile." Various writers specified that the use of violence to defend
one's religion, civil rights, property, or existing government was legitimate
under sacred law. Or, as Samuel Nowell observed, "it is lawfull by war to
defend what we have lawfully obtained and come by, as our possessions, lands
and inheritance. . . ."[28]

Roger Williams once observed that each society would "labour to maintaine
their Wars to be defensive." Certainly many early American writers perforce
labored diligently to convince their readers that nearly every imaginable kind
of war could be construed as a defensive, and therefore a justifiable, war. Like
Grotius, many colonists defended the legitimacy of a war to recover something
that had been lost. Even then, some writers qualified their remarks to insist that
the war must be only "commenc'd for the *Recovery* of something of great
Importance unjustly taken from us, which we cannot do well without, nor after
Application, obtain by milder Measures." Some writers considered warfare fair
and just if undertaken to liberate those peoples whose civil or religious liberties
were oppressed by despotic rulers. It also was generally considered proper to
make war to rescue those unfortunates taken captive by an enemy. Even wars
of revenge were sometimes considered to be defensive, but frequently the colonists did not even attempt to justify them as defensive wars; some just wars
were waged, these writers maintained, simply for the sake of vengeance. Soldiers
were admonished to fight to avenge comrades who had been "butcher'd and
mangled." The bones of those unfortunates, the colonists were told, lay "whi-

27. Williams, *A Sermon*, p. 27; Nowell, *Abraham in Arms*, pp. 1, 17; Malone, "Indian and
English," p. 156; Symonds, *Virginia*, p. 42; Edmund Bland, *The Discovery of New Britaine* (Ann
Arbor, Mich., 1966), p. 4; [Anon.], *A Brief Relation of the State of New-England . . .* , in Force,
Tracts, vol. IV, no. 11, p. 5; *Planters Plea*, in ibid., vol. II, p. 5; Jameson, *Johnson's Wonder-
Working Providence*, pp. 42, 80.

28. John Smith, *New England Trials . . .* , in Arber, *Works of Smith*, vol. I, p. 272; Thomas
Prentice, *A Sermon Preached at Charlestown . . .* (Boston, 1745), p. 9; Haven, *A Sermon*, p. 31;
Elisha Fish, *The Art of War Lawful . . .* (Boston, 1774), p. 8; Carmichael, *Self-Defensive War*, p.
13; Samuel Adams to Thomas Young, 17 October 1774, in Harry Alonzo Cushing, ed., *The Writings
of Samuel Adams*, 4 vols. (New York, 1904), vol. III, pp. 162–63; [Thomas Paine], "Thoughts on
Defensive War," [1775], in Philip S. Foner, ed., *The Writings of Thomas Paine*, 2 vols. (New
York, 1945), vol. II, p. 53; Richardson, *The Necessity*, p. 9; Gibbs, *Right Method of Safety*, pp.
9–10; Nowell, *Abraham in Arms*, p. 3.

tening in the Sun to this Day, whilst their Blood, which the Earth has Swallowed up, still cries for Vengeance." Even the New Haven General Court alleged that it "may be considered . . . a just war" to "get satisfaction" from an enemy that had launched detrimental attacks.[29]

Still another example of "defensive" warfare was preventive war. Actions taken by a state to alter the balance of power might provoke a legitimate military response from its neighbor. Should a despot who manifested belligerent tendencies accede to power, that state's adversaries might launch a surprise attack "to prevent . . . Insults and Depredations for the future." A people deemed to be irretrievably hostile might justly be attacked in order to "avoid the blow." Some tribes of Indians were frequently seen in this light, as were the French, with their alleged schemes of universal monarchy. Some justified preventive civil wars to topple tyrants who violated the laws they had sworn to maintain. Clergyman Simeon Howard thought even an inconsequential affront might justify a preventive war. He reasoned that an unavenged indignity might instill a permanent mood of appeasement. If the sword is always left to "rust in its scabbard," he added, "people will awaken one day to find their liberty has vanished."[30]

The arguments delineated here reflect the philosophic ruminations of the colonial elite. Although they believed what they said publicly, they espoused other ideas regarding warfare more privately. In this realm, the leadership elite discerned positive virtues for engaging in what could be described only as offensive warfare. Combat seemed the only means by which some benefits could be attained. "Sea coal" from the mines of Cape Breton was an alluring commodity, for it would not only solve New England's fuel shortage problems but also preserve the region's timber for the profitable naval construction industry. Fish and furs, likewise, were economically important and capable of increasing prosperity in provincial America and laying "a foundation for a superiority of British Power on the Continent of Europe." The acquisition of these items, however, hinged on the conquest of portions of French Canada. But there were additional factors that made the seizure of Canada desirable. For instance, French maritime competition would be dealt a severe blow if Britain acquired the region. The Canadian wilderness could also be carved into homesteads for the land hungry New Englanders. Benjamin Franklin and Governor William Shirley of Massachusetts each played on this theme in their pleas to London. Franklin depicted the colonists as so destitute of arable land that many had fled to the cities hoping to escape a life of agrarian tenantry. He predicted that various "Trades, Occupations and Offices" were growing overcrowded. This potentially explosive social situation, he added, could be eradicated by the acquisition of new territory, even if it required the removal of "the Native to give his own

29. Phillips, *Souldiers Counselled,* pp. 15–16; Lockwood, *The Worth and Excellence of Civil Freedom,* p. 35; Buffinton, "Puritan View of War," p. 83.

30. Prentice, *A Sermon,* p. 9; Appleton, *Origin of War examin'd,* p. 21; Phillips, *Souldiers Counselled,* p. 24; Lathrop, *A Sermon,* pp. 14, 23; Howard, *A Sermon,* pp. 20–21, 33.

People Room." Those who accomplished this feat, he predicted, would be remembered as the "Fathers of their Nation."[31]

The merchant class stood to gain the most by the acquisition of Canada's precious commodities, and, not surprisingly, leading merchants, or their political lackeys, customarily were the leading spokesmen for still additional invasions of the French provinces. Political leaders spearheaded such drives; for example, Governor George Thomas of Pennsylvania exhorted his colony to join in King George's War by arguing that the welfare of the entire province hinged on the well-being of the merchant class. "Even the Farmer, who is too apt to consider the Landed and Trading Interests in Opposition to each other," must realize that he will have to "confine his Produce to Consumption of his own Family, if the Merchant is disabled" from acquiring Canadian goods that will increase his access to foreign markets. Wars did lead to economic boom times for some members of society. King George's War and the French and Indian War led to what historian Carl Bridenbaugh called "unparalleled" prosperity for some maritime colonies; and the families who made fortunes from these conflicts frequently intermarried, producing the first urban gentry in the colonies.[32]

Astute politicans did not need to be told of the political advantages that might be bestowed through warfare. Governor Shirley is perhaps the best example of a politician who used warfare to build a political machine. Shirley, who had risen in the imperial bureaucracy because of Britain's recurrent warfare, quickly discovered that as merchants, speculators, and contractors prospered, they attached themselves to his administration. A symbiotic relationship developed between the governor and those businessmen with interests in Maine and those who stood to profit either by the acquisition of portions of Canada or by the elimination of French competition. Shirley extended military commissions to men who, in private life, were seeking to extract fortunes from the region over which France and Britain squabbled. William Pepperell, whom Shirley appointed to lead the expedition against Louisbourg in 1745, was a timberman who hoped to gain free access to the forests of Maine. To be commissioned a colonel in an expeditionary force was, as Shirley knew, an enviable honor. Colonels were permitted deductions in the purchase of their clothing, they handled the money designated for soldiers' salaries, they were allotted the opportunity to sell luxuries to the rank and file troops, and, of course, they were permitted a healthy cut of the spoils acquired from the enemy. These men were often akin to Samuel

31. Carl Bridenbaugh, *Cities in Revolt . . .* (New York, 1955), p. 26; Carl Bridenbuagh, *Cities in the Wilderness* (New York, 1938), p. 151; Gerald S. Graham, ed., *The Walker Expedition to Quebec, 1711* (Toronto, 1953), pp. 257–58, 260–61, 266–67; William Shirley to the Duke of Newcastle, 7 July 1744, in Charles H. Lincoln, ed., *The Correspondence of William Shirley,* 2 vols. (New York, 1912), vol. I, p. 132; Shirley to Newcastle, 14 January 1744, ibid., vol. I, pp. 161–36; Shirley to the Lords of Trade, 10 July 1745, ibid., vol. I, p. 243; Shirley to Newcastle, 29 October 1745, ibid., vol. I, p. 285; Benjamin Franklin, *Observations Concerning the Increase of Mankind* [1755], in Labaree, *Papers of Franklin,* vol. IV, pp. 227, 231.

32. Robert E. Wall, "Louisbourg, 1745," *NEQ* 37 (March 1964), p. 70; Bridenbaugh, *Cities in Revolt,* pp. 43, 45, 140.

Vetch, the New Yorker who is blandly described by his biographer as a "colonial enterpriser"; Vetch was a venal hustler who lobbied for an attack on French Canada, traded with the French during the ensuing war, and then requested of London that he be named governor of Canada if it was acquired or, if not, that he be designated governor of either New York, Maryland, Virginia, or Massachusetts. Shirley appointed his friends to positions of exalted martial rank, and those he appointed grew steadfast in their zeal for Shirley. The governor, moreover, lobbied with key officials in London "to distribute part of the conquer'd Lands" among his friends. As Shirley's biographer has observed, the governor was cognizant that "War had increased his political capital; the discontinuance of war threatened to reduce it." Thus, "he had motives to avoid peace" since demobilization only brought on problems such as deflation and shrunken patronage powers.[33]

Governor Shirley had greater motives for his wartime operations than simply to manipulate a political machine that enhanced his chances of getting a few bills through the Massachusetts Assembly. He actively lobbied for the governorship of both New York and the Leeward Islands. Moreover, he proposed a union of all the mainland colonies headed by a president-general, and he did not rule himself out for that post if Whitehall acceded to the scheme. He also begged for financial rewards from conquered provinces. As he was "likely to leave some Debts undischarged and a large Family unprovided for," he implored London to grant him "a few Veins of Coal lying on the Back Part" of Cape Breton Island. He often begged for a special pension as a reward for his military service. Finally, in the aftermath of the successful attack on Louisburg in 1745, Shirley was bitterly disappointed to learn that he was merely given the rank of colonel in a newly created American regiment, whereas Pepperell was knighted. The governor complained loudly to London that the expedition had been "wholly formed, set on foot, and carried into execution, in New England by myself." His importunings fell on deaf ears, however, and Shirley was left to concoct still another grand military scheme that might bring him financial security and satiate his vanity. This plan, which he proffered first in 1746, and ultimately sold to the colonists as a defensive war, involved nothing less than "securing the whole northern continent as far fack as the French settlements of the Mississippi, which are about 2000 miles distant."[34]

33. Shirley to Newcastle, 29 October 1745, in Lincoln, *Correspondence of Shirley*, vol. I, p. 245; G. M. Waller, *Samuel Vetch: Colonial Enterpriser* (Chapel Hill, N.C., 1960), pp. 63–64, 79, 83, 100, 168; Schutz, *Shirley*, pp. 42, 84–85, 92, 120.

34. Shirley to Newcastle, 1 September 1750, in Lincoln, *Correspondence of Shirley*, vol. I, p. 509; Shirley to Newcastle, 23 November 1752, ibid., vol. II, pp. 1–4; Shirley to Thomas Robinson, 24 December 1754, ibid., vol. II, p. 117; Shirley to Newcastle, 27 July 1745, ibid., vol. I, pp. 254–55; Shirley to Newcastle, 20 November 1745, ibid., vol. I, p. 291; Shirley to Newcastle, 1 April 1758, ibid., vol. II, p. 599; Shirley to Newcastle, 12 May 1758, ibid., vol. II, p. 602; Shirley to Newcastle, 13 June 1759, ibid., vol. II, pp. 603–4; Schutz, *Shirley*, pp. 105, 108.

Shirley was hardly unique. The notion that portions of French Canada could be acquired or that French competition could be mitigated or eliminated by military means dated back to the early days of the Jamestown settlement. With their own colonists on the verge of starvation, the London Company in 1613 directed Samuel Argall to raid French territory in Canada. John Winthrop entertained the same impulse in 1644, and another generation of Massachusetts authorities launched a full-scale invasion of Acadia in 1690 and an attack on Quebec the following year. In 1707 American colonists made their first formal request of aid from London to assist in an invasion of Canada—an appeal made, incidentally, on the grounds that the more money made by American settlers, the more British manufactured goods America could import—and expeditionary forces pushed northward in 1709 and again in 1711. It fell to Shirley and his contemporaries to push for renewed attacks in the 1740s and 1750s, until Britain at last acquired these besieged regions in 1763. Then, in 1775 the rebellious American provincials invaded Canada to strip it from the parent state. Without exception, the leadership elite in each generation characterized its military endeavors as "just" and "defensive" wars, with General Washington even depicting the invasion by the Continental army as a magnanimous gesture by which English colonists would liberate the Canadians from the English.[35]

It is more difficult to determine how the inarticulate colonists reacted to this recurrent warfare, but it is probably safe to assume that they welcomed the outbreak of war with considerably less relish than did the colonial leaders. Certainly warfare sometimes so stimulated the economy that a portion of the prosperity trickled to middle- or working-class colonists. Wars often created short-lived jobs in certain fields, principally in the shipbuilding and attendant maritime industries; losses of foreign or coastal markets while a war was in progress frequently induced merchants to turn to the interior for a substitute market, which stimulated the economy in the frontier regions and even assisted in the development of some interior cities, such as Lancaster, Pennsylvania.[36] Most important, however, warfare and the acquisition of new lands often went hand-in-hand. Because of these factors it was not unheard of for the inarticulate to urge the commencement of war or to welcome an announcement of hostilities with genuine zeal. Those engaged in the maritime trades about Boston, for instance, were often as keen for war with France as were their employers; and western farmers, who found the supply of land diminishing in the face of a rapidly growing American population, were frequently no less zealous.

35. Jeremiah Dummer to Lord Dartmouth, 3 January 1711, in Graham, *Walker Expedition,* pp. 266–67; Richard Van Alstyne, *The Rising American Empire* (New York, 1960), pp. 10–19; "To the Oppressed Inhabitants of Canada," in Worthington C. Ford, ed., *The Journals of the Continental Congress,* 34 vols. *(Washington, D.C., 1904–1937), vol. II, p. 69.*

36. Bridenbaugh, *Cities in Revolt,* p. 51.

While there was often a beneficial side to conflict, it was more common for war to be accompanied by unsettling events. The evidence indicates that these unpleasant characteristics of warfare were sufficiently apparent to the mass of colonists to mitigate their enthusiasm. One of the first effects of warfare was civilian deprivation, either because the interruption of trade produced shortages or because inflation, which was endemic to colonial wars, skyrocketed prices beyond the purchasing abilities of most people. Many citizens in the northern colonies, for instance, shivered through wartime winters because wood was unavailable or too expensive to acquire. Sometimes deprivation occurred because precious commodities were siphoned off by the army. Boston experienced a bread shortage in 1709 when the Canadian invasion force bivouacked in the city for weeks prior to launching its expedition. And, of course, if the men of the family were in the army, the family farm could not be operated at full capacity. At times the manpower to produce goods simply did not exist. Boston, in the space of three years in the early 1740s, lost 20 percent of its male population, most of them in their prime working years. The combination of these forces often triggered an economic depression on the homefront, usually shortly after the war ended, but occasionally while it was still in progress. Moreover, several recent studies have indicated that wars usually accelerated the process of concentrating wealth and power in the hands of an elite class. Although wars were not the only force producing a maldistribution of abundance and power, by the time of the Revolution a smaller number of people held a greater percentage of the wealth, than during the previous two or three generations; officeholding took on unmistakably oligarchical features, the middle class contracted, and society may have grown less democratic. No one has suggested that the mass of colonists were fully aware of these trends, but there is evidence that the disaffected in the Revolution sought, in Gary Nash's words, to reform the "structural problems in the economy" that had arisen during the eighteenth century.[37]

Wars had additional ramifications for many people. They made widows and orphans. Conflicts sundered families for months or years. Many were disgruntled at the changes in morality that usually accompanied warfare. Typical was the Bostonian who remarked that while the American soldiers stationed in his city in 1749 "Scatter some Money in Town, yet we grow very tired of them."[38]

37. Bridenbaugh, *Cities in the Wilderness,* pp. 151, 178, 204; Bridenbaugh, *Cities in Revolt,* pp. 59–60; Leach, *Arms for Empire,* pp. 262–69; James A. Henretta, "Economic Development and Social Structure in Colonial Boston," *WMQ,* 3d Ser. 22 (January 1965), pp. 75–92; James A. Henretta, *The Evolution of American Society, 1700–1815* (Lexington, Mass., 1973), pp. 95–107; Alan Kulikoff, "The Progress of Inequality in Revolutionary Boston," *WMQ,* 3d Ser. 28 (July 1971), pp. 375–412; Bruce C. Daniels, "Emerging Urbanization and Increasing Stratification in the Era of the American Revolution," in Ferling, ed., *American Revolution,* pp. 15–30; Gary Nash, "Social Change and the Growth of Prerevolutionary Urban Radicalism," in Alfred Young, ed., *The American Revolution . . .* (DeKalb, Ill., 1976), pp. 5–32; Marvin L. Michael Kay, "The North Carolina Regulators, 1766–1776: A Class Conflict," in ibid., pp. 71–123.

38. Bridenbaugh, *Cities in Revolt,* p. 60.

Some colonists had an even more direct interest in these wars; they faced the real prospect of service in the military forces that were raised.

Despite Governor Shirley's and his cronies' aspirations for war, the average man was far less enthusiastic. Men went to considerable lengths to avoid service, including rioting when press gangs descended upon their towns. Few, however, went so far as the Puritan who pleaded to be excused from service because of a recent marriage, and who cited Deuteronomy 24:5 as his justification: "when a man hath taken a new wife he shall not goe out to warr. . .but he shall be free at home one year." The colonial leadership was compelled to resort to a wide variety of tactics to secure enlistees. Massachusetts authorities were so worried about induction prospects during King Philip's War that they issued a special proclamation explaining the causes of the conflict and justifying waging the war. Bounties were offered in every war to secure enlistments. Colonies commonly offered land, clothing, or cash, sometimes paying the latter only when the soldier produced the scalps of those he had killed in the war. At times the authorities played on religious prejudices or patriotic zeal to attain soldiers, and nearly every war was depicted as the last conflict that would trouble the generation. Those who were garnered for service often left much to be desired. British leaders during the French and Indian War generally thought provincial armies were composed of "riff-raff" and the "Lowest Dregs of the People, both Officers and Men." A Pennsylvanian concurred, noting that the volunteers from his colony consisted of "a parcel of Mutinous Dutch Rascals." Nor did those who served always perform valiantly. On the remote Pennsylvania frontier during the French and Indian War, Colonel George Washington, serving his initial command, was plagued by deserters who often "went off in a Body," sometimes as many as a score or more fleeing in a single day. And, according to an English administrator, colonial forces often waited to pursue the Indians until they were certain the foe had evacuated the region.[39]

If the colonists were preoccupied with the issues of war, the articulate settlers were additionally concerned with the agents of conflict—the warrior. "The Time is not (we may fear) yet come, when Men may beat their Swords into Plowshares," a Massachusetts clergyman reminded his congregation. It was necessary, therefore, to train the citizenry in the marital arts. Their "Hands should be taught to War, and their Fingers to fight. They should know how to use the

---

39. Pauline Maier, "Popular Uprisings," *WMQ* 27 (January 1970), pp. 8–9; Leach, *Flintlock and Tomahawk*, pp. 123–24, 186; "The Organization of John Van Etten's Company," in Labaree, *Papers of Franklin*, vol. VI, pp. 349–50, 353–54; Graham, *Walker Expedition*, pp. 300–1; Warren B. Johnson, "The Content of American Colonial Newspapers Relative to International Affairs, 1704–1763," (Ph.D. diss., Univ. of Washington, 1962), p. 369; Ward, *"Unite or Die,"* pp. 245–51; Stanley M. Pargellis, *Lord Loudon in North America, 1756–1758* (New Haven, Conn., 1933), p. 99; "Letters of Capt. Shippen," *PMHB* 36, no. 4 (1911), p. 432; Leach, *Arms for Empire*, p. 432; [Anon.], *Edward Randolph; Including His Letters and Official Papers . . .* (Boston, 1899), p. 64.

Sword, the *Spear,* the *Gun,* and all other *Martial Weapons.*'' Repeatedly, society's spokesmen, particularly the clergy, extolled the warrior ethic. Soldiering,
according to one cleric, was an act of ''true manliness and grandeur,'' it was
a ''just, honorable'' endeavor that tended to ''banish . . . littleness and mean-
ness, and fill men with greatness of spirit.'' Good soldiers, he added, deserve
singular respect. But what made a good soldier? Some thought the best warriors
were those who freely volunteered their service. Others believed it was the
soldier who could be trained to manifest ''patience under hardships, . . . fortitude, . . . obstinate perseverence, and military obedience.'' General Washington believed natural bravery, longing for rewards, and fear of punishment
combined to mold the best soldier.[40]

The colonists probably devoted more attention to the qualities of good soldiering than did their counterparts in Europe. Certainly, the reason was that the
European armies were composed largely of men barely distinguishable from
criminals and, as such, were considered by the elite simply as soldiers ''fit to
kill or be killed.'' In America, on the other hand, the concept of the citizen-
soldier remained in vogue. The treatment of such men, living in a more egalitarian society than prevailed in Europe, required extensive consideration. Of
course, the task of making soldiers was abetted by the manner in which young
boys were socialized. From an early age colonial boys were taught the alleged
virtues of masculine, or manly, traits. Once aware of their designated role, as
Philip Greven has demonstrated, a struggle set in between the qualities of ''se-
duction, temptation, effeminacy,'' on the one hand, and ''manliness, industry,
fame, and watchfulness'' on the other hand; it was a battle of ''hard versus soft,
rugged versus indolent, manly versus effeminate.'' Most men accepted the
masculine identity and, probably subconsciously, deemed the very qualities
attributed to the soldier—rationalism, strength, industry, courage, willfulness,
self-confidence, bravery—as identical to the traits they sought to exhibit as
males.[41]

Above all else the colonists prized two virtues in their soldiers: courage and
discipline. Courage, it was presumed, was an inherent virtue for only a few
men, a part of their ''natural Constitution,'' which enabled them to ''brave
hardships and the risk of life with a cheerful face.'' But what was meant by
courage? The articulate took pains to show that much that was considered
courageous behavior was, in fact, low and unseemly deportment. Those who
engaged in the duel, for instance, postured in a courageous manner, but in reality

40. Oliver Peabody, *An Essay to revive and encourage Military Exercises . . .* (Boston, 1732),
pp. 16, 18–19; Nathaniel Robbins, *Jerusalem's Peace Wished . . .* (Boston, 1772), pp. 14, 20;
Prentice, *A Sermon,* p. 29; Wright, *Sullivan Expedition,* vol. 5, p. 2; Berhard Knollenberg, *Washington and the Revolution: A Reappraisal* (New York, 1941), p. 111.
41. David Ogg, *England in the Reigns of James II and William III* (Oxford, Eng., 1955), p. 328;
Philip Greven, *The Protestant Temperament* (New York, 1977), pp. 125, 246–47, 284–85, 322.

the nefarious practice was "seldom undertaken but from the ignominious Power of Fear" of ridicule by one's peers. Nor would a truly valiant soldier consider killing his adversary "in a little underhand and sneaking manner." The soldier of real virtue and courage was a man of "Moral Prudence" filled with "generous Compassion to the Vanquished." Moreover, the foolhardy soldier who would rush blithely and pugnaciously into combat was more rash than courageous. Courage could not be distinguished by "Show, or Pomp and Appearance." The truly courageous warrior, therefore, was the man who would be intransigent in the face of danger, fearing "neither guns nor swords, nor any other instruments of death." Manifesting boldness, fidelity, hardness, fortitude, sobriety, and orderliness, he must be able to "stand like brazen walls against the fiercest onsets of his enemy," to "let not the Roar of Cannon, nor the infernal Yell of Barbarians affright" him. He was a brave soldier, Cotton Mather told his fellow Puritans, whose *"Blood chills* not when . . . call'd out to dy alone in *cold Blood,"* who could "Laugh at *Fear"* and "shout among the loud Drums and the shrill Clangors of the Trumpet *Ha, Ha!"*[42]

The good, courageous soldier anticipated travail. He knew, indeed, that it was adversity that "causeth him to *play* the *Man."* The superior warrior, therefore, properly entered combat fixed with a "suitable Suspicion and proper Apprehension" of his foe. But he did not approach the war zone in the hope of gaining either booty or revenge. Likewise, the soldier who delighted in "shedding human Blood" would be an "impotent" warrior. The best soldier was the man of "calm, deliberate Resolution . . . cooled by Reason, governed and conducted by Discretion," the man who acted only from a "sincere Desire to Defend the people of God, from a crew of *Unjust* Men."[43]

The opposite of courage was cowardice, and the early colonists spilled great amounts of ink fulminating against such conduct. In combat, a clergyman exclaimed, the coward would "quake with fear, his face gather paleness, his knees smite one another, and [he will be] supremely anxious for his own safety."[44] Sometimes cowards never reached the battlefield. Those men were deemed cowards who, instead of defending their country, "unman themselves with sensual Pleasure and Debauchery." So, too, were men who

42. Mather Byles, *The Glories of the Lord of Hosts* . . . (Boston, 1740), pp. 20–21; [Thomas Paine], *The American Crisis,* in Foner, *Writings of Paine,* vol. I, p. 63; Robbins, *Jerusalem's Peace Wished,* p. 14; Samuel Stillman, *A Sermon Preached* . . . (Boston, 1770), p. 17; William Linn, *A Military Discourse, Delivered in Carlisle* (Philadelphia, 1776), p. 7; William Hubly, *The Soldier caution'd and counsel'd* (Boston, 1747), p. 11; Williams, *A Sermon,* p. 10; James Cogswell, *God, The Pious Soldier's Strength* (Boston, 1757), p. 28; Cotton Mather, *Military Duties, Recommended* . . . (Boston, 1687), p. 12.

43. William McClenachan, *The Christian Warrior* . . . (Boston, 1745), pp. 7–8; Cogswell, *God, The Pious Soldier's Strength,* p. 15; Cotton Mather, *A Discourse Delivered* . . . (Boston, 1689), p. 26.

44. Stillman, *A Sermon,* p. 10.

if, instead of searching out the Enemy, they keep out of their Way, lest they should search out and find them; if they lie sleeping or rioting in Forts and Places of Safety, while their Country is ravaged, perhaps in their very Neighborhood . . . or . . . when they lay themselves open to false alarms, by being credulous to every Account that magnifies the Force of the Enemy; when they are tedious or divided in their Consultations, and slow and faint in the Execution; when they consult rather what would be most *safe for themselves,* than most *beneficial to their Country;* when they keep skirmishing at a Distance, instead of making a bold Push, and bringing the War to a speedy Issue by a decisive Stroke; when they are fond of prolonging the War, that they may live and riot at the public Expence; when they sell themselves and their Country to the Enemy for a Bribe . . . they do the Work of the Lord deceitfully.[45]

Discipline was regarded as the second great virtue of soldiers. Unless the warrior was obedient to the commands of his superiors, all the courage he could muster would be wasted. The "first principle of military education," Mercy Otis Warren contended, was explicit obedience. New England spokesmen believed training and discipline to be essential because of the prevalence of the "levelling spirit of our Plantations." Proper military training, another clergyman noted, "civilizes them [the soldiers], takes down their Temper, tames the Fierceness of their Natures, forms their minds to virtue, learns 'em to carry it with a just Deference to *Superiours*. . . ." A Southerner, on the other hand, believed "Our men are the best crude materials for soldiers. . .in the world, for they possess a docility and patience which astonish foreigners," but he concurred that their innate habits of insubordination required constant tending. Some believed the soldier should be reduced to an unthinking automaton. Nathaniel Appleton, a clergyman, suggested that the best soldier would merely "presume that the Government have good Reasons" for sending him into combat. Another writer agreed, contending that the "true Hero disdains to ask any Questions." The soldier, therefore, must be "obedient. . . , diligent and faithful, just and honest in his Place and Station." A "discontented, murmuring Spirit in an Army," another commentator noted, "is like a Fever in the Body; or Fire in a City." Many colonial writers asserted that discipline was essential lest the armed troops become a menace to those they were recruited to defend. It was imperative for the soldier to exhibit *"loyalty* to his Prince," and it was equally essential that the "soldier never make use of arms, but when he is ordered by the constituted guardians of our rights and liberties." A familiar litany, therefore, was the admonition to "keep up martial Discipline: a Souldier is the worst of creatures that is not under Discipline." Many believed that the virtues of trainband activities, so long as the soldiers were kept properly subordinated, carried over into civilian life. Township activities, as well as those of the church, the school, and the militia, in the estimation of John Adams, produced a citizenry

45. Samuel Davies, *Curse of Cowardice* (London, 1759), pp. 13–14.

characterized by fortitude, temperance, patience, justice, knowledge, skill, trust, ingenuity, dexterity, and industry.[46]

Training, of course, was essential to refine inherent skills and to develop physical strengths. Honed to perfection, these attributes would make a "compleat Champion." It was a rare man who "by an intuitive glance [could] distinguish between what is only difficult and what is absolutely impossible." Hence, discipline was the means by which most could achieve the other cardinal virtue, courage. Most writers perceived that fear in combat was not only natural, but even desirable. Courage was a quality to be instilled. It was commonly acknowledged that not all men were brave but that "most men have more courage than they know of." Most commentators believed that rigorous, repetitious training would produce the enigmatic fortitude that society exalted. Even so, a "sudden Panic, occasioned by some unforeseen Accident, may seize on the most hardy resolute Soldier, which may . . . unman him, shake his Resolution." And the panic could trigger a pell mell retreat, an event often more dangerous than standing before the enemy. Thus, courage could never be guaranteed. But, with proper discipline cowards frequently continued to fight, and often a "little Handful of Chast, Sober, Devout Persons, a small Army," had been victorious.[47]

Rigid training alone would not suffice to mold a superior soldier. Colonial leaders generally believed their subjects were more virtuous, enlightened, less obsequious, and more materialistic than European commoners. Because of their virtue and acumen, the leadership believed, Americans would fight willingly only in wars that were "just," or at least properly justified by the governing elite. Although even after training most soldiers did not possess a truculent, sanguine spirit, the cadre's belief in the "Equity or Justice" of the encounter, one writer noted, would "strengthen every Nerve and Sinew in the noble Soldier." Buoyed by a sense of right, "human nature [would] rise above itself, in acts of bravery and heroism." It behooved the leadership, therefore, that "rea-

46. Mercy Otis Warren, *History of the American Revolution* . . . (Boston, 1805), p. 219; Douglass, *Summary*, vol. I, p. 352n; Jameson, *Johnson's Wonder-Working Providence*, p. 34; Jeremiah Wise, *Rulers the Ministers of God* . . . (Boston, 1729), p. 31; Appleton, *Origin of War examined*, p. 22; Byles, *Glories of the Lord*, p. 21; Ebenezer Bridge, *A Sermon Preach'd* . . . (Boston, 1752), p. 11; Stephen Payne Adye, *A Treatise on Courts Martial* (New York, 1769), pp. 16–17; Joseph Willard, *The duty of the good and faithful Soldier* . . . (Boston, 1781), p. 11; Ebenezer Gay, *Well-accomplished Soldiers* . . . (Boston, 1738), p. 17; Stillman, *A Sermon*, pp. 7–8; Lathrop, *A Sermon*, pp. 35–36; Nowell, *Abraham in Arms*, p. 18; Lyman H. Butterfield et al., eds., *The Diary and Autobiography of John Adams*, 4 vols. (Cambridge, Mass., 1964), vol. III, p. 195.

47. Richardson, *Necessity*, p. 10; Israel Evans, *A Discourse delivered at Boston* . . . (Philadelphia, 1779), p. 19; Benjamin Franklin, "A Dialogue between X, Y, and Z . . . ," in Labaree, *Papers of Franklin*, vol. VI, p. 304; Paine, *American Crisis*, in Foner, *Writings of Paine*, vol. I, p. 63; Hubly, *Soldiers caution'd*, p. 11; Cogswell, *God, the Pious Soldier's Strength*, p. 16; Byles, *Glories of the Lord*, pp. 17–18; Cotton Mather, *Things to be Look'd for* . . . (Cambridge, Mass., 1691), p. 78.

sonable Satisfaction should be given . . . that the War is lawful, and the Cause better than their Lives.''[48]

Soldiers normally were prepared for war in one of two ways: they were told the conflict was for the salvation of their religion, or they were told that the conflict was essential for the protection of their liberties. Repeatedly, warriors were told they were rational and moral agents sent to protect society. Typically, one clergyman admonished soldiers on the eve of battle that the troops were not to "aim chiefly at the gaining of Honour or Wealth," but to assist God in pursuing the destruction of Satan. Indeed, to "grow into a great nation is a very great blessing of God," one writer intoned, even if blood was spilled in the process. Often, another pastor suggested, wars were "highly *necessary*" to "preserve and defend the pure Worship of GOD.''[49]

From the days of John Smith, rhetoric concerning the defense of liberty was the principal tool for motivating soldiers. The crusty early Virginia captain, for instance, believed his troops fought best when they believed they were struggling to "defend the innocent and the humble." The colonists believed God had bestowed liberty and property upon them. To fight in defense of liberty, in fact, was to grapple for those "Priviledges which Christ hath so dearly purchased" for mankind.[50] The battle was actually easier, the risk of injury more remote, when defending liberty, for he

> Who fights, to take our liberty away,
> Dead-hearted fights, and falls an easy prey.[51]

If the civilian population was filled with an equal zeal, the soldiers would be even more worthy. One expedition that plunged onto the frontier in pursuit of Indians was applauded by the settlers, who regarded the troops as "intrepid adventures who . . . would have done honor to a Brutus or a Caesar." Properly emotional, the soldiers, according to one eyewitness, "shewed the utmost ardor to engage" the foe.[52]

But the colonists were materialists, too. Rewards and bounties were common inducements to exact more from the soldiers. General Washington quickly learned that cash sometimes could procure more satisfactory behavior than any

48. Gibbs, *Right Method of Safety,* p. 13; McClenachon, *Christian Warrior,* pp. 6–7.

49. Gibbs, *Right Method of Safety,* p. 13; McClenachan, *Christian Warrior,* p. 6–7; Hamilton, *Farmer Refuted,* in Syrett and Cooke, *Hamilton Papers,* vol. I, p. 155; Gay, *Well-accomplished Soldiers,* p. 8; Williams, *A Sermon,* p. 16–17; Cogswell, *God, the Pious Soldier's Strength,* p. 16; Phillips, *Soldiers Counselled,* pp. 15, 32; Symonds, *Virginia,* p. 35.

50. Smith, *New England Trials,* in Arber, *Works of Smith,* vol. I, p. 272; Nowell, *Abraham in Arms,* p. 10; Richardson, *Necessity,* pp. 6, 9.

51. Hugh Henry Brackenridge, *The Battle of Bunkers-Hill* . . . , in Montrose J. Moses, ed., *Representative Plays of American Dramatists,* 3 vols. (New York, 1964), vol. I, p. 246.

52. Wright, *Sullivan Expedition,* vol. 6, p. 5.

rhetorical flourish or harsh disciplinary code. The general, for instance, got the troops into bearable quarters at Valley Forge only when he offered cash prizes to the group that most rapidly built the best hut and one hundred dollars to the soldier who designed the best roofing material for the cabins. With these enticements, Thomas Paine noted, the soldiers worked "like a family of beavers, every one busy."

Although few colonists were pacifists, it was an age when religion played an overweening role in the lives of most people. War and Christianity—not just war for the sake of religion—had to be reconciled in the minds of the populace. Pacifism, which denounced all war as immoral, was labeled a "strange piece of dotage befallen this crazy headed Age." War was a fact of life—a "Law of Nature," of God—in this imperfect world, and it was proper to be prepared for its eventuality. Soldiers were told that the Scriptures contained no denunciation of "just" warfare or of the military profession. The history of the ancient Hebrews, the chosen people, was an epic of nearly uninterrupted war, and the warlike deeds of their leaders, particularly Abraham and David, were touted repeatedly by colonial ministers. Much was made of the biblical stories of John the Baptist and Jesus welcoming centurions. Gilbert Tennent reasoned, moreover, that if Jesus taught *"Heads of Families* to be upon their *Guard* against Thieves . . . what were invading hordes but thieves." When God told each disciple to be a "souldier of Jesus Christ," it was said, He meant they were to be warriors in the fullest sense of the term. Lawful soldiering, therefore, not only was not immoral, according to Cotton Mather, it was "a Needful, yea, and a very *Noble* Thing."[53]

The colonial leadership, in fact, believed that the Christian soldier was the best soldier. Articulate colonists fretted over the licentiousness of warriors. Souls might be lost in the encampments, and, worse still, the sins of the military might be transmitted to the civilians. Lamentable as it might be, "the Contagion of Vice . . . is perhaps no where stronger than in the Army." Backsliding into profanity and tippling was the least of the problem. Some were anxious that witnesses to the horror of war might grow less resolute in their Christian faith. On the other hand, the dangers implicit in soldiering tended to *"rectifieth his Arms"* by enlarging "his Views beyond the Limits of this short Life."[54]

And as the soldier thought more of the next world and less of pleasure on this earth, his virtue as a warrior increased. Only dedicated Christians could view

53. Smith, *A New Age*, vol. II, pp. 998–1000; Nowell, *Abraham in Arms*, pp. 5, 9; Tennent, *The late Association*, p. 17; Clark, *Christian Bravery*, pp. 22–25; Ruggles, *Usefulness and Expedience of Soldiers*, pp. 3–4; Ebenezer Pemberton, *A Sermon preached . . .* (Boston, 1756), pp. 8–9; Peabody, *Essay to Revive*, pp. 14–16; Williams, *A Sermon*, pp. 4–7; Jameson, *Johnson's Wonder-Working Providence*, p. 165; Mather, *Things to be look'd for*, p. 74.

54. Davies, *Curse of Cowardice*, p. 10; Samuel Webster, *Rabshakeh's Proposals Considered . . .* (Boston, 1775), p. 30; Samuel Cooper, *A Sermon Preached . . .* (Boston, 1751), pp. 13–14; Joseph Parsons, *Religion recommended to the Soldier* (Boston, 1744), p. 12.

the "slaughter and death spread before them, in all its gloomy horrors, with so rational a courage." Only the religious zealot could see death as a relief to the pain of life: The Christian warrior would be characterized by firmness and an intrepid spirit, by "boldness . . . and a readiness to endure hardness." Some writers deprecated the maxim of Machiavelli that religion made men cowardly; they argued that the most valient soldiers had always been "the most eminent for the Religion." Christianity, they stressed, transformed "effeminate Cowards" into "valiant Heroes." Resoluteness was but one virtue of the Christian soldier. Loyalty, obedience, was an additional byproduct of religious zeal, for the Christian was certain to realize that disloyalty was "a sin of the first Magnitude."[55]

Christianity in the army camp produced a further benefit: it "engageth the *Providence of GOD* on our Side." God, according to this logic, would work his wonders through the "godly grave Fathers" of the government, and this, in turn, rendered "every common Soldier among you . . . a Magistrate" licensed to engage in the acts of war. Hence, if transgressors invited the wrath of God, righteousness coaxed the favor of the Deity, imparting "wisdom to the simple, knowledge to the ignorant, strength to the weak, and courage to the faint-hearted." The ideology did not fall on deaf ears. Time after time, for example, John Smith in his histories of early Virginia attributed narrow escape from certain doom to Divine intervention. His troops, likewise, accepted the principle. Once, surrounded by natives in a primeval forest, a commander barked to the Indians that "we are not afraid . . . for that any one of us were able to deale with forty through the protection of our great God."[56]

Concomitantly, such rhetoric was steadfastly accompanied by the doctrine that to suffer or to die in battle would earn the soldier glory in heaven and on earth. Generations were told that, should the Christian warrior perish in a "just" war, "he falls not unnoticed by the Father of Spirits." Although Jesus was silent on such matters, it sufficed that the Old Testament acknowledged that fallen Jewish warriors were regarded by God as "the *Worthies* of the Kingdom." Hence, a Boston clergyman told a company of soldiers that for those killed, the "Field of Blood shall become a Field of Triumph," and that on Judgment Day all soldiers who perished would "rise above the Ruins of *this* World, and become Inhabitants of the Regions of Immortality and Glory, with Jesus." Soldiers killed in battle were to be held as martyrs among the living, too. Those who perished in battle, it was said, died not because they were poor soldiers "but rather because earths honours are too scant for them." Those about to enter

55. Haven, *A Sermon*, p. 19; Parsons, *Religion recommended*, pp. 13–17, 20; Williams, *A Sermon*, p. 20; Phillips, *Soldiers Counselled*, p. 21; Stillman, *A Sermon*, p. 7; Hull Abbot, *Jehovah's Character as a Man of War* . . . (Boston, 1735), p. 26; Pemberton, *A Sermon*, p. 12.

56. Parsons, *Religion recommended*, p. 14; Jameson, *Johnson's Wonder-Working Providence*, p. 165; Adams, *The Grounds of Confidence*, p. 8; John Smith, *A True Relation* . . . , in Arber, *Works of Smith*, vol. I, pp. 7, 92; Bland, *Discovery of new Brittaine*, p. 4.

battle were reminded that if they succumbed to the enemy their names would be "enroll'd in the Annals of eternal Fame . . . and handed down from Generation to Generation."[57] Indeed, poets did enshrine in a literary Valhalla many of those who died in combat. Upon learning of the death of General James Wolfe at Quebec, one writer admitted

> For my ambition, is to die like Wolfe
> Wept by his country, and by many a bard,
> Of silver-tongued, high-storied in his urn.

The same poet believed dead soldiers mingle with one another

> By crystal currents, on the vale of Heaven,
> High in full converse of immortal acts,
> Achiev'd for truth and innocence on earth.[58]

Despite the official line lauding the avocation of soldiering, the mass of people manifested ambivalent views toward practitioners of the art. Some military heroes apparently won the genuine affection of the colonial populace. A British militarist like General George Howe, who died at Ticonderoga during the French and Indian War, posthumously garnered the respect of the inhabitants of the region where he died. General Wolfe, the British victor at Quebec in 1759, may have been the most widely celebrated figure among the colonists. His only rival for the honor was William Pitt, who attained larger-than-life proportions for contriving the political-military strategy that won the Great War for Empire in 1763. Some colonial soldiers gained widespread respect among contemporaries. Sir William Phips became something of a hero for what Professor Douglas Leach accurately described as "a piddling victory." Phips was perhaps the most widely revered colonist before Franklin. Philadelphia's Benjamin Franklin is best remembered today for his scientific experiments, but a large part of the popularity he attained in his lifetime was derived from his energetic military conduct during three colonial wars. He took the lead in raising volunteer companies in pacifist Pennsylvania, and, already middle-aged, he accompanied soldiers to the wil-

---

57. Jonathan Hamer, *The Character and Duties of a Christian Soldier . . .* (Boston, 1790), pp. 11–12; Abbot, *Jehovah's Character*, p. 25; Prentice, *A Sermon*, p. 22; Jameson, *Johnson's Wonder-Working Providence*, p. 166; Cogswell, *God, the Pious Soldier's Strength*, p. 31; Davies, *Curse of Cowardice*, p. 16; Linn, *Military Discourse*, p. 18; *Boston Gazette and County Journal*, 13 June 1757.

58. Brackenridge, *Battle of Bunkers-Hill*, in Moses, *Representative Plays*, vol. I, pp. 260–61. This dogma of Christian salvation through soldierly suffering went virtually unchallenged. An occasional critic dissented, usually arguing that excessively laudatory remarks tended to "inflame the Ambitions of Men" and to create potentially dangerous "*Pagan* Heroes." Later, as the American Revolution wound down, some pastors denounced the concept as theologically unsound. See Cooper, *A Sermon*, pp. 13–14, and Willard, *Duty of a good and faithful Soldier*, p. 8.

derness areas of his colony. The Puritan colonists also showered their soldiers with special thanksgiving fetes and made popular figures of successful military leaders, such as Colonel Benjamin Church. There is considerable evidence that large numbers of colonists assembled to applaud the troops in every war as they marched off to battle. Repeatedly, diarists made notations that the "spectators, who were very numerous, appeared very affected" by the troops' departure, or that the soldiers were surrounded by cheering mobs of deeply moved colonists and embarked "amidst the benediction of friends and connexions." The presence of "Many pretty Girls . . . upon the shore" weeping and waving, knowing that "we had many harships to encounter and many of us should never return," recurred with the outbreak of each war, and it always deeply moved—and nearly intoxicated—the male warriors. In some colonies the scene was repeated every generation, and young boys, seeing the attention and affection lavished on the soldiers, often longed from an early age for the opportunity to march off to battle. The civilian population at times was so caught up in the martial fervor of the hour that they reacted spontaneously with contempt for soldiers who had mutinied. When rebellious Kentucky soldiers marched home from a planned campaign in the West during the American Revolution, they were denied food and admission to their fort by the civilian inhabitants.[59]

On the other hand, those colonists who lived in close proximity to soldiers frequently saw warriors in a different light. Bostonians were shocked by the brutal discipline, including the painfully lengthy executions of British regulars stationed in their city in the 1760s. Chroniclers in most colonial wars spoke of the "many outrages" perpetrated by soldiers; these depredations normally involved plundering raids, but at times there were allusions to "every other act of violence that a lawless banditti think fit to show." Moreover, grasslands were rendered ungrazable, trees were toppled, cattle and sheep were slaughtered, and milk and milk cows were stolen in areas where armies encamped. Nor was it uncommon for fights, even small-scale battles, to erupt between soldiers and civilians. Inevitably, jealousies flared over the soldiers' dating and working practices (troops often took the civilians' women and their jobs) as well as over encroachments on private property. To victims of human lust, the soldiers appeared more as "dirty creatures" than as heroes. A traveler to a region that had recently been occupied by an American army found the "unhappy people" radically transformed by their experience. "They feared everybody whom they saw, and loved nobody." When questioned, "they gave such an answer as would please the inquirer. . . . Fear was apparently the only passion by which

59. Ira Gruber, *The Howe Brothers and the American Revolution* (New York, 1972), pp. 51–52; Leach, *Arms for Empire,* p. 91; Roberts, *March to Quebec,* p. 546; *Diary of Samuel Richards . . .* (Philadelphia, 1909), p. 9; "Diary of Lieutenant James McMichael, of the Pennsylvania Line, 1776–1778," *PMHB* 16, no. 2 (1892), p. 141; John Bakeless, *Background to Glory* (Philadelphia, 1957), p. 59.

they were animated. . . . They were . . . obsequious." Although the populace gathered to mingle with embarking soldiers, the returning warrior was often shunned. He might bear a camp disease that could decimate the community. In fact, a hundred people in one church in Danbury, Connecticut, perished of diseases spread by returning troopers in 1775. Philip Fithian, a soldier-diarist, noted that the town in which his regiment was stationed was as "sickly as the Army." He added that "Four Funerals, all Citizens, went past our Door this Evening!"[60]

The attitudes that soldiers acquired in the army, many civilians feared, might produce a breakdown in the morality of society. The incidence of profanity, gambling, drunkenness, and sexual promiscuity was thought to increase during wartime, and soldiers were often avoided lest their alleged licentiousness spread. At war's end, veterans were normally eschewed. With their service completed, the formerly deferential society quickly resumed its prewar posture. A dead soldier was more likely to be honored than a live veteran.

If the colonial leadership was concerned with the training of its soldiers, it was no less interested in the quality of its officers. As mentioned in a previous chapter, the earliest New England settlers took pains to retain professional militarists until their plantations were securely settled, while the London Company hired veteran officers to oversee the conquest of early Virginia. In the latter instance, it was not long before the deeds of Captain John Smith were being celebrated—most notably, though not exclusively, in the histories written by Smith himself—as the reason for Virginia's successful planting.[61]

Many of the qualities deemed essential for soldiers were also regarded as necessary for officers. But in deferential early America it was presumed that officers would be drawn from among the "better sort," even if elected by the militia companies, a common practice as late as the American Revolution. Massachusetts actually restricted officeholding, including military rank, to freemen. One pre-Marxian New England clergyman even suggested that it behooved the rich to serve, since "Riches are . . . the main temptation to war." Why would an affluent colonist consider forfeiting the comforts of his class for the trials of the military? Of course, many, though they might welcome a war, wanted no part of the military. But other patricians hurried to lead armies. They were drawn by forces as diverse as nationalism, peer pressure, adventure, and

60. Shy, *Toward Lexington*, pp. 307–9, 381–90; "A Diary of Trifling Occurrences," *PMHB* 82 (October 1958), p. 440; Leach, *Arms for Empire*, p. 265; Timothy Dwight, in Barbara M. Solomon, ed., *Travels in New England and New York*, 4 vols. (Cambridge, Mass., 1969), vol. III, p. 345; R. G. Albion and L. Dodson, eds., *Journal of Fithian* (Princeton, N.J., 1924), p. 209; Bridenbaugh, *Cities in Revolt*, pp. 121–22.

61. Gabriel Archer, *A relaytion of the Discovery . . .* , in Arber, *Works of Smith*, vol. I, p. xlix; Smith, *Map of Virginia, ibid.*, vol. I, pp. 107, 142, 147–48; Smith, *Generall Historie, ibid.*, vol. II, pp. 485–86; William K. Boyd, ed., *William Byrd's Histories of the Dividing Line* (New York, 1967), p. 3.

the booty promised by conflict. General Nathanael Greene provided an additional explanation: becoming an officer afforded "an Opportunity of traveling the shortest Road to the greatest heights of Ambition."[62]

There were no academies for officers—none were proposed until after the Revolution, and then only for engineers and artillery officers—and the militia drills were designed more for the recruits than for the leaders. Generally better educated than yeomen and artisans, the elite were largely expected to acquire military skills through their own initiative, an expectation that persisted because colonists presumed war was immutable and "the art of war is only to be learned in war." Several treatises on military leadership were published in England or America during the colonial era, and periodic militia muster days could be of some assistance, although in many instances the officer learned from experience, if he and his underlings survived, on the battlefield. Many, like Washington, believed the task was "not so very difficult for any man of common sense who applies himself to it."[63] Indeed, Washington had attained the rank of colonel in the Virginia militia by his twenty-first birthday, though his conduct on his initial command, against the French at Fort Necessity in 1754, left much to be desired.

The first lesson for officers to learn was that they were not only to give orders, but to take them as well. Those leaders who were heedless of the commands of their superiors could be "more harmful to ourselves than to our enemies." To exceed an order in the hope of accomplishing a noble feat was "an error on the right side, but still it is an error."[64]

To lead adequately, an officer required the respect of his troops. Since he was expected to demand courage of his men, the leader must likewise exhibit courage. If the officer was capable of noble and bold acts in the "midst of pressing dangers," it was believed his troops would be suitably inspired. But this frequently proved to be one of the most difficult colonial military procedures to achieve. Before the conflict at Bunker Hill, the first pitched battle of the Revolution, many men believed there was "much more cause for fear that the officers would fail in a day of trial than the privates." Frequently, the fears were not misplaced. Too often the leaders reacted like the colonel at Bunker Hill who "no sooner came in sight of the enemy than a tremor seiz'd him & he began to bellow, 'Retreat! retreat! or you'l all be cut off!' which so confused

---

62. Sharp, "Leadership and Democracy," p. 257; Howard, *A Sermon*, p. 40; Nathanael Greene to Samuel Ward, 14 July 1775, in Richard Showman, ed., *The Papers of General Nathanael Greene* (Chapel Hill, N.C., 1976), vol. I, p. 99.

63. Roger Stevenson, *Military Instructions for Officers* . . . (Philadelphia, 1775), pp. iv–v; Robert Dankin, *Military Collections and Remarks* (New York, 1777), p. 38; James T. Flexner, *George Washington and the American Revolution* (Boston, 1967), p. 263. Not all contemporaries agreed with Washington. One popular manual insisted that if "a Man is not born with a Military Genius, all the Directions that can be given, will never make a General." See Adye, *Treatises on Courts Martial,* (New York, 1769), p. ii.

64. Simes, *Military Guide,* p. 175.

& scar'd our men, that they retreated most precipitately.'' Another officer at that battle sent his men to the hill promising to "overtake them directly"; he never appeared. Later, even Washington, beset by officers who resigned when "danger approaches," remarked caustically that he feared "being left alone with the soldiers" to face the enemy.[65]

In addition to a courageous demeanor certain other qualities were believed essential for leaders in combat. The colonists believed inspired rhetoric could inflame and mobilize troops, but it was not enough merely to give commands and speeches. Several martial guides indicated that the officer must set a proper example, and this required an air of "suitable dignity," of "Proprietie," and of magnanimity. One training manual suggested that officers should dress "as if they were to mount guard at a royal palace." Few contemporaries accepted such advice, and most counseled that the officer must leave such "littlenesses to those below him." The soldiers were acknowledged to be sufficiently perceptive to see through contrived behavior. Dignified behavior alone could not earn respect. Competency was the crucial element that characterized the respected officer. The good leader was not only to appear to be knowledgeable, he was to have mastered the major treatises of his calling. Cotton Mather believed the superior officer required "some insight into all the *Liberal Arts,* especially those of the *Mathematics,*" and he regaled New England's officers with the tale of Julius Caesar's exemplary conduct; "being forc'd to swim for his life in an extremity," Caesar "employ'd one hand to preserve from the damage of the water, certain BOOKS which he had a special value for." It was well known that professional soldiers, such as Miles Standish, read Caesar's *Commentaries* and other military classics. That there was much idle time and boredom in the military regimen was admitted, but the best officer, a general noted, would use the leisure to attend the "Minutia of Military Matters." However, knowledge and demeanor counted for little if they were not employed in moments of exigency. Unless officers could "preserve presence of mind, possess themselves fully, think clearly, judge wisely and act with calmness, firmness and resolution, in times of great confusion and tumult, in the midst of the most pressing dangers and perplexing distresses," they would inevitably fail.[66]

The extraordinary officer, it was believed, would inspire feelings that transcended respect. He would arouse a mingling of the passions of love and fear. Love would be kindled through combining the aforementioned qualities with

65. Clarke, *A Sermon,* p. 19; Bolton, *Private Soldier,* pp. 132–35; Herbert T. Wade and Robert A. Lively, eds., *This Glorious Cause* (Princeton, N.J., 1958), pp. 22, 25.

66. *Plan of Exercise, for the Militia of the Province of Massachusetts Bay . . .* (Boston, 1768), p. 35; Simes, *Military Guide,* pp. 1–2; Richard Lambert, *A New System of Military Discipline Founded upon Principle* (Philadelphia, 1776), p. v; Fausz and Kukla "Letter of Advice," p. 123; Mather, *Things to be look'd for,* n.p.; Cotton Mather, *Military Duties, recommended . . .* (Boston, 1687), p. 77; Dankin, *Military Collections,* p. 145; Leach, "Military Systems of Plymouth," p. 344; "Orders of the Day," 28 July 1776, in Showman, *Greene Papers,* vol. I, p. 267; Clarke, *A Sermon,* p. 19.

the "principles of piety." In addition, soldiers would cherish those commanders who were demonstrably concerned for the welfare of their troops. Soldiers were always suspicious that vainglorious officers might throw away their lives to gratify their own "Pride and Ambition, or Rancour and Revenge." Officers, therefore, were exhorted to demonstrate a proper respect for the enemy's capability, and to be cognizant of where the "Enemies skill and advantage lyes." The commander should know when and where to fight, to know, for instance, that it was "ill fighting with a wild Beast in his own Den." Through such precautionary measures, the troops would know they would never be hurled capriciously into a Molochan encounter. The troops would know their leaders would not act rashly and they would not be "sacrificed to the gay Humours of a Battle."[67]

For maximum respect the soldiers' love of the officer had to be counterbalanced by a measurable fear. Already it was widely believed that the earliest colonies survived because the settlers feared their own rulers as much as the enemy. Early chroniclers stressed that "fearing our power," the inhabitants "chose rather to subject themsleves to us, than . . . to expose & lay themselves open" to the enemy. The officer, of course, was not tendered license to exhibit "violent impatience, or insupportable brutality." Such base conduct merely triggered insubordination, resentment, and acts of revenge. Still, such unbecoming conduct as "sloath, pride, and indignitie," as well as carelessness, negligence, insolence, and dishonesty, required punishment. The officer was to be "cool and sedate," to manifest a superior air. He must gain the "proper submission" of his troops. Otherwise, the officer "will soon lose all command over the men." Meting out discipline was difficult, for it compelled the officer to walk the thin line between the tyrant and the weakling. The officer was to seek to imitate that favorite figure of eighteenth-century philosophers, the benevolent despot. Being an officer was rendered all the more difficult because it required techniques uncharacteristic of some and considered un-Christian by others. Many of the early officers in the Revolution, according to General Greene, were destroyed because they neglected "their duty . . . through fear of offending their soldiers." The manuals attempted to counter such anxiety by assuring that discipline would not provoke a loss of esteem. Instead, the soldiers ultimately would understand that severity sprang from "generosity and humanity."[68]

67. Clarke, *A Sermon*, pp. 18–19; Bridge, *A Sermon*, p. 10; Richardson, *Necessity*, p. 3; Fausz and Kukla, "Letter of Advice," pp. 117–19; Drake, *Hubbard's History of the Indian Wars*, p. 87; Barnard, *A Sermon*, pp. 13–14; Simes, *Military Guide*, p. 192; *An Account of our Late Troubles in Virginia*, in Force, *American Archives*, vol. I, p. 5.

68. Hamor, *A True Discourse*, p. 15; *Plan of Exercise*, pp. 33–36; Stevenson, *Military Instructions for Officers*, p. 53; Smith, *General Historie*, in Arber, *Works of Smith*, vol. II, pp. 485–86; Bridge, *A Sermon*, p. 10; William Livingstone, *A Review of the Military Operations in North America . . .* (London, 1758), p. 7; Theodore Thayer, *Nathanael Greene: Strategist of the American Revolution* (New York, 1960), p. 63.

Many men failed as officers, not just in the Revolution, as General Greene reported, but in each war. Contemporaries offered numerous explanations for these failures. Some attributed the failures to the militia tradition of electing officers, since it resulted in leaders who resembled "heads of a Mob, who must support their preheminence by unworthy Condesensions & Indulgences subversive of order & of the very Existence of an Army." Or, by the same token, election elevated "ackward, illiterate, ill-bred" men to posts that required an understanding of the nuances of military science. It was also hinted timorously that elitism led to placing unworthies in command, men who lacked courage and skill. Some writers believed that overly indulgent and mild behavior was the greatest failing of officers; others thought the contrary was true. Too many officers resembled the Pennsylvania captain who was described by his commanders as a "Bully," a person of "profligate and debauched morrels, a mean Cringing and servile flatterer, crouching at the Col[onel's] Feet." Finally, some lost esteem—though not necessarily with their subordinates—because they were thought to be too cautious. Thomas Paine once suggested that as a class all officers were too restrained, too likely to be immobilized by lack of sufficient information. Ultimately, not even Washington could escape these criticisms. Soldiers and civilians alike quibbled over the commander's methods, with Congress, at one point, even accusing the general of "too great delicacy in exerting military authority." Benjamin Rush blamed Washington's problems on amateurish, sycophantic, intemperate, and cowardly adjutants. Joseph Reed and Thomas Mifflin of Pennsylvania were less kind. Reed thought Washington was suited only "to command a regiment," whereas Mifflin believed he was "fit only to be the head clerk of a London countinghouse."[69]

The most striking aspect of American attitudes toward war and warriors before the mid-eighteenth century was their unchanging, lockstep nature. Whether in the early seventeenth century or the middle of the succeeding century, the colonists, living in a milieu of recurrent warfare, deemed war to be inevitable, and urged preparedness as a safeguard for the inevitable conflict. They persisted in sanctioning only wars that could be labeled as "just" struggles, but, as with their contemporaries in Europe, virtually any conflict in which they became embroiled might be so defined. Both seventeenth- and eighteenth-century colonists identified certain virtues as those requisite for a good soldier. The warrior,

69. Milton W. Hamilton, *Sir William Johnson: Colonial American, 1715–1763* (Pt. Washington, N.Y., 1976) pp. 150, 178; Page Smith, *John Adams*, 2 vols. (New York, 1962), vol. I., p. 287; Bruce T. McCully, "Catastrophe in the Wilderness: New Light on the Canada Expedition of 1709," *WMQ*, 3d Ser. 11 (July 1954), pp. 450–51; "Memoirs of Brigidier-General John Lacey, of Pennsylvania," *PMHB* 25, no. 1 (1901), p. 353; "Journal of a Physician on the Expedition Against Canada, 1776," *PMHB* 49 (October 1935), pp. 333, 340–42, 352–53; "Military Operations Near Philadelphia in the Campaign of 1777–78: Described in a Letter from Thomas Paine to Dr. Franklin," *PMHB* 2, no. 3 (1888), p. 285; Ford, *Journals of Continental Congress*, vol. IX, pp. 1013–14; David Hawke, *Benjamin Rush: Revolutionary Gadfly* (Indianapolis, Ind., 1971), pp. 191, 206–7.

they thought, must be disciplined and obedient, and he must act with valor in the face of danger. The attributes he was to exhibit still smacked of chivalric behavior. Although every colonial war brimmed with atrocities, the limits to which a soldier should go in obeying the orders of his superiors was never questioned. Clearly, the soldier was to be an automaton who trusted the moral wisdom of his social betters, who were, of course, his civil and military leaders.

These were the attitudes of the elite. There is much evidence to suggest that the mass of colonists were not always enthusiastic at the occurrence of a new round of warfare. Often they had little to gain and much to lose. The wars, after all, were normally fought for the economic, as well as the political and social, benefit of the elite. But defiance never reached mass proportions. If there were war protests, they were individual, isolated acts of opposition to war, or, even more likely, acts opposing compulsory service in the conflict. Mass remonstrance had to await a more republican age and an era in which warfare was less commonplace. Men still protested by not volunteering or by requesting deferment from service. Whatever the militia tradition, the armies of the colonial era were often composed of the luckless and the hopeless from the bottom of society. The greater one's social rank, the greater the likelihood of perceiving the war as ''just'' and of watching the conflict from the sidelines.

Chapter Four

The Warriors

Anxiety . . . fatigue and hardship

War in America, this book has argued, occurred with considerable frequency and regularity, and the conflicts were often waged with a severity at least as great as the warfare of sixteenth- and seventeenth-century Europe. But what of the men who fought in these wars?

The experience of war—as perceived by the men who served in the armies—can be discerned best in the Revolutionary era. Many soldiers in many wars kept diaries or subsequently compiled memoirs of their experiences. But, while soldiers who served in earlier Indian or intercolonial conflicts frequently left behind such documents, they did not do so in the same volume as their Revolutionary War counterparts; moreover, though the dangers of combat might elicit common emotional responses regardless of the age, the nature of Indian warfare in the early seventeenth century was so different from fighting a French army in the mid-eighteenth century that the experience of the soldiers in the two wars were vastly dissimilar. By focusing on the Revolution, however, one can attempt to understand how soldiers, not politicians or clergymen or other opinion shapers, actually experienced army life, from camp drudgery to combat, and some understanding might be gained of their feelings for those responsible for placing them in these circumstances.

America's rebel soldiers sustained incredible deprivation during the War for Independence. The suffering of the luckless troops quartered at Valley Forge in the winter of 1777-1778, in fact, has become part of the national mythology. One soldier complained of "Poor food—hard lodging—Cold Weather—fatigue—Nasty Clothes—nasty Cookery. I can't Endure it—Why are we sent here to starve and Freeze." Another soldier complained of having received just half a day's allowance of food in eight days. As often as not, alleged one soldier, when the troops were provided with "beef" it was actually horse meat. The bread frequently "had nearly as much flesh as bread being . . . full of worms." It "required a deal of circumspection in eating it," he added. One soldier claimed that for four days he had tasted only "a little black birch bark which I had gnaw'd off a stick of wood." Other men, in their desperation, boiled their shoes for food. Some troops purchased foodstuffs wherever they could locate a seller. Others lived by stealing provisions. "I would have taken victuals or drink from the best friend I had on earth by force," one trooper ruefully acknowledged.[1]

The deprivation experienced at Valley Forge almost paled beside the forlorn experiences of the men in Benedict Arnold's 1775 invasion of Canada. Few American soldiers have endured the miseries to which these men were subjected. Although the expedition was undertaken in the autumn and winter months in the northeastern corner of the mainland colonies, and, of course, into Canada, the troops were dispatched with an inadequate number of tents. The general shortage of provisions was exacerbated by the destruction of many of the serviceable goods the men did possess; since few of the men were familiar with the bateaux provided to transport the items through the swampy terrain, it was not uncommon for a diarist among the troops to record that the soldiers "lost all the Baggage, Arms, & Provisions of 4 men" when several craft capsized. On the eve of entering Canada, General Arnold noted that his "detachments are as ready, as naked men can be. . . ." Food supplies for the expedition quickly dwindled, and much that remained was palatable only to someone facing starvation. The men first substituted salt pork and flour for the accustomed regimen. Soon their diet consisted of water and flour, a drab concoction which the men christened "Lillipu." Ultimately, the men ate soap, candles boiled in water, gruel, wood, boiled rawhide and leather, carcasses of animals discovered in the forests, and even the pet dogs that had accompanined some of the soldiers. The latter fare, which was made into a green stew, was eaten with gusto, particularly by those who did not realize the contents of this culinary delight.[2]

Lack of food was not the only deprivation experienced by Arnold's troops. "Every step we made sunk us knee-deep in a bed of wet turf," one soldier lamented. "My feet were pained and lacerated by the snags of the dead pines a foot and more below the surface of the moss." Then, as winter set in, their poorly constructed shoes disintegrated, leaving the men to walk upon "the hard frosty ground" in bare feet. Fires could not be fashioned from damp wood. The troops were often unable to find dry ground or, having at last discovered such a place, they were frequently aroused in the middle of the night by a rising tide. The only thing which seemed to flourish in this misery was vermin of every

1. "Valley Forge, 1777–1778: Diary of Surgeon Albigance Waldo, of the Continental Line," *PMHB* 21, no. 3 (1887), pp. 306–7; Benjamin Talmadge, *Memoirs of Talmadge* (New York, 1958), p. 25; Herbert T. Wade and Robert A. Lively, eds., *This Glorious Cause* (Princeton, N.J., 1958), pp. 235–36; George Sheer, ed., *Private Yankee Doodle* (Boston, 1962), pp. 103, 109, 150, 158, 172.

2. Martin H. Bush, *Revolutionary Enigma: A Reappraisal of General Philip Schuyler of New York* (Pt. Washington, N.Y., 1969), p. 61; Benedict Arnold to Washington, 13 October 1775, in Roberts, *March to Quebec*, p. 73; Journal of Arnold, ibid., p. 60; Journal of Dr. Santer, ibid., pp. 203, 210, 213, 218–19; Arnold to Gen. Montgomery, 25 November 1775, ibid., p. 96; Journal of Capt. Meigs, ibid., p. 181; Lynn Montross, *Rag, Tag and Bobtail* (New York, 1952), pp. 57–58.

description, unwelcome creatures that soon covered the men and added to their discomfort.[3]

Many of Arnold's men in Canada and Washington's men at Valley Forge ached for combat, not from lust for action but as a possible respite from their plight in camp. Victory would likely mean plunder. Defeat might be fatal, but, as a survivor later recalled, "death would have been a welcome messenger to have ended our woes." How "happy would we have been to have no other danger to face but the enemy," he added. Conditions were so wretched that one Valley Forge veteran, who may have had difficulty getting veterans of other campaigns to agree, claimed that combat is the "great scarecrow" to civilians, but it was not more exacting than the "anxiety . . . fatigue and hardship" of the camp.[4]

The miseries of these two groups of soldiers were not uncharacteristic of the soldiers' fate in the Revolution. Shortages of tents, uniforms, blankets, and shoes persisted to the end of the conflict. Nothing, however, prompted as much complaint as inadequate or poor food. Occasionally food existed, but only in a barely edible condition. A Pennsylvanian complained of meal that was "hardly ground," and he claimed it would have been fed to the livestock back home. Soldiers protested that what seemed to be good meat was, in reality, mostly bone. Sometimes the food spoiled. Meal was often musty, while the meat "had such a stench it could not be eaten." Good food was sometimes rendered less palatable by the lack of salt and other spices. Or the food was prepared improperly. Soldiers often claimed that decent cooks were quickly sequestered by the officers, leaving the unskilled men to cook for themselves. General Greene admitted that the unavailability of firewood forced many of his regiments "to Eat their Provision Raw." But often food was simply in scarce supply. The worst deprivation occurred on long marches. Sometimes the troops for days on end had nothing but dampened flour "daubed upon a flat stone and scorched one side." In what seemed an endless march through South Carolina, one northern soldier complained that in two weeks he had been allotted just one half pound of flour and some occasional beef that was "so miserably poor that scarce any mortal could make use of it." Instead, these men lived "chiefly on green apples and peaches, which rendered our situation truly miserable"; these soldiers were "purg[ed] . . . as well as if we had taken jallop, for the men, all the way as we went along, were every moment obliged to fall out of the Ranks to evacuate."[5]

3. Journal of Capt. Topham, in Roberts, *March to Quebec,* p. 267; Journal of John Henry, ibid., p. 310; Journal of Dr. Senter, ibid., p. 206.

4. Journal of George Morison, ibid., pp. 523, 528; Sheer, *Private Yankee Doodle,* p. 289.

5. Allen Bowman, *The Morale of the American Revolutionary Army* (Pt. Washington, N.Y., 1976), pp. 17–20; Sheer, *Private Yankee Doodle,* p. 55, 76–77; "Memoirs of Gen. Lacey," PMHB 25, no. 1 (1901), p. 346; "Sullivan's Expedition to Staten Island in 1777: Extract from the Diary of Captain Andrew Lee," *PMHB* 3, no. 2 (1879), pp. 172–73; Greene to Samuel Ward, 31 December 1775, in Richard Showman, ed., *Greene Papers* (Chapel Hill, N.C. 1976), vol. I, p. 173; William Seymour, "Journal of the Southern Expedition, 1780–1783," *PMHB* 7, no. 3 (1883), p. 288.

The water often caused as many problems as did the supply of food. Water near encampments frequently became brackish. The water "was quite yellow," one soldier noted, and "No sooner had it got down than it was puked up by many of the poor fellows." The water often was contaminated by an army itself. Soon after waste and the pollutants from laundry were spilled into a stream, the water was rendered "very Dirty and muddy."[6]

Many times troops suffered for prolonged periods with inadequate supplies of clothing and blankets. Early in the war, Congress legislated to outfit each enlistee in the Continental army with two hunting shirts, two pairs of overalls, a leather or woolen coat, a hat or cap, one pair of trousers, two shirts, two pairs of hose, and two pairs of shoes. Nevertheless, during an entire winter campaign in the South, General Greene had coats for only 10 percent of his troops. A visitor to a Virginia regiment discovered some troops "with one coat, some hoseless, with their feet peeping out of their shoes; others with breeches that put decency to blush." A British officer thought "no nation ever saw such a set of tatterdemalians. There are few coats among them but what are out at elbows and in a whole regiment there is scarce a pair of breeches." Even the troops in Philadelphia celebrating the first anniversary of the Declaration of Independence "paraded thro' the streets with great pomp, tho' many were barefoot & looked very unhealthy." Numerous soldiers complained of endless cold nights, of sleeping under leaves, or of huddling together in a vain attempt to stay warm. One contingent, without blankets or shelter, discovered that the "only way to avoid freezing was to be constantly walking, running, or jumping." Another, according to a bitter new recruit, just kept "marching and counter-marching, starving and freezing." Even so, these troops were lucky. Soldiers who got lost while on night patrol were known to die of exposure. In one horrid instance, a crew of eighty on a privateer perished from the cold during a storm.[7]

Those who died quickly and relatively painlessly in the cold may have been fortunate. The chronic inadequacy of food and other provisions produced incredible suffering among thousands of soldiers. The common cold, respiratory diseases, and a wide variety of apparent viral ailments were endemic to the camps of the Revolutionary armies. At best, these ills could immobilize an entire army; at worst, soldiers so weakened by deprivation and these minor ills could become susceptible to more serious ailments. Malaria and dysentery, usually

6. Journal of Dr. Senter, in Roberts, *March to Quebec,* p . 205; Charles K. Bolton, *Private Soldier* (New York, 1902), p. 77; *Elijah Fisher's Journal* . . . (Augusta, Me., 1880), p. 7.

7. Bolton, *Private Soldier,* pp. 52, 94, 102; Bowman, *Morale of the Revolutionary Army,* pp. 17–20; Sarah Fisher, "Diary of Trifling Occurrences," *PMHB* 82 (October 1958), p. 438; *Personal Recollections of Captain Enoch Anderson,* Historical Society of Delaware, *Papers* (Wilmington, Del., 1896), vol. XVI, p. 28; Hiram Bingham, *Five Straws* (Cambridge, Mass., 1901), p. 12; Sheer, *Private Yankee Doodle,* p. 47; *Diary of Samuel Richards,* p. 22: "Journal of Sergeant William Young* . . . 1776–1777," *PMHB* 8, no. 3 (1884), p. 257; *Diary of Colonel Israel Angell* . . . (Providence, R.I., 1899), pp. 32, 36.

referred to as "the flux," repeatedly struck at the soldiery. But smallpox probably frightened the soldiers more than any enemy. Colonel Jeduthon Baldwin of Massachusetts left a graphic account of his successful three-month battle with the disease. He was one of 29,000 soldiers who fell ill with smallpox in May 1776. At the outset, Baldwin's appetite waned and he grew listless. He also developed severe headaches "over my eyes" that left him "very full of pain & distress"; on the second day, chills tore through his body, and he was scarcely able to lift his head. After five days the fever abated, but a sore throat developed and the "hard head ache" persisted. He was without energy and quickly grew faint if moved. The fever returned a few days later, accompanied now by the pox, which provoked "an extream fire and itching [and] made me Very uncomfortable." Sixteen days after his ills commenced, Baldwin at last seemed well. Three months later, he suffered a relapse and endured a similar period of headaches, "fever and ague."[8]

Conditions in Baldwin's environment must have resembled those witnessed by General John Lacey of Pennsylvania. He toured a camp of New England soldiers where he saw "some men in and some out of Tents sick on the bare ground—infected with Fluxes, Fevers, Small Pox and over run with legions of Lice. . . . The Lice and Maggots which seemed to vie with each other, were creeping in Millions over the Victims." Lacey departed hastily to acquire some "good old ·Spirits" and become "handsomely Drunk" in order to forget the horrors he had seen. But the sight of troops so inflicted with "rhumatism" from exposure that they were unable to care for themselves "any more than a new born infant," of men with "every joint . . . inflexible and swelled to an enormous size," of soldiers who could not see, speak, or walk tightly packed into a barn for shelter, of men infested with "large maggots, an inch long, Crawl[ing] out of their ears" were not sights easily forgotten.[9]

Those luckless troops who were wounded or grew ill could expect only inadequate care. At the outset of the fighting, some colonies endeavored to recruit quality physicians for their militia, grilling each candidate for hours on the nuances of anatomy, physiology, surgery, and medications. In Massachusetts, half the initial candidates were rejected. But these exacting standards did not last. Philip Fithian noted, shortly before his death in 1775 from the camp disease, that he had "no physician to attend him but an unskilled quack of a Surgeons mate, & no nurse but an unknowing country lad." Another soldier remembered watching a comrade die of complications from a superficial wound that had been "dressed by an ignoramus boy of a surgeon." The wounded

8. Wade and Lively, eds., *This Glorious Cause,* p. 189; Thomas W. Baldwin, *The Revolutionary Journal of Col. Jeduthan Baldwin, 1775–1778* (Bangor, Me., 1906), pp. 46–52, 72–77.

9. "Memoirs of Gen. Lacey," pp. 203–4, 206; Journal of Dr. Senter, in Roberts, *March to Quebec,* pp. 205–6; "Journal of a Physician," PMHB 49, (October 1935), p. 336.

soldier who complained that he was left unattended because "the surgeon . . . was at a game of backgammon and could not attend to minor affairs" may have been fortunate. He may have been better cared for, though not looked after, than the unfortunate militiaman whose shattered arm "was taken off by . . . a black-smith, with a shoemaker's knife and carpenter's saw"; the smitty "stopped the blood with the fungus of an oak." Nor were those lodged in hospitals always in good hands. One physician described his own hospital as a "dirty, stinking place" in which some patients were "dead, some Dying, others at the point of death, some Whistling, some singing & many Cursing & swearing." For the most part, the ill and wounded were "left to take care of themselves," or they were administered a variety of concoctions containing gin, rum, mustard seed, horseradish roots, vinegar, molasses, and spruce beer.[10]

Under these conditions, the death rate from illnesses could be astronomical. For thirty months after July 1776, never less than 16 percent of the troops were incapacitated by illness; at times more than one-third of the army was on sick call. When an epidemic swept a camp, soldiers by the score might die daily. A chaplain who visited Ticonderoga in August 1776 reported that about thirty men perished each day. These disasters left little opportunity for customary burial procedures. Corpses were hurriedly buried without a coffin. Sometimes large pits were dug to accommodate scores of victims.[11] A visitor to a camp saw

several Corps brought, carried by four Soldiers in a blanket, one holt of each corner. On their arriving at the pit or Grave, those next to it let go of the blanket, the other two giving a Hoist rolled the dead body into the pit where lay several bodies already deposited in the same way, with no other covering but the Rags in which they dyed, heads and points as they happened to come to the place. In this manner the burial continued all day.[12]

In such an extraordinary situation the body was buried "as soon as the breath had left the unfortunate Victim." In the evening a new hole was prepared for the following day, the dirt from the excavation being utilized to cover those just buried. Often not enough healthy men were available for burial detail, and the bodies continued to pile uncovered in full view of the ill.[13]

The deprivations faced by these men, and the fear that inadequate supplies might produce illness and death, prompted many soldiers to prey on the civilian

10. James Thacher, *Military Journal of the American Revolution* . . . (Hartford, 1862), p. 28; Albion and Dodson, *Fithian's Journal*, p. 242; Sheer, *Private Yankee Doodle*, pp. 70, 274; *Diary of Lieut. Anthony Allaire* (New York, 1968), p. 27; "Journal of a Physician," p. 332; Montrose, *Rag, Tag and Bobtail*, pp. 45–46.

11. Charles Lesser, ed., *The Sinews of Independence: Monthly Strength Reports of the Continental Army* (Chicago, 1976), pp. xxx–xxxi; Jeanette D. Black and William G. Roelker, eds., *A Rhode Island Chaplain in the Revolution* (New York, 1972), pp. 26–27.

12. "Memoirs of Gen. Lacey," pp. 203–4.

13. "Journal of a Physician," p. 332; "Diary of Trifling Occurrences," pp. 417, 420; Bush, *Revolutionary Enigma*, p. 61.

population. Loyalists and Quakers were often singled out for plunder by troops on an expedition, but they were by no means the only victims of the practice. Some Maryland troops burned the furniture and woodwork in the houses where they were barracked in a frenzied attempt to ward off the biting cold. Troops stationed about Cambridge, Massachusetts, chopped down civilians' trees and fences for firewood, and even threatened to tear down houses until the Assembly stopped their destruction by authorizing predatory raids on Tory estates. Many troops refused to fret over such occurrences, believing that a "country laid waste" was a "natural consequence" of warfare. Timothy Dwight was shocked at the "scenes of desolation" he discovered in Westchester County, New York, in the wake of the American army—which he characterized as composed of "self-taught officers and raw troops" who frequently engaged in "fruitless and visionary" pursuits. He found people whose houses were torn down, "furniture . . . extensively plundered or broken to pieces. The walls, floors, and windows . . . injured . . . by . . . violence. . . . Their cattle were gone. Their enclosures were burnt . . . and in many cases thrown down." General Montgomery's army that invaded Canada apparently was more restrained, but it bullied the civilian population for supplies until the populace's hostility to any American endeavor was assured.[14]

Some of the plundering that civilians experienced was wrought not by disciplined soldiers, but by deserters from the service who lived in the hills or forests and periodically emerged to forage for necessities. Nevertheless, most of the perdition was wrought by soldiers, many of whom maintained an ill-disguised hatred for civilians. A physician attached to the Connecticut Line lamented that there "are but few families for the soldiery to Steal from," and later, when a soldier in his care died he stormed that the trooper's "memory ought to be respected, more than those rich [civilians] who supply the world with nothing better than Money and Vice." Another officer complained of the "Rascally Stupidity" of civilians, particularly those who controlled the public purse strings and compelled the soldiers "to put up with what no troops ever did before"; he also fretted over the likely postwar treatment of the veterans, certain that "Insult & Injury in a triplicate Proportion" would be their reward. A Pennsylvania captain gleefully told General Anthony Wayne how he had drawn "crowds to the doors and windows" when he rode through recently liberated Philadelphia, and he added that he "had the happiness of treating some of the male Butterflies with the most humiliating contempt."[15]

14. Charles Royster, "The Continental Army in the American Mind, 1775–1783," (Ph.D. diss. University of California, Berkeley, 1978), pp. 88, 133, 471; Solomon, *Travels of Dwight,* vol. III, pp. 339, 345; Bush, *Revolutionary Enigma,* p. 59.

15. Bolton, *Private Soldier,* p. 172; "Valley Forge," *PMHB* 21 (1897), pp. 306, 319; Ebenezer Huntington to Andrew Huntington, 7 July 1780, and 2 August 1781, in Charles F. Heartman, ed., *Letters Written by Ebenezer Hartman during the American Revolution* (New York, 1915), pp. 87–88, 94; Henry Archer to Anthony Wayne, 28 July 1779, in Harry Dawson, *The Assault on Stony Brook* (Morisiana, N.Y., 1863), p. 121.

The leadership of the army, of course, attempted to curtail such occurrences. General Washington thought it "disgraceful" that "our countrymen and fellow citizens, dread our halting among them," and he repeatedly issued orders aimed at prohibiting unlicensed foraging. Other officers likewise attempted to discourage the practice. General Greene feared that a "few unprincipled rascals may ruin the reputation of a whole corps of virtuous men," and General Sullivan labeled it "a very scandalous practice unbecoming soldiers . . . to make free with and rob [civilians] of their property." Still, the nefarious practice continued, for it was not a simple task to compel men in desperate straits to abide by the law; nor were officers such as Washington, who in fits of desperation railed that "the people in the country can be forced to give information" necessary to the army, always willing to enforce the military law.[16]

Those soldiers who escaped illness, and many who did not, endured a steady regimen of grinding physical toil. While in camp, a work day of twelve hours or more was common for those on fatigue duty, which involved principally cooking, cutting wood, and building entrenchments and barracks. Work commenced at about six in the morning and continued, with one hour for breakfast, until noon; work resumed at about two o'clock and continued without abatement until sunset. The length of the work day was comparable to that of farmers and artisans, but the nature of the work was more onerous. The "fall business in Flaxseed time is nothing to be compared to the Fatigues I undergo Daily," one farmer-soldier assured his wife. Some details were less arduous than others, but far less pleasant. To the "Camp Colour men" fell the unhappy duty of cleaning the area of all "nausances," defined in written orders as "filth, bones, &c.," and of "throwing the Same into the pits and Covering the filth therein with fresh dirt every morning"; these men additionally faced the even less enviable task of covering "the excrements in the holes of their Respective Regiments every morning."[17]

Still, most troops probably preferred the loathsome tasks and the boredom of camp life to the endless, and what often must have appeared pointless, marches. Washington's forces were extraordinarily mobile. One soldier mentioned marching forty-five miles in twenty-four hours. Another calculated that his outfit had marched 160 miles during the last three weeks of November 1781, followed by 281 miles in December and 60 additional miles in January; his diary typically

16. Washington's General Orders, 23 July 1777, in Fitzpatrick, *Writings of Washington,* vol. VIII, pp. 455–56; Wade and Lively, *This Glorious Cause,* p. 71; "Orderly Book of the Second Pennsylvania Continental Line, Col. Henry Bricker," *PMHB* 36, nos. 1–2 (1912), p. 45; "The Orderly Book for Capt. William Coits' Company at Cambridge, April 23d, AD 1775," in CHS, *Coll.,* vol. VII (Hartford, 1899), p. 28; "Journal of Boyze Wells," *ibid.,* vol. VIII, p. 293; Joseph Brown Turner, ed., *The Journal and Order Book of Captain Robert Kirkwood . . .* (Pt. Washington, N. Y., 1970), p. 181; Bolton, *Private Soldier,* p. 172.

17. Wade and Lively, *This Glorious Cause,* p. 32; Ebenezer Huntington to Joshua Huntington, 25 June 1775, in Heartman, *Huntington Letters,* p. 16; Turner, *Journal of Kirkwood,* p. 122, 144; "Orderly Book of Capt. Coits' Co., CHS, *Coll.,* vol. VII, pp. 32, 46–47.

notes marches on successive days of sixteen miles, sixteen miles, twenty-three miles, ten miles, and eleven miles. One company marched nearly eight hundred miles in six months in 1777, followed by marches totaling over seventeen hundred miles between April and December of 1780, over two thousand miles in 1781, and in excess of twelve hundred miles in the first four months of 1782.[18]

The men marched, of course, under all kinds of conditions. At times they tromped in merciless heat, choking on the dust raised by thousands of feet, whereas in other seasons they were rendered "as wet as Rain could make us and Cold to numbness"; soldiers noted in their journals that they slogged through mud up to their knees, that their wagons bogged down repeatedly in the quagmire of the roads, and that, when at last their trek ended, they were prevented, either because of the weather or from a desire to conceal their strength and movements, from building fires.[19] Nor was it only the feet and legs of the troops which suffered. After one long march, several men "had the flesh worn from their shoulders, even to the bone" by their weapons and baggage. In the minds of many soldiers the physical anguish was exacerbated by a feeling that the exercise had been useless. Men marched, made camp, and then were uprooted to march again before they could enjoy their camp. One trooper wrote with rancor that he had spent the summer "Digging & Building of forts to Cover our heads," only to be obliged to move as the British drew near. As the British closed in on his new encampment he complained that "now we are hear and not one shovell full of Durte to Cover us." More characteristic was the soldier who complained of marching until midnight, then establishing a camp "as Comfortable as we could but jist as we got a shelter bilt and got a good fire and Dried some of our Cloths and began to have things a little Comfortable . . . Come orders to march and leave all we had taken so much pains for. . . ."[20]

Occasionally the troops marched until they encountered an adversary. Then the pain of camp duty and training gave way to the terror of battle, an ordeal of agony and spasmodic fear unlike anything ever experienced by these men. The thought of battle was sufficient to knot a man's stomach, to leave his mouth dry with nervous anticipation. Few displayed their anxiety to the comrades, but instead masked their feeling with a false display of joviality "as if they were Wholly at peace." On the eve of combat they spent their time "either sleeping, swimming, fishing, or Cursing and Swearing, most generally the Latter." One observer was fooled by their jocosity and bravado. They "laugh at death," he thought, "mock at Hell and Damnation, & even call the Deity to remove them out of this World."[21]

18. "McMichael Diary," *PMHB* 16, no. 2 (1892), p. 153; "Itinerary of the Pennsylvania Line from Pennsylvania to South Carolina, 1781–1782," *PMHB* 36, no. 2 (1912), pp. 273–92.

19. Turner, *Journal of Kirkwood*, pp. 274–77; "Journal of Sgt. Young," p. 257; Cook, *Journals of the Sullivan Expedition*, p. 9; Montrose, *Rag, Tag and Bobtail*, pp. 56–57.

20. Wade and Lively, *This Glorious Cause*, p. 217; *Elijah Fisher's Journal*, p. 7.

21. "Journal of a Physician," pp. 339, 352; Ebenezer Huntington to Jabez Huntington, 4 March 1776, in Heartman, *Huntington Letters*, p. 30.

But these men did confide in their families. They often thought of death, and they prepared their wills and put their business in order "in case that my maker should . . . ordain that I should not live to Come off the Hill." Some men were fatalistic in the face of battle. "Heaven is the Prize for which we all contend," one soldier believed. Some were idealistic, claiming to fear not "Tory *George, & his* "War-worn Army!" All wondered what combat would be like. "When two such powers impinge there must be a dreadful Impulse," Philip Fithian speculated. Typically, Fithian immediately tried to shake off his fear: "I prefer my Situation here . . . to any Situation whatever of *Eligence, Safety,* or *Ease.*"[22]

Eventually the confusion and noise of combat descended on the men. Fear, paralyzing to some, numbing to others, was the predominant sensation. Private Fithian, the young man brimming with Whig principle and pretended dauntlessness, summarized the shock of his first battle in the briefest of diary entries: "O doleful! doleful! doleful!—Blood! Carnage! Fire!" Another, less poetically, registered his feelings: "Good God, how the balls flew,—I freely acknowledge I never had such a tremor." To the common soldier, a battle often seemed a melee of events to be endured, not understood. With difficulty, men described the encounters in which they had participated. King's Mountain, for instance, simply "appeared volcanic," to one soldier, as there "flashed along its summit and round its base and up its sides, one long sulphurous blaze." Most found some aspects of battle surprising. "Such an explosion of fire I never had idea of before," one trooper noted at Saratoga. Some were struck by their unquenchable thirst and the ungovernable quavering they experienced in the grip of fear. Panic, which most men swore they could avoid, but which set in so frequently, startled many survivors. "Like electricity," one veteran reflected, panic "operates instantaneously—like sympathy it is irresistible where it touches." Many commanders spoke of the impulse to flight upon "the discharge of a few Booms of the Enemy." The opposite of panic, what seemed to be a soldier's absolute indifference to his own welfare, indeed the appearance of inviting a fatal wound, occurred frequently and never ceased to amaze the soldiers.[23] A Pennsylvania captain, for example, watched with incredulity at Yorktown while a

militia man . . . possessed of more bravery [than] prudence, stood constantly on the parapet and d—d his soul if he would dodge for the buggers. He had escaped longer than could be expected, and growing fool-hardy, brandished his spade at every ball that was fired, til, unfortunately, a ball came and put an end to his capers.[24]

22. Wade and Lively, *This Glorious Cause*, p. 73; Albion and Dodson, *Fithian's Journal*, pp. 130, 210.

23. Albion and Dodson, *Fithian's Journal*, p. 281; Wade and Lively, *This Glorious Cause*, p. 21; Hank Messick, *King's Mountain* (Boston, 1976), p. 140; Smith, *A New Age,* vol. I, pp. 925, 927, vol II, p. 1413; Bush, *Revolutionary Enigma*, p. 45.

24. "Diary of Captain James Duncan, of Colonel Moses Hazen's Regiment, in the Yorktown Campaign, 1781," *Pa. Archives,* 2d Ser., XV, p. 748.

Some soldiers, to the mortification of their comrades, chose suicide by their own hand as a quicker reprieve from their anguish.[25]

Although not unanticipated, no one could fathom the incredible carnage wrought by battle until it had been experienced. Physicians sometimes broke after a prolonged period of "beholding mutilated bodies, mangled limbs and bleeding, incurable wounds." A soldier might be expected to waffle when he saw his comrades take "a musket-ball through his cheeks, cutting its way through the teeth on each side, and the substance of his tongue." Others saw men with half their faces "torn off by a cannon-ball, laying mouth and throat open to view." Men were decapitated or rendered paraplegics within a moment of the commencement of a battle. Many unravelled when they saw soldiers "split like fish to be broiled." Those who had not previously experienced the scores of wounded men "weltering in their blood . . . in the most horrid tortures" could never be adequately prepared for such a sight. Many men broke into tears when confronted with a view of their buddies lying "in heaps on all sides," or when they heard the "groans of the wounded" pierce the otherwise silent night. Equally surprising and disturbing was the bovine indifference to suffering which some callous men exhibited. With horror, one soldier related a scene he witnessed at the Battle of Monmouth, where a "wounded captain . . . lying on the ground and begging his sergeant, who pretended to have the care of him, to help him off the field or he should bleed to death. The sergeant and a man or two he had with him were [too] taken up in hunting after plunder" to provide assistance.[26]

Perhaps the best account of a first engagement by an enlisted soldier was provided by Joseph Martin, a private in the Connecticut line. Martin first underwent combat when British regulars invaded Long Island in 1776. As his company marched toward the front lines, with the sounds of battle growing unmistakably nearer, Martin grew nauseated, his gait became more awkward as his leg muscles involuntarily tightened, he was suddenly thirsty and he felt a decided urge to eliminate. His first sight of war was of the wounded who had been returned to a hastily contrived field hospital. It was a sight that "daunted me," he reflected. Suddenly, an officer collapsed under the strain. He "ran around among the men . . . sniveling and blubbering, praying each one if he had aught against them, or if *he* had injured anyone that they would forgive him, declaring at the same time that he, from his heart, forgave them if they had offended him." Had the man "been at the gallows with a halter about his neck," Martin reflected, "he could not have shown more fear or penitence." Not much further down the road Martin witnessed death for the first time. His company saw men from a

25. "Diary of Samuel Bixby," MHS, *Proc.*, 1st Ser., XIV (March 1876), pp. 286, 288.

26. Thacher, *Military Journals*, pp. 113–14; Sheer, *Private Yankee Doodle*, p. 37, 131; Smith, *A New Age*, vol. I, p. 927, vol. II, p. 1431.

retreating Maryland outfit driven into a millpond. Those who could swim survived, but those who lacked this ability and "could not procure anything to buoy them up, sunk." Martin's company paused to assist, and "took out a number of corpses" from the pond. Then the march resumed, but the company walked into a trap. It was "fired upon by a party of British from a cornfield and all was immediately confusion." Quickly, "the demons of fear and disorder seemed to take full possession of all and everything on that day." Officers and men scattered, "endeavoring by all sober means to escape from death or captivity. . . . The men were confused, being without officers to command them." Martin escaped his first combat encounter.[27]

As in all wars, untested men wondered how they would perform in combat, and they particularly speculated at whether they could kill another man. Those men who left accounts of their battle activities during the War for Independence were not inclined to mention inaction because of paralyzing fear, but they did discuss their feelings about killing. In one breath they told of taking "as deliberate aim at him as ever I did at any game in my life," and candidly confessing in the next breath that "I hope I did not kill him, although I intended to. . . ." And they acknowledged their reluctance to kill. "When we got so near we could fairly see them they looked too handsome to be fired at; but we had to do it," a soldier at Bunker Hill remembered.[28] In all likelihood, that was not the full story.

Unlike many modern wars wherein technology has depersonalized killing, the American Revolution was the kind of war in which soldiers frequently saw their adversaries. Men formed ranks and marched toward one another; a volley might be fired at point-blank range into a massed regiment, or the battle might conclude with hand-to-hand combat following a bayonet charge. Of course, psychological studies were not made following the War for Independence, but an abundance of evidence—much of which has been exhibited previously in this study—indicates that men perceived their situation much the same as the combat soldiers in World War II, who were subjected to elaborate studies and tests. The technology of war differed in these two eras. There were no aerial attacks in the Revolution, nor were there tanks or machine guns; perhaps most important, whereas men are thought to panic in modern wars because the enemy is often unseen, the adversary usually was quite visible during the Revolution. Yet, at bottom, battles always involved noise, confusion, the terrible sights of tangled destruction, and, above all else, the churning presence of inextinguishable fear.

Recent studies indicate that fear reaches its zenith just before the battle commences. The soldier experiences a pounding heart, rapid pulse, tense muscles, a sinking feeling in his stomach, dryness of mouth and throat, constant per-

---

27. Sheer, *Private Yankee Doodle*, pp. 22–24, 26, 36, 41.
28. Ibid., p. 127; Wade and Lively, *This Glorious Cause*, pp. 20–21.

spiration, and an involuntary desire for elimination. Psychologists have concluded that every "soldier engaged in any form of combat is apprehensive before, and fearful during, the action. The situations of war, for the civilized man, are completely abnormal and foreign to his background." Men enter combat wondering why they were so unfortunate to be in this ghastly predicament; they question the purpose of the war, and they speculate whether they will survive and how they will perform. The soldier does not seriously consider being wounded until he has seen his comrades maimed. He is more fearful of artillery shells and bayonets than of bullets. He worries most about wounds to the face and genitals; then he fears wounds in the abdomen, chest, and extremities. He has little hatred for the enemy; indeed, he even tends to empathize with his adversary. During combat, well over half the American soldiers in World War II acknowledged that they "lost their heads for a moment, couldn't control themselves and were useless as soldiers for a little while." Many experienced tremors, grew weak or dizzy, alternately sobbed or laughed uncontrollably, were disoriented. Older men and married men performed less well than their comrades in battle. The longer men were subjected to the uncertainties of the front lines (in the Revolution most engagements were short-lived, although the battle for New York, and the struggles at Saratoga and Yorktown, lasted for weeks), the greater the likelihood of jumpiness, carelessness with officers, freezing during fighting, loss of appetite, and laconic behavior toward one's comrades. The strongest feeling of the soldiers, aside from fear, was a reluctance to kill an adversary. One soldier in four failed to fire his weapon in battle, and 75 percent of the combat troops made ineffective use of their firearms. A few soldiers were rendered totally ineffective, and in their "severe anxiety" physicians witnessed a "disintegration of the entire personality." These men displayed "varying degrees of stupor, mutism, and amnesia," and some were plagued by headaches, nightmares, depression, sensititivity to noise, irritability, even choking sensations, fainting spells, vertigo, cramps, speech defects, and loss of sight and hearing.[29]

Soldiers entered combat during the Revolution fearful of death and wounds, but also anxious about being captured. Thousands of colonial soldiers were apprehended and languished in British prison camps. Never a pleasing prospect in any war, the possibility of capture in a civil war is fraught with special

---

29. John Dollard et al., *Fear in Battle* (Washington, D.C., 1944), pp. 2, 4, 8, 20, 38; Roy R. Grinker and John P. Spiegel, *War Neurosis* (Philadelphia, 1945), pp. 1, 4–5, 9, 11, 14–16, 22–25, 30–33, 115; Abra Kardiner and Herbert Spiegel, *War Stress and Neurotic Illness* (New York, 1947), pp. 6–7, 9, 17, 23, 33–34, 47–49, 73, 96–143; Samuel Stouffer et al., *The American Soldier*, 2 vols. (Princeton, N.J., 1949), vol. II, pp. 72–77, 91, 111, 123; S. L. A. Marshall, *Men Against Fire: The Problem of Battle Command in Future War* (New York, 1964), pp. 9–10; Eli Ginzberg et al., *The Ineffective Soldier: Lessons for Management and the Nation*, 3 vols. (New York, 1959), vol. I, p. 133, vol. II, p. 102, vol. III, p. 53.

psychological terrors. Actually, with the exception of the treatment of Loyalist prisoners, both sides generally made sincere efforts to afford their captors the most humane treatment possible. The policy of leniency partially arose from the humanitarianism of the Enlightenment, but more realistically it arose from the pragmatic realization that deliberate ill-treatment could provoke the foe into retaliatory measures. The United States, of course, complained of the British treatment of the rebel prisoners. General Washington spoke of their "barbarous usage"; Congress publicized accounts of the prisoners' "utmost distress," and even claimed that some captives had been "barbarously mangled and put to death." Stories of the massacre of surrendered troops circulated, such as the allegation that the victorious British following the battle at Fort Trumbull, Connecticut, in 1781 butchered as many as seventy of the American prisoners, even loading a wagon with the wounded and pushing it into a "steep declivity . . . whence it descended until it was stopped at a considerable distance by an apple tree. A number of these unhappy men died instantly by the shock."[30] Although there was some truth to the charges, the American leadership primarily was interested in the propaganda benefits to be derived from such allegations.

The British command normally sought to exchange its prisoners. Failing that, some captives simply were released if they pledged not to reenlist. But most colonial prisoners were dispatched to New York, where they were lodged in an assortment of compounds, including public jails, city halls, abandoned warehouses, colleges, and churches. Some were transported from the colonies; many were confined in Canada, the West Indies, Florida, Portugal, England, Ireland, and even Africa. Others remained in America, but were incarcerated in prison ships. In most instances, the British segregated officers and enlisted men, frequently not even jailing the former, and sometimes permitting them great latitude in their freedom to roam. At its peak in 1776, Britain detained more than 4,500 colonial prisoners of war.[31]

The worst prison conditions existed on the prison ships. The vessels were poorly ventilated, a problem soon exacerbated by overcrowded conditions. The captives, moreover, were expected to cook their food in water procured from the area where waste and human excrement were dumped. In virtually every prison, problems arose from shortages of food, clothing, blankets, and medical supplies. There was seldom a shortage of vermin, however, and, all too often, contagious diseases ravaged the prison population. Every prison quickly established a punishment code. Disobedience could result in a sentence of half rations, flogging, solitary confinement, or even execution. Nor were sadistic guards unheard of. Even so, while much suffering occurred, the mortality rate among

30. Montross, *Rag, Tag and Bobtail,* p. 183; Ford, *Journals of the Continental Congress,* vol. VII, pp. 277–78; Solomon, *Dwight's Travels,* vol. III, p. 369.

31. Larry G. Bowman, *Captive Americans: Prisoners During the American Revolution* (Athens, Ohio, 1976), pp. 7–12, 30, 42–45.

prisoners, considering the appalling state of medicine, was astonishingly low. Colonel Ethan Allen, leader of New England partisan forces, spent nearly two years in captivity, during which time he suffered from "goal distemper," was abused by a pathological commandant, and was "cruelly pinched with hunger"; yet only 2 percent of those captured with Allen perished in captivity. Larry Bowman, in the most recent study of prison conditions during the Revolution, is undoubtedly correct in concluding that the British were "not guilty of a conscious policy of concerted cruelty." Nevertheless, prison was a fate that no one would wish upon himself.[32]

Most American troops entering combat could only conjecture—and one can imagine the atrocity tales that circulated about the campfires—what life in a British prison might be like. Of course, they almost certainly had heard the official propaganda, and they might have surmised what prisoner of war conditions were like from firsthand knowledge of how the British were treated while in the custody of the rebels. During the rebellion the colonists captured fewer prisoners than Great Britain, so its captives normally were exchanged quickly. Nevertheless, some prisoners were detained and conditions were not always desirable. Sometimes information was solicited by flogging captives. One British general described his lodgings as an inadequately heated "dungeon of twelve or thirteen feet square, whose sides are black with grease and the litter of successive criminals." Another officer complained that his cell lacked "bedding of any sort," and he was outraged that his servant was not permitted to join him. Others allegedly were incarcerated in "black-hole[s], decorated with a pair of fixed chains."[33]

The harassment of the captives by the rebel population did not make life any more pleasant. A British major and his fellow captives confined in Hartford barely escaped a lynching when the townspeople learned that General Montgomery had perished in the invasion of Canada; some locals dropped in to "insult us daily," the officer recalled, and he added that they repeatedly were told that they were to be executed in reprisal for the British treatment of colonial prisoners. A female camp follower captured along with Burgoyne's army was frequently spat upon by the local citizenry where she was confined. In another compound the British officers were told that for every American village destroyed

32. Ibid., pp. 12–19, 42–48, 124; Daniel Sterling, ed., "American Prisoners of War in New York: A Report by Elias Boudinot," *WMQ*, 3d Ser. 13 (July 1956), p. 381; George McGowen, *The British Occupation of Charleston, 1780–82* (Columbia, S.C., 1972), pp. 60–61; R. Livesay, ed., *The Prisoners of 1776; a Relic . . . Compiled from the Journal of Charles Herbert* (Boston, 1854), pp. 30–35, 50, 56–57, 61, 65–66, 81–98, 101, 108, 115–16, 122, 127, 142–50; Bolton, *Private Soldier*, p. 188; Thacher, *Military Journals*, pp. 75–76; Journal of John Henry, in Roberts, *March to Quebec*, pp. 383–84, 412–13, 455–57, 592–94; Ethan Allen, *A Narrative of Col. Ethan Allen's Captivity . . .* (Walpole, N.H., 1807), pp. 40–64.

33. Rankin, *Francis Marion*, 88–89; "Major French's Journal," CHS *Coll.*, vol. I (Hartford, 1860), pp. 190–91, 206–8, 212–13, 220, 223; Montross, *Rag, Tag and Bobtail*, pp. 184.

by the redcoats, a captured general would be decapitated and his head, salted down in a barrel, would be sent to the British command.[34]

Often the British surrendered when they were promised a speedy release from captivity, but some prisoners, in violation of such accords, were detained for prolonged periods. General Burgoyne's army, which surrendered at Saratoga upon a promise of hasty repatriation, was confined in America for nearly four years. These luckless soldiers were marched first to New England, then to Virginia, and finally north again to Pennsylvania. But they might be considered fortunate to have been captured alive. In the passion of war, many defenseless soldiers were simply murdered on the battlefield. The worst atrocities of this sort occurred in the partisan warfare in the South, but every major encounter probably experienced some manifestations of this conduct.[35]

Some soldiers became inured to the anxiety and suffering of camp life and battle. "Nothing new this day, unless it is new to dig graves," a soldier laconically remarked in his diary. But most never grew accustomed to the spectacle. "Death is a Subject not to be attended to by Soldiers," a physician noted. The men continued to curse and revel, he thought, in the hope that such behavior would expiate the realities of mortality about them. "How strange it is," the physician thought, "that we have death sent into our Camp so repeatedly. . . . And we take so little notice of it. . . ."[36]

Men, of course, did take note of the suffering about them, and they protested against their miseries in a variety of ways. The easiest, least dangerous means of recrimination was to refuse to reenlist when one's term of service expired. Not that it was always pleasant or even safe to depart from the army under these perfectly legal means. Those packing to leave were the target of jeers and depredations by their officers. General Charles Lee even smashed the butt of a musket over the skull of one soldier who tried to persuade a comrade to come with him. Yet, so many soldiers refused to reenlist at the end of the first year of hostilities that some historians, such as Don Higginbotham, believe it "was the much berated militia that pulled Washington through the . . . crisis." Late in 1775 Washington reported that less than 150 men in a regiment of 650 men agreed to reenlist. The problem persisted through the next year, prompting Thomas Paine, in his now famous words, to characterize some men as "summer soldiers and sunshine patriots." Frequently, Washington spoke of his fears that the rebellion might collapse for lack of troops, and, in despair, he was driven to complain of the "egregious want of Public Spirit" that prevailed. Nor was

34. "Major French's Journal," vol. I, pp. 190–91, 197, 206; Montross, *Rag, Tag and Bobtail,* p. 184.

35. Robert M. Calhoun, *The Loyalists in Revolutionary America, 1760–1781* (New York, 1973), pp. 492–96; Gross, *Minutemen,* p. 127.

36. "Diary of Bixby," MHS, *Proc.,* XIV: p., 288; "Journal of a Physician," pp. 332, 337–39, 342.

it just the common soldier who went home. Officers resigned, too. At the end of 1775, Washington told Congress that up to 50 percent of all officers beneath the rank of captain were quitting the army. By 1778 so many officers were departing that Washington, alarmed and caustic, wondered aloud if he would be left alone with his privates and corporals to wage the war. Arrears in pay induced many officers to quit, but many others departed when "fatigued through wet and cold" they returned to their tent to find a letter from home "filled with the most heart-aching tender complaints a woman is capable of writing," and begging him "to consider that charity begins at home."[37]

Other soldiers sought escape from the horrors of military life by deserting. Nearly a full year before the woes of Valley Forge, Adjutant Alexander Hamilton reported that "hardly a day passes without some deserter" bolting from the ranks. During periods of great suffering, the desertion rate dramatically increased. Joseph Galloway, the Loyalist intelligence official from Pennsylvania, reported nearly 1,500 defections—a figure that included civilian as well as military activity—during the winter of 1777-1778. A recent study indicates that about ten soldiers deserted each day from Washington's camp at Valley Forge. During the long course of the war, roughly two of every ten soldiers deserted. Even more might have departed, but, when challenged, officers sometimes made concessions—as General Montgomery was compelled to do to keep his Canadian invasion force intact—of more abundant food and clothing, or even cash bounties.[38]

Men deserted for numerous reasons. Many deserting soldiers reflected the poor state of recruiting. Some of these "hungry lean fac'd Villians" took their enlistment money, then took leave of the army at the first opportunity. Some deserters were of foreign birth, and the ideological and nationalistic sentiments that motivated others were alien to them; one contemporary, for instance, estimated that early in 1778 three out of four deserters had been born abroad.[39]

But most deserters simply skipped out because of the difficulties and dangers that confronted them daily. Not all men fled with the intention of never returning. Some absented themselves from duty, as an officer reported, "to produce a draught of milk from the cows in a farmer's yard." Many intended to escape

37. Don Higginbotham, *The War of American Independence* . . . (New York, 1971), p. 104; Paine, *American Crisis*, in Foner, *Writings of Paine*, vol. I, p. 50; John Todd White, "Standing Armies in Time of War" (Ph.D. diss., The George Washington University, 1978), p. 131; Washington to Congress, 28 November 1775, in Fitzpatrick, *Writings of Washington*, vol. IV, p. 121.

38. Hamilton to the N.Y. Committee of Public Safety, 20 March 1777, in Syrett and Cooke, *Hamilton Papers*, vol. I, pp. 209–10; Galloway to Dartmouth, 20 January 1778, in Benjamin Stevens, ed., *Facsimiles of Manuscripts in European Archives* . . . (London, 1889–98), vol. XXIV, no. 2078; Charles Lesser, ed., *Sinews of Independence* (Chicago, 1976), pp. 54–74; Royster, "Continental Army," p. 131; Bush, *Revolutionary Enigma*, p. 50.

39. Bowman, *March of the Revolutionary Army*, pp. 14–15; Joseph Galloway, "An Account of the Deserted Soldiers . . . ," in Stevens, *Facsimilies*, vol. XXIV, no. 2094.

temporarily from the hazards of battle or from the fatigue of camp duty, like the private who was discovered "stowed . . . away snugly in an old papermill." A few soldiers deliberately overstayed legitimate furloughs, figuring that "my country should give me a day to return to camp." One private was prepared to return when his lieutenant arrived home on leave and encouraged his subordinate to linger for another week; the young private no doubt joyfully "remained another week and then went with the officer to camp and had no fault found." Many, however, deserted with the hope of never returning, and many struck out because they believed the soldiers were forgotten by the civilians back home. "[W]e doubt the Willingness of our Countrymen, to Assist us," wrote one soldier, who probably spoke for many. "You cannot blame us," he added. "I despise My Countrymen. I wish I could say I was not born in America. . . . I am in Rags, have lain the Rain on the Ground for 40 hours past, & only a Jerk of fresh Beef & that without Salt to dine on this day. . . ." Amid such distress the bounties afforded by home grew more alluring. "How impatient of Home am I at this Distance, in so inclement a Season, when a little unwell—Home, Home, Home, O Dear Home," a private lamented to his diary.[40] The wives of the recruits could send an appeal no less alluring than those proffered by the mates of officers. "Not a Day Passes my head," an officer noted, "but some Soldier with Tears in his Eyes, hands me a letter to read from his Wife Painting forth the Distresses of his Family in such strains as . . . *Pray Come Home*. . . ." Under these pressures many walked away determined "not [to] trouble the army much more." After all, one soldier explained to his wife, "I have spent three years in the war [and] have Been Exposed to Every hardship, Venter'd my Life & Limbs, Broke my Constitution, wore out all my clothes & has got Nothing for it . . . seems two much for any man to Bare. . . ."[41]

On occasion some troops grew so disconsolate that they mutinied. Upon learning that they were being sent deep into western Indian country, some Kentucky troops under George Rogers Clark, who had promised the men they would not have to leave Kentucky, "Debated on the subject" and most "determined to follow their Officers," although one company did mutiny and returned to Harrodsburg. An aide to General Washington claimed at the outset of the war that Boston was overrun with Indians and soldiers, and, he added, "it is hard [to] say which is the most irregular and Savage. The former are mutinous for want of liquor, the latter for want of pay, without which they refuse to march." Despite occasional rumblings, the leadership succeeded in controlling disaffection fairly well. Washington, for instance, fretted over the the possibility of mutiny at Valley Forge, and many European officers were frankly flabber-

---

40. Sheer, *Private Yankee Doodle*, pp. 64–65, 156–57; Ebenezer Huntington to Joshua Huntington, 3 May 1779, in Heartman, *Huntington Letters*, pp. 77–78; Huntington to Andrew Huntington, 1 July 1780, ibid., pp. 87–88; Albion and Dodson, *Fithian's Journal*, p. 134.

41. Ebenezer Huntington to Joshua Huntington, 3 May 1779, in Heartman, *Huntington Letters*, pp. 80–81; Ward and Lively, *This Glorious Cause*, p. 238.

gasted that a revolt did not occur. At one point the troops did make demands for better conditions and even fired their weapons through the night in violation of military law. The officers first tried to cajole the troops, then "endeavored to soothe the Yankee temper . . . with an abundance of fair promises." The grumbling ceased, but conditions remained the same. The "officers had been too crafty for us," one hoodwinked soldier sadly confided to his diary. Toward the end of the war the games ended. Late in 1780 several Connecticut regiments mutinied, and in January of 1781 troops of the Pennsylvania line revolted. These men were frustrated because of inadequate provisions and lack of pay; in addition, most believed they had enlisted at the beginning of 1778 for a three-year tour, but the high command now claimed their enlistments were for the duration of the war. During the early stages of the revolt, some soldiers hunted down officers and settled old scores. Later, more than a thousand soldiers marched from the camp, some heading for the Congress to make their demands on the civilian authorities. In a savage reprisal, the ringleaders were apprehended and executed. However, three weeks later several New Jersey regiments mutinied, and during the spring a Virginia regiment revolted and marched home.[42]

At the outbreak of hostilities officers, like the soldiers who served under them, existed in abundance. Caught up in the patriotism of the moment, and lured by the dream of fame and adulation, many men accepted a position of high rank. Most who joined probably anticipated a short, glorious war; if the war was prolonged, officers, unlike common recruits, always enjoyed the luxury of resigning their post. As the realities of the war and army life grew apparent, many officers exercised that option, leaving the American forces with what many regarded as a woeful coterie of junior officers and an abundance of senior leaders. Some politicians, like John Adams, thought too many officers were "ackward, illiterate, ill-bred" types, but he concluded that this had occurred because of republican "jealousy. . .of men of learning, and a wish to exclude them from the public councils and from military commands." Few agreed, however, that republicanism was the culprit. Many observers thought the officers themselves, deliberately or not, forced good men from the service. Some characterized their fellow officers as tyrants and, despite their collegial air, referred to comrades as profligate bullies. A sizable band of political leaders seethed against the officer corps. Benjamin Rush, while a member of Congress, and following a tour of duty in the Continental army, termed General Greene "timid, speculative, without enterprize," and he labeled General Sullivan a "proud, vain, lazy, ignorant drunkard." Rush and others even thought the problems stemmed from the very top of the army, from the "slackness and remissness" of Washington, and they campaigned for the commander's removal, imagining

---

42. Bakeless, *Background to Glory*, pp. 57, 59; Tench Tilghman, *Memoir of Lieut. Col. Tench Tilghman* . . . (Albany, N.Y., 1876), pp. 97–98; Sheer, *Private Yankee Doodle*, p. 184; Higginbotham, *War of American Independence*, pp. 403–4; Thayer, *Greene*, pp. 397–98; Royster, "Continental Army," p. 533.

"a general murmur in the people . . . against the weak conduct" of the Virginian.[43]

From the outset the officers of the Continental army adopted the view of European officers. They saw themselves as a special caste, within both the army and society generally. Although they were hardly the only men who gave up economic enterprises at home to risk life and limb, they manifested an air of selflessness. An spirit of élan emerged quickly among officers. They depicted the army as a "place for sociability, friendship, and happiness" for those within this elite cadre. Certain badges of honor—codes of conduct—sprang up among army leaders. To an officer, one explained, "honor is so feelingly alive that it must smart and agonize at the least show of aspersion." A "rage of duelling," commonplace in the officer corps of many European armies, grew fashionable in the Continental army among men who believed their honor had been besmirched. Failure to attain promotion was regarded as such a blow to one's personal honor that it drove some officers to quit the army; at least one officer, Abiel Leonard, a chaplain, committed suicide when he was not elevated to a more important command. More than anything, the officers longed for fame and flattery, a craving that led some to act recklessly, exposing their men to unnecessary risks.[44]

These attitudes aroused suspicions in a society pledged to increased egalitarianism. John Adams grew weary "with the wrangles between military officers, high and low. They quarrel like cats and dogs. They worry one another like mastiffs, scrambling for rank and pay like apes for nuts." In addition, he concluded early in the war that it was unwise to "trust your generals, with too much power, for too long," and he argued that it "becomes us to attend early to the restraining" of officers. Not even General Washington was above suspicion. Adams was relieved that General Gates, not Washington, had captured Burgoyne's army at Saratoga, lest the "glory of turning the tide of arms" would have produced an "idolatry and adulation . . . [so] unbounded, so excessive as to endanger our liberties." Similarly, Congressman James Lovell was ecstatic at Washington's lack of success in the encounters at Germantown; he regarded the commander's difficulty as *"the* day of salvation offered by Heaven to us." Samuel Adams carefully watched officers, fearful that they all harbored a lust for military dictatorship. Congress occasionally was so concerned that it berated officers for their comments and conduct, and in one instance even required an outspoken officer to apologize in person before Congress. Thomas Jefferson and

---

43. Smith, *Adams,* vol. I, p. 287; James Warren to Elbridge Gerry, 31 August 1777, in C. Harvey Gardiner, ed., *A Study in Dissent: The Warren-Gerry Correspondence, 1776–1792* (Carbondale, Ill., 1968), p. 79; Hamilton to Washington, 25 March 1783, in Syrett and Cooke, *Hamilton Papers,* vol. III, p. 306; "Memoir of Gen. Lacey," pp. 196, 353; Hawke, *Benjamin Rush,* pp. 266–67, 214; Royster, "Continental Army," p. 276.

44. Perhaps the best account of the officer mentality is contained in Royster, "Continental Army," pp. 311–30, the study upon which I relied for this paragraph.

many others feared that officers were "trained to monarchy by military habits." These people overreacted, although a few officers openly castigated the "weakness of republics" and yearned for royal or military government. Some officers aroused suspicion merely by derogating the militia, others by castigating civilians for their indifference and niggardly appropriations.[45]

Many officers were filled with contempt for the men. They believed that "a proper subordination" by such soldiers was unlikely because they perceived "little distinction" between social classes. Where "so thorough a levelling spirit predominates," Joseph Reed complained, "either no discipline can be established, or he who attempts it must become odious and detestable." Militia troops were thought to be the worst of the lot. They were "not to be depended upon for more than a few days," one officer remarked, "as they soon get tired, grow impatient, ungovernable. . . ." Upon taking command Washington was shocked to find uninhibited fraternization between officers and men, including instances of officers shaving enlistees. The commander was particularly contemptuous of New England fighting forces, where, he thought, "an unaccountable kind of stupidity . . . prevails but too generally among the officers . . . who are nearly of the same kidney with the privates. . . ." General Washington once raged that "nothing . . . but the breaking of Two or Three officers in every regiment will effect a radical *cure* of [the] negligence, inattention, and in fact downright disobedience" of the troops. Indeed, Washington commenced his service by almost immediately making "a pretty good slam" against these alleged incompetents; in a few days he dismissed or arrested two colonels, one major, and four captains, believing that such draconian measures would stimulate the officers who survived the purge to be equally zealous in whipping their men into fighting shape.[46]

Various officers issued orders prohibiting some activities and requiring others. In part, the intention was to maintain proper hygiene, as well as an environment that would assure continued civilian support, but in large measure the disciplinary

45. John Adams to Abigail Adams, 22 May 1777, in Charles Francis Adams, ed., *Familiar Letters of John Adams and his Wife Abigail Adams* (Boston, 1876), p. 276; John Adams to Horatio Gates, 18 June 1776, in Edmund C. Burnett, *Letters of Members of the Continental Congress,* 8 vols. (Washington, D.C., 1921–1936), vol. I, p. 497; Hawke, *Benjamin Rush,* p. 185; Bernhard Knollenberg, *Washington in the Revolution* (New York, 1941), p. 192; Higginbotham, *War for American Independence,* pp. 266–67; Thomas Jefferson, "Anas," in Paul L. Ford, ed., *The Writings of Thomas Jefferson,* 10 vols. (New York, 1892–1899), vol. I, p. 157; Louise B. Dunbar, "A Study of Monarchical Tendencies in the United States from 1776–1801," University of Illinois *Studies in the Social Sciences* (March 1922), vol. X, p. 40–45.

46. Philip Schuyler to Washington, 15 July 1775, in Jared Sparks, ed., *Correspondence of the American Revolution,* 8 vols. (Freeport, N.Y., 1970), vol. I, p. 4; Bolton, *Private Soldier,* p. 128; Robert Pugh, "The Revolutionary Militia in the Southern Campaign, 1780–1781," *WMQ,* 3d Ser. 14 (April 1957), p. 157; Higginbotham, *War for American Independence,* p. 101, Washington to R. H. Lee, 29 August 1775, in Fitzpatrick, *Writings of Washington,* vol. III, pp. 450–51; Royster, "Continental Army," p. 145.

measures were designed to disabuse the soldiers of any civilian instincts they might have retained. After all, the task of controlling men faced with seemingly omnipresent shortages of the necessities of decent living was not an enviable task. Moreover, only unthinking, regimented automatons could be expected to stand firm in the face of a withering fire by the enemy or to remain unflinching when confronted by a terrifying bayonet charge. "Discipline, discipline, discipline is the great thing wanted. There can be no order nor cleanliness in any army without discipline," one revolutionary remarked. Gambling was among the prohibited activities, since it served only "Sordid purposes." The men were required to shave, bathe, and change clothing twice each week. Attempts were made to dictate the proper length of one's hair. Regular attendance at worship services was required. Chaplains, in fact, frequently were put to work by the leadership to whip up fervor for fighting among the men. Officers sometimes suggested topics or instructed the pastors on what would be suitable for the army. The chaplains culled many of their messages from Old Testament exhortations to Israel's warriors, one of their favorites being Jacob's charge to his army to "Be of good courage and let us play the men for our people . . . and the Lord will do that which seemeth his good." Not surprisingly, chaplains were used to read important public statements, such as Congress' "Declaration of Causes and Necessity of Taking up Arms," to the assembled troops. Of course, "all prophain Cursing and Swering and all Indesant Langue" was outlawed. And, not only was "all posable Care [to] be taken that no Lewd Women Com into the Camp," but the troops were warned against "offering any insult to the female sex in Particular or . . . offering any money to entice any Women."[47]

Soldiers additionally were prohibited from fighting among themselves, and no soldier was permitted to challenge another to a duel. To curtail fighting, "reproachful, or provoking . . . Gestures" were forbidden. Explicit orders governing the cleaning of the camp and the latrines were issued, as were instructions and orders concerning the collection of firewood, the preparation of food, and the washing of clothes. Some of the orders were designed to protect the troops from one another, to prevent accidental or deliberate injuries; for instance, at the outset of the war officers were notified to fine troops around Boston who tried to catch British-fired cannon balls before they stopped bouncing. Many actions were expressly forbidden. These included being absent without permission, causing false alarms, giving aid to the enemy, selling equipment or being intoxicated while on duty, being disobedient, and exhibiting negligence toward one's weapon. It was difficult to secure compliance with even the most sensible

47. John Adams to Abigail Adams, 13 April 1777, in Adams, *Familiar Letters*, p. 259; Turner, *Journal of Capt. Kirkwood*, pp. 58, 142; Royster, "Continental Army," pp. 255, 262–64; "Orderly Book of Col. Bicker," p. 34; Montrose, *Rag, Tag and Bobtail*, p. 185; "Orderly Book of Coits' Company," CSM, *Coll.*, vol. VII, pp. 28, 32; "Journal of Wells," ibid., vol. VIII, p. 293; *The Militia Act; together with the Rules and Regulation for the Militia* (Boston, 1776), pp. 25–40.

order. One soldier, for example, indicated that most troops preferred to deposit their "Excrement about the fields Promiscuously," rather than use the proper facilities. What was permitted, even encouraged, were "Games of exercise for amusement."[48]

Officers tried to attain compliance through a variety of tactics. Blandishments, bribes, and offers of additional liquor in return for essential work were commonplace. Sometimes professional workers were hired to replace troops in the construction of facilities; such a practice was recommended because the artisans "will cost incomparably less, and . . . will work a great deal more, and give less trouble . . . and not consume such an immense quantity of tools of all kinds." But, if necessary, discipline could be attained and the will of intransigent soldiers could be broken by macabre punishments.[49]

The leadership felt no moral constraints in ordering a variety of physical punishments, although most leaders, with an eye toward morale, attempted to mingle the velvet glove with the mailed fist. Still, most officers believed that brutality was sometimes required, and many leaders were impatient with what they regarded as leniency. Joseph Reed, Washington's secretary, believed that the time-honored military punishment of thirty-nine lashes was ineffective. He urged even harsher codes, believing that the men were so "contemptible" of this form of excoriation—"it is very frequent for them," he claimed, "to offer to take as many more [stripes] for a pint of rum"—that disorder was rampant. Alexander Hamilton likewise exhorted his chiefs to order more drastic punishments. "An execution or two, by way of example, would strike terror, and powerfully discourage the wicked practices going on" among the troops. Hamilton believed corporal punishment merely tended to "excite compassion" for the victim and to "breed disgust" toward the officers.[50]

Initially, Washington modestly punished even serious offenders. In 1775, for instance, he ordered a deserter to forfeit nine days' pay, to perform latrine duty for six days, and to wear at all times during the ensuing week a sign bearing the word "Deserter." This attempt to mobilize peer pressure as a deterrent against a multiplicity of practices was made in an endless variety of ways. Some officers attempted to embarrass soldiers who refused to reenlist by cursing them in the presence of their comrades and denouncing them as the "worst of all creatures." At times the soldiers themselves took the initiative. Captain Simon

48. Wade and Lively, *This Glorious Cause*, pp. 32–33; "Diary of Bixby" vol. XIV, p. 289; Journal of Dr. Senter, in Roberts, *March to Quebec*, p. 199; *Militia Act*, pp. 25–40; "Orderly Book of Capt. Coits' Company," vol. VII, pp. 32, 46–47, 75, 77; Turner, *Journal of Capt. Kirkwood*, pp. 122, 156, 181; Montross, *Rag, Tag and Bobtail*, p. 185.

49. Wade and Lively, *This Glorious Cause*, p. 72; Turner, *Journal of Capt. Kirkwood*, p. 271; Du Coudray Memoir, 29 August 1777, in Worthington C. Ford, ed., *Defenses of Philadelphia in 1777* (Brooklyn, 1897), pp. 44–45.

50. Montross, *Rag, Tag and Bobtail*, p. 44; Hamilton to N.Y. Committee of Correspondence, 20 March 1777, in Syrett and Cooke, *Hamilton Papers*, vol. I, p. 237.

Thayer, who served under Arnold during the invasion of Canada, noted the time several soldiers seized four men who refused to do their share in a work detail and "led them from place to place with Halters round their necks, exposing them to the ridicule of the soldiers, as a punishment Due to their effeminate courage."[51]

However, whatever constraints Washington might have displayed initially were quickly abandoned. In fact, the civilian authorities at times were compelled to restrain the commander. At one point Washington requested that the maximum number of lashes that the army was permitted to apply to an offending culprit should be increased from thirty-nine to five hundred. Congress refused, and set the maximum in the Articles of War at one hundred lashes. Many Congressmen believed discipline was essential for "preserving the health and spirits of the men," but they also felt that soldierly attributes could be acquired without resorting to "cruelty, severity, tyranny." Still, during the Battle of Long Island, when the fate of the rebellion seemed to hang on its outcome, Washington ordered that any soldier attempting "to skulk, lay down, or retreat, without orders . . . be instantly shot as an example." When the fighting commenced, the General rode among the troops and "laid his Cane over many of the Officers who showed their men the Example of running."[52]

Flogging was the preferred form of punishment. An established ceremony normally accompanied the practice. The troops were assembled and the convicted soldier was marched—quite literally marched, for he stepped to a drummed cadence—to the punishment area, where, after his shirt was removed, he was tied to a tree or post. The sentence was read and the "drummer" began to administer the flogging. A "whip formed of several small knotted cords" was the usual tool. Often the lash "cut through the skin at every stroke," providing a ghastly sight, as was intended, for the soldiers who were compelled to watch the spectacle. While the lash ordinarily was laid on the back, there is evidence that some were whipped on the "naked Buttocks." Additional humiliations were often conjured up. Some men, for instance, were "dress'd in Petticoats & Caps" for their flogging. Often, following the final stripe, salt was rubbed liberally into the lacerated flesh to heighten the torment. Those unfortunates sentenced to an excessive number of lashes, usually any number over thirty-nine, commonly suffered their punishment at intervals of two to three days. This procedure, a physician noted, meant that "the wounds are [still] in a state of inflammation" when the lashing resumes, and "the terror of the punishment is greatly aggra-

51. Smith, *A New Age,* vol. I, pp. 570, 580; Journal of Capt. Thayer, in Roberts, *March to Quebec,* pp. 273–74.

52. Stuart Bernath, "George Washington and the Genesis of American Military Discipline," *Mid-America* 49 (April 1967), pp. 83–100; Maurer Maurer, "Military Justice under George Washington," *MA* 27 (Spring 1964), pp. 8–16; Montross, *Rag, Tag and Bobtail,* p. 120; Tilghman, *Memoir of Lt. Col. Tilghman,* p. 137.

vated." It must have been aggravated, too, by the knowledge that errors could be made. "We found," a soldier scribbled in his diary, "that one of the men that was flogg'd Yesterday was not sentenced by the Court Martial but Receiv'd his Punishment through Mistake." This was not the only instance of such a grievous error. The victims frequently bit on a bullet during the punishment, and sympathetic jailors often clandestinely furnished their prisoners with a stiff belt of rum just prior to the beating. Sometimes, too, drummers, either from compassion or from fear of reprisal, made the flogging appear to be worse than it really had been.[53] Still, it was a brutal and dreaded punishment and, if it failed to eliminate disorder in the army, it was not because of any slackening by those who ordered the lashings.

Other forms of punishment often were inflicted. Some men were compelled to "ride the wooden horse" or to stand in the pillary. Others were dry-shaved, and still others had their hair curled or plaited in the prevailing feminine fashion. Also, soldiers were made to run the gauntlet. This practice called for the bare-backed victim to walk, not run, between two rows of men furnished with sticks or switches. A drummer held a bayonet-equipped rifle to the chest of the victim and backed very slowly down the line, insuring that each soldier was permitted to strike the condemned man. Sometimes men died from the floggings received, whether at the whipping post or from the ordeal of the gauntlet.[54]

Between forty and seventy-five American soldiers were executed during the Revolution. Most faced capital punishment for mutiny or desertion. Once, in fact, a sergeant was executed for leading a mutiny for back pay, even though the promised pay was fifteen months in arrears. Some died for striking officers or for repeatedly committing offenses. Hanging was the customary form of execution, although some men were dispatched by firing squads and, in at least one instance, much to the mortification of Washington, a soldier was decapitated and the severed head was impaled on a tall pole for exhibition near the camp.[55] Most condemned soldiers, however, were sentenced to the gallows. As with floggings, other soldiers were compelled to watch for the lesson it presumably taught. The execution was preceded by an excrutiatingly lengthy ceremony, during which the victim was marched to the gallows, the sentence slowly read, and prayers were said. A hood was draped over the victim's head. After an agonizing moment, the trap was sprung. Following the execution, the body frequently was allowed to dangle for up to twenty-four hours. The ceremony itself was expected to so chasten the assembled troops as to deter any further malfeasance. Often, therefore, a reprieve was announced at the last moment, or, in some instances, one luckless soldier might be executed but others, with the noose already about their necks, pardoned.

53. Rankin, *Francis Marion*, p. 21; Thacher, *Military Journals,* pp. 186–87.
54. Thacher, *Military Journals,* p. 186–87; Rankin, *Francis Marion*, p. 26.
55. Royster, "Continental Army," pp. 141, 463; Bolton, *Private Soldier*, p. 171.

Orderly books demonstrate the zeal, as well as the lack of uniformity, with which punishments were prescribed. In a nine-month period of 1777, the following punishments were carried out in one Delaware battalion: four men were executed, forty-eight flogged, two ran the gauntlet, thirteen were fined, four were reduced in rank, two were imprisoned for the duration of the war, and eight were given dishonorable discharges; in addition, nine were convicted but either were pardoned or reprimanded, and twenty-five others were tried but acquitted. In the space of one month in this battalion, these sentences were executed: thirty-nine lashes for theft of clothing, fifty lashes with a cat o' nine tails for desertion, fifteen lashes and dishonorable discharge for desertion, four hundred lashes for "Drawing his Bayonet on Lt. Bowman," one hundred lashes for stealing an army horse and wagon, one hundred lashes administered over four days for stealing army equipment, fifteen lashes for intoxication, fifty lashes for desertion, one hundred lashes and a dishonorable discharge for "fraud & Extortion," and execution by firing squad for desertion.[56]

Soldiers carried out these punishments against soldiers, but they also carried out punishments against civilians, including female camp followers. Civilians were jailed, whipped, drummed out of camp, and executed for spying, stealing, inciting desertion, spreading venereal diseases, engaging in fraudulent endeavors, and illegally selling liquor to the soldiers. Because of the sexual overtones, perhaps the strangest punishment was that meted out by a Connecticut commander for some unrecorded offense; the soldier who observed the punishment recorded that "3 men whipt about 3 hundred lashes apeace & 1 woman 2 & 52 on bear rump."[57]

One of the most noticeable aspects of army life to men subjected to such a brutal regimen was the extraordinary difference between their lot and the life enjoyed by the officer caste. The army, of course, was modeled on the prevailing caste attitudes of civilian society in the 1770s. Many leaders of America's rebellion did not find it hypocritical to embrace the new republican principles while openly fretting over the growing power of the people. As can be seen from Elbridge Gerry lamenting that "the people . . . feel rather too much their own importance" and the South Carolina clergyman trembling at the prospect that "every silly clown, and illiterate mechanic" might govern, the old class values of the ruling elite died slowly. In addition, the American army was still patterned on the European model, and in this age, according to Professor Corvisier, the Continental "military hierarchy conformed fairly closely to the social hierarchy" of the ancien regime. In Washington's army of the rebellion, therefore, as in American society in general, a wide gap existed between the living conditions and perquisites of the rulers and the ruled. It should not be surprising, therefore, that men might be punished for intemperance while they daily witnessed officers appearing openly in an inebriated state. Moreover, the very

56. Turner, *Journal of Capt. Kirkwood,* pp. 50–96, 128, 181, 256, 261.
57. *The Military Journals of two Private Soldiers* (New York, 1971), pp. 37–38.

leader who might have a man flogged for excessive drinking was powerless to do more than complain about "Effeminate officers, who [would] rather pass their time in tippling than turn it to the profit and advantage of their country." Soldiers might be punished brutally for accidentally discharging a weapon, but the duel, in which one officer might deliberately kill or maim another officer, was regarded as a mark of honor within the officer caste. The common soldier additionally could readily perceive that substantially different supplies were allotted to officers. On General Sullivan's expedition against the Indians in Pennsylvania and New York in 1779, officers were furnished with a quart of whiskey for every pint issued to the men; moreover, officers were ordered to see "that water be immediately mixed with the soldiers' whiskey." At the same time in 1779 that soldiers were complaining of monotonous sustenance and inadequate food supplies, and Washington was urging Congress to increase the quantity of victuals, the commander, in one week, dined on ham, bacon, roast beef, greens, beef-steak pies, crab, and apple pie. Officers and men possessed unequal shares of clothing. Expecting rapid movement in the fall of 1777, the men were told they could keep one blanket, two sets of clothes, and one great coat, but officers were permitted to possess virtually unlimited supplies. In 1776 General Gates noted that he spent the equivalent of five times the annual pay of a private on clothes. A colonel in the Canadian invasion force was robbed of the following items: one hat, six coats and jackets, six shirts, four pair of stockings, one pair of shoes, two handkerchiefs, a compass, ink pot and knife, numerous papers, and about forty dollars. Housing accommodations usually differed, too. At Valley Forge twelve soldiers were lodged in each fourteen-by-sixteen-foot hut, but private dwellings were built, by the men, for the highest ranking officers, and among the lower-grade officers only two to four men shared a cabin. Washington apparently deemed it a sacrifice to stay in a hut. He quickly moved to a private home, the Hewes's farmhouse. In addition, although it was customary for women to be permitted to accompany European armies in the eighteenth century, and whereas Washington and other generals encouraged their wives to be camp followers, the leadership frequently attempted to drive the wives and female companions of the ordinary soldiers from the encampments. Of course, discrepancies in pay also existed. A lowly lieutenant normally earned about four times the pay for privates. In 1776 officers' pay was increased by about 20 percent per month, but enlisted men continued to draw the same meager rates.[58]

58. Merrill Jensen, *The Founding of a Nation* (New York, 1968), pp. 626, 629; Corvisier, *Armies and Societies*, p. 154; Merrill Jensen, *The New Nation* (New York, 1958), p. 33; Journal of Capt. Thayer, in Roberts, *March to Quebec*, p. 257; Cook, *Journals of the Sullivan Expedition*, p. 120n.; Montross, *Rag, Tag and Bobtail*, p. 331; Baldwin, *Revolutionary Journal of Col. Baldwin*, pp. 59–60; Turner, *Journal of Capt. Kirkwood*, pp. 165, 271; Joan Hoff Wilson, "The Illusion of Change: Women and the American Revolution," in Young, *American Revolution*, pp. 422–23; Wade and Lively, *This Glorious Cause*, p. 40.

Soldiers, of course, were required to perform certain tasks that were unthinkable for officers. The leaders of the army simply did not clean latrines or sweep camp streets. On the customarily lengthy marches, officers often rode on horseback, but the soldiers always walked. Distinct differences existed between the punishments levied against officers and enlistees. Officers might be dishonorably discharged, but they were not flogged, made to run the gauntlet, pilloried, or incarcerated on a bread and water diet; no American officer was executed by the American army during the War for Independence. And officers could resign their commissions, but if a soldier departed, even because his promised pay was not forthcoming, he could be, and sometimes was, executed. Other differences must have been more than just barely perceived. Those who were affluent were not likely to be compelled to serve in the army, and if they chose to serve they automatically entered as officers. Furthermore, the only real contemporary heroes were officers; foot soldiers may have been lauded, but none were inducted into the pantheon of national heroes as were General Montgomery, Dr. Joseph Warren, or General Washington. Even more galling must have been the realization that the "young ladies here are very fond of the soldiers, but much more so of the officers."[59]

The men frequently bridled at the leadership elite's failure to provide adequate direction. An unwise decision to use batteaux, coupled with inadequate training in the use of these crafts, produced unnecessary miseries for Arnold's men during the invasion of Canada. Repeatedly, supplies were low or nonexistent because of malfeasance—or so the men suspected—on the part of the officers. Soldiers must have felt that officers cared more about catching the eye of their superiors than caring for their men. Even fellow officers criticized Hamilton for having "wantonly exposed the lives of his men" with his foolish acts of bravado at Yorktown. Of course, officers often were blamed for the high mortality rate, sometimes because of battlefield blunders and sometimes because of the inexcusable camp conditions. Who was to blame, the soldier wondered, for the selection of improper and unwholesome sites for camps? Who should be censured when severely ill patients drowned because no one removed them from a floodplain during a heavy rainstorm? One private bitterly noted the indiscretion of officers, and recalled that the very officers who denied the men liquor suddenly offered it, although as "our stomachs being empty the whiskey took rank hold and the poor brain fared accordingly. . . . Had the enemy come upon us at this time, there would have been action worth recording." Another soldier thought it unpalatable that five days after the considerable death rate at Monmouth, the commander invited several "gentlemen and Ladys [for] a Bawl at Head Quarters with great Pomp." Many officers raised the ire of their men by acting deceitfully. Even Washington, knowing that northern soldiers feared serving in the South

59. "Orderly Book of Col. Bicker," pp. 30–59; *An Ordinance for Regulating the Militia of New Jersey* . . . (Burlington, N.J., 1776), pp. 14, 22, 25; *Militia Act*, pp. 25–40; Jensen, *A New Nation*, p. 33; "Diary of Lt. McMichael," p. 141.

John Trumbull, *The Death of General Warren at the Battle of Bunker's Hill*
(Copyright Yale University Art Gallery)

John Trumbull, *The Death of General Montgomery in the Attack on Quebec*
(Copyright Yale University Art Gallery)

After Benjamin West, *Death of General Wolfe* (Yale University Art Gallery) Gift of William L. Andrews

Charles Willson Peale, *George Washington at the Battle of Princeton*
(Yale University Art Gallery) Given by the Associates in Fine Arts and Mrs. Henry B. Loomis
in memory of Henry Bradford Loomis, B.A. 1875

because of its reputation for pestilential fevers, made his Yorktown-bound army in 1781 believe its destination was New York City.[60]

Resentment toward the officers often threatened to blow up, and sometimes individuals or small groups, did erupt. Once a death sentence was commuted at the last moment following "secret and open threats" by the soldiers against the officers who had sanctioned the execution. "I believe it was well" that the commutation was ordered, a private stated, for the condemned man's "blood would not have been the only blood that would have been spilt: the troops were greatly exasperated." A Pennsylvanian witnessed the execution of a Virginian who had shot an officer, then he calmly recorded that the murderer was "certainly justified" in his deed. Another soldier longed for the courage to drill an officer who needled him. "I heartily wish," he wrote, that "some person would make an experiment on him to make the sun shine thro' his head with an ounce ball. As previously described, full-fledged mutinies occasionally erupted, and during these riots some soldiers hunted down and murdered officers who angered them.[61]

Securing nonmilitia soldiers had never been an easy task in the colonial years. Many colonists had fled Europe because of their strong antipathy to warfare and, having made their escape, they were not about to join a military force in the New World. Nor did these predominately rural peoples wish to abandon their farms during the planting season or at the harvest. As Daniel Boorstin had indicated, moreover, many colonists did serve in the local militia force, but the seemingly omnipresent possibility of an Indian attack or a slave uprising made them reluctant to volunteer for service in a force that might be dispatched hundreds of miles from their neighborhood.[62] Furthermore, with the passage of each year the traditions of service in a regular army grew more remote to this militia-conscious people. But certainly, too, colonists disdained service because of the horrors involved; the military was, after all, a place of degrading and brutal punishments, of difficult and frequently menial tasks, and, obviously, of dangerous pursuits.

Despite the changed nature of war during the struggle for independence, and in spite of the considerable idealism that accompanied the conflict, recruiting remained an arduous task. As in the colonial wars, the Revolutionary authorities resorted to a variety of ploys to persuade men to join. Ministers, particularly in New England, acted as de facto recruiting agents. Sermon after sermon was

60. Willard M. Wallace, *Traitorous Hero: The Life and Fortunes of Benedict Arnold* (Freeport, N.Y., 1970), pp. 65–69; "Diary of Capt. Duncan," *Pa. Archives*, 2d Ser., vol. XV, p. 749; Journal of Arnold, in Roberts, *March to Quebec*, p. 55; Bolton, *Private Soldier*, pp. 202–3; "Journal of a Physician," p. 344; Sheer, *Private Yankee Doodle*, p. 79; *Elijah Fisher's Journal*, p. 9; Flexner, *Washington*, p. 442.

61. Sheer, *Private Yankee Doodle*, p. 46; "Extracts from the Journal of Lieutenant John Bell Tilden, Second Pennsylvania Line, 1781–1782," *PMHB* 19, no. 1 (1895), p. 52; Montross, *Rag, Tag and Bobtail*, p. 134.

62. Boorstin, *The Americans*, pp. 347–48, 351, 355.

preached to whip up enthusiasm for the war; many pastors also authored patriotic newspaper essays. One clergyman was said to have "preached his whole parish into the army and then to have gone himself." When recruiters in Boothbay, Maine, failed to raise a single enlistee after four days, the local pastor tried his hand and succeeded in filling an entire company with a single fiery sermon. The "Art of War becomes Part of our Religion," one minister remarked with candor. Often the town folk assisted the recruiters. Once a local leader convinced a ne'er-do-well to enlist, then told the recruiter—who, apparently, was less concerned about the potential abilities of the recruit than in the commission he would pocket for having secured another warm body—that the new soldier "would do to stop a bullet as well as a better man . . . as he was a truly worthless dog. . . ."[63]

Most enlistees were offered some sort of payoff to sign up. In 1776 Congress tendered a grant of one hundred acres to all volunteers, and a further bounty of ten dollars for those who joined for three years; Congress also offered an annual stipend of twenty dollars for each soldier who enlisted for the duration. The following year Congress established quotas for each state, which, in turn, set quotas for each county. If volunteers could not be secured quickly, negotiations commenced for more attractive bounties. Harvard, Massachusetts, for instance, offered up to £30 for a three-year enlistment, although this subsequently was changed to a bounty of eighteen calves. The states frequently supplemented these local bounties. An additional kind of payoff was utilized in some northern states. Slaves who agreed to serve for the duration were promised their freedom upon the successful termination of hostilities. About five thousand blacks served in the Continental army, and another considerably smaller group of recent freedmen served in various maritime capacities. Even officers were payed to join, though they received greater compensation than the men they would lead. Colonel John Laurens reported in 1777 that officers could receive two hundred acres to join, privates could receive fifty acres. Recruiters, too, were given incentives to hustle. In 1777 Congress established specific districts for recruiters, and offered them a bounty of eight dollars per man enlisted and five dollars for each deserter apprehended. Some fraud existed, however. One bitter soldier who had been bilked, alleged that the recruiters "will promise them they will give them so and so [but] after they have got them to Enlist they are Cheated out of one-half they ought to have. . . ."[64]

---

63. Charles W. Akers, "Religion and the American Revolution: Samuel Cooper and the Brattle Street Church," *WMQ,* 3d Ser. 35 (July 1978), pp. 487, 493; Alice M. Baldwin, *The New England Clergy and the American Revolution* (New York, 1928), pp. 125–26; Bolton, *Private Soldier,* pp. 38–39.

64. Higginbotham, *War of American Independence,* pp. 390–93; Royster, "Continental Army," pp. 113, 201; Bolton, *Private Soldier,* pp. 49–50; Philip S. Foner, *Blacks in the American Revolution* (Westport, Conn., 1975), pp. 56, 67, 69–70; Benjamin Quarles, *The Negro in the American Revolution* (Chapel Hill, N.C., 1961), pp. 68–93; *The Army Correspondence of Colonel John Laurens in the Years 1777–8* (New York, 1969), p. 66; *Elijah Fishers' Journal,* p. 14.

Some enlistments were solicited by a combination of fast talk and alcohol. Many men signed up under the influence, but few were as lucky as the drunken Maryland carpenter whose release was granted when his enraged wife accosted the authorities with "every vile name she could think of." Recruiters also used barbecues and even dances to fill their quotas. The general patriotic fervor that swept the colonies netted some recruits, particularly in the early days of the conflict. Many men joined in those days in the belief that the war would be short and relatively bloodless. These men, one such idealist noted, "had a fixed expectation and a strong desire of meeting the british in real combat. Those feelings absorbed the more *tender* ones." Another recruit of this ilk was "unconscious of danger, and animated by a hope of applause from [his] country." It was, in the words of a popular poem of the day, "Fame and dear freedom" that induced many to volunteer.[65]

Some enlisted for psychological reasons they could not hope to fathom. One recruit spoke of his father's pride upon "seeing me dressed in military uniform, with epaulets on my shoulders, and a sword by my side." Another enlistee mentioned that when he agreed to serve he was the center of attention in his village for a few shining hours. The wholehearted support of the endeavor by women helped provoke men to join. "It was not necessary to urge anyone to enlist," one soldier wrote. "I presume," he added, "that female influence . . . was never more evident than at this time: they appeared to vie with their brethern in sustaining the idea of a fixed and determined resistance."[66]

Many men were forcefully persuaded to join. One soldier claimed a recruiter told him he would see that his grain and fields would be destroyed if he refused to serve. Another soldier acknowledged that he enlisted to escape jail for some offense at home. Those already in the army were urged to reenlist, and some were threatened with suicidal missions or the prospect of inadequate food supplies during the remaining weeks of their tour if they refused to continue to serve.[67]

Three Revolutionary War soldiers left behind accounts of their enlistments. Philip Fithian, a young teacher and minister who joined the New Jersey militia as a chaplain, enlisted in November 1775. A recruiter played on Fithian's emotions, telling him that the people in his community believed those who refused to serve were "dull" and lauding his brother who had enlisted as a "Brave Youth" whose "Bosom is warmed with genuine patriotic Fire!" Fithian

65. Bolton, *Private Soldier*, pp. 38–39; Norton, "What an Alarming Crisis," in Crow and Tise, *Southern Experience*, p. 217; Rankin, *Francis Marion*, p. 10; *Diary of Samuel Richards*, pp. 9, 46; Journal of John Henry, in Roberts, *March to Quebec*, p. 303; "The American Hero," in Mason I. Lawrence and Georgia B. Bumgardner, eds., *Massachusetts Broadsides of the American Revolution* (Amherst, Mass., 1976), p. 61.

66. *Memoir of Col. Talmadge*, pp. 7–8; *Diary of Samuel Richards*, pp. 8–9.

67. "Diary of Trifling Occurrences," p. 247; Journal of Moses Kimbell, in Roberts, *March to Quebec*, p. 433; "Journal of Simeon Lyman of Sharon, August 10 to December 28, 1775," in CHS, *Coll.*, vol. VII (Hartford, Conn., 1899), pp. 128–29.

was weakened by this pitch of the older recruiter, but not to the point that he was yet willing to enlist. Next, apparently, the captain of the local militia company, an important person in Fithian's small world, worked on the impressionable youth. Sensing his vulnerability, the captain extolled the "Fortitude" and "Virtue" of Fithian's brother, and suggested that his name would be entered "on the Roll of American Heroes." Fithian waited, studied a Prussian military manual, then enlisted, certain that the colonists were "preparing with a Confidence of Success, to rival the whole World in Military Honour."[68] A few months later, in the shabby surroundings of a filthy army hospital, Fithian died of a camp disease.

Joseph Plumb Martin joined the Connecticut line as a private late in 1775. Whatever his feelings about the colonists' quarrel with Great Britain, the young Martin, still a teenager when the war erupted, initially believed it best to "Stay at home out of harm's way." He began to waver when he saw men paid to enlist, but he continued to resist the temptation to join. He broke when the local company, which included many of his friends, marched and drilled about the tiny village of Milford. Martin feared "they will come swaggering back . . . and tell me all their exploits, all their 'hairbreath 'scrapes,' and poor Huff will not have a single sentence to advance." He also noticed how the "Worthy young ladies" swooned over the soldiers and how the townsfolk prayed and mourned for those who were preparing to depart for the front. He asked his grandparents with whom he lived to grant their permission for him to enlist. They refused, but when they discovered that he planned to run away to "engage on board a man-of-war," his grandfather relented, realizing the youth was "resolved to go into the service in some way or other and he had rather I would engage in the land service if I must engage in any." So Martin joined, although he refused to sign on for a full year. It "was too long a time for me at the first trial," he thought. "I wished only to take a priming before I took upon me the whole coat of paint for a soldier." Having joined, the youngster felt like a new person; indeed, he believed for the first time that he was regarded by his neighbors as an adult, and he "felt a little elevated" at his newly acquired stature. When his first tour of duty ended, Martin returned to Milford, having "learned something of a soldier's life, enough . . . to keep me at home." But Martin reenlisted. This time, deaf to the cheers and flirtations of those in Milford, he joined solely for the fiscal bonus he received. Martin served in a distinguished manner for the duration of the conflict, seeing combat on Long Island, Saratoga, and Yorktown, and enduring some of the worst moments of the war, including the winter at Valley Forge.[69]

James Thacher of Massachusetts differed from the two previous enlistees in that he was anxious to join, but was restrained by his friends. They thought him

---

68. Albion and Dodson, *Fithian's Journal*, vol. I, p. 131, vol. II, p. 20.
69. Sheer, *Private Yankee Doodle*, pp. 5–9, 14–15, 24, 45, 57, 61.

"too young to possess a maturity of judgement." Thacher, in fact, acknowledged that he was emotionally immature, and he admitted that he was "unable to resist the impulse of enthusiasm which characterizes the times." His friends tried to dissuade him by arguing that he would be executed as a traitor should he fall into the hands of the British. But Thacher wanted to join. He sought out James Otis, a local gentryman and one of the most vociferous of the provincial firebrands, for "advice," almost certainly knowing what counsel he would receive. Otis immediately "applauded my enterprise," and the puffed-up youngster enlisted as a physician, certain that "Our rulers are the most competent judges" of his fate. Under "their banners I shall venture," he wrote. Thacher also served for the duration, and he lived to witness what he referred to in his diary as the "last act of the drama," the British surrender at Yorktown.[70]

Who did serve in the Revolutionary forces? Probably about 100,000 men, of a total population in excess of 3 million persons, actually bore arms at one time or another between 1775 and 1783. Washington hoped to have 75,000 soldiers in the field for the campaign of 1777, but his peak strength was 18,472, and that was attained on October 1, 1778. The armies included British deserters, slaves, free blacks, indentured servants, even children twelve to thirteen years of age. The bulk of these forces, however, consisted of young adult and teenage white freemen. A recent study of Maryland recruits in 1782 indicated that about 40 percent were foreign-born. The average age of the native-born soldier was twenty-one years, but the median age of the foreign-born was twenty-nine years. Many had only recently completed a period of indentured servitude. Economically, the average soldier among these Marylanders was in the bottom third of his state. Some troops in the Continental army were conscripted, but most enlisted. "As a group," John Shy has written, "they were poorer, more marginal, less well anchored in the society. Perhaps we should not be surprised; it is easy to imagine men like this actually being attracted by the relative affluence, comfort, security, prestige, and even the chance of satisfying human relationships offered by the Continental Army."[71]

The soldiers are "so sick of this way of life, and so home sick," General Greene wrote at the end of the first year of the war, that most were unlikely to reenlist. He was correct. Perhaps as many as 80 percent of those who bore arms in 1775 were home again by early 1776. Thomas Paine railed at the "summer soldier" in 1776, and in 1781, a few months before Cornwallis's defeat at Yorktown, another patriot lamented that if "the Salvation of the Country had depended on their staying Ten or Fifteen days, I don't believe [the soldiers]

70. Thacher, *Military Journals*, pp. 20–21, 28, 302.

71. Howard Peckham, *The War for Independence* (Chicago, 1958), pp. 199–200; Higginbotham, *War for American Independence*, pp. 370, 394; Edward C. Paperfuse and Gregory A Stiverson, "General Smallwood's Recruits: The Peacetime Career of the Revolutionary War Private," *WMQ*, 3d Ser. 30 (January 1973), pp. 120–23, 126: Bolton, *Private Soldier*, p. 236; Shy, *A People Armed*, p. 173.

would have done it.'' Most soldiers, this writer anguished, believed that ''he was a good Soldier that served his time out,'' and nothing beyond. Daniel Morgan, the Virginia laborer who rose to the rank of general, wondered ''what is the reason we cant Have more men in the field—so many men in the country Nearby idle for want of employment.'' John Adams knew precisely the answer to Morgan's query. It hardly was ''credible,'' he thought, ''that men who could get at home better living, more comfortable lodgings, more than double the wages, in safety, not exposed to the sickness of the camp, would bind themselves during the war. . . .''[72]

The experience of war, then, was a blend of monotony and anticipated danger, of brutal discipline and an exacting regimen that circumscribed one's personal liberties, of exhilaration mingled with churning terror, of physical toil, needless tasks assigned by callous taskmasters, deprivation, disease, indecency, guilt, hatred, loneliness, homesickness, inequities, and, above all else for most men, the ardent, ever-present longing for the end of one's tour of duty.

But this was the experience of those in the army. Some—the political leaders who shared responsibility for the war—had the luxury of facing the war well out of harm's way. The warmaker's experience of war, the subject of the next chapter, generally has been neglected by scholars, but it is as important to an understanding of the dynamism of conflict as is an understanding of the experiences of those on the front lines.

72. Nathanael Greene to Samuel Ward, 10 December 1775, in Showman, *Greene Papers,* vol. I, p. 160; Boorstin, *The Americans,* p. 369; Butterfield, *Adams D&A,* vol. III, p. 388.

Chapter Five

The Political Warrior

Oh that I was a Soldier!

When a war of the magnitude of the colonists' struggle for independence erupted, men were drawn to the conflict in diverse ways. Until the spring of 1775, for instance, Nathanael Greene was a relatively obscure Quaker blacksmith and iron master in East Greenwhich, Rhode Island. Largely self-taught—he received some guidance from his hometown physician and from Ezra Stiles, then a local clergyman, later the president of Yale College—and driven by a passion to be accepted and respected by his peers, Greene eventually became a successful businessman and a member of the colonial assembly. As the war approached, he grew increasingly interested in the martial arts, reading all the popular manuals he could lay his hands on. His attempt to secure a commission in a local infantry company was rejected, however, because of a personal "blemish," a limp. He was permitted a place in the company as a private, and he was called to the field the day after the Lexington-Concord engagements. Those skirmishes caused Rhode Island to increase its military strength, and the assembly promoted Private Greene to Brigadier General Greene, commander of the Army of Observation. This choice was made because of Greene's reputation as a martial scholar and his work on legislative defense committees.[1]

John Sullivan, on the other hand, parlayed a highly successful legal career in Durham, New Hampshire, into a major's commission in the colonial militia. Later, the thirty-five-year-old Sullivan was elected to the Continental Congress, and in 1775 he adroitly used his political connections to secure a brigadier general's commission in the Continental army. Henry Knox, a Boston bookseller, developed an early interest in military matters, reading manuals in his spare moments and even joining a British-commanded militia of artillery as a teenager in the 1760s. After a few years, he helped establish a colonial-commanded artillery company, and he was made its second in command. He acquired a

1. Theodore Thayer, *Greene* (New York, 1960), pp. 15–51.

sufficient reputation as a leader to be offered a commission in the British army. He, of course, rejected the offer, and on April 20, 1775, the day following the battles at Lexington and Concord, he fled Boston for Cambridge, where he volunteered his services to Artemas Ward. Three months later, General Washington, impressed with Knox's knowledge and administrative ability, took the young artillerist under his wing.

Anthony Wayne, of Chester County in Pennsylvania, was the grandson of a commander of English dragoons and the son of a captain who fought with the Pennsylvania militia during the French and Indian War. Wayne left no doubt, even as a young boy, that he hoped to be a soldier also. During idle moments, including school recess, his uncle claimed Wayne played at "rehearsals of battles, sieges, etc." But there was no chance for a provincial to advance in the British army, and the colonial militia was mostly an inactive social club; Wayne, therefore, turned to surveying, the "occupation [that] resembled in this country more nearly that of a soldier than any other." When relations soured with Britain, however, Wayne plunged into politics for the first time. A year after his initial election to the Provincial Congress, and nearly nine months after the war with Britain erupted, Wayne was commissioned colonel in the Pennsylvania line.[2]

Joseph Galloway, also of Pennsylvania, had never served in the military before the Revolution, nor had he expressed any interest in such pursuits. He was an affluent lawyer in Philadelphia, perhaps even the wealthiest man in the colony, and after 1756 he served almost continuously in the assembly, usually as its speaker. But when relations with Great Britain soured Galloway used his influence in the legislative body, as well as in the Continental Congress, to abort the plans of the radical colonists. He desperately hoped to avoid a war, believing that a conflict would destroy colonial freedoms and, perhaps, even precipitate French or Spanish rule over what had previously been British territory. When the war commenced, Galloway retired from politics and lived in seclusion at his country estate for nearly two years. Late in 1776, however, Galloway cast his lot with the British, and General Howe employed the Loyalist as quasi-military intelligence official and police commissioner of occupied Philadelphia.[3]

Like the common soldiers examined in the previous chapter, each of these men was caught up in the events of the Revolutionary era. Some, like Galloway, were dragged into activities they had never sought because of the outbreak of a war they had hoped would not occur. For others, however, the war offered an opportunity to further a career or an opening for the commencement of martial activities that previously could only be fantasized.

---

2. Charles P. Whittemore, *A General of the Revolution* (New York, 1961), pp. 4–19; North Callahan, *Henry Knox* (New York, 1958), pp. 17–32; Charles J. Stille, *Major-General Charles Anthony Wayne* . . . (Philadelphia, 1893), pp. 5–15.

3. John E. Ferling, *The Loyalist Mind* (University Park, Pa., 1977), pp. 7–64.

But how did the political elite experience the war? How did those men who played an active role in the furor and agitation against British policies in the 1760s react once hostilities commenced in the 1770s? What pressures did the war impose on the leaders?

A study of this scope obviously cannot scrutinize all the political figures of the era. But two men, John Adams and Dr. Joseph Warren, might be studied. There was probably no such thing as a "typical" politician. But this portion of the study is concerned with the experience of war, and Adams and Warren can provide some insight into how the politician, the nonmilitarist, reacted to war. These two men were selected for scrutiny because they knew one another and had somewhat similar backgrounds, and because each gained prominence in the politically turbulent milieu of Massachusetts. The two, however, experienced the coming of the war in quite different ways, and each reacted in a distinctly different manner when the war occurred. Here, therefore, we will seek to explain not how all men experienced war, but how these two men came to grips with the killing they were partially responsible for unleashing.

John Adams was born into comfortable surroundings in Braintree, Massachusetts, in 1735. The family thrived, principally from a farm and malt brewery that the Adams had operated for nearly a century, but also from the income that John's father brought home as the town's shoemaker. John Adams, Sr., was a figure of authority in the village, a deacon in the church, a selectman, an officer in the local militia. His affluence, his marriage into the prominent Boylston family, and social deference to the wealthy assured him an opportunity of leadership.[4]

Young John's childhood was typical of boys raised in small towns. He excelled in school, of course, grinding his way through the town's primary and Latin schools, and eventually shining under the guidance of a private tutor. Otherwise, he recalled these years as a time of "constant Dissipation among Amusements," years of hunting and fishing and of discovering one's self and the surrounding world. However much young Adams might have frittered away his earlier years, he had developed, by this teenage years, an insatiable lust for success and recognition. He openly acknowledged that he was ambitious to the point of perversity. He was admitted to Harvard College at age fourteen, and he studied with such tenacity, so he claimed, that his inclination for both athletics and women were vitiated.[5]

Deacon Adams expected his son, after four years at Harvard, to embark on a career as a Congregational minister, like most graduates of the day. His son,

4. Page Smith, *Adams,* 2 vols. (New York, 1962), vol. I, pp. 1–10; Peter Shaw, *The Character of John Adams* (Chapel Hill, N.C., 1976), p. 3.

5. Smith, *Adams,* vol. I, pp. 11–14; Shaw, *Character of Adams,* pp. 4–7; L. H. Butterfield et al., eds., *Adams D&A,* 4 vols. (Cambridge, Mass., 1964), vol. I, p. 131, vol. III, pp. 261–62; L. H. Butterfield et al., eds., *The Earliest Diary of John Adams* (Cambridge, Mass., 1966), p. 91.

however, had other ideas. He accepted a post as Latin schoolmaster in Worcester, a town about fifty miles southwest of Boston. Soon he was dissatisfied, and he often lamented his "unhappy Fate" in the confidentiality of his diary. He thought teaching an affliction; he was bored and during classes he found himself day-dreaming that he was a political leader, even a dictator. More than anything else, however, Adams realized that teaching in a remote village would not fulfill his lust for renown. Page Smith, Adams' biographer, noted that the young master was driven to be "a person of consequence in this world." Adams mentioned that he craved to achieve more than "Persons who have had less Advantages than myself." It was not wealth that he sought; indeed, he acknowledged that he would not change places with his wealthiest pupil. What he did harbor was a desire for distinction, and he concluded that unless he altered his career plans he would live in obscurity. He was, he said, "enslaved" by a desire for fame.[6]

If he was to succeed, Adams believed he must work and study to the exclusion of most earthly delights. He tried to begin his daily toil with Latin at sunrise, and to devote his afternoons and evenings to reading English authors. Soon he had no time for other pursuits, and he had no friends. He lashed himself for any frivolous behavior. "A poor Weeks Work!," he scolded in his diary, chiding himself for daydreaming away precious time. "Dreams and slumbers, sloth and negligence," would prove the ruination of his plans, he lamented. He began one academic term in Worcester by resolving not to neglect his time as he had the previous year. "May I blush whenever I suffer one hour to pass unim-proved," he exclaimed. His goal was notoriety. "How shall I gain a Reputation! How shall I Spread an Opinion of myself" as a man of learning, he wondered.[7]

Nothing he saw in Worcester persuaded him to forgo teaching for a career in the church. He concluded that the local parson, presumably typical, was an effeminate drone. Besides, the occupation was too sedentary for his taste. Ad-ditionally, he was shocked to learn of the bigotry and intellectual rigidity that seemed to characterize many clergymen; he was too liberal to ever expect to receive a parish. But he was unhappy teaching, and thought of medicine as an alternative career, although he finally decided that good physicians, like most clergymen, were too poorly paid. Ultimately, Adams decided on a legal career. The decision was made in part because his mentors and comrades at Harvard had suggested that he was an accomplished speaker, and that he would make a better lawyer than clergyman. His decision also probably represented a not unnatural defiance of his father, a seeking after personal independence by dic-tating his own destiny.[8] More than anything, however, legal pursuits might open the door to the recognition he demanded.

6. Butterfield, *Adams D&A*, vol. I, pp. 8, 14, 22, 35, 100; Smith, *Adams*, vol. I, p. 28.

7. Butterfield, *Adams D&A*, vol. I, pp. 22, 26, 35, 39, 41–42, 78.

8. Ibid., vol. I, p. 74, vol. III, pp. 262–63; Adams to Charles Cushing, 1 April 1756, in Charles Francis Adams, ed., *The Works of John Adams, Second President of the United States: With a Life of the Author*, 10 vols. (Boston, 1850–56), vol. I, p. 30; Shaw, *Character of Adams*, pp. 7–9.

Even as Adams began his legal studies he was haunted by feelings of guilt at his career plans. Necessity drove him to this career, he scribbled in his diary, but his inclination really was to preach. He feared that his virtue would be compromised by practicing law, and he resolved at the outset never to commit any injustice as a barrister. Yet, he chose a legal career because he knew it was the principal avenue to the most important political offices, a means to "greater Glory." He also admitted that the French and Indian War caused all of Worcester to be preoccupied by politics, and, he concluded, that probably also influenced his plans. His guilt sprang from the defiance of his father. He knew he was the first Adams "who has *degenerated* from the virtues of the house so far as not to have been an officer in the militia or a deacon."[9]

Adams's anxiety was so pervasive that he fell ill, the first of his bouts with stress-induced ailments that would flare in moments of tribulation. Finding himself quite ill, he visited two physicians; each concluded that his exacting study regimen had weakened him, corrupting his blood. For a year and a half he attempted to cleanse himself by converting to a strict vegetarian diet and abstaining from alcholic beverages. He pursued his cure at his father's house, until, at length, Deacon Adams again converted his son to the use of a little meat and alchohol. Nurtured by his father, Adams, not surprisingly, soon recovered.[10]

His anxiety at undertaking legal studies was triggered additionally by his feelings of inadequacy. He repeatedly bemoaned his ignorance. He feared that he would be treated with contempt, or, worse yet, that he would be ignored because of his shortcomings. He imagined that those about him sneered at his failings, that they mocked his ignorant declamations with sarcastic retorts. He castigated himself for his vain and ostentatious manner, admitting that he behaved in such a manner to disguise his alleged intellectual shortcomings. Moreover, one of his first trips to Boston after moving to provincial Worcester was a disaster. Thrown into the company of sophisticated urbanites, he grew "so disordered" that he could not utter half the declamations he wished to make. And he was awed by the barristers that he encountered. He wondered how to succeed in this calling, and he repeatedly plagued his friends and his teachers with questions concerning the achievement of notoriety. One manner, he concluded, was to converse familiarly with the common people "in their own Style, on the common Tittletattle of the Town"; however, he found such behavior alien and unbecoming. Another route to success was to ingratiate himself with the merchant community and the emerging young gentlemen in Boston, but he decided that would take too long and would require both greater art and patience than he possessed. Or he could curry the favor of other attorneys, but that too

9. Butterfield, *Adams D&A*, vol. I, pp. 43, 73, vol. III, p. 263; Butterfield, *Earliest Diary*, p. 91; Shaw, *Character of Adams*, pp. 12, 18, 35. The italics in the "degenerated from . . ." quotation were added by the author.

10. Butterfield, *Adams D&A*, vol. III, p. 269.

was tedious and, in addition, likely to arouse their jealousy. The best route to fame, he concluded in 1759, was to look for a popular cause and proclaim his feelings. To "cut a flash, strike amazement to catch the Vulgar. . . . A bold Push, a resolute attempt, a determined Enterprize" it would be. In the meantime, he was sufficiently cunning to bluff his way, and he possessed more than an adequate dose of ambition to get him through his legal studies.[11]

Fortunately, for a young man so beset by feelings of guilt and inadequacy in his chosen profession, an alternative existed for John Adams. Just as he graduated from Harvard, the French and Indian War erupted. Adams was nearly nineteen years old and apparently in excellent health. He admitted never having been in higher spirits, and at the time he bragged of his physical prowess. He admitted to an overweening enthusiasm for athletics, another sign of his robust behavior. Moreover, Massachusetts needed troops and actively recruited in Adams's neighborhood. The province, in fact, paid a handsome bonus to enlistees and a good salary to officers. This should have intrigued Adams, who, as a would-be law student, needed money for tutorial fees, room, and board, but who believed he no longer could request assistance from his father since he still had three younger sons to care for. In addition, his father, whom he so hoped to please, not only was an officer in the Braintree trainband, but may have participated in Massachusetts' invasion of Canada in 1745.[12] Finally, military heroics perhaps afforded the fastest route to fame for a young man in the provinces. But Adams elected to teach, not become a soldier.

Adams did want to be a soldier, however. "I longed more ardently to be a Soldier than I ever did to be a Lawyer," he later remarked. Three large contingents of British troops, commanded by Lord Loudon, General Amherst, and George Augustus, Viscount Howe, passed through Worcester during the war, and Adams eagerly turned out to watch them drill. Later, in Boston, he watched the local militia companies perform. Both Adams and his close friend Oxenbridge Thacher watched enviously as the soldiers paraded; Adams did not disguise his covetousness, nor did he disagree with Thacher who remarked that he felt inferior to those soldiers who paraded "with their Guns upon their shoulders." In his despair Adams's health again deteriorated. He was too ill to enlist, he claimed; his service was confined to carrying a military dispatch from Worcester to Newport, Rhode Island, a mission that he regarded as so arduous that it harmed his health.[13] When reminiscing, at the age of eighty-five, Adams claimed he had tried unsuccessfully to attain a captain's commission in 1755. His recollection was probably faulty, since he mentioned nothing about this in his diary or autobiography.

11. Ibid., vol. I, pp. 42, 54, 69, 78, 96, 100; Smith, *Adams*, vol. I, p. 47.

12. Butterfield, *Earliest Diary*, p. 91; Butterfield, *Adams D&A*, vol. III, pp. 257, 263; Shaw, *Character of Adams*, pp. 46–47.

13. Adams to Abigail Adams, 13 February 1776, in L. H. Butterfield et al., eds., *Adams Family Correspondence*, 4 vols. (Cambridge, Mass., 1963 —), vol. I, p. 347; Butterfield, *Adams D&A*, vol. I, p. 110, vol. III, pp. 266–67, 267n.

Adams's feeling of inferiority dogged him during these early years. Following tea and discussions with Worcester's elite, including its trainband leaders, Adams often engaged in verbal self-flagellation for his failure to measure up to their greatness. "I am dull," he told himself. "My Brains seem constantly in . . . great Confusion, and wild disorder. . . . I have never any bright, refulgent Ideas. . . . Drank Tea at the Colonels." When he moved to Boston his companions were in the militia, and Adams found himself alone on the drill days. On one such day he noted that he was isolated and lacked company. When Adams completed his legal training, he returned to Braintree. His reception was less than overwhelming. His practice bumped and struggled, and he found the town's political affairs monopolized by the local militia elite.[14]

Adams even lost his first love to a militia officer. Upon returning to Braintree, he met Hannah Quincy, and shortly thereafter he found himself beguiled by "that face, those eyes, that shape." He found that he was unable to sleep, and when sleep came he dreamt only of Hannah. They dated for six months, from about December 1758, until May or June 1759. She wished to marry, and Adams acknowledged that he was ardent for matrimony. But they did not marry, and Adams claimed the failure of the relationship was partially due to circumstances, partially to his better judgment. He alleged that he was about to propose marriage one evening when Jonathan Sewall and Hannah's sister broke in upon them in the Quincy parlor. Given an opportunity to reconsider, he later claimed, he decided to abandon her in order to further his study and his career.

Adams's explanation does not ring true, however. Instead of marrying Adams, Hannah met Bela Lincoln, a captain in a Boston militia company; Lincoln courted the belle in his uniform. The couple soon were married, and Adams spread the rumor that he had broken off the courtship because "she repelled me." Privately, however, Adams called her marriage a mortal disappointment, and he spoke of how she had dashed his wishes. His remorse was so pervasive that he could not eat for a time, and he even abstained from drinking tea, for it reminded him of the hours he had spent with Hannah. He fell ill again, his first serious illness since the crisis over a career choice.

A full eighteen months after he last courted Hannah, Adams described Lincoln in the most vitriolic terms. Captain Lincoln, he thought, was a brute, a primitive rustic. After attending a party at which the Lincolns were present, Adams claimed the Captain treated Hannah "as no drunken Cobbler, or Clothier would have done"; the Captain was an inelegant boor, an ostentatious and ill-bred swine, a man of vulgar tastes who treated his wife with disdain. Adams believed Hannah was mortified by her husband, and Adams also conjectured that she realized her error in rejecting her first suitor.[15] Adams's subsequent statements belie his

14. Butterfield, *Adams D&A*, vol. I, pp. 21–22, 131; Smith, *Adams*, vol. I, p. 43.
15. Smith, *Adams*, vol. I, pp. 49–50; Butterfield, *Adams D&A*, vol. I, pp. 87–88, 118–19, 176–77.

claims that he rejected Hannah, and indicate strongly that she refused the young lawyer for the Harvard-educated militiaman.

In May 1761, Deacon Adams succumbed to an epidemic of influenza that ravaged Braintree. John Adams's inheritance at last made him a man of status in his hometown. He plotted against those who controlled local politics, and schemed to enhance his own power by finding important local posts for his brothers.[16] Meanwhile, his legal practice grew more lucrative. And in October 1764, Adams married Abigail Smith of Weymouth. Like his earlier flame, Hannah, Abigail was a descendant of the Quincy's on the maternal side.

Shortly after his marriage, news arrived in the colonies of the Stamp Act. For the next half dozen years, relations deteriorated between the provinces and the parent state, but during these crises Adams played a minor, at times almost an indifferent, role. Although he reproved the Stamp Act, Adams's rage was due as much to the personal threat posed by the act as to any bitterness wrought by ideological considerations. After many years of struggle without friends and companions he had "just become known, and gained a small degree of Reputation, when this execrable Project was set on foot for my Ruin." He played a minor role in the subsequent provincial protest movement, drafting a moderately worded anti-Stamp Act resolution (he later admitted that the resolve "conceded too much to the . . . Enemy"), which was adopted at the Braintree town meeting. His actions did not enhance his reputation to any significant degree. While the zealous opponents of the Stamp duties had been "caressed" by their fellow citizens, Adams querulously lamented that he was neglected by the citizenry of Braintree. There was no adulation, and he was not elected to the general court. Feelings of guilt at his conduct crowded in upon him. He feared that his actions merely indicated a scheming for money and power. He wondered whether he had acted on behalf of his family or his country. Adams quickly moved from Braintree to Boston.[17]

The family lived in Boston for four years, but he could not entirely escape the growing crisis. When news of the Townshend Duties reached Massachusetts, Adams played a role identical to that which he had undertaken in the previous crisis. He quietly drafted resolutions. He refused the requests of Joseph Warren and other firebrands to address public rallies, asserting "That way madness lies." He also rejected a lucrative government offer of an admiralty court position. But the so-called Boston Massacre of March 5, 1770, momentarily drew Adams into the vortex of the imperial crisis. On the evening of the shooting, Adams was meeting with a small club of young barristers when the pealing of alarm bells caught their attention. All rushed for the center of town expecting

16. Smith, *Adams,* vol. I, pp. 59–71.

17. Shaw, *Character of Adams,* pp. 52–53; Butterfield, *Adams D&A,* vol. I, p. 337, vol. III, pp. 282–83.

to assist in dousing a fire. Along the way, however, they were alerted that British soldiers had fired into a crowd of Bostonians, killing several of the inhabitants. Adams shortly was overcome with concern for his wife, for she was pregnant and he feared the news of the shooting might have a detrimental effect on her.[18] He hurried home, away from the potential danger.

In the weeks that followed, Adams agreed to defend the British soldiers charged with the killings. Other Boston attorneys, or at least those who were firmly committed to the popular cause, refused to take the case. Adams claimed he was moved to act out of the principle that all men were entitled to a fair trial; moreover, he believed a judicial mockery would disgrace Massachusetts and corrupt the morality of his fellow citizens. But Adams, who had revered soldiers and longed to wear a uniform, had never joined Warren, James Otis, Samuel Adams, and the other radicals in their baiting of the British troops. He, in fact, denounced those "busy Characters" who had labored so diligently to distress the soldiers and to provoke difficulties with the troops. His defense of these luckless soldiers was entirely in keeping with the attitudes he had displayed for so long toward those in the military. Of course, too, defending the soldiers tallied exactly with one of the prescribed routes to fame he had considered a few years earlier. This was "a Cause to speak to," a perfect opportunity "to cut a flash." Despite his ideals, Adams believed he was damaged by the case. Some of the Boston radicals, including Samuel Adams, took pot shots at him in the press. He brooded over the charges that were whispered against him, claiming that he not only lost half his legal business but that his hard earned political popularity had been damaged severely. Adams almost certainly exaggerated the damage, as Peter Shaw has observed, for he was elected for the first time to the Massachusetts Assembly while the case was being adjudicated.[19]

Whatever the feelings of his contemporaries, Adams believed the fame he had pursued for so long had been destroyed on the shoals of his defense of the British soldiers. Characteristically, he suffered another stress-induced illness. The toil of the trial exhausted him, provoking chest pains and a shortness of breath; he was so convinced that his life was in jeopardy that he abandoned some of his legal business and all public endeavors. He fled Boston for "still, calm, happy" Braintree. Even in his hometown, however, he imagined that he was the object of insult and ridicule. Hence, when Britain repealed the Townshend Duties and a three-year lull in the imperial crisis followed, Adams soon found that his health quickly improved. He returned to Boston, where he lived until a few weeks before the outbreak of the war three years later.[20]

Back in Boston, Adams wanted nothing to do with the radicals who periodically attempted to fan the flame of discontent toward Britain. He rejected their

18. Butterfield, *Adams D&A*, vol. III, pp. 287–88, 291–92.
19. Ibid., vol. III, pp. 292–94; Shaw, *Character of Adams*, p. 58.
20. Butterfield, *Adams D&A*, vol. II, pp. 7, 11, vol. III, pp. 296–97.

entreaties to deliver a memorial address commemorating the Boston Massacre, claiming again that his feeble health precluded such an exercise. Moreover, the thirty-seven-year-old Adams alleged, he was too old to make speeches; he told his friends that he hoped to avoid even thinking about public affairs. Principally, Adams played the Sybarite during these years. His years of long struggle and unremitting study, not to mention his inheritance, had left the Adams family with a most comfortable existence. He was flattered to learn how many of his college chums lived less opulently than his family. He boasted that few earned the money or possessed the good that he had acquired. Some of the radicals chided Adams for his behavior, and Adams lamented that two-thirds of the inhabitants of Boston probably shared the feelings of the agitators. James Otis, for instance, accused Adams of having no interest in anything save getting enough to live in easy circumstances. And Otis told Adams that the radicals would not count on him if the smoldering crisis with Britain once again flared. "Youl never learn military Exercises," he tongue-lashed the younger barrister. "That You have an Head for it needs no Commentary, but [you have] not an Heart." Adams, hurt, attributed this "Rant" to envy and jealousy, but privately he admitted his hopes for continuing his lucrative law practice in Boston hinged upon "Peace of Mind" and the avoidance of politics.[21]

On New Year's Day, 1773, Adams acknowledged that he had never been happier. The crisis with England seemed such a thing of the past that the contented John Adams decided to seek public office once again, and in May he was elected to the assembly. Four months later news of the Tea Act shattered the colonists' solitude, prompting the final crisis that ultimately would result in hostilities with Great Britain. During the next few hectic months, a time of considerable agitation and, of course, of the Boston Tea Party, Adams maintained a low profile, his time consumed more by family business (he purchased his father's homestead, a forty-eight-acre estate, and plunged into the planning of how best to improve the tract) than by the imperial controversy. During the period of fundamental crisis for his colony, Adams can best be described, to borrow Peter Shaw's terminology, as a "fellow traveler," philosophically disturbed by Britain's policies, but unwilling to play an activist role in opposing these distasteful measures.[22]

As late as April 1774, Adams refused to believe the imperial squabble would degenerate to the point of open warfare. He doubted that there was sufficient resolve on either side to bring the thorny imperial questions to a complete decision, and he suspected the quarrel would simmer for years with each side occasionally compromising a bit. But a few weeks later news of the Coercive Acts reached America. Adams now believed war was certain. He had reached another crisis point in his life, and, characteristically, he fell ill. Once again he considered scuttling his political ambitions, noting that "My own Infirmities . . . and the public News coming alltogether have put my Utmost

21. Ibid., vol. II, pp. 65–67, 73–74; Smith, *Adams*, vol. I, p. 136.
22. Butterfield, *Adams D&A*, vol. II, p. 76; Shaw, *Character of Adams*, p. 75.

Philosophy to the Tryal.'' As the crisis deepened during the summer, he lamented that he had never ''suffered such Torments in my Mind;'' he grew weak and lethargic. He sent the family back to Braintree, but this time Adams not only continued to support the popular cause, he emerged by the fall of 1774 as one of the faction's leaders. The popular party immediately seized upon Adams's capabilities and reputation for moderation, elevating him to the Continental Congress.[23]

Peter Shaw has suggested that the key to Adams's commitment to the rebel cause was his subconscious displacement of guilt. Adams felt pangs of guilt at his defiance of legitimate authority, but he succeeded in convincing himself that it was the imperial authorities who had broken with the old values, which he defended. In short, Adams ''legitimized his rebellion by upholding the principles of those he rejected.''[24]

Adams also knew by mid-1774 that war with Britain was certain, and he convinced himself of the efficacy of hostilities. As a delegate to the First Continental Congress he censured those who ''shudder at the prospect of blood.'' Three days after the fighting at Lexington and Concord, Adams, curiously, could not resist riding the same route over which the redcoats had marched. Despite his earlier bravado, the still smoldering scenes of war sent Adams reeling to his bed with the alarming symptoms of still another illness. A few days later, Adams's head and spirits felt better. But as Britain brought in reinforcements and the first full-scale bloodletting loomed, Adams relapsed. He described his condition as ''quite infirm.''[25]

Despite these occasional setbacks, Adams was little troubled by the likely outcome of the war. From the outset he harbored no doubt of the colonists' ability to defend the country and win the war. America had sufficient manpower and virtue to contest the British. Moreover, he was certain America would gain experience with each day of fighting. He thought the colonists could expect deep divisions, perhaps even a civil war, to occur in the parent state, and he believed the French would assist the colonists in humbling Great Britain. Only when Britain invaded New York in 1776 did Adams doubt the certainty of victory, and, typically, he once again fell ill. He was ''not a little concerned about my Health,'' he noted at this point, and he added that he had every reason to fear that he risked irreparable physical damage.[26]

23. Smith, *Adams*, vol. I, pp. 152–53; Adams to Abigail Adams, 12 May 1774, in Butterfield, *Adams FC*, vol. I, p. 107; Adams to Abigail Adams, 1 July 1774, ibid., vol. I, p. 119.

24. Shaw, *Character of Adams*, pp. 73–74.

25. Adams to William Tudor, 29 September 1774, in Adams, *Works*, vol. IX, p. 346; Adams to Joseph Palmer, 26 September 1774, in Burnett, *Letters of Members of Congress*, vol. I, p. 48; Adams to Abigail Adams, 7 May 1775, in Adams, *Familiar Letters*, pp. 53–54; Adams to Abigail Adams, 29 May 1775, in Butterfield, *Adams FC*, vol. I, p. 207; Adams to Abigail Adams, 10 June 1775, ibid., vol. I, p. 213.

26. Butterfield, *Adams D&A*, vol. III, p. 328, vol. II, pp. 3, 76; Adams to Abigail Adams, 11 February 1776, in Butterfield, *Adams FC*, vol. I, p. 346; Adams to Abigail Adams, 11 July 1776, ibid., vol. II, p. 44.

Adams never displayed any moral reservations about the killing that had been unleashed by the conflict. Just as he succeeded in allaying his guilt feelings concerning his rebellious conduct, he convinced himself that others were to blame for the bloodshed. He believed, in part, that the war arose out of the depths of the colonial experience, an inevitable occurrence that fell by coincidence to his generation to conduct. The English government and the colonies had been on a collision course from the beginning of Anglo-American experience, he thought. The two had often clashed over important issues. The collision simply occurred in 1775. The war, in his estimation, was also divinely inspired. Adams and his colleagues merely carried out God's will. He never thought of the war as divine punishment, however. Indeed, it was to have a cathartic effect, to prepare America for the tasks God had appointed them. He saw the conflict in geopolitical terms, as well. The Americans deserved Canada and Florida, and friendly relations with Britain were doomed so long as these dominions lay beyond the new country's sphere of influence.[27] This war would, therefore, prevent future wars.

He blamed the ministry for the war, too. Those rulers had precipitated the conflict because of their jealousy of America's growing power. Adams believed the morality of resisting what he defined as tyranny counterbalanced any reservation at killing. He thought warfare was justified if it saved even one victim of despotism. This war was of timeless consequence, for the lives and liberties of unborn millions hung in the balance. He also saw the conflict as a *"people's war,"* a bloodletting that sprang from the dissatisfaction of average citizens. Adams was simply the instrument by which the war was guided, and in this sense he had no feelings of culpability for the killing that had been unleashed. Finally, he convinced himself that the British officers were largely to blame for the agonies of the war. He reproached General Howe as callous and depraved, and he alleged that the General had committed offenses against both men and God. He labeled American deaths as murders, and he left no doubt who the murderers were.[28]

One reason, perhaps, that Adams expressed so little concern for the moral implications of his actions is that he took precautions to avoid the scene of fighting. He never witnessed a battle, although some major encounters, such as the battles of Brandywine and Germantown, occurred near his residence. Only on two occasions did he even visit the wounded. When he retraced the route of the British army three days after the incidents at Lexington and Concord,

27. Butterfield, *Adams D&A,* vol. II, p. 276; John R. Howe, *The Changing Political Thought of John Adams* (Princeton, N. J., 1966), pp. 44–48; Adams to Abigail Adams, 11 February 1776, in Butterfield, *Adams FC,* vol. I, p. 346; Smith, *Adams,* vol. I, p. 395.

28. Smith, *Adams,* vol. I, pp. 261, 485; Adams to Abigail Adams, 20 August 1777, in Butterfield, *Adams FC,* vol. II, p. 321; Adams to Abigail Adams, 19 Aug. 1777, *ibid.,* vol. II, p. 319; Adams to Abigail Adams, 13 April 1777, *ibid.,* vol. II, p. 207; Adams to Abigail Adams, 27 April 1777, *ibid.,* vol. II, p. 255.

he undoubtedly spoke with injured civilians and militiamen, and he may even have stumbled upon the funerals of some of the victims of that tumultuous day. By the end of the day he was physically ill. Two years later, he visited a military hospital and cemetery in Philadelphia. He previously had resisted the temptation to visit these facilities, knowing full-well the disturbing scenes of horror he would find. After all, his brother, who had enlisted in 1775, died that same year of a contagious disease in an army camp. The night after his visit to the Philadelphia hospital, Adams sank into a pensive mood. He wrote his wife that he had never been so moved. The scene was "enough to make the Heart of stone to melt away." It also was sufficient to deter Adams from inspecting such places in the future, although the visit had the additional effect of driving Adams, like a "galley slave bent on his oar," according to one scholar, to correct the abuses that had led to the misery and death he had witnessed.[29]

Disease, Adams learned that day, "has destroyed Ten Men for Us, where the Sword of the Enemy has killed one." The graves he saw were filled with men who had perished of various camp diseases, a largely preventable calamity that had resulted from the lack of tents, clothing, soap, food, and medicine. But, he claimed, the shortages of these commodities could not account for all the army's ills. The unspeakable misery and the languishing deaths he had seen were attributable to those officers and jobbers who directed and serviced the army. For Adams, this explanation afforded the final means of extricating himself from the horrors that accompanied the fighting of the war.[30]

"Nothing in this contest has ever given me so much pain as the sufferings of the soldiers in sickness," he asserted. The problem stemmed in part from inadequate supplies. The men needed wholesome provisions, adequate fuel, and, of course, they had to be paid. But he laid much of the blame at the feet of the officer corps. He agreed with his friend Robert Treat Paine that the army too often was run like a "Slop Shop." The illnesses that had decimated the troops, he thought, stemmed from a lack of discipline. The notion of cleanliness had to be drilled into the troops. In addition, rigorous physical training would harden their bodies and render the troops less susceptible to disease. But the officers either shirked their duties, or they kept the soldiers constantly at work and always dirty so that, without wives to care for them, the men gradually lost their health.[31]

This was not the first time Adams would turn his wrath on the officers. While he generally lauded Washington and most other high commanders, he was

29. Butterfield, *Adams D&A*, vol. III, p. 255; Adams to Abigail Adams, 13 April 1777, Butterfield, *Adams FC*, vol. II, p. 209; Gilbert Chinard, *Honest John Adams* (Boston, 1933), pp. 109–10.

30. Adams to Abigail Adams, 13 April 1777, in Butterfield, *Adams FC*, vol. II, p. 209.

31. Adams to Abigail Adams, 21 March 1777, in Adams, *Works*, vol. IX, p. 458; Butterfield, *Adams D&A*, vol. I, p. 179; Adams to Col. Daniel Hitchcock, 10 October 1776, ibid., vol. III, pp. 443–44.

frequently contemptuous of lesser figures. As a group, he moaned, the officer corps did not shine; privately, he confessed his contempt for many officers. There was a dearth of genius and spirit among them, he charged. He groped to find good officers, but he realized that their appointments were too political to assure a high caliber of leaders. Many officers were incompetent and acted out of fear, while others were moved to act by anger; moreover, rash behavior by those pursuing glory had repeatedly led to failure.[32] Some simply failed because of inadequate diligence and patience. Many leaders were not zealous because they hoped for a prolonged conflict, and they openly proposed the toast: "A long and moderate war."[33]

Adams exhibited little patience for those who failed in battle, but for those who could not function in a moment of crisis, or for officers who acted in a cowardly manner, he prescribed the most extreme penalties. He admitted that he could more easily witness the destruction of American cities than countenance ignominy. On several occasions he proposed the execution of cowardly officers, contending that they deserved the most infamous death. To be surprised by the enemy, on the other hand, was such a capital crime that it caused him to reflect on how generals in antiquity had been nailed to gibbets for such ineptitude.[34] He insisted that he would not intervene to save even his own brother if he was condemned for such inexcusable conduct. Adams toyed with the prospect of an even more savage reprisal against common soldiers when their companies broke and fled under fire. He thought he might almost consent to the execution of every tenth soldier from such a disgraceful outfit. In the Roman Army, he reflected, such a terroristic policy restrained dismayed soldiers.[35]

Adams was severely critical of the strategy of the Continental army, but his judgments were so contradictory they revealed his lack of military expertise. At times he suggested the only sensible ploy was that of "ambuscade, and ambush," and he outlined a strategem that amounted to the implementation of guerrilla warfare. He thought it wise not to hazard a decisive battle, but to harass the enemy with frequent assaults. Yet at other times he railed at General Washington for failing to fight, calling his tactics injudicious. Once he claimed he would have stood firm and defended a post even if it had cost half his army.[36] Adams

32. Adams to Gen. Samuel Parsons, 19 August 1776, in Butterfield, *Adams D&A*, vol. III, p. 448; ibid., vol. III, p. 439; Adams to Abigail Adams, 3 June 1776, in Butterfield, *Adams FC*, vol. II, p. 6.

33. Adams to Abigail Adams, 2 September 1777, in Butterfield, *Adams FC*, vol. II, p. 336; Butterfield, *Adams D&A*, vol. I, p. 33; Adams to Benj. Rush, 8 February 1778, in Adams, *Works*, vol. IX, p. 473.

34. Adams to William Tudor, 26 September 1776, in Butterfield, *Adams D&A*, vol. III, p. 438; Adams to Col. D. Hitchcock, 10 October 1776, *ibid.*, vol. III, p. 444; Adams to Gen. S. Parsons, 2 October 1776, *ibid.*; Adams to John Sullivan, 23 January 1776, in Adams, *Works*, vol. IX, p. 407.

35. Adams to Henry Knox, 29 September 1776, in Butterfield, *Adams D&A*, vol. III, p. 441.

36. Adams to William Tudor, 29 August 1776, in Adams, *Works*, vol. IX, p. 438; Adams to Tudor, 26 September 1776, in Butterfield, *Adams D&A*, vol. III, p. 440.

also urged the army's leadership to engage in retaliatory measures against the British. Strangely, he distinguished between revenge—which, he said, Jesus had proclaimed to be immoral, lest in warfare men became devils''—and "retaliation.'' The colonies, he thought, must retaliate at times in order to gain the respect of the enemy. It might even be necessary, he admitted, to perpetrate "Cruelties which would disgrace Savages,'' because to shrink from such horrors "would be cruelty to ourselves, our Officers and Men.''[37]

This intermittent carping at the army's leadership in all likelihood stemmed from Adams's troubled feelings over his own role in the war. Congressman Adams was plagued by guilt over his failure to serve in a military capacity in a war that he helped create. Indeed, Adams not only did not serve in a military unit, he rejected the implorings of his colleagues in Congress to undertake a nonmilitary, though hardly a risk-free, mission to Canada early in 1776. Congress believed the American armies under Montgomery and Arnold might succeed if only the Canadian population could be wooed from its loyalty to Britain. But Adams refused to accompany the other emissaries on the grounds that his command of French was inadequate, a curious excuse in light of his willingness to undertake the diplomatic mission to France itself the following year, and of his tutoring his son, John Quincy, in French in preparation for that trip.[38]

Adams's old feelings of awe toward the military frequently appeared during the war. For instance, he often spoke of the beauty of the military regimen. He repeatedly indicated his longing to bear arms. He fervently wished he could have been lying in ambush between Concord and Boston that fateful day in April 1775, to drill some unsuspecting redcoat. Once the war had commenced he announced that everyone must become a soldier. "I hope there is not a gentleman in the Massachusetts Bay, not even in the town of Boston, who thinks himself too good to take his flintlock and his spade,'' he added. "Such imminent dangers level all distinctions.'' He thought of quitting Congress and accepting a commission as a colonel.[39] He admitted often experiencing a desire to be in dangerous situations. He too longed to march into combat, and he hoped something would occur when it "will be proper for me'' to don a uniform. When General Howe's army approached Philadelphia in August 1777, Adams postured his indignity that Congress would flee to the hinterland rather than stay to fight.

---

37. Butterfield, *Adams D&A*, vol. II, p. 265; Adams to Col. Hitchcock, 10 October 1776, *ibid.*, vol. III, pp. 443–44; Adams to Abigail Adams, 14 March 1777, in Butterfield, *Adams FC*, vol. II, p. 175; Adams to Abigail Adams, 2 June 1777, *ibid.*, vol. II, p. 253.

38. Adams to Abigail Adams, 18 February 1776, in Butterfield, *Adams FC*, vol. I, p. 349; Butterfield, *Adams D&A*, vol. II, pp. 272–73. Adams acknowledged, however, that his "Ignorance of the Language was very inconvenient and humiliating to me'' while on the diplomatic mission to France in 1778 and thereafter. See, Butterfield, *Adams D&A*, vol. IV, p. 49.

39. Adams to Abigail Adams, 24 August 1777, in Butterfield, ed., *Adams FC*, vol. II, p. 327; Smith, *Adams*, vol. I, pp. 196–97; Adams to Abigail Adams, 7 May 1775, in Adams, *Familiar Letters*, pp. 53–54; Adams to Samuel Cooper, 30 May 1776, in Adams, *Works*, vol. IX, p. 382; Adams to Gen. Parsons, 19 August 1776, in Butterfield, *Adams D&A*, vol. III, p. 448.

"We are too brittle ware," he remarked sarcastically, and he noted that the Roman senators had refused to flee from the invaders. For his part, Adams claimed to harbor "a strong Inclination to meet them [the British] in the Field."[40]

Adams, moreover, was convinced that he could become an effective officer quite easily. He repeatedly stated that only courage and reading were necessary to become an effective officer. In addition, he believed that of all the high American officers only General Charles Lee, a former officer in the British army, was better read in the military manuals than himself. "Oh that I was a Soldier! — I will be. — I am reading military Books. — Ever Body must and will, and shall be a soldier," he proclaimed rather forlornly a month after the war commenced.[41]

Beneath the veneer, however, Adams knew he would never be a soldier. Perhaps in private he even acknowledged that James Otis had been correct years ealier when he admonished the "fellow traveling" Adams that he had no heart for the military life. At any rate Adams conjured up a variety of excuses for never accepting the rank of colonel that he dreamed of, and which he could have had for the asking. If he had come from one of the southern or middle states, he once remarked, he probably would have been an officer, but there was such an abundance of qualified leaders in New England that his services were not required. He usually claimed he was too old, though he was younger than military activists such as Philip Schuyler, Alexander McDougall, Francis Marion, Horatio Gates, and George Washington, to name just a few. He was too old and too worn from his early studies, he once complained, to seriously consider becoming a soldier. A "shattered Constitution," prevented his assuming a military Command," he wrote. Were it not for this "insuperable Difficulty" he certainly would have joined. Because of his infirmities he thought he could best serve America as a Congressman. Not everyone could be a soldier, he told a correspondent. Besides, the country would need some experienced statesmen following the war. Once he even proposed legislation which made dual service in the armed forces and the Congress illegal.[42] But only once did Adams disclaim any interest in serving in a military capacity. In the early, dark days of 1777, on the eve of his visit to a military hospital, he confided to his wife that the military life held "no Charm for me." He added that he had

40. Adams to Abigail Adams, 13 February 1776, in Butterfield, *Adams FC*, vol. I, p. 347; Adams to Abigail Adams, 19 August 1777, ibid., vol. II, p. 319.

41. Smith, *Adams*, vol. I, p. 305; Adams to Henry Knox, 29 September 1776, in Butterfield, *Adams D&A*, vol. III, p. 442; Adams to Abigail Adams, 29 May 1775, in Butterfield, *Adams FC*, vol. I, p. 207

42. Adams to Abigail Adams, 13 February 1776, in Butterfield, *Adams FC*, vol. I, p. 347; Adams to Gen. Parsons, 19 August 1776, in Butterfield, *Adams D&A*, vol. III, p. 448; Adams to Jonathan Mason, 18 July 1776, in Adams, *Works*, vol. IX, p. 423; Adams to Samuel Chase, 14 June 1776, ibid., vol. IX, p. 397.

"nothing of Caesar's Greatness in my Soul," at last confirming Otis' allegation.[43]

Like a man seeking to purge himself of guilt for his nonmilitary role, Adams plunged into his congressional chores with an almost abnormal vigor for this man of normally toilsome deportment. He quickly became, in the words of his biographer Page Smith, a "kind of *de facto* Secretary of War." Nothing seemed beyond his grasp. "Recruitment, discipline, supply, even tactics and strategy—it sometimes seemed that Adams was trying to fight the whole war singlehanded." In the Second Continental Congress, Adams served on ninety committees, acting, as Peter Shaw indicated, "virtually as a war department," and "he handled a daily, crushing burden of administrative details."[44]

Adams soon grew to believe that the suffering he endured as a statesman was every bit as severe as that to which the common soldier was subjected. "The Fatigues of War are much less destructive to Health than the painfull, laborious Attention to Debates and to Writing" imposed upon the legislator, he exclaimed; such an extraordinary statement that one can only presume Adams either had no knowledge whatsoever of the life of the common soldier or that he was unable to perceive his own role with even a modicum of realism. He found his work a drudgery, and he complained of the solitude and the melancholy life forced upon him by the war. "I am a lonely, forlorn, Creature" in the halls of Congress, he wailed to Abigail; "there is not one Creature here, that I seem to have any kind of Relation to." He thought himself a man of peace, yet he was forced daily to attend to the ghastly details of war. The atrocities of the conflict "harrow me beyond Description," he moaned.[45]

Adams emphasized the dangers and hardships forced on him by the war. Even though he never acknowledged to those close to him that he believed Britain would crush the rebellion—indeed, he steadfastly maintained that the rebels could not be suppressed—he was a portrait of pathos to others. He often described the miseries of politicians, and he claimed to take comfort in the knowledge that renowned statesmen in antiquity had died on the scaffold or while languishing in jail. The war wounded Adams in the pocketbook, too, and he frequently inveighed against the lawyers who remained at home and grew rich. He too longed to enter private practice, but while "there are many dangerous things to be done" he could not contemplate resignation. He endured the deprivation, he said, because of his ideals, and, he added, he was compelled to tend to politics and war so that his sons might have the liberty to study at college. He

43. Adams to Abigail Adams, 16 March 1777, in Butterfield, *Adams FC,* vol. II, p. 176.

44. Smith, *Adams,* vol. I, pp. 289, 293; Shaw, *Character of Adams,* p. 101.

45. Adams to Abigail Adams, 11 July 1776, in Butterfield, *Adams FC,* vol. II, p. 44; Adams to Abigail Adams, 22 May 1776, ibid., vol. I, pp. 412–13; Adams to Abigail Adams, 17 February 1777, ibid., vol. II, p. 163.

characterized his activities as his duty. It was necessary that his "Interests are sacrificed as they have been" to ensure the "Happiness of others."[46]

Like a soldier at the front, Adams longed for the serenity of his home in Braintree. He was burdened by public business, he complained, when all he wished was the company of his family. He yearned for rural pleasures; he deplored the smoke and noise of the city in which he toiled. He endured political intrigue and the misery of warfare when he desired only "private Peace." He ached at the abandonment of his family. "What Pleasures has not this vile War deprived me of?" he asked. One of the pleasures forfeited to the conduct of the war, he concluded, was his health. "I have hazarded all very often," he claimed. His work load, he believed, was so great as to destroy younger men. But, he added, adopting a military metaphor, "I cannot excuse myself from these duties, and I must march forward until it comes my turn to fall."[47]

Adams knew there were those who envied the station he had attained, and he resented their feelings. Named to the American negotiating team in Paris—and, thus, having achieved the recognition and fame for which he had toiled unremittingly—he emphasized the dangers and rigors of his mission. He claimed the toil of negotiation tore at his strength and caused him greater suffering than any of his other wartime duties. He yearned to escape the trenches in which he imagined himself, and, as he put it in a characteristic phrase, "retreat like Cincinnatus, to my plough."[48]

Adams believed he endured great risk as a statesman during the War for Independence, and his assumptions were not without foundation. Some danger was attendant to the decision to rebel against the lawful government. Moreover, he subjected himself to several arduous journeys, though until 1778 his political obligations necessitated less travel than he would have undertaken as a practicing lawyer in rustic Massachusetts. His greatest wartime hazards were the Atlantic crossings and an extensive overland trek from Spain to France. He first sailed in February 1778, and returned about fifteen months later; he embarked for France again in November 1779, and did not return until long after the war concluded. Peril stalked every ocean voyager. The vessel could capsize in rough seas; the passengers were susceptible, because of the weakness of prolonged

46. Adams to James Warren, 25 June 1774, in Adams, *Works,* vol. IX, p. 339; Adams to Warren, 15 March 1775, ibid., vol. IX, p. 355; Butterfield, *Adams D&A,* vol. III, p. 342; Adams to Abigail Adams, 12 May 1780, in Butterfield, *Adams FC,* vol. III, p. 342; Adams to Abigail Adams, 28 April 1776, ibid., vol. I, p. 399.

47. Adams to Abigail Adams, 28 April 1776, in Butterfield, *Adams FC,* vol. I, p. 399; Adams to Abigail Adams, 16 July 1776, ibid., vol. II, p. 50; Adams to Abigail Adams, 16 March 1777, ibid., vol. II, p. 176; Adams to Abigail Adams, 23 September 1778, ibid., vol. III, p. 91; Adams to Benjamin Highborn, 29 May 1776, in Adams, *Works,* vol. IX, p. 380.

48. Adams to James Warren, 16 March 1780, in *Warren-Adams Letters: being chiefly a correspondence among John Adams, Samuel Adams, and James Warren,* MHS, *Coll.,* 2 vols. (Boston, 1925), vol. II, pp. 129–30.

seasickness, to more serious ailments; there was no escape if an epidemic struck the craft; pirates were a constant menace; and, in a presteam power era, a ship adrift for days could be depleted of precious beverages and foodstuffs. Adams's problems were compounded by the fact that he sailed in the wartime. If his ship was captured by a British vessel, Adams could look forward to a prolonged incarceration, a fate that befell Henry Laurens, United States minister to Holland, who consequently spent fifteen months in British jails. If imprisoned, and if America lost the war, Adams, as a traitor, could anticipate the most horrid manner of execution. Adams faced this personal danger twice during his initial crossing. About a week out, three British frigates appeared and gave chase. Eventually one closed in on the *Boston*, Adams's ship, and caused the American envoy a few considerably unpleasant hours. Adams exhorted the crew to fight to the death, and, he freely acknowledged, in doing so his motives "were more urgent than theirs," for he did not wish to be captured. But apparently he did not offer to stand and fight for his life alongside the crew. He scurried to his cabin and watched the action through a porthole. In the end the fight was aborted when a fortuitous storm arose and tossed the vessels far from one another.

Three weeks later Adams experienced another close call. This time the *Boston* overtook a smaller British ship bound with cargo for New York. Seeking a prize, and not anticipating a struggle, the *Boston* drew aside its quarry. Since there appeared to be no danger, Adams remained on deck to enjoy the proceedings. Without warning, the British vessel fired broadside into the *Boston*, and before Adams realized what had occurred explosives were flying over his head. He does not record his next move, although no additional shots were fired and the *Boston* soon claimed its cache. Adams's second Atlantic crossing was relatively uneventful, though it too was arduous and not without risk. The voyage ended in Spain, from whence he crossed the mountains into France. Conveyed by mule and carriage, Adams completed the exhausting journey of one thousand miles in six weeks.[49]

Safe at last in Paris, Adams commenced his diplomatic activities, only to encounter persistent roadblocks and, additionally, to learn of moves afoot in Philadelphia to recall him. He fell ill once again. For nearly a week the physicians despaired for his life. He survived the illness, likely still another stress-induced ailment given the anxieties of his new assignment and his awareness of the machinations at home. And he survived the war, certain though he was that the wartime strain had destroyed his health. He almost always was physically safe during these years of conflict. But for Adams the war was a mental hell.[50]

49. Butterfield, *Adams D&A*, vol. IV, pp. 12, 24, 202–38.

50. Adams to James Warren, 16 March 1780, in *Warren-Adams Letters*, vol. II, p. 130; Adams to Abigail Adams, 9 October 1781, in Butterfield, *Adams FC*, vol. IV, p. 224; Adams to Abigail Adams, 24 August 1777, ibid., vol. II, p. 327; Adams to Abigail Adams, 4 November 1775, ibid., vol. I, p. 320.

John Adams had moved slowly from fellow traveler to radical to revolutionary. He helped precipitate the conflict and he longed to bear arms alongside the men he sent to the front, but he could not overcome the deep inner reservations that inevitably surfaced to restrain his ardor. Haunted by his failure to fight, Adams assumed the congressional direction of the war, laboring exactingly over the thousands of petty details which were involved in a struggle of this magnitude. He even managed to convince himself that he was as much a soldier as those on the picket; in addition, Adams sincerely believed that his service was as difficult as and perhaps fraught with even greater danger to one's health than were the activities of the soldier who slogged through battles. The mental anguish, the product of his political choices and of his realization of personal limitations, was the price Adams paid to be a "warrior."

Dr. Joseph Warren, like his friend John Adams, was haunted by the anxieties of rebellion and killing, but his inner turmoil was manifested in a totally different wartime behavior. Like Adams, Warren reached adulthood in Massachusetts as that colony became the firestorm of the imperial conflict. But, whereas Adams at first remained aloof and indecisive, Warren quickly immersed himself in the machinations of Boston's radicals, and he assumed far more radical positions than his lawyer friend. When war came—an occurrence that disturbed Warren far less than it grieved Adams—Warren knew from the outset that he would be, that he had to be, an active participant in the bloodletting.

Joseph Warren was born in Roxbury, Massachusetts, in 1741, five and a half years following John Adams's birth in nearby Braintree. The Warren family had been in the colonies for more than a century, and Warren's ancestors included sailors, craftsmen, and, beginning with his grandfather, farmers as well. Joseph's father was affluent by the standards of rural Massachusetts. His estate, which included ninety acres, a substantial house, and a collection of outbuildings, was valued at £1,345 in 1755. This affluence assured the family a prominent place in Roxbury society, and, indeed, Joseph's father was a selectman by the time his first son was born. Joseph's maternal ancestry was equally prominent, his grandfather having served Roxbury as a physician for several years.

Warren's boyhood was not exceptional. He studied in the local Latin school, grew up amidst the Puritan and Yankee environment of mid-eighteenth-century Roxbury, and engaged in the usual work and pranks of rural adolescents. But at age fourteen two events of consequence occurred. Joseph enrolled at Harvard College in 1755, missing being a fellow student of John Adams by only a term. Only a few weeks after his matriculation, young Warren's father was killed in a farming accident. For the time the new financial constraints imposed on Joseph's widowed mother jeopardized his education, but local benefactors, recognizing that he was "possessed of a genius which promised distinction," provided the additional funds to assure its continuation. Warren's college years were filled with far more pranks and high jinks than the sober Adams ever contemplated, but he ultimately graduated with high marks in 1760. Like Adams, he spent a short time—one year in Warren's case—as a schoolmaster. During this year he decided to pursue a medical career, and he was accepted to serve an apprenticeship under a London-trained physician in Boston. He began his medical practice in 1763.

Within five years, Warren possessed the most prosperous medical practice in Boston. He saw about twenty-five hundred patients annually, including the elite of the city. He also trained several of the physicians of the next generation. Most important, perhaps, he treated and became perhaps closer to the lower economic classes of the town than any other man of his social station in Boston. He saw the poor on his rounds, held the commission to treat the inmates of the almshouse, and lived with them in quarantine stations when an epidemic gripped Boston.

Despite his exalted social position, Warren did not grow wealthy. In fact, he experienced some economic difficulty. Physicians were well paid in the eighteenth century, but not as well as flourishing merchants or barristers. Moreover, the economic burden of maintaining both the family farm and his dependent, aged mother fell to Joseph. And after 1764 he had his own family to support. He married Elizabeth Hooten that year, and she swiftly bore him four children.[51]

Unlike Adams, Warren plunged into the forefront of the squabble during the first crisis, the Stamp Act furor. He fired off several letters to the local press criticizing the provincial administration, a tactic he once again pursued during the Townsend Duty turbulence which followed two years later. In addition, Warren not only joined a political club of affluent lawyers and clergymen, he helped form the North End Caucas, a rough and tumble club of artisans and small merchants. The ends sought by the two groups did not always coincide, and the means they employed to achieve their ends were often as different as night and day. Warren, for instance, as a member of the less affluent organization, spent considerable time and effort directly harassing the redcoats stationed in Boston after 1768, a tactic that annoyed many in the elite clubs, including John Adams. He also frequently surfaced at town meetings to "harangue," a ploy that Adams deplored, telling Warren it would only lead to violence. Warren was the only Bostonian to deliver two "Massacre Day" orations in 1772 and in 1775; in addition, he largely wrote John Hancock's address for the anniversary in 1774. Even in this early period Warren seems to have foreseen that war between the colonists and Great Britain was inevitable, and he purportedly told one acquaintance that "nothing would satisfy him short of heading the political and military affairs of North America" during the conflict.[52]

---

51. The preceding biographical sketch is based on John Carey, *Joseph Warren: Physician, Politician, Patriot* (Urbana, Ill., 1961), pp. 1–32, 47.

52. Richard Frothingham, *Life and Times of Joseph Warren* (Boston, 1865), pp. 50–51; Cary, *Joseph Warren*, pp. 65, 68, 84, 105.

In his letters and public addresses Warren played on the popular themes that alienated the colonists from the parent state, but from the early days his cant took on a decidedly radical, even violent, tone. Warren emphasized four themes: colonists—deserved to be remembered as heroes by their successors because the sacrifices they had made had "civilized" the continent without real assistance from Great Britain; Americans were a particularly virtuous people; a cabal of corrupted English ministers were promulgating new policies that jeopardized provincial sanctity; and the colonists would fight and die to preserve what they held dear.

He spoke frequently of how the early settlers who, faced with slavery at home, emigrated to America, their "ark dancing upon the waves," only to find "the land swarming with savages, who threatened death, with every kind of torture." In this "most unnatural and violent state" they "fought battles" interminably to secure the region. They were compelled to defend "their dear bought possessions with . . . the bravery of the hero." But the English government looked upon these life and death struggles with indifference, leaving "our ancestors to bear the severest hardships" and to undergo the "most rugged toils" alone.[53]

Warren believed the provincials were the most virtuous of people. Over the decades American "vigilence, fortitude, and perseverence" had secured the most "inestimable rights and privileges." He believed, long before Thomas Paine made the phrase more familiar, that Providence had made America "an asylum for oppressed and injured virtue." Indeed, it was the "noble attachment to a free constitution . . . which glowed in the breast" of the early settlers that drew them to America. Their struggles made the country a "land of liberty, the seat of virtue, the asylum of the oppressed, a *name and a praise* in *the whole earth.*"[54]

Now, charged Warren, and it was a common accusation during the tumultuous years, Great Britian had been captured by a small clique of plotters who hoped to gain greater power and wealth through the subjugation of the colonists. He spoke of the "Egyptian darkness" that pervaded the "court atmosphere" of this "capricious ministry" in London. He characterized the monarch who led the cabal as a "tyrant," a "man-hater." He thought Britain's ministers were guided by "rage and malevolence." Warren described "the pit they have digged for us." He complained that "virtue . . . fled from the councils of the parent

53. Warren to Edward Dana, 19 March 1766, in Frothingham, *Warren,* p. 21; Boston Massacre Oration, 1772, in [Anon.], *Biographical Sketch of Gen. Joseph Warren, Enhancing the Prominent Events of his Life, and his Boston Massacre Orations of 1772 and 1775* (Boston, 1857), pp. 21, 24, 31; Boston Massacre Oration, 1775, ibid., p. 48.

54. Warren to Stonington Comm., 24 August 1774, in Frothingham, *Warren,* pp. 345–46; Warren to East Haddam Comm., 1 September 1774, ibid., p. 354; Boston Massacre Oration, 1772, *Biog. Sketch of Warren,* pp. 19, 32.

state.''[55] Britain was ruled by a "ravenous pack of dependents," "villains," a "miscreat host," and a "malicious group of harpies" who were cheered by "venal sycophants" into "diabolical designs."[56]

But the major thrust of Warren's message was that the colonists would fight British armies to preserve their freedoms, their virtue. Well before others thought war was likely, Warren belabored—almost reveled in—that assumption. His rhetoric bulged with violence, his thoughts seemed to drip with a ghoulish preoccupation with blood and death. The "mistress we court is LIBERTY," he wrote, and "it is better to die than not to obtain her." American liberty was imperiled by the British, who had "promiscuously scattered death" in the colonies, who had "open'd the sluices of New-England's blood, and sacreligiously polluted our land with the dead bodies of her guiltless sons."[57]

He believed no sacrifice was too great when a people defended its liberties. Who "would shun the warfare? Who would stoop to waste a coward thought on life?" he asked. He urged his compatriots to "act like *men*," and, like himself, to "pant for the field" upon which they could battle the oppressors. He told his friends that they must not shrink from the possibility that they would "lose their lives in defense" of freedom, or that their "blood and treasure" might be expended in the struggle. No one's blood should be "esteemed too rich a libation for [liberty's] alter." In fact, America was already being described in his speeches as "my bleeding country" six weeks prior to the commencement of hostilities. Frequently he called it a "sanguinary theatre" even before the incident at Lexington and Concord.[58]

Warren characterized Britain as a nation of "noisy cowards," but he was convinced that the colonists had "courage enough to fight." He knew many would "perish in the attempt" to resist Britain's policies, that war would "deluge

55. Boston Massacre Oration, 1772, in *Biog. Sketch of Warren,* p. 29; Warren to Arthur Lee, 21 December 1773, in Frothingham, *Warren,* pp. 288–89; Warren to Norwich Comm., 27 August 1774, ibid., p. 351; Warren to Stonington Comm., 24 August 1774, ibid., p. 345; Warren to Preston Comm., 24 August 1774, ibid., p. 347; Warren to Middletown Comm., 17 November 1774, ibid., p. 393.

56. Frothingham, *Warren,* pp. 392, 395–96, 405; Boston Massacre Oration, 1772, in *Biog. Sketch of Warren,* p. 55. Warren helped write the Boston Massacre speech for 1774, an oration delivered by John Hancock. Since Warren's style is clearly discernible, Hancock's oration will hereinafter be cited as reflecting Warren's ideology. See John Hancock, *An Oration; delivered March 5, 1774, at the Request of the Inhabitants of the Town of Boston: To Commemorate the Bloody Tragedy of the Fifth of March 1770* (Boston, 1774), especially p. 10 for the above paragraph.

57. Warren to Samuel Adams, 15 June 1774, in Frothingham, *Warren,* p. 317; Boston Massacre Oration, 1772, in *Biog. Sketch of Warren,* p. 27; Hancock, *An Oration,* p. 9.

58. Warren to Stonington Comm., 24 August 1774, in Frothingham, *Warren,* pp. 345–46; Warren to Preston Comm., 24 August 1774, ibid., p. 347; Warren to East Haddam Comm., 1 September 1774, ibid., p. 354; Warren to Josiah Quincy, 21 November 1774, ibid., p. 395; Boston Massacre Oration, 1772, in *Biog. Sketch of Warren,* p. 31; Boston Massacre Oration, 1775, ibid., pp. 44, 53.

your country in blood," that the contest would be "sever," but that "an honorable death in the field" was preferable to nonresistance. "We fear not death," he inserted in John Hancock's Massacre Day Oration. "Our hearts . . . can witness that we fear not death," he injected into a resolution he drafted. He added that "Patriotism . . . impels us to sacrifice everything dear, even life itself. . . . Surely our hearts flutter no more at the sound of war, than did those of the immortal band of Persia, the Macedonian phalanx, the invincible Roman legions."[59] The coming battle, of course, was for the preservation of the colonists' virtue. We "shall be instrumental in calling back that virtue" of our fathers, he said. "Your fathers," he again noted, "look from their celestial seats with smiling approbation on their sons, who boldly stand forth in the cause of virtue." He argued that Britain's liberty, as well as the colonists', would be "preserved by the virtue of America."[60]

The violence manifest in Warren's rhetoric was also evident in his behavior. Twice in 1769 he engaged in fist fights with British troops quartered in Boston. That same year he issued a challenge to an assailant of James Otis. John Adams knew Warren well enough to suspect—to fear—that the doctor would "influence some dirty tool to stir up revenge and bloodshed." Because of his violent demeanor, many feared for Warren's life, and early in 1775 rumors swirled throughout Boston of assassination plots allegedly being fomented against the agitator.[61]

Unlike Adams, the adventurous Warren's activities never waned in the long prewar clashes with Britain, and after the fall of 1773, when news of the Tea Act reached Boston, Warren became enmeshed daily in the plots, the propagandizing, the strategy sessions that molded and shaped public opinion and colonial policy. Working around his busy medical schedule, Warren established a close relationship with the leader of the town's artisans, Paul Revere. He engaged in limitless activities for the local Committee of Correspondence, and he even composed a snappy "liberty song." He was made leader of Boston's Masons, and he helped mobilize them for his radical endeavors. That he played an active role in planning the Boston Tea Party goes without saying, although his precise role in this clandestine affair is unclear; Warren's most recent biographer, John Cary, believes he was on board one of the British ships that fateful evening, actually directing the "Mohawks" in their illicit activities. Warren

59. Warren to Samuel Adams, 10 February 1775, in Frothingham, *Warren*, p. 415; Warren to Arthur Lee, 3 April 1775, ibid., pp. 447, 452; Warren to Provincial Congress of Mass., 20 April 1775, ibid., p. 466; Warren to Govt. of Connecticut, 2 May 1775, ibid., p. 476; Hancock, *An Oration*, pp. 10, 12, 14.

60. Warren to Comm. of Public Safety, 17 November 1774, in Frothingham, *Warren*, p. 393; Boston Massacre Oration, 1775, in *Biog. Sketch of Warren*, p. 58.

61. Cary, *Joseph Warren*, pp. 84, 90, 174.

assumed an even more prominent place in radical councils in 1774, particularly from early August onward when the Adamses and others departed for Philadelphia and the initial meeting of the Continental Congress. In fact, Warren emerged as president of the Boston Committee of Safety, the de facto city government, now that the Coercive Acts prohibited town meetings.[62]

By late 1774 it was apparent to all but the most naive that war was certain. Warren was prepared. Through the winter he served with clandestine parties that spied on the activities of the British army. The work was not without risk, but Warren insisted that he was determined to share all dangers with his colleagues. He directed a last-minute propaganda barrage to prepare the populace for war, frankly explaining that the "sudden destruction" of the colony was at hand unless the citizenry was "cooly and resolutely" prepared to defend itself. He delivered the last peacetime Massacre Day Oration, a speech which outdid all its predecessors in its fatalistic and radical tone. He spoke of their generation drawing near the "melancholy walk of death," of "stronger passions" supplanting the "softer movements of the soul," of the likelihood that they would "fly to arms," and of "death [that] grins a hideous smile, secure to drench his greedy jaws in human gore, whilst hovering furies darken all the air."[63]

Early in the evening of April 18, 1775, Warren learned from his spy network of General Gage's plans to dispatch redcoats to the Concord arsenal the following morning. Warren made the decision to send Paul Revere and William Dawes on their famous ride to alert the militia. In all likelihood, Warren knew that the long-awaited clash was only hours away. In fact, expecting as much, he hurried to Lexington as quickly as business permitted. He arrived too late for the initial skirmish of the war on Lexington Green, but he was there in time to direct the militia, though neither a military officer nor an elected official to any legitimate body, in the ambush of the retreating British soldiers. At Menotomy, in one of the hottest engagements of that day, Warren was nicked by a musket ball, but his skin was not broken. The following day, and for the next several weeks, he acted, to quote his biographer, as a self-appointed and "semiofficial commander-in-chief" of the Massachusetts militia, directing generals, securing food and equipment, conferring with Indians, recruiting physicians for militia service, and preparing plans for an attack on Boston. Warren did not become a military officer until June 14, when the Provincial Congress appointed him a major-general.[64]

During these feverish spring weeks Warren seemed to engage in an emotional dance of death, as if he not only knew that he soon would perish, but longed to die. He courted danger, and on May 27 he was in the midst of a brief and

62. Ibid., pp. 123–25, 127, 134, 150.
63. Ibid., pp. 171–72; Boston Massacre Oration, 1775, in *Biog. Sketch of Warren*, pp. 53–55.
64. Cary, *Joseph Warren*, pp. 183–87, 206–9, 216.

inconsequential, though dangerous, firefight with British regulars at Hog's Island, an engagement that left several men dead and wounded on both sides. In the meantime he prayed to "the God of armies" for sustenance, but he appeared resigned to his fate. "I think I have done my duty," he reflected.[65] He told Elbridge Gerry that he believed it "sweet and becoming to die for the country." Another friend claimed Warren told him that he would "mount the last round of the ladder or die in the attempt." To another friend he exclaimed that he hoped he would "die up to my knees in blood!"[66]

On the morning of June 16 a thousand-man militia force under Colonel William Prescott began to construct redoubts atop Brede's Hill. Everyone presumed the British would strike soon to dislodge the militiamen; preparation would take some time, but it was apparent that a major battle was imminent. Warren decided without hesitation, and against the objections of several friends, that he must participate. His spy network surreptitiously arranged for him to sneak into occupied Boston that evening so that he might transact some final business. Back in Cambridge shortly after midnight, Warren languished for several hours with a "nervous headache." Cannonading began in the early daylight hours of June 17. Though ill with a crushing headache, Warren walked to the top of Brede's Hill early in the afternoon. Again some troops attempted to dissuade him from fighting, and Colonel Israel Putnam, Warren's subordinate, attempted to surrender his command to the physician-warrior. Warren refused. "I am here only as a volunteer," he replied. "I know nothing of your dispositions; nor will I interfere with them. Tell me where I can be most useful." Putnam directed him to the redoubt, telling him that he would "be covered" in that area. Warren protested, exclaiming, "Don't think I came to seek a place of safety, but tell me where the onset will be most furious." Nevertheless, armed with a pistol, Warren took up the position to which Putnam had directed him.[67]

In the redoubt Warren and Prescott, with about 150 men, looked down on more than two thousand redcoats. Soon after the British charged, and in the ensuing confusion of the battle no one was certain what had occurred. The best evidence is that Warren issued some orders during the battle and remained in the redoubt and fought until a retreat was ordered by Prescott. By that time, the British had reached the vicinity in which Warren was entrenched, and about thirty militiamen already had been bayoneted. Warren thereupon joined the retreat, but as he was scampering down the hill he was struck by a musket ball in the rear of the skull. He died instantly.[68]

65. Ibid., pp. 105–6, 215–17; Warren to Gen. Gage, 20 April 1775, in Frothingham, *Warren*, p. 287.

66. Frothingham, *Warren*, pp. 452, 510.

67. "Colonel David Putnam's Letter Relative to the Battle of Bunker Hill and General Israel Putnam," CHS *Coll.*, vol. I (Hartford, Conn., 1860), p. 247; Frothingham, *Warren*, pp. 513–16; Cary, *Joseph Warren*, pp. 218–20.

68. Cary, *Joseph Warren*, pp. 220–21.

Not everyone was disappointed in Warren's fate. Patrick Henry was overjoyed, for he knew that the ensuing propaganda barrage would help the war effort. Upon learning of Warren's demise, Henry exclaimed, "I rejoice to hear it. His death will do a great deal of good. We wanted some breeches to be made upon our affections to awaken our patriotism still more and to prepare us for war." John Adams, though genuinely distraught over the fate of his friend, had grown to distrust Warren as too radical, too zealous, in his popular activities. Adams even feared that "too much admiration" would be directed toward the martyred Dr. Warren.[69]

Nor were many surprised at Warren's battlefield death. He had pursued this fate too openly. As Mercy Otis Warren later observed in her history of the rebellion, the doctor "rather incautiously courted the post of danger, and rushed precipitately on his fate. . . . Yet, if the *love of fame* is the strongest passion of the mind, and human nature pants for distinction in the flowery field," nothing could have saved Warren from his rendezvous with combat and death.[70]

Whatever Adams's and Warren's roles in the conflicts with Great Britain before 1774, both men were activists by the eve of hostilities. Each man knew his actions helped precipitate the war. One man desperately longed to fight, but could not make himself endure the hardships and hazards of war. He struggled to convince himself that statecraft was the equivalent of martial endeavors in terms of toil, sacrifice, and danger. The other man desperately wished to fight and, knowing that death was possible, even likely, hastened into combat.

Neither man could escape the war he helped make. Adams avoided the terror and dangers that beset the common soldier. But he experienced the same loneliness and homesickness, and, though not driven by a drill sergeant, he nevertheless compelled himself to suffer through unremitting toil. For Adams it was a painful, emotional experience, a bloodletting spree which filled him with a sense not unlike that born by many soldiers when they first spilled the blood of a foe. But, ironically for Adams, war earned him the fame and recognition he had pursued with less success in more peaceful fields.

For Warren, the war was a liberating experience, a cataclysm which permitted the fulfillment of his deepest drives and his inner turmoil. Ironically, the experience of war snuffed out his life.

69. Conner, *Autobiography of Benj. Rush*, p. 111; Cary, *Joseph Warren*, pp. 105–6.
70. Warren, *History of the American Revolution*, vol. I, pp. 222–23.

Chapter Six

The Revolutionary War Experience

A Christian Sparta

A revolutionary upheaval can produce dire change, sweeping away the most discernible vestiges of the old, discarded past. Or it can be a time when a people, particularly a colonial people seeking independence and nationhood, identity, and a meaning to their existence, can draw—consciously in some instances, unconsciously in others—upon the disjointed past and weave the fragmented, confusing threads of their experience into a cohesive, comprehensible pattern.

The colonists' crisis with the parent state was an instance of the latter sort of revolution. Ultimately, the dispute was soluble only by war. In the protracted struggle that followed, the colonists drew on their experiences in the conquest of wilderness America, on their encounters with the terror and perversity inevitable in war. Under the exigencies of the moment, they also reexamined their assumptions about themselves and their goals and scrutinized their philosophy and long-held beliefs. Some ancient verities were discarded as anachronistic. The colonists saw themselves as a hybrid of the European and the American, and they fashioned their culture and their conduct of the war accordingly.

In at least four ways the colonists' experience of war helped shape the events of the era of the rebellion. First, while attitudes toward war, and the nature of conflict itself, were changing in eighteenth-century Europe, the colonists' attitudes remained in lockstep. When, after 1763, relations with Britain deteriorated as a result of largely extraneous causes, the colonists' military ethos, as well as their plentiful experience with war, did nothing to restrain them from embarking on a course of violence. Their experiences, in fact, may have helped, if only subliminally, to propel them toward conflict.

Second, events in the initial year of the war manifested that fundamental alterations in the nature of America's military organization were essential if the colonists were to win the war. The colonists, who had paid lip service to the presumed merits of a militia force, realized that a standing army was probably necessary if independence was to be attained. The colonial experience facilitated the transition to the Continental army.

Third, the colonial leadership of these years, a generation tempered in part by the impetuous militant ferment of their age, articulated a world view that can be characterized only as aggressive and expansionist. Its fulfillment hinged on the use of force, for which the colonists had been prepared by the long years of colonial warfare and the ideology, culture, and hubris that accompanied conflict. By 1763 it not only was obvious that the colonists lacked a free hand in satisfying their ambitions, it was clear to some that their aspirations could be achieved only outside the aegis of the Empire. War had become an accepted agent for change. It would once again be the central tool to meet these men's goals.

Finally, the war with Britain reflected the colonists' experience with conflict, so that the nature, if not the outcome, of the War for Independence was colored by the American past.

Until the middle of the eighteenth century, many of the concerns and much of the rhetoric of the colonists about war and warriors resembled the prevalent attitudes of the articulate in Europe. On both sides of the Atlantic, commentators drew similar distinctions between ''just'' and ''unjust'' wars. The colonists were as inclined as the continentals to view war as inevitable. Although European wars were contested by professional soldiers, the soldierly virtues cherished on the continent were nearly identical to those propounded by Americans.

Nevertheless, there were important differences. For one thing, Americans may have been more directly, and, perhaps, even more indirectly, affected by war than were European citizens after the middle seventeenth century. In America, wars occurred with considerable frequency. Battles flared in inhabited regions and played havoc with a provincial economy that depended on foreign trade. Most important, the colonists did not hire troops, they fought themselves; men might suddenly be compelled to abandon their families, property, and work for service in the trainband. When an American politician, clergyman, or orator philosophized about soldiering, his was not idle speculation, but commentary that bore directly on the lives of a large percentage of the population. Whether the average colonist inculcated the alleged virtues of a soldier's life is impossible to discern; but there can be no question that in the world of the colonists, martial pursuits were esteemed, military sacrifice was extolled as heroic, and the qualities of courage and obedience were offered up as the most exemplary models of behavior for the citizen-soldier.

A second difference in attitudes toward war concerned the long, largely futile European history of attempts to control the ravages of warfare. In the middle ages, edicts had been issued to outlaw war at certain times and among certain segments of society. In more recent years, efforts had been made to establish formal rules for military conduct and to provide a rudimentary international law to govern the waging, and hopefully the avoidance, of warfare. Although some colonists obviously had read Grotius and other Europeans of like persuasion, these ideas remained foreign to the colonies. The colonists remained too much the pawns of European statesmen to exert any real influence in the mitigation of conflicts. Nor did the colonists manifest genuine interest in instituting rules governing clashes with the native Americans. Indeed, it was often native Americans who solicited accords which might have minimized the tragedies of those wars by confining the fighting to the adult male population or restricting hostilities to a few months in each year.

After about 1750, however, much more substantive differences emerged between European and American views of warfare and warriors. As mentioned in an earlier chapter, the religious wars that plagued Europe for about one hundred years after the 1520s produced untold suffering among civilians as well as soldiers. Invading armies, swelled by wives, children, prostitutes, and servants, spread abroad like a "plague of locusts." Even worse, much of the misery was produced by "friendly" troops. As a respected historian recently noted, the "homeland often had to suffer as severely as, if not more than, the enemy "territory" from the "murder and arson, plundering, extortion and robbery" of their own army. In addition, the European literati soon concluded that the close proximity of soldiers and civilians produced a deterioration in morality and an upswing in intemperance, prostitution, swearing, and godlessness.[1]

In the aftermath of these wars, revolutionary changes occurred in Europe's warfare and in its attitudes toward war. As the wars of righteousness receded and for the moment disappeared, dynastic wars for limited objectives emerged. Most common were wars fought for the balance of power, an elusive, mystical ideal; in fact, if several monarchs concluded that hostilities had resulted in a less satisfactory balance, the sides might be changed, even in the middle of the war, and the fighting resumed. The changes in warfare resulted, in part, from what Professor Eric Robson called "a natural revulsion from the horror" of the religious conflicts.[2] But the European economy and modern technological advances altered the nature of war as well. In this age of mercantilist domination, the bourgeoisie came to be regarded as a nonmilitary segment of the population, a class whose primary function was to manage the new industrial and commercial enterprises; not only was this class considered more valuable to the state if its time and talents were not squandered through service in the armed forces, but the bourgeoisie was also to be protected from those who were compelled to serve. Simultaneously, wealthy nation-states improved their transportation facilities and established magazines stocked with foodstuffs along the new highways; now, as armies in the field could be fed more easily, the need to pillage the civilian population in a war zone was dramatically reduced.

1. J. W. Wign, "Military Forces and Warfare, 1610–1648," in G. N. Clark et al., eds., *The New Cambridge Modern History,* 13 vols. (Cambridge, Eng., 1969–1970), vol. IV, p. 206.

2. Eric Robson, "The Armed Forces and the Art of War," in ibid., vol. VII, pp. 165–66, 174–75.

Still another factor that altered the nature of warfare in Europe after the mid-seventeenth century was the changing nature of the continental armies. In most instances armies remained quite large, even larger than previously; for a hundred years before 1550, for example, no general commanded more than 50,000 troops, but Louis XIV put more than 100,000 men under arms, and Peter the Great raised an army of 200,000 men. What did change was the composition of these armies. The old policy of raising conscripts from nearly all segments of society fell into abeyance. Armies increasingly were drawn from three segments of society. The officer caste, as had been true for centuries, virtually was reserved for those of aristocratic lineage, although the percentage of bourgeois officers steadily increased. Still, most people apparently continued to believe that a relationship existed between noble birth and military capabilities. In every European country officers were almost universally aristocrats, and often they commenced service as quite young men. James Wolfe was a second lieutenant at age fifteen, for example, whereas Wellington held similar rank at seventeen years and had risen to the rank of major general by the age of thirty-two. Each higher rank was purchased by the monied noblemen, thus excluding all but the wealthiest from the highest positions.

The common soldiers were drawn from two sources: foreign mercenaries sometimes constituted two-thirds of an army, and the remainder of the legions were conscripted—actually, kidnapped or hoodwinked into "volunteering" in many instances—locally from among marginal peasants and the unemployed. This, too, altered warfare. Among troops who were brutally disciplined, even tortured, desertion became a problem as never before. The Prussian army under Frederick William I averaged more than one thousand desertions annually; in Saxony about one of every two troops deserted between 1717 and 1728. The rear guard in the British army no longer existed so much for protection from enemy strikes as to apprehend runaways from their own forward ranks. In Prussia commanders dared not move an army at night or through a large forested region for fear of desertion. Throughout Europe, reconnaissance patrols which had been used traditionally for gathering intelligence had to be curtailed; likewise, because of the desertion rates, battlefield victories were seldom followed by sustained attacks to destroy a crippled foe.[3]

After about 1700, even Britain's military situation changed markedly. The permutation reflected the fact that warfare had become, in the words of one

3. Clark, *War and Society* (Cambridge, Eng., 1958), pp. 98–113; Maurice Ashley, *Louis XIV and the Greatness of France* (London, 1963), pp. 198–200; Robson, "Armed Forces," in Clark, *New Cambridge Modern History*, vol. VII, p. 186; Paul E. Kopperman, *Braddock* (Pittsburgh, Pa., 1977), p. 109; Louis Ducross, *French Society in the Eighteenth Century* (London, 1926), pp. 291–95; John W. Fortescue, *The History of the British Army*, 13 vols. (London, 1910–1930), vol. I, p. 579; Andre Córvisier, *Armies and Societies* (Bloomington, Ind., 1979), pp. 70, 177; Martin Kitchen, *A Military History of Germany* . . . (Bloomington, Ind., 1975), pp. 10–11, 21–23; Christopher Duffy, *The Army of Frederick the Great* (New York, 1974), pp. 65–66.

historian, "a sport of kings, rather than [an] issue between peoples." Moreover, conflicts waged to secure a balance of power could have important economic manifestations. Of the nations frequently active in Europe's wars, only Britian, in part because of its ideological proclivities, and, in part, because its insularity militated against the dangers of foreign invasion, had successfully resisted standing armies and relied on its militia trainbands. Even though Britain's antipathy to a standing army remained intact, its frequent participation in the wars of the eighteenth century resulted in changes in traditional policy. During the final years of the seventeenth century, a British army which ranged from about twenty thousand men in peacetime to nearly seventy thousand in wartime, augmented by an approximately similar number of mercenaries, was established. During the three-quarters of a century before the American Revolution, its composition and problems were akin to those of its counterparts in Europe, although some observers, such as the Earl of Chesterfield, regarded it as "the worst-officered [army] in all Europe."[4]

All these factors—the substitution of dynastic warfare for wars of religion; the reaction to the terrible suffering produced by the wars of the early sixteenth century; the technological and economic revolutions that had transpired; and the reliance upon the dregs of society as the backbone of the various armies—had transformed the nature of war in Europe. Although wars were often declared, leaders now contrived to reduce the frequency of battles. When armies contested one another, the results of the struggle could still be woeful, as demonstrated by the death of nearly 10 percent of Prussia's population during the Seven Years' War. During battles the forces volleyed at close range, stopped cavalry charges with bayonets, and even grappled in hand-to-hand combat. Hence, engagements were approached, if at all, with considerable care. "We fight more like Foxes than Lyons," the Earl of Orrery remarked. The Duke of Alva concurred, noting in 1760 that it "is the business of a general always to get the better of his enemy, but not always to fight, and if he can do his business without fighting, so much the better." Warfare grew more defensive. The desecration and atrocities that had occurred in the earlier religious wars were muted considerably. Moreover, perhaps never before or since were civilians less touched by the warfare that swirled about them. The ideal of Frederick the Great, in fact, was that when he was at war, the civilian population should not be aware that war was being pursued. Even the percentage of the armies that perished from combat-

4. C. G. Cruickshank, *Elizabeth's Army* (London, 1966), pp. 1–2, 12–13, 16–17, 19, 23, 160–62; Lois G. Schwoerer, *"No Standing Armies!"* (Baltimore, 1974), pp. 8–17, 19–32, 162, 180–83; T. H. Breen, "Persistent Localism: English Social Change and the Shaping of New England Institutions," *WMQ*, 3d Ser. 32 (January 1975), pp. 13–14; Correlli Barnett, *Britain and her Army, 1509–1970* (New York, 1970), pp. 79–115, 141–42, 172; Fortescue, *History of the British Army*, vol. I, pp. 283, 291–94; J. G. A. Pocock, *The Machiavellian Moment* (Princeton, N.J., 1975), p. 415; Caroline Robbins, *The Eighteenth-Century Commonwealthmen* (New York, 1968), pp. 103–5; Basil Williams, *The Whig Supremacy, 1714–1760* (Oxford, Eng., 1939), pp. 204–6, 208.

related factors declined during this century. By the mid-eighteenth century conflict in Europe had grown as distinct from the warfare of the medieval years as it would be from the catastrophic wars of the twentieth century.[5]

As the transactions of war became increasingly removed from the eyes of the citizenry of Europe, and as the issues over which wars were waged grew more remote from the interests of the inhabitants, a strong revulsion against war sprang up on the continent. Those who denounced war were considered spokesmen of the Englightenment, a broad, epochal intellectual transformation which touched much of northern Europe in the eighteenth century. Enlightenment writers usually had bourgeois roots, or at least they appealed primarily to readers of that class. The bourgeoisie, a class of merchants and burgeoning industrialists, a class whose livelihood hinged on trade, increasingly found war a meaningless, even detrimental, undertaking. Perhaps of greater importance, war was pursued at the behest of the nobility, and the Englightenment most assuredly amounted to a concerted attack by the bourgeoisie on many of the values of the nobility; among the virtues held paramount by the ancien regime were those of courage, loyalty, selflessness, and austerity, all of which found their fullest expression when war was waged. Moreover, as a scholar noted recently, the soldier, as never before, had become

the King's man, for he wore the King's coat. And it was the King's coat indeed; for by the close of the century there was already a tendency in monarchs of an absolutist cast to consider military uniforms as their traditional attire.[6]

These writers, in addition, were appalled at the manner in which militarism had permeated society. In Prussia, for instance, retired military officers controlled numerous offices, the bureaucracy existed largely to serve the army, and the economy was geared to the interests of the armed forces. As Professor Corvisier has demonstrated, the ancien regime was "filled with a military spirit." Even its "social values were military values." Throughout Europe, moreover, an aura of violence seemed to shroud life. The practice of dueling remained popular in many circles, as did the spectacles of trial by combat and public executions. Soldiers were expected to act cruelly (Louis XIV's troops were ordered to stamp out the *papier timbre* insurrection in 1675 by skewering children on their swords) and enraged mobs of civilians often acted equally brutishly,

5. Howard Mumford Jones, *Revolution and Romanticism* (Cambridge, Mass., 1974), p. 30; Walter L. Dorn, *Competition for Empire, 1740–1763* (New York, 1940), pp. 80–99; Theodore Rapp, *War in the Modern World* (Durham, N.C., 1959), pp. 28–42; John Wolf, *The Emergence of the Great Powers, 1685–1715* (New York, 1951), p. 173; Richard Preston and Sydney Wise, *Men in Arms* (New York, 1970), p. 141; Robson, "Armed Forces," in Clark, *New Cambridge Modern History*, vol. VII, p. 163; Montross, *War Through the Ages*, pp. 347–414; Zook and Higham, *History of Warfare*, pp. 102–16.
6. C. B. A. Behrens, *The Ancien Regime* (London, 1967), pp. 119–20;

torturing and desecrating its victims and pillaging the property of suspected foes.[7]

The antiwar writers of the European Enlightenment found the origin of conflict in the alliance of church and nobility, particularly in the person of the monarch. While the prince fought to increase his honor and wealth, the masses "languish in misery and servility." The concept of an inevitable link between monarchy and war began to gain currency in the seventeenth century, but it was Montesquieu who did most to popularize the notion in subsequent years. "The spirit of monarchies is war and aggression, the spirit of republics is peace and moderation," he claimed.

Likewise, Voltaire thought war was the natural conduct of rulers. With little circumspection, he alluded to rulers as "Bloodthirsty animals" who would never seek real peace, who were indifferent to the primary interests of their subjects, and who were addicts to military glory. Why people would "die for the pretended interests of a man whom [they] know not" was beyond his comprehension. He believed the very idea of a "just war" to be "contradictory and impossible. . . . There are only offensive wars." To attack a neighbor for the sake of territorial enlargement was immoral. To defend what had been acquired by some previous monarch was nonsensical. To attack another country so that it might not, generations removed, attack your country was folly. All warfare was organized, legitimized crime.

Diderot labeled war-making rulers the "shame and scourge of mankind," and he considered their warriors to be "master-butchers." Rousseau pursued the same logic, arguing that the "whole life of kings is devoted solely to two objects: to extend their rule beyond their frontiers and to make it more absolute within them."[8]

To the antiwar writers, however, the monarch was not solely culpable. Warfare remained a pervasive fact of life because of the structure of the European states. Monarchs, after all, did not function in a vacuum. They were surrounded by a military caste, whose raison d'être was war. There were ministers who advised the princes and who discovered that war was a godsend, for by maneuvering their monarch "into difficulties from which he cannot escape without their aid," they rendered themselves indispensable. Likewise, the church lent its moral sanction to these conflicts; its clergy blessed the regimental flags of the war machine and exhorted the masses to march gaily to the slaughter. Moreover, some writers despaired for peace so long as a state system existed, for the very system excited economic rivalries that culminated in warfare. None denied that

7. Michael Roberts, *The Military Revolution, 1560–1660* (Belfast, Ire., 1956), pp. 20–23; Corvisier, *Armies and Societies,* pp. 4–11, 118.

8. Souleyman, *Vision of World Peace,* pp. 115–24, 126, 140; Constance Rowe, *Voltaire and the State* (New York, 1968), pp. 135, 138, 142–43; Alfred Vagts, *History of Militarism* (New York, 1959), p. 76.

human nature, particularly man's inherent credulence, his insatiable lust for wealth, and his superstition, helped popularize warfare, but most believed that the state system, and the system of the states of the ancien regime, exacerbated these natural qualities to the point that war was tolerated, even welcomed. On the continent, while some writers tinkered with notions of international organizations as an effective palliative for war, most philosophers had no hope for peace unless fundamental changes were made in the institutions and environments in which men functioned.[9]

Even the art of much of eighteenth-century Europe, though often produced by quite different psychological and meditative factors from the written word, reflected the changing mood of the continent. As with the philosophes, the ceremonial art of the royal court was eclipsed by that which appealed to middle-class tastes. The earlier art which had celebrated the virtues of the ancien regime was supplanted by portraits, still lifes, landscapes, and works that celebrated rusticity and the humble family, an imagery that, in the words of one scholar, reflected anew "a longing for . . . the tranquil and secure joy of living." It was an era for "de-heroizing and humanizing," a time to "reduce their size and bring them closer" to the common man. Now, art extolled the wise ruler, not the warrior-king, and warriors were depicted as men of "downright lunacy" and vanity.[10]

In Great Britain somewhat different winds stirred in the eighteenth century. Although the state had frequently been embroiled in conflict, Britain's wars were waged in distant climes by the flotsam and jetsam of society. Unaccustomed to the direct ravages of conflict, and unsympathetic to the plight of the masses, the articulate in Britain were not concerned by repeated warfare for the same reasons as their counterparts in Europe. What alarmed many writers in Britain was that a monarch might, through repeated episodes of conflict, accumulate a standing army which ultimately could be used at home to snuff out the liberties of the citizenry. Much was made of the histories of France and Denmark where such occurrences had resulted in arbitrary governments. Those fears had been temporarily laid to rest by the Glorious Revolution of 1688, a bloodless constitutional reconstruction that resulted in the balancing of the old contending interests of English society; monarchy, aristocracy, and the commoners were mixed neatly into one government, so that each checked the others to prevent licentious or tyrannical behavior. For a time most Englishmen believed they had discovered the solution to the ancient riddle of reliable government; even the

9. Peter Gay, *The Enlightenment*, 2 vols. (New York, 1969), vol. II, pp. 401–7; Souleyman, *Vision of World Peace*, pp. 50–52, 105–50.

10. Arnold Hauser, *The Social History of Art*, 4 vols. (New York, 1952), vol. II, pp. 461, 502–3, 514, 525; Robert Rosenblum, *Transformations in Late Eighteenth Century Art* (Princeton, N.J., 1967), pp. 55, 57, 59–60; Arno Schonberger and Halden Soehner, *The Roccoco Age* (London, 1968), p. 55; Julius S. Held and Donald Posner, *17th and 18th Century Art* (New York, 1971), pp. 314, 317, 320; Paul Hazard, *The European Mind, 1680–1715* (New Haven, Conn., 1952), p. 324.

European philosophes agreed, for, like Montesquieu, most beamed at "this beautiful system." But as the eighteenth century progressed, a small coterie of radical voices in Britain expressed concern that the constitutional revolution was perhaps not the final solution. These radicals, labeled the "Real Whigs" by Professor Bernard Bailyn, asserted that the monarch was breaking the constitutional bonds that restrained him, raising once again the specter of despotism.[11]

Paradoxically, while important shifts of opinion concerning war surfaced in Europe and Britain, the American attitude did not change demonstrably. As late as 1769 many colonists might have sympathized with the youthful Alexander Hamilton's lament: "I contemn the grovling and condition of a Clerk or the like, to which my Fortune, &c., condemns me. I wish there was a War." When war occurred many responded by hastening to enlist. When King George's War flared, the sixteen-year-old William Franklin, Benjamin's son, attempted to sign on as a privateer. His plans were thwarted by his father, although the elder Franklin did secure a commission for his son in a company of volunteers about to invade Canada. The attitudes of Hamilton and young Franklin were not isolated phenomena. On the eve of his opposition to Britain's colonial policies, Oxenbridge Thacher of Massachusetts grew despondent as he watched British troops march through his village en route to combat in the French and Indian War. "I wish my self a soldier," he told a similarly depressed young John Adams. "I look upon these private soldiers with their Guns upon their shoulders, as superior to me."[12] Adams concurred.

From the beginning the colonists lauded their soldiers. As noted in an earlier chapter, in some instances London financiers had dispatched professional soldiers to direct the colonists; in other cases the colonists had hired career soldiers to assist in establishing a beachhead in America. Many of the earliest histories written about the colonies praised the exploits of these soldiers. John Smith's adventures were recorded by numerous pamphleteers, making him one of the most popular of men in the colonial era; similarly, New Englanders early on applauded the "brave Englishmen bred to arms in the Dutch Netherlands" who had "spread a terror over all the Tribes of Indians around about" them, and who acted in a manner akin to "those inspired Heroes of who we read [in] History in the Eleventh Chapter to the Hebrews." Even a stern Puritan such as Cotton Mather could put aside his notions of predestination to acclaim soldiers as the most "noble" among men and the "Favorites of Heaven"; Mather urged the citizenry to display "extraordinary *Mark of Respect*" for their warriors, and

11. Bernard Bailyn, *The Ideological Origins of the American Revolution* (Cambridge, Mass., 1967), pp. 61–63, 73–76; Gordon S. Wood, *The Creation of the American Republic, 1776–1789* (Chapel Hill, N.C., 1969), pp. 10–11, 33; Robbins, *Eighteenth Century Commonwealthmen*, pp. 22–108, 320–77.

12. Hamilton to Edward Stevens, 11 November 1769, in Syrett and Cooke, *Hamilton Papers*, vol. I, p. 4; David F. Hawke, *Franklin* (New York, 1976), p. 75; L. H. Butterfield et al., eds. *Adams D&A*, 4 vols. (Cambridge, Mass., 1964), vol. I, p. 110.

he acknowledged that "their very Countenances methinks carry Loveliness in them." In keeping with these sentiments, Mather declared in 1697 that *"Canada must be Reduced,"* and he penned a laudatory biography of Sir William Phips, the New Englander who led the expedition against the French province.[13]

Mather's notions were in keeping with the prevailing mood. Following successful wars, while the populace gave thanks for the destruction of the enemy, the magistrate and elders often provided the returning heroes with a feast. Moreover, in its first quarter-century, Massachusetts had two governors other than John Winthrop. It temporarily dumped Winthrop in 1634 in favor of Thomas Dudley, a man with military experience, and in 1649, upon Winthrop's death, the colony reelected John Endicott, who had led the initial expedition against the Pequots in 1637; Winthrop, himself, had succeeded Endicott nearly two decades earlier.[14]

America's respect for its soldiers—and, until the imperial squabble erupted, even for British troops—remained largely unchanged in the eighteenth century. Following the capture of Louisbourg in 1745 a poet characterized New England's "fearless" invasion force as "godly Soldiers." Another lyricist believed that colonial leaders "May vie with Marlborough and Blake for fame." William Douglass, a popular mid-eighteenth-century American historian, was one of the first colonial writers to compare American warriors to Rome's Cincinnatus. He thought it "very laudable" and deserving of "places of profit or honor" that "some of our good farmers, artificers, and other labourers" leave their several occupations for a short time, to serve their country upon an exigency." The clergy, as might be expected, continued to extoll the virtues of warriors. Valorous soldiers were declared to be "Characters of Praise" to be "Consecrated to Posterity"; citizens were reminded of their "lasting Obligation" to their protectors. Likewise, secular leaders were not to be heard denouncing their wars or their warriors.[15]

News of victories was greeted with peeling bells, cannonades, fireworks, and bonfires. Upon the British successes in Canada in the French and Indian War, General Wolfe and Jeffrey Amherst became instant heroes in the colonies. Even the Marquis de Montcalm, the fallen French commander, was romanticized

13. Phillip Vincent, *A True Relation,* MHS, *Coll.* 6: p., 40; Cotton Mather, *Things to be Look'd for* (Cambridge, Mass., 1691), pp. 74–75; Cotton Mather, *Military Duties* (Boston, 1689), p. 36; Cotton Mather, *The Life of Sir William Phips* [1697] (New York, 1929), pp. 68–69.

14. Hosmer, *Winthrop's Journal,* vol. I, p. 238; Edmund S. Morgan, *The Puritan Dilemma* (Boston, 1958), pp. 86–87, 103–9, 113; Francis J. Bremmer, *The Puritan Experiment* (New York, 1976), p. 11.

15. Samuel Niles, *A Brief and Plain Essay . . .* (New London, Conn., 1747), p. 2; William Douglass, *A Summary* 2 vols. (Boston, 1755), vol. I, pp. 353n, 356–57; Hull Abbott, *Jehovah's Character* (Boston, 1735), p. 25; James Cogswell, *God, The Pious Soldier's Strength* (Boston, 1757), pp. 25–26; Ebenezer Bridge, *A Sermon* (Boston, 1752), p. 13; Nathaniel Robbins, *Jerusalem's Peace Wished* (Boston, 1772), p. 20.

posthumously by his provincial foes. The colonies named newly founded hamlets after soldiers and donated scarce monies for the erection of statues to military heroes. Nor were colonial men alone in making heroes the soldiery. Mercy Otis Warren, in her history of the Revolution, in all likelihood reflected the sentiments of many women when she romanticized "every manly arm which had been raised on the blood-stained field." So, too, did the South Carolina belle who remarked that she had "no husband to fight against them (though, by the bye, if I had one who refused to enter the field in his country's cause, I believe I should despise him from my soul)."[16]

While more pacifistic themes began to predominate the culture of Europe, colonial art seemed to reflect and romanticize the struggle that had established Europe in America. Painting in the colonies, since it was dependent on patronage, was virtually restricted to commercial portraiture. Ironically, though, the earliest artwork rendered by an Englishman in America was John White's depiction of a pitched battle between native Americans and European sailors under explorer Martin Frobisher. Throughout the colonial years some popular art, such as the commonplace weathervane shaped in the form of an Indian firing an arrow, and many mass recreational forms, such as hunting and shooting matches, reflected the violence that permeated primitive America.

After the middle of the eighteenth century, other forms of artistic expression grew more fashionable. Historic painting grew especially popular, and several young colonial artists—one might almost say particularly American artists—demonstrated extraordinary abilities as painters of epic events. Such painters were, in reality, historians, craftsmen in search of what a professor at the Royal Academy called the "entire man, body and mind"; subconsiously, perhaps, some of the artists sought to capture as well the soul of the society responsible for the majestic events portrayed. The theme of conflict and the agents of violence were predominant in the works of many of these artists. The most influential painting of this genre produced by an American was Benjamin West's *Death of General Wolfe,* first exhibited in 1771. The dead warrior was mythologized. One modern critic, in fact, compared the "overtones of martyrdom" in the work to contemporary versions of the crucifixion of Jesus. Wolfe lies in the arms of a surgeon and his adjutant, dying under a sky mingled with acrid white smoke and ominous black clouds. The general is surrounded by comrades, including Indian allies who seem more intrigued than mortified by events, and by a messenger, who is depicted as an American frontiersman and, significantly, bears the news of the momentous victory at Quebec. The entire scene is cast in an eerie red hue. What was most startling to contemporaries was that West painted these figures in the clothing they had actually worn during

16. Douglas Leach, *Arms for Empire* (New York, 1973), p. 241; John Shy, *Toward Lexington,* (Princeton, N.J., 1965), p. 147; Mercy Otis Warren, *History of the American Revolution* (Boston, 1805), vol. I, pp. iii–iv; Caroline Gilman, ed., *Letters of Eliza Wilkinson* (New York, 1969), p. 22.

the battle rather than in the togas of antiquity, a deliberate undermining of the old dictum that "modern dress could not be admitted into pictures where Heroism" was characterized.

This school of art reached its zenith during the Revolutionary War. Innumerable painters depicted battle scenes, though none surpassed John Trumbull, a native of Connecticut and a student under West in the mid-1780s. Trumbull, like his mentor, sought not only historical accuracy, but he endeavored to define the heroism of the warriors. His most famous works, *The Death of General Warren at the Battle of Bunker's Hill* and *The Death of General Montgomery in the Attack on Quebec,* reveal unmistakenly his indebtedness to West. The stricken combatants as portrayed by Trumbull have been described as "drooping Christ-figures," and, indeed, it has been suggested that both works display "Christian overtones" of martyrdom and apostolic fervor. In both paintings the mortally wounded soldier is floodlighted in a scene otherwise dark with gloomy smoke and clouds, a forbidding scene broken only be the gaily fluttering battle flags that swirl about the dying thane. Also, in both works the eyes of virtually all the nearby combatants are riveted on the wounded leader, and all, even the foes, are expressing horror at the impending loss.

Portraiture persisted, of course, and artists such as Charles Willson Peale utilized this format to lionize the young nation's warriors. His George Washington, painted in 1779 but intended to depict the victorious commander following his triumphs at Trenton and Princeton two years earlier, portrayed the general in keeping with what Professor Kenneth Silverman has termed his image of the "Christian Hero, a conqueror whose military prowess was fully matched, and thankfully tempered, by benevolence to mankind, domestic virtue, and reason." General Washington is floodlighted in the foreground, while in the rear armies, actually prisoners, march and an aide cares for the commander's horse. The implements of war abound. Washington stands over the battle flags of his defeated British and Hessian foes, and he leans rather jauntily on a cannon. A trace of smugness tugs at the corners of Washington's mouth, yet he does not appear overbearing, and he certainly manifests no airs of the martial tyrant. Peale magnificently captured the citizen-general, this Cincinnatus who, without pomposity or affectation, has overcome the professional warrior, and who is fully cognizant of the magnitude of his deed.[17]

The colonists' martial enthusiasm mounted as relations with Britain steadily deteriorated through the 1760s and 1770s. In fact, John Adams believed a pertinent rumor, "propogated with . . . dispatch," was sufficient to send many

17. Louis B. Wright et al., *The Arts in America* (New York, 1966), pp. 167, 178, 234, 236, 245–47; Julian David Proun, "Style in American Art, 1750–1800," in Charles F. Montgomery and Patricia E. Kane, eds., *American Art: 1750–1800, Towards Independence* (New Haven, Conn., 1976), pp. 36, 83; Kenneth Silverman, *A Cultural History of the American Revolution* (New York, 1976), pp. 24, 90, 175–76, 430, 466.

men scurrying for their weapons. Thousands of New Englanders—perhaps as many as twenty thousand men from one county and six thousand from another in Massachusetts—prepared to descend upon Boston with swords drawn in September 1774, when word spread that the British fleet had shelled the city. A few weeks later a similar rumor produced identical results in Philadelphia; Joseph Reed reported that perhaps "thousands would have gone at their own expense, to have joined in the revenge." John Adams noted that "the People seemed really disappointed when the News was contradicted," although many were able to vent their violent emotions in "tory hunts" within their neighborhoods. Adams added that the colonists were "more warlike . . . than they were during the last War. A martial Spirit has seized all the Colonies."[18]

More than six months before the first shot in the War for Independence was fired, several colonies adopted laws organizing companies of soldiers, some of which drilled as often as three days a week; the following spring the provincial assembly in Massachusetts urged the creation of an army of thirty thousand. The people of America, as the governor of Virginia exclaimed, had "put themselves in a posture of war." Soon, in fact, the rebel leadership, many of whom still hoped, even longed, for a negotiated settlement, feared its ability to maintain control of these armed men. One activist anguished that the militiamen were so "uneasy" that it would be difficult to restrain them much longer; they "urge us and threaten" to attack the redcoats, he added. Most advisors of the British ministry debunked such occurrences, but a professional soldier, General Thomas Gage, understood perfectly what was afoot, and he advised that his government could "get the better of America" only if it dispatched approximately twenty thousand trained soldiers, accompanied by a few contingents of Canadian troops who were specialists in the manner of war indigenous to America.[19]

Once again, as they so frequently had done in the earlier conflicts, the colonists viewed war as the means of expiating their evil ways and reforming American society. Much of this logic came from America's pulpits, where the colonists' radical clergy, its so-called "Black Regiment," preached jeremiads alleging that "by our universal declension, manifold offenses, [and] abuse of divine blessings" the colonists had provoked God into "this severe controversy." In this crisis, however, many secular agitators played on the same theme. The country was swept by the feeling that corruption and debauchery had multiplied at an alarming rate since the defeat of France in 1763; "luxury of every kind," a radical intoned, "has flowed in from abroad." While the continental culture would "refine the Taste," it contained elements "which can seduce, betray,

18. Butterfield, *Adams D&A*, vol. II, pp. 160, 235; Merrill Jensen, *Founding of a Nation* (New York, 1968), pp. 536–42.

19. Jensen, *Founding of a Nation*, pp. 549, 553, 556, 558; Gen. Gage to Berrington, 3 October 1774, in Clarence E. Carter, ed., *The Correspondence of General Thomas Gage*, 2 vols. (New Haven, 1931), vol. II, p. 656.

deceive, deprave, corrupt and debauch it." David Rittenhouse, the Philadelphia scientist, believed that "by our connections with Europe . . . our fall will be premature." Men at first were corrupted in their personal affairs, but they soon carried their vices into the public sector. Samuel Adams thought "private and publick Vices, are in Reality . . . nearly connected," and he added that there "is seldom an Instance of a Man guilty of betraying his Country, who had not before lost the Feeling of Moral Obligations in his private Connections." Adams believed the diminution of public virtue ultimately led to the extinction of liberty. Like the clergy, Adams thought that divine force provoked these dire consequences. "Communities are dealt with in this World by the wise and just Ruler of the Universe. He rewards or punishes them according to their general Character." America, the radical Whigs charged, had slid alarmingly toward degradation. It "never was, perhaps, in a more corrupt and degenerate State than at this Day," a radical concluded in 1775.[20]

But the blood spilled in the war with the parent state would serve as atonement for the national sins. America could redeem itself, said John Adams, by adopting the "great, manly, and warlike virtues." As Professor Gordon Wood has noted, belief in the principle that the "virile martial qualities—the scorn of ease, the contempt of danger, the love of valor—were what made a nation great" swept across the colonies. War, conjectured Samuel Adams, afforded the "golden opportunity of recovering the Virtue & reforming the Manner of our Country," of "restoring the ancient purity" for which their ancestors had struggled. "I think," he added in 1774, "our Countrymen discover the Spirit of Rome or Sparta."[21] Even after three years of war, some felt the reformation of the American character insufficient. More war was required, Benjamin Rush thought, "to purge away" the "impurity" which ate at the vitals of the new nation. Only at war's end did Samuel Adams conclude that the Spartan spirit he believed essential in 1774 at last had been attained. The new nation was "the Christian Sparta."[22]

20. Wood, *Creation of the Republic*, pp. 107–8, 110, 115; John Adams to Abigail Adams, April-May 1780, in L. H. Butterfield et al., eds., *Adams FC*, (Cambridge, Mass., 1963), vol. III, p. 333; Samuel Adams to James Warren, 4 November 1775, in Harry Alonzo Cushing, ed., *Writings of Adams,* 4 vols. (New York, 1904), vol. III, p. 236; Samuel Adams to John Scollary, 30 April 1776, ibid., vol. III, p. 286.

21. John Adams, *Thoughts on Government* . . . , in Charles Francis Adams, *Works,* 10 vols. (Boston, 1850–1856), vol. IV, p. 199; Wood, *Creation of the Republic,* p. 52; Samuel Adams to James Warren, 4 November 1775, in Cushing, *Writings of Adams,* vol. III, p. 235; Samuel Adams to Elbridge Gerry, 29 October 1775, ibid., vol. II, p. 231; Samuel Adams to Richard Randolph, 1 February 1775, ibid., vol. III, p. 176; Samuel Adams to Thomas Young, 17 October 1774, ibid., vol. II, p. 163.

22. Rush to John Adams, 8 August 1777, in L. H. Butterfield, ed., *Letters of Benjamin Rush,* 2 vols. (Princeton, N.J., 1951), vol. I, p. 152; Samuel Adams to John Scollay, 30 December 1780, in Cushing, *Writings of Adams,* vol. IV, p. 238. An extensive analysis of the sense of national degradation and transformation can be found in Wood, *Creation of the Republic,* pp. 36–124.

Many colonists entered the crisis with extraordinary aplomb. Whereas in Europe a great fear of trained soldiers existed among the populace, most colonists seemed not to have shared in that anxiety. The Americans fancied themselves as hearty, resourceful frontiersmen, and gullibly swallowed tales of their prowess with the "rifle gun." In addition, they were confident that a citizen army, motivated by the ideology of freedom, would be a match for professional automatons; indeed, they believed their commendable service in the two most recent intercolonial wars had demonstrated their martial capabilities. Many were anxious to duplicate the exploits of earlier settlers. "The People are recollecting the Achievements of their Ancestors," Samuel Adams reported, "and whenever it shall be necessary for them to draw their Swords . . . they will shew themselves to be worthy of such Ancestors." Some, like Dr. Rush, believed that Charles Lee, major-general in the Continental army and formerly an officer in the British legions, had done the most to lessen "in our soldiers their superstitious fears of the valor and discipline of the British army." Lee lauded the conduct of Americans in earlier wars, observing that he could recollect instances when British regulars panicked and were "saved from destruction by the valour of a few Virginians," but he could not remember "a single instance of ill behavior in the Provincials." Valorous regulars undoubtedly were superior to raw recruits, he admitted, although he contended that the colonists could acquire "all the essentials necessary to form infantry for real service . . . in a few months." Thomas Paine calculated additional American advantages: it had a sufficient population to grapple with England; it could build and staff a quality fleet in short order; its international credit was excellent; and it could anticipate foreign assistance.[23]

Although the colonists believed fervently in their own martial capabilities, they belittled British prowess. General Lee thought the redcoats "expert in the tricks of their parade," but "they knew not how to fight." Their leadership was inadequate, too, he added, suggesting that no British general was the equal of the late General Wolfe. Many attributed the alleged British shortcomings to a creeping degeneracy which had engulfed the parent state; "how fallen is the nation!" a colonial polemicist proclaimed.[24] Political divisiveness, coupled with the inevitably unreliable mercenaries, added to Britain's woes.

23. Shy, *Toward Lexington*, p. 380; Jensen, *Founding of the Republic*, pp. 541–42; [Charles Lee], *Strictures on a Pamphlet . . .* (Boston, 1775), pp. 14, 16; Shy, *A People Numerous*, pp. 146–47; Samuel Adams to Arthur Lee, 29 January 1775, in Cushing, *Writings of Adams*, vol. III, p. 171; Don Higginbotham, *War of American Independence* (New York, 1971), p. 89; [Charles Lee], *General Lee's Letter to General Burgoyne . . .* (New York, 1775), p. 6; [Thomas Paine], *Common Sense* [1776], in Philip S. Foner, ed., *Writings of Paine*, 2 vols. (New York, 1945), vol. I, pp. 31–39.

24. Charles Lee, *Strictures* (Boston, 1775), pp. 8, 10, 14; Philip Davidson, *Propaganda and the American Revolution, 1763–1783* (Chapel Hill, N.C., 1941), pp. 161–63; Paine, *Common Sense*, in Foner, *Writings of Paine*, vol. I, pp. 36, 50, 53, 56; Paine, *American Crisis*, in ibid., vol. I, pp. 63, 65, 67, 70, 75, 79, 96, 112, 114–15, 143.

These vitriolic attacks on British soldiers fell on fertile ground, for many colonists had long entertained the notion that amateurs were superior to professionals in the martial arts. The concept may have been as old as the colonies. At any rate, a century and a half before the Revolution John Rolfe expressed the belief that ''a plain soldier that can use a pick-ax and spade is better than five knights.'' The idea was nourished by the colonists' record of triumph in the wars with the native Americans, as well as by occasional colonial achievements during the intercolonial wars, such as the seizure of Louisbourg in 1745. Furthermore, the idea was abetted by occasional British failures, the most sensational, of course, being the rout of General Edward Braddock in 1755. In fact, Braddock not only failed disastrously, but contemporaries additionally concluded, in part because of the post-battle allegations of some of the redcoat survivors, that the Americans ''did the moast Execution of Any'' that day on the Monongahela. Finally, the colonists simply believed that free men fighting for a cause made better soldiers than spiritless professionals. ''There is a certain enthusiasm in liberty,'' as Hamilton put it, ''that makes human nature rise above itself, in acts of bravery and heroism.''[25]

If anything, the colonists, extremely aware of their violent disposition, displayed nearly as much fear of one another as of the prowess of the redcoats. On the eve of independence, a considerable fear existed in the South that the northern states someday might annex their comrades south of Pennsylvania. The Loyalists whipped up much of this anxiety. ''The northern colonies, inured to military discipline and hardships'' were depicted as likely to ''carry devastation and havock over the southern'' region. One Tory even predicted that the inhabitants of the ''Northern districts'' would become the ''future Goths, Vandals, Huns, or Franks'' of America. A north-south alliance was portrayed as unnatural. One was more likely to see the ''wolf and the lamb to feed together as Virginians to form a cordial union with the saints of New England.'' In the inevitable clash, these writers predicted, the southern states would be ''easy objects of conquest.'' Not only were southerners unused to warfare, they contained ''a dangerous enemy [of slaves] within their own bowels.'' But the Loyalists were not alone in perceiving these dangers. John Adams heard other members of Congress express concern that New England, ''full of Veteran Soldiers,'' would ''conceive Designs unfavourable to the other Colonies.'' A congressman from New York expressed his dread of the New Englanders, and he too alluded to the ''Goths and Vandalls'' to the north.[26]

25. Darrett B. Rutman, ''Militant New World,'' (Ph.D. diss., University of Virginia, 1959), p. 763; Kopperman, *Braddock*, pp. 95, 107–8, 302n; Hamilton, *Farmer Refuted*, in Syrett and Cooke, *Hamilton Papers*, vol. I, p. 155.

26. [Joseph Galloway], *A Candid Examination* . . . (New York, 1775), p. 47; Jonathan Boucher, *A View of the Causes and Consequences of the American Revolution* . . . (London, 1797), lxxii; Jonathan Boucher, *Reminiscences of a American Loyalist, 1778–1789* (Pt. Washington, N.Y., 1971), p. 134; John Adams to James Warren, 6 June 1775, in Burnett, *Letters of Members of Congress*, vol. I, p. 153; Butterfield, *Adams D&A*, vol. II, p. 107.

Despite its alleged antipathy to war, America lavished immediate, and immense, attention upon its new heroes, the military activists. America's first
intercolonial thanes, Dr. Warren and General Montgomery, were acquired in
the initial months of the War for Independence. Of Warren it was claimed that
"His Virtues shall remain when we have left the Stage: His praises shall be
spoke for many an age to come."[27] Soon a carefully orchestrated canonization
of the fallen physician-patriot commenced. Warren was described as the "godlike
Warren" who had ascended to the military heroes' "own native heaven, where
angels' plaudits to his deeds are given." "WARREN the great, the good, is
now no more," still another commentator mourned, but "He's left this earth,
to hail those blessed abodes . . . where NORTHS shall vex not, and the virtuous
rest." Posthumously, Montgomery, likewise, was rendered larger than life. He
was depicted as having been a "great, disinterested, affectionate" man of the
"utmost benevolence." Soon, too, playwrights made him the central figure in
their propaganda pageants. Nor was it long before "that great CHIEF Washington" and his fellow officers were acclaimed. "The praise is due to WASH-
INGTON, Whose glory now, and ever shone," one poet expostulated.[28] Another
lyricist exclaimed

> Honor commands great Washington I sing,
> The noble feat of Count de Grasse must ring. . .
> Brave Greene I sing, with all his Patriot Sons,
> But most adore Great Godlike WASHINGTON. . .
> Great Washington doth thunder thro' the plain,
> And piles the field with mountains of the slain;
> His foes they tremble and his name adore,
> Confess his might.'till time shall be no more.[29]

What has been suggested here—that Enlightenment concepts attacking war
did not strike a responsive chord in the colonies; that Americans lived in an
environment of considerable violence; and that the colonists not only were
prepared to do battle with Britain in 1775 if a peaceful reconciliation could not
be produced, but their violent history perhaps rendered Americans psycholog-
ically eager for conflict—flies in the face of much that has been written about
colonial life. The colonists customarily are depicted as leading tranquil lives,
isolated on this huge continent by the vast Atlantic barrier from the recurrent
dynastic discord of Europe, from the conflicts that not infrequently spilled over
to America, but tended to be confined to the remote frontier of the New World.

27. *New England Chronicle*, 23 June 1775, in Frothingham, *Warren*, p. 535.
28. Conner, *Autobiography of Rush*, p. 111; Frothingham, *Warren*, pp. 535–41; William Smith,
An Oration in Memory of General Montgomery . . . (Philadelphia, 1776), pp. 32–34; *A Poem, His
Lordship Humbled* . . . , in Lawrence and Bumgardner, *Massachusetts Broadsides of the American
Revolution* (Amherst, Mass., 1976), p. 107.
29. *A Poem*, in Lawrence and Bumgardner, *Massachusetts Broadsides*, p. 107.

Of course, many historians have observed the impact of various war-related occurrences on the lives of the colonists, even preparing the ground for the American Revolution. It frequently has been noted, for example, that the removal of the French and the Spanish threats following the French and Indian War caused many colonists to deem further British protection superfluous. In addition, this last intercolonial war helped plunge Britain into economic difficulties, which in turn prompted the parent state to initiate the new revenue-raising measures that aroused the colonists. These wars, moreover, placed British soldiers and colonists in close proximity to one another, leading the English to deride the provincials as their backward country cousins, while the colonists, bridling at the haughty demeanor of their British comrades, lost whatever affection they once had for the elite of the parent state.[30]

Two additional points frequently have been made by scholars. One is that the colonists, far from prizing any military ethic had long shared Britain's aversion to standing armies, and that the presence of British regulars in Boston, and the subsequent occurrence of inflammatory incidents such as the Boston Massacre, helped precipitate the War for Independence. The second point is that Americans desired separation from Britain in order to escape warfare. Franklin's famous remark that America must go its own way or forever be dragged into wars, and Paine's contention of an inevitable symbiotic relationship between monarchy and warfare are often cited as evidence for this contention. Each idea conveys the impression of a peace-loving, nonviolent folk, a burgeoning nation of colonists who sought freedom in order to liberate themselves from standing armies and who fought this war with Britain so they might avoid fighting future wars. Each idea merits consideration.

That the colonists, or at least the Bostonians, were anguished by the presence of British troops after 1768 is incontrovertible. The soldiers frequently were joustled and cursed by Boston rowdies, and following the Boston Massacre an enormous, and quite successful, campaign of invective against the troops was waged in the press and from the pulpit. The British soldiers were alleged to have raped and plundered numerous civilians, mugged and pistol whipped many innocent evening pedestrians, incited slaves to run away, and provoked a high incidence of prostitution, gambling, drinking, swearing, Sabbath-breaking, and additional forms of debauchery. More important, however, as Bernard Bailyn has indicated, was the Bostonian's fear ''not simply of armies but of *standing armies,* a phrase that had distinctive connotations, derived, like so much of their political thought, from the seventeenth century and articulated for them by earlier English radicals.''[31] These fears were never better expressed than by Samuel Adams:

30. In particular, see Lawrence H. Gipson, ''The American Revolution as an aftermath of the Great War for Empire, 1754–1763,'' *Political Science Quarterly* 65 (March 1950), pp. 86–104.
31. Oliver M. Dickerson, ed., *Boston Under Military Rule, 1768–1769* (New York, 1970), pp. 11, 15–17, 26, 34, 38–39, 42–43, 47, 63, 71, 79, 93; Bernard Bailyn, ed., *Pamphlets of the American Revolution, 1750–1776* (Cambridge, Mass, 1965), vol. I, p. 41.

A standing Army, however necessary it may be at some times, is always dangerous to the Liberties of the People. Soldiers are apt to consider themselves as a Body distinct from the rest of the Citizens. They have their Arms always in their hands. Their Rules and their Discipline is severe. They soon become attached to their officers and disposed to yield implicit Obedience to their Commands. Such a power should be watched with a Jealous Eye. . . . Men who have been long subject to military Laws and inured to military Customs and Habits, may lose the Spirit and Feeling of Citizens. And even Citizens, having been used to admire the Heroism which the Commanders of their own Army have displayed, and to look up to them as their Saviors may be prevailed upon to surrender to them those Rights for the protection of which against Invaders they had employed and paid them.[32]

Writing in part about their attitude toward standing armies, Professor Bailyn has suggested that it was the "meaning imparted to the events after 1763 by this integrated group of attitudes and ideas that lies behind the colonists' rebellion."[33]

While the colonists' concerns after 1768 were real and undoubtedly played some role in the emotional furor that helped trigger hostilities, the extent of their alleged deep-seated anxieties may be questioned. There is little evidence, for instance, of consternation among the colonists regarding the British regulars who were stationed among them for varying intervals during the hundred years before the Revolution. Although British redcoats first arrived during the war with the Dutch for New York, and thereafter came periodically to help suppress colonial rebellions, fight the French and Spanish, or police newly acquired territories, friction was so rare that, as Professor Shy has noted, "one has to search" for signs of "attacks on the very idea of regular troops in America *before* the [Boston] Massacre."[34]

Occasionally, feathers were ruffled, though grievances usually concerned questions of who was to pay to quarter the troops, or the arrogance of the redcoats rather than fears that these troops jeopardized colonial liberties. John Adams admitted, for instance, that the "Treatment of the Provincial officers and soldiers by the British officers during [the French and Indian] War, made my blood boil in my veins." Rumors persisted of British commanders who had treated the provincials as "slaves," who had, with an "arrogance unchecked . . . lorded it over and insulted" colonial officers, and whose conduct resulted in "the great injury and oppression of many poor people." Still, the English mistrust of standing armies lingered, and that tradition, coupled with the intemperate political climate of 1768 (the frightening Stamp Act crisis only recently had ended and the colonists were, at that moment, instituting economic

32. Samuel Adams to James Warren, 7 January 1776, in Cushing, *Writings of Adams,* vol. III, pp. 250–51.
33. Bailyn, *Ideological Origins,* p. 94. The best recent survey is John Todd White's doctoral dissertation, "Standing Armies"; see especially pp. 49–57.
34. Shy, *Toward Lexington,* p. 376.

boycotts in protest of the Townshend Duties), guaranteed that the arrival of redcoats would provoke almost as much anxiety as if an invading French or Spanish army had been spotted suddenly nearing Boston Harbor. In *The Federalist,* in fact, Hamilton alludes to this very point, suggesting that the sensational atmosphere of the 1760s and 1770s "quickened the public sensibility" and aroused old, largely forgotten anxieties.[35] Astute observers in Whitehall should not have been taken by surprise by the colonists' outbursts toward the "lobster backs," even though their clamorous and vituperative rhetoric was almost without precedence.

For a people who allegedly harbored such long-standing antipathies toward standing armies, it was ironic, not to mention surprising, that the colonists established their own regular force in a remarkably short time following the commencement of war with Great Britain. Several factors contributed to the relatively easy transition from the militia force used at the outset of the rebellion to the Continental army. One was that the colonists' aversion to standing armies may, as Professor Charles Lofgren has suggested, simply have been "exaggerated" by later generations.[36] The evidence introduced in an earlier chapter would indicate that the colonists, at best, were ambivalent toward warriors. Undoubtedly they brought some of the long-standing English biases toward standing armies to the New World. On the other hand, their recurrent warfare led them to heap praise upon their own warriors and, before 1763, upon the English regulars who came to their assistance. Their troops, and the warrior ethic in general, were eulogized far more than they were deprecated. Moreover, although some suspicion and apprehension lingered, it was counterbalanced by the pervasive spirit of republican virtue, a phenomenon discussed later in this chapter, which swept the colonies during the rebellion.

The slide toward a regular army also arose from the steady deterioration in America's military position following the early success at Bunker Hill. It quickly became clear that the nature of America's armed forces had to be altered if the rebellion was to be continued. Samuel Adams, quoted at length on the dangers of a standing force, watched the war's progression for only a few months before advocating princely land and cash bounties for long-term enlistments; eventually, he sat on a congressional committee which recommended virtually dictatorial powers for General Washington. Dr. Warren wasted even less time than Adams before he urged the appointment of a national "Generalissimo." "A summer's

35. Richard Kohn, *Eagle and Sword* (New York, 1975), p. 5; Richard H. Kohn, "The Murder of the Militia System in the Aftermath of the American Revolution," in James Kirby Martin, ed., *The Human Dimensions of Nation Making* (Madison, Wis., 1976), p. 307; "Daniel Dulany's Newsletter, 9 December 1775," *PMHB* 3, no. 1 (1879), pp. 14, 21; Jack P. Greene, "The South Carolina Quartering Dispute," *South Carolina History Magazine* 60 (October 1959), pp. 311–15; *The Federalist,* 26:161.

36. Charles A. Lofgren, "Compulsory Military Service under the Constitution: The Original Understanding," *WMQ,* 3d Ser. 33 (January 1976), p. 71.

experience has now taught us better'' than to rely on the militia, Paine likewise concluded; "they will not do for a long campaign,'' he added, and he reasoned that the "only way to finish a war with the least possible bloodshed, or perhaps without any, is to collect an army'' and keep it under arms at all times.[37] In short, the very success of the rebellion seemed to hinge on the creation of a regular army.

An additional factor that aided in the transition to a standing army during the Revolution was that the colonists' commitment to militia forces had deteriorated considerably by 1775. In fact, while the colonists paid excessive lip service to the militia concept, their actual attachment to this kind of military force was probably less intense than historians have generally believed. The major colonial conflicts, engagements with Indians as well as the important intercolonial conflicts, which included invasions of French Canada and Spanish Florida, were fought principally by armies raised for the occasion. Troops were secured by bribery, coercion, offers of bonuses, skullduggery, and, if necessary, conscription. If called up at all, the militia was usually kept at home as a purely defensive unit. In fact, while the militia remained active and performed credibly in some colonies, elsewhere it might be used so seldomly that it virtually ceased to exist for generations. John Shy has noted, for instance, that Governor Alexander Spotswood of Virginia was unable to muster his colony's militia in 1713 when Virginia's frontiers were menaced by the Tuscarora because the various units had fallen into a state of neglect and inattention nearly fifty years previously.[38]

Moreover, well before the Revolution, many colonists had concluded that the militia had grown worthless as the scope of colonial warfare increased. Simply put, many citizens not only had no interest in fighting wars hundreds of miles from their homes, but they actively balked at the prospect of such service. As a result, the early setbacks during the Revolution, especially Britain's rather easy seizure of New York and parts of New Jersey in 1776, confirmed the worst suspicions of many colonists. By September of that year Congress passed resolutions that permitted enlistments for the duration of the war. John Hancock succinctly addressed the issue. "Without a well disciplined Army,'' he stated, "we can never expect success agst [*sic*] veteran troops; and it is totally impossible we should have a well disciplined Army, unless our Troops are engaged to serve the war.'' Hence, the colonies quickly established an interprovincial army under a military commander-in-chief. The civilian authorities, however, never delegated unrestricted powers to the general. From the moment of his appointment Washington knew that his position would only "continue in force, until revoked by this, or a future Congress.''[39]

37. Ford, *Journals of the Continental Congress,* vol. VI, pp. 1045–46; William Wells, *The Life and Public Services of Samuel Adams,* 3 vols. (Boston, 1865–1868), vol. II, pp. 307, 456, 458; Frothingham, *Warren,* p. 485; Paine, *American Crisis,* in Foner, *Writings of Paine,* vol. I, p. 54.

38. Shy, *A People Armed,* pp. 27–32.

39. White, "Standing Armies,'' pp. 90–93, 112, 145; Ford, *Journals of the Continental Congress,* vol. II, p. 96.

An additional point often made by historians is that the colonists declared independence in order to increase the odds against future warfare. The point is true, but misleading. It would be more accurate to argue that the colonists hoped to escape wars which England believed necessary; by escaping Britain, the Americans would be free to engage in the conflicts they deemed essential to their interests and aspirations. There is no evidence to suggest any concerted disenchantment in America with Britain's imperial wars before relations with the parent state soured. The wars may, in fact, have been more popular in the colonies than in the parent state. Parliament was advised by American representatives that the colonists freely participated in the Empire's wars and that they made "no distinction of wars, as to their duty of assisting in them." Britain's "speedy succour" in the recurrent intercolonial wars frequently was applauded.[40]

However, following Spain's retrenchment and the French abandonment of mainland America in 1763, carping about America's frequent involvement in these wars began to surface among the colonists. Increasingly, the complaint was voiced that Britain waged these wars "solely for her own benefit." Franklin, in fact, told the House of Commons in 1765 that the French and Indian War "was really a British war." Some colonists, for the first time, insisted that the wars had been detrimental to American interests and security. John Dickinson suggested that the acquisition of new territory further dispersed colonial settlement, creating additional problems of defense; some insisted that the newly procured lands would affect property owners adversely by reducing land values in the original colonies. James Otis even candidly acknowledged that Britain's acquisition of foreign sugar islands hindered the American smuggling activities, and he ominously warned that in the future the colonists might be inclined to fight only when their interests were clearly jeopardized.[41]

Having reached the revolutionary conclusion that the intercolonial wars were no longer in their interest, the colonists proceeded to a second revelation. Before the 1760s, articulate colonists were in agreement that war was endemic to Europe, but that Britain's august constitutional structure served as a bulwark against malevolent rulers who might be inclined to precipitate hostilities. The Anglo-American crisis of the 1760s and 1770s exploded that concept, and left the colonists with the belief that England, like its counterparts on the continent,

40. *The Examination of Benjamin Franklin*, in Labaree, *Papers of Franklin*, vol. XIII, pp. 150–51; John Morgan et al., *Four Dissertations* . . . (Philadelphia, 1766), p. 108.

41. Merrill Jensen, ed., *English Historical Documents*, 12 vols. (London and New York, 1955), vol. IX, pp. 655–56; [James Otis], *The Rights of the British Colonies Asserted and Proved* (Boston, 1764), pp. 43, 58; [Daniel Dulany], *Considerations on the Propriety of Imposing Taxes in the British Colonies* . . . (Annapolis, Md., 1765), pp. 17–18; *The Examination of Benjamin Franklin*, in Labaree, *Papers of Franklin*, vol. XIII, pp. 150–51; [John Dickinson], *Letters from a Farmer in Pennsylvania to the Inhabitants of the British Colonies* (Philadelphia, 1769), pp. 43, 50; [James Otis], *A Vindication of the British Colonies* . . . (Boston, 1765), p. 4; Stephen Hopkins, *The Rights of Colonies Examined* (Providence, R.I., 1765), p. 21.

was governed by a thoroughly base, privileged elite who had but one aim: the perpetuation of its rule through the acquisition of the riches of others abroad. Having pillaged the homelands and Ireland "to the last farthing," the suspicion grew that England's profligate rulers now were turning to America to pick it clean.[42]

For some, such as Thomas Paine, who popularized the notion, the epitome of the privileged orders was Britain's monarch; that country's frequent wars, according to Paine and others, could be traced to the "evil of monarchy." The monarch was the "principal ruffian" of the state, an official who "hath little more to do than to make war and give away places." It was the presence of British troops in Boston after 1768 that convinced many colonists of the king's implication in the "plot" to eliminate American liberties, and these same circumstances convinced many of the inevitable link between monarchism and recurrent warfare. The monarchical system, therefore, "instead of making for peace . . . makes against it, and destroys the very foundation it seems to stand upon." Paine, in fact, concluded that England had been at war more often than it had enjoyed peace for nearly five hundred years. Franklin, who had done as much as any colonists to assist Britain in the intercolonial wars, and who shortly before had considered moving from the colonies to the parent state, suddenly claimed that Britain quarreled with other nations, then went to war with these foreign powers, then obliged the colonists to enter the conflict, then took the credit for protecting America from enemies it otherwise would not have had. By 1775 he had concluded that if the colonists did not detach themselves from this "old rotten state," the monarch and his ministers would "ever drag us after them in all the plundering wars which their desperate circumstances . . . and rapacity may prompt them to undertake."[43]

The idea that America could escape *unwanted* wars by separating from Britain had grown to be part of the conventional wisdom by 1775 and 1776. In part, the notion grew from the visionary image the eighteenth-century colonists had of themselves. North America, a pristine continent, had afforded its immigrants the unique opportunity of beginning anew, of eradicating the worst evils and institutions of the Old World. The suggestion by a European that the "epoch

42. Arthur A. Buffinton, "Puritan View of War," CSM, *Pub.*, XXVIII: 67–86; Ebenezer Pemberton, *A Sermon* (Boston, 1756), p. 6; Gilbert Tennent, *The late Association* (Philadelphia, 1748), pp. 6–7; Mather, *War is Lawful*, pp. 8–9; Nathanial Appleton, *The Origin of War* (Boston, 1733), pp. 14, 18; Paine, *American Crisis*, in Foner, *Writings of Paine*, vol. I, pp. 124, 146–47; Paine, *Common Sense*, ibid., vol. I, pp. 12, 15–16.

43. Paine, *American Crisis*, in Foner, *Writings of Paine*, vol. I, pp. 81–82, 124, 147; Gerald Stourzh, *Benjamin Franklin* (Stanford, Calif., 1970), p. 111; Franklin to Joseph Galloway, 25 February 1775, in Albert H. Smyth, ed., *Writings of Franklin*, 8 vol. (New York, 1905–1907), vol. VI, p. 312; Garry Wills, *Inventing America* (Garden City, N.Y., 1978), p. 40; White, "Standing Armies," pp. 58–59, 62, 68–69; Burgh, *Political Disquistions*, vol. II, pp. 341–42, 344, 348–49, 355–57, 429, 447, 450–51, 465.

has become one of the total fall of Europe," that everything European "turns into rottenness," and that "all hastens to renew itself in America" seemed quite logical to many colonists, particularly to those who had seen Europe at first hand.[44] The Americans, as Professor Russel B. Nye, has noted, believed they were

building a new society from which all the flaws and inequalities of Europe could be erased; none of the old institutions . . . were successfully transplanted to the New World. . . . The idea that men could shape their world for the best was especially appealing to Americans, who believed that they already had done a good deal toward accomplishing exactly that.[45]

Some perceptive colonists recognized the absurdity of such ideas. Franklin regarded men as "Beings very badly constructed" whose natural qualities were not likely to be altered drastically. For all his optimism, Paine acknowledged that governments were necessary evils because of the "inability of moral virtue to govern the world." Nevertheless, these colonists believed that if America could substitute republican government for monarchical rule, the corruption that characterized Europe and had triggered that continent's endless wars, could be tempered through what Gordon Wood has called the "regenerative effects" of republican government. In England, Paine asserted, "the monarchy hath poisoned the Republic," but in America, with its independent governments stripped of monarchical and aristocratic privilege, "a new era for politics is struck—a new method of thinking has arisen." The very Revolution which promulgated these changes would "give a new turn to human affairs" by launching a moral reformation. War would be rendered anachronistic.[46]

Other writers discovered additional reasons for believing that separation from Britain would forestall undesired warfare. Some thought an independent United States could isolate itself from Europe. The Atlantic Wall offered the shield, they suggested, and continued agrarianism afforded the means of avoiding contact with the Old World. A more important radical element believed that an independent America, loosened from Britain's constrictive mercantile policies, would become a commercial polity. These writers denied that war and commerce went hand-in-hand, and, in fact, they insisted that trade actually mitigated contention. The very forces which impelled Britain and Europe to annex others—the

44. Adrienne Koch, ed., *The American Enlightenment* (New York, 1965), p. 20; Wood, *Creation of the Republic,* pp. 47, 106–7; Bailyn, *Ideological Origins,* pp. 55–93; Louis Hartz, *The Liberal Tradition in America* (New York, 1955), pp. 53–54.

45. Russell B. Nye, *This Almost Chosen People* (East Lansing, Mich., 1966), pp. 2–3.

46. Wood, *Creation of the Republic,* pp. 57, 66, 68–69, 91–93, 100–1, 120; Paine, *Common Sense,* in Foner, *Writings of Paine,* vol. I, pp. 16–17; [Thomas Paine], *Letter to the Abbe Raynal* (Philadelphia, 1782), in ibid., vol. II, p. 243; Felix Gilbert, *To the Farewell Address* (Princeton, N.J., 1961), pp. 65–66; Lawrence Kaplan, *Colonies to Nation* (New York, 1972), p. 93.

search for additional wealth—would lead the same states to seek America's riches, but the dictates of commerce would compel these powers to act peacefully. Why go to war, a colonist wondered, when what was desired could be procured peacefully through commerce? To make war under these conditions would be akin to "setting the bull-dog upon a customer at the shop door." These writers, as Drew McCoy has demonstrated, adapted the traditional anti-mercantile biases of classical republicanism to their own republican sympathies. They suggested that commerce and industry would elevate a people "above a level of savage subsistence . . . thereby securing the virtues of the American people." This was essential for the salvation of republicanism, which, in turn, was essential to the preservation of the peace. Hence, the political system was the key to peace, but the preservation of that system hinged upon the economic system.[47]

Some feared that a weak, independent America would invite European interventionism and, consequently, more warfare would occur than the colonists had ever experienced while tied to Britain. But most radicals brushed aside such anxieties. The realities of international affairs, in addition to virtuous American republicanism, they argued, would act as a deterrent against war. Many thought it inconceivable that any European power would attempt to gain by conquest what Britain, after nearly two centuries of nurturing, had been unable to retain. Moreover, even the worst despot would have to act temperately, for an attack on America would so imperil the European balance of power that other nations would rush to assist the new nation. "They would not let any one nation engross us," a radical speculated, "lest such an acquisition should enable that nation to be too powerful for its neighbors. Thus are the small states in Europe kept independent." In addition, some believed the European powers would be too preoccupied in the foreseeable future to encroach on the United States. With several "young monarchs upon the principal thrones of Europe [and] two old ones looking with hatred and revenge" against them, one pamphleteer conjectured, Europe would be troubled with its own contentions for years to come. Some in the colonies thought it incomprehensible that European autocrats would tolerate America's new republican regimes, but no place existed for such pessimistic speculation in the radicals' rhetoric. For one thing, the expense of attempting to subjugate America, as well as to police the trade of sullen colonists, was thought to be a deterrent for even the most deluded despot. In addition,

47. Benjamin Franklin, "Positions to be Examined," in Labaree, *Papers of Franklin*, vol. XVI, p. 109; Stourzh, *Benjamin Franklin*, pp. 100–11; Drew R. McCoy, "Benjamin Franklin's Vision of a Republican Political Economy for America," *WMQ*, 3d Ser. 35 (October 1978), pp. 622, 627; Paine, *Common Sense*, in Foner, *Writings of Paine*, vol. I, p. 20; Paine, *American Crisis*, ibid., vol. I, p. 145; [Thomas Paine], "Thoughts on Defensive War," ibid., vol. II, p. 56; [Thomas Paine], "The Forester to Cato," ibid., vol. II, p. 68; Gerald Stourzh, *Alexander Hamilton and the Idea of Republican Government* (Stanford, Calif., 1970), pp. 142–45; [David Ramsay], *An Oration on the Advantages of American Independence* . . . (Charleston, S.C., 1778), pp. 8, 11.

many thought it indisputable that all European princes, regardless of their de-
basement, would find that the advantages of free trade with America outweighed
their anxiety over republicanism. Finally, it was presumed that every power
would realize that any attempt to overrun America would only drive the colonists
back into the arms of Britain, thereby strengthening an Old World rival.[48]

Some fatuously hoped that Britain would be influenced similarly by the sub-
tleties of international politics. Perhaps the ministry would apprehend the advantages of free trade with an independent America over a union with recalcitrant
colonists; or, perhaps, because it had stood alone so often against its European
rivals, Britain would realize that the friendship of the United States was essential.
As the young Hamilton put it, the parent state might understand that it would
"reap from us . . . a degree of stability and lasting prosperity."[49]

Therefore, an independent United States was more secure and more likely to
avoid unwanted wars than a colonial America, in the estimation of these writers.
Once independent, a Virginian concluded in this vein, "all nations of Europe
will protect us and keep us so. . . . This will be much better than to be under
the protection of . . . the most powerful nation in the world."[50]

Hence, by 1776 the colonists did hope to free themselves of Britain's wars,
and that desire played an important role in the decision for independence. But,
as mentioned earlier, it is misleading to suggest that the colonists severed their
ties with the parent state in order to avoid war. It was unwanted, inexpedient
wars that the radical colonists hoped to avoid. Many revolutionaries, in fact,
embraced expansionist and aggressive notions that were no less ambitious than
the schemes of the imperial overlords in Whitehall. A full generation before the
Revolution, the governor of Nova Scotia, warned of the likelihood of an assault
on his province by the colonists to the south. By 1776 the feeling had grown
strong in the colonies that Britain's assistance was no longer necessary, but was,
indeed, an unwelcome restraint on the fulfillment of American designs. Many
Americans believed, as Professor Richard Van Alstyne stated, that they had a
"pre-emptive right to the continent." Much of the western region, Florida, the
fisheries in the North Atlantic, and Canada, including Nova Scotia, Cape Breton
Isle, and Newfoundland, were believed to be the natural possessions of the
United States. Of course, endeavors to seize these lands, whether in the colonial
invasion of Canada in 1775 or in George Rogers Clark's western campaign later
during the war, were couched in terms of national security. The invasion of
Canada was portrayed as a defensive gesture "dictated by the law of self-

48. [Jacob Green], *Observations on the Reconciliation of Great-Britain and the Colonies* (New
York, 1776), pp. 8–10, 13; [Anon.], *Remarks on a Late Pamphlet entitled Plain Truth* (Philadelphia,
1776), pp. 9–13.

49. Abbe Raynal, *The Sentiments of a Foreigner* . . . (Philadelphia, 1775), p. 25; Hamilton, *The
Farmer Refuted,* in Syrett and Cooke, *Hamilton Papers,* vol. I, p. 161;

50. Arthur Lee, *An Appeal to the Justice and Interests of the People of Great-Britain* . . . (New
York, 1775), pp. 36–37; *Virginia Gazette,* 17 February and 24 August 1776.

preservation." General Washington assured the Canadians that the American armies were not sent to plunder but to assist in securing the rights of Englishmen. Otherwise, the Canadians also ran the risk of being "transported into foreign countries to fight battles in which you have no interest, and to spill your blood in conflicts from which neither honor nor emolument can be derived." The war in Canada also was depicted as essential to avoid future conflicts. Acquisition of Canada by the United States "wd ensure a safe & lasting peace," whereas if Great Britain or some other power controlled the region, international tension would be unavoidable. Paine argued that since the "seeds of almost every former war have been seen in the injudicious or defective terms of the preceding peace," it followed logically that the United States should fight a war to acquire Canada in order to prevent a future war to acquire the region.[51]

Some radicals were less circumspect. "Canada must be ours," John Adams asserted. Jefferson believed the colonists required Canada to "complete the American union." Samuel Adams insisted openly that the United States should procure Quebec, Nova Scotia, and the Newfoundland fisheries by arms or by treaty. "Florida too is a tempting object," he added. The new nation, he continued, would be on "solid Footing" only when it attained "what Nature designs we sh[ould] have." "Will it ever do," a radical asked, for Britain to have "Canada, Nova Scotia and the Floridas, or any of them? We will have perpetual Wars with Britain while she has a foot of Ground in America." Others stressed the notion that it was America's destiny to expand. "Nature, in her distribution of favors, seems to have appointed" these regions to America, a radical observed.

America's right to the wilderness frontier lying to the west was not even debated, and the revolutionaries pursued a dual policy with regard to this region. On the one hand, armies such as Clark's or Sullivan's were dispatched strategically according to the exigencies of the war. On the other hand, the rebels, especially after the French entered the war in 1778, acted always with an eye on the eventual peace settlement; campaigns sometimes were planned so as to strengthen the American hand at the bargaining table. Washington, therefore, in planning the Sullivan expedition, remarked that the Continental army "should be ready to strike an important blow . . . for opening a door for a further progress" into these unsettled lands. The radicals were in agreement that these

51. Richard Van Alstyne, *Rising American Empire* (Oxford, 1960), pp. 8–9; [Anon.], *The Power and Grandeur of Great Britain* . . . (New York, 1768), p. 22; Force, *American Archives,* vol. II, p. 1838; Ford, *Journals of the Continental Congress,* vol. II, p. 69; Gustave Lanctot, *Canada and the American Revolution, 1774–1783* (Cambridge, Mass., 1967), p. 65; Albert K. Weinberg, *Manifest Destiny* (Baltimore, 1958), pp. 18–24; Thomas Jefferson to Francis Eppes, 12 November 1775, in Julian P. Boyd et al., eds., *Jefferson Papers* (Princeton, N.J., 1950-), vol. I, p. 264; Jefferson to John Randolph, 29 November 1775, ibid., vol. I, p. 269; Samuel Adams to Sameul Cooper, 21 February 1779, in Cushing, *Writings of Adams,* vol. IV, p. 128; Thomas Paine, "Peace and the Newfoundland Fisheries," in Foner, *Writings of Paine,* vol. II, p. 206.

vast British territories would provide "treasures [which] might supply what the mediocrity of her own production denies her."[52]

Many radicals conceived of an independent American power that would grow boundlessly. The new nation's burgeoning population would soon sweep across the undeveloped West, its actions "conducted with an energy peculiar to new societies." United States' ships would "ride triumphant on the ocean, and . . . carry American thunder around the world. . . . The wealth of Europe, Asia, and Africa . . . will flow in upon America."[53] An exuberant radical bard, moved by the wartime alliance with France after 1778, was moved to write that

> If (so Heaven permit!) the union to stand
> 'Twixt potent Gallia, and our rising land,
> Firm leagu'd in one, what mortel pow'r can hope
> With those so formidably great to cope?
> So great, so happy, that the world shall own
> No clime, no empire is so pow'rful known.[54]

In part, it was these unabashed expansionist desires that prompted the movement for the creation of a standing American army following independence. Of course, as was suggested elsewhere in this chapter, the experience of fighting European regulars, both before and during the Revolution, demonstrated the weaknesses of a militia force. Trainbands had come to be ridiculed as "the mimicry of soldiership." They were depicted as costly, inefficient, and unreliable.[55] Accompanying these complaints, however, was the realization that a militia was structured for defensive purposes, but that if America was to acquire additional territory it required an offensive war machine. In 1783 a congressional committee chaired by Hamilton, and acting on the recommendations of Generals Washington and Knox, proposed the retention of a regular force following the war with Britain. The report acknowledged that a militia was satisfactory in the event of defensive wars because such conflicts afforded the time to "levy and form an army," a "work of leisure and peace." But the expansionists' schemes

---

52. Samuel Adams to James Warren, 3 November 1778, in Cushing, *Writings of Adams*, vol. IV, p. 90; Paine, "Peace," in Foner, *Writings of Paine*, vol. II, p. 198; John Adams to James Warren, 26 July 1778, in Adams, *Warren-Adams Letters*, vol. II, p. 36; David Humphreys, *The Glory of America* . . . (Philadelphia, 1783), p. 16. The Washington quotation is in Dave Richard Palmer, *The Way of the Fox* . . . (Westport, Conn., 1975), p. 158.

53. Raynal, *Sentiments of a Foreigner*, pp. 25–26; *Pennsylvania Evening Post* (Philadelphia), 17 February 1776; Ramsay, *An Oration*, pp. 8, 11, 20–21.

54. Humphreys, *The Glory of America*, p. 16.

55. Hamilton to Aedanus Burke, 1 April 1790, in Syrett and Cooke, *Hamilton Papers*, vol. VI, p. 333; Josiah Quincy, *The Journals of Major Samuel Shaw* . . . (Boston, 1847), p. 22; Gerry to James Warren, 6 October 1777, in Gardener, *Study in Dissent*, p. 86; Ebenezer Huntington to Jabez Huntington, 25 November 1776, in Charles F. Heartman, ed., *Huntington Letters* (New York, 1915), p. 53; Kohn, *Eagle and Sword*, pp. 7–8.

required that troops be maintained "within certain districts, the jurisdiction and property of which are not yet constitutionally ascertained," and which were not "within the original claims of any of the states." Moreover, navigation prerogatives on the Mississippi and the Great Lakes, as well as control of the fisheries, "demand the joint protection of the Union, and cannot with propriety be trusted" to individual militia forces. Hamilton, acting in part upon the advice of Washington and other high officers, would have solved the quandary by creating regular army of four infantry regiments and one artillery regiment with a corps of engineers, erecting five arsenals capable of arming thirty thousand troops for a three-year period, and maintaining a restructured network of state militias.[56]

Congress rejected the plan, but the proponents of a national force soon saw their aspirations fulfilled. Less than four years after Congress balked at Hamilton's plan, the Constitutional Convention meeting in Philadelphia granted the new Congress the power to create a regular army for two-year periods. Even though the convention refused to consider a reformation of the state militia forces, the nationalists, in Professor Richard Kohn's words, had "achieved their most important military aim—empowering the government to create a national army—with spectacular ease." The ease with which the victory was won should not have come as a surprise. As one of *The Federalist* essays observed, only two state constitutions contained statements that might be construed as a prohibition against standing armies, and the wording in these cases actually merely suggested that such forces "ought not" to be maintained.[57]

During the fight to ratify the Constitution the anti-Federalists, the opponents of the proposed charter, marshalled forces against the prospect of a standing army. Their arguments essentially were restatements of the ancient English fears of standing armies. The heart of their attack was that soon "uncontrolled power" would be in the hands of an elite officer corps, "about 50 . . . of the *well born*," which, in turn, would establish a "military king" over America. When that occurred, liberty would be eradicated in the new nation. In addition, some anti-Federalists contended that the troops would consist largely of men of "little or no property," the type who would not hesitate to blindly follow their officers. Others complained that the sturdy yeomen conscripted into regular service would be "subjected to corporal punishments of the most disgraceful and humiliating kind, and to death itself" by the arrogant, professional officers. Some expressed fears that a standing army would spread vice and corruption, eroding the virtues of the new republican society. Still others were anxious lest the creation of a standing army might arouse fears about the intentions of the United States,

56. Syrett and Cooke, *Hamilton Papers,* vol. III, pp. 381–84; Kohn, *Eagle and Sword,* pp. 52, 393–96.

57. Kohn, *Eagle and Sword,* pp. 75–78; Lofgren, "Compulsory Military Service," pp. 64–66; *The Federalist,* vol. 24, p. 148n.

perhaps provoking an invasion by a coalition of concerned European powers.[58] The anti-Federalists, however, were as ineffectual in their attacks on these sections of the Constitution as they were in proposing other deletions and additions.

The Federalist, or nationalists who propounded the concept of a standing, regular force, denigrated the militia and alleged that national security considerations necessitated the army. War had grown too complicated for a militia force, Hamilton contended. It now was "a science to be acquired and perfected by diligence, by perseverance, by time, and by practice." The War for Independence demonstrated that "the steady operations of war against a regular and disciplined army can only be successfully conducted by a force of the same kind." Many nationalists suggested that "Conquest or superiority among other powers is not or ought not ever to be the object" of the United States, but they championed the acquisition of the "immense tracts of uncultivated [Indian] lands" to the west.[59]

Yet, even in the pending Indian wars, where the nature of the struggles had not changed substantially for generations, Hamilton believed the use of militia troops to be an antiquated practice. He thought it "impracticable" that militiamen would consent to "be dragged from their occupations and families" to staff garrisons in peacetime on the now remote Indian frontier.[60] Hamilton also argued that the American colonies were sufficiently imperiled as to require a regular army. He adroitly implied that the force was designed solely for defensive purposes. He resurrected the ancient fears of encirclement, contending that the British presence in Canada, Spanish troops in Florida, and "our natural enemies," the "savage tribes on our Western frontier," jeopardized the new nation's interests. He quoted the Abbe de Mably's prophesy that "NEIGHBOURING NATIONS . . . are naturally ENEMIES of each other."[61] The danger was increased, he added, by the likelihood that Britain and Spain, traditionally European rivals, would become natural allies as a result of commercial affinity. The nationalists discerned a plethora of potential conflicts, including contention over the fisheries, commercial clashes such as over "the trade to China and

---

58. Jackson Turner Main, *The Anti-Federalists* . . . (Chapel Hill, N.C., 1961), pp. 127–40, 146–48; Cecelia M. Kenyon, ed., *The Antifederalists* (Indianapolis, Ind., 1966), pp. 57–58, 65, 72–73, 188, 227, 229, 295; Morton Borden, ed., *The Antifederalist Papers* (East Lansing, Mich., 1965), pp. 8, 17, 19, 64, 66–67, 74–76, 213; John Back McMaster and Frederick D. Stone, eds., *Pennsylvania and the Federal Constitution, 1787–1788,* (Lancaster, Pa., 1888), vol. I, pp. 155–56, vol. II, p. 585; Paul Leicester Ford, ed., *Pamphlets on the Constitution of the United States* (Brooklyn, 1888), pp. 10–11; Jonathan Elliot, ed., *The Debates in the several State Conventions on the adoption of the Federal Constitution . . . ,* 5 vols. (New York, 1888), vol. III, pp. 411, 423–24, 428, 611.

59. *The Federalist,* vol. 25, p. 157; Max Farrand, ed., *The Records of the Federal Convention of 1787,* 4 vols. (New Haven, Conn., 1966), vol. I, p. 402.

60. *The Federalist,* vol. 24, p. 151.

61. Ibid., vol. 6, p. 33.

India,'' and struggle for hegemony on America's inland waterways. Preparedness, which was feasible only with a standing army, was the keynote. America must appear to be of sufficient strength so as ''not to *invite* hostility or insult.''[62] Moreover, since the ''ceremony of a formal enunciation of war has of late fallen into disuse,'' America, without a regular army, ''must receive the blow, before we could even prepare to return it.'' America was becoming a commercial giant, he added, and any army must be kept at all times to prevent attacks from maritime rivals on the ''dockyards . . . and sometimes the fleet itself.''[63] Finally, Hamilton added, congressional power to keep an army ''ought to exist without limitation'' because it is *''impossible to foresee or define the extent and variety of national exigencies. . . .''*[64]

The Federalists also attempted to allay lingering anxieties concerning a standing army. Some dismissed such a force as a necessary evil, others simply argued that the ''prudence of congress must be trusted.'' One writer thought that before ''a standing army can rule, the people must be disarmed,'' and that had not occurred in the new nation. Most nationalists maintained that a combination of republican virtue and adequate constitutional safeguards would restrain the military elite. If ''no rational Englishman apprehends the destruction of his rights,'' one activist queried, ''Ought then an American to have greater fears of a president, than an Englishman has of his king?''[65]

One of the more pressing fears arose from the alleged link between standing armies and monarchical government, with many persisting in the belief that the creation of a regular army would inevitably lead to the displacement of the president by a monarch. Hamilton confronted those fears with a convoluted argument. Whereas Paine had contended that monarchy made war inevitable, Hamilton asserted that war made monarchy inevitable. Since the existence of a regular army in the American colonies would serve as a deterrent against war, and since ''it is of the nature of war to increase the executive at the expense of the legislative authority,'' it therefore followed that monarchical government and executive tyranny were unlikely in a tranquil America.[66]

62. Ibid., vol. 4, pp. 18–19.

63. Ibid., vols. 24–25, pp. 150–56.

64. Ibid., vol. 23, p. 142.

65. Ibid., vol. 4, pp. 18–19; McMaster and Stone, *Pennsylvania and the Federal Constitution*, vol. I, p. 101; Ford, *Pamphlets on the Constitution*, pp. 56, 235.

66. *The Federalist*, vol. 8, p. 43. Although the nationalists succeeded in establishing a standing army, the force was, to them, disappointingly small. Nevertheless, as historian Marcus Cunliffe has noted, among those men ''who held national office or were close to the centers of power,'' particularly within the federal executive branch, there ''existed a real sentiment in favor of a standing army.'' These men were ''contemptuous of the militia,'' but they realized ''it would be politically disastrous to declare their contempt in public.'' Thus, throughout the late eighteenth and nineteenth centuries, in ''covert, qualified ways the argument for an American standing army was maintained—successfully.'' See Marcus Cunliffe, *Soldiers & Civilians* (Boston, 1968), pp. 147–48.

Viewed from these perspectives neither the colonists' fear of standing armies nor their revulsion against the very notion of war were as strong as has frequently been alleged. The colonists did not relish the presence of a standing army, and their anxieties in this quarter helped arouse bitterness and suspicion over British policies. The Declaration of Independence indicted George III for having "kept among us in time of peace standing armies," but not so much for keeping the armies as for doing so "without the consent of our legislatures." Similarly, the Americans were no longer willing to be dragged endlessly into the wars of Europe, conflicts whose nature had changed in the course of the eighteenth century and which grew to have less and less meaning for the colonists, particularly following France and Spain's humiliating defeat in the French and Indian War. Nevertheless, the experience, ideology, and objectives of the newly independent United States coalesced in the 1780s to lead the new nation to conclude that it required a standing force to fulfill its aspirations, and that such a force would be safe within the new constitutional framework erected at the end of the Revolutionary epoch.

This is not to say that the colonists were unanimous in these beliefs. The most vocal opponents of the rebellion, the Loyalists, or Tories, denounced the uprising for many reasons, but one reason for their hostility to the idea of separation from Britain was an abiding fear that independence could lead only to endless, ruinous warfare in America. Indeed, the Loyalists frequently began their attack on the radicals by denying that Britain had repeatedly dragged America into its wars. They denied that Britain was a dissolute country forever perched on the precipice of war; the Tories asserted it was the colonists—as in 1754, when their forces were too feeble to withstand even the "militia of Canada"—who often had implored the parent state to send military assistance. Many Loyalists additionally denied the allegedly inevitable link between monarchism and warfare, arguing that war was as likely to occur under republican governments; in fact, according to an Anglican curate in New York, the Roman Republic had wrought more distress and misery than "any three monarchs . . . in the whole compass of ancient history." The Loyalists, like their radical adversaries, were less than sanguine in their expectations that war could ever be eradicated; therefore, their principal concern was not so much to avoid warfare as to ensure that American society would be intact when war occurred.[67]

---

67. *New York Gazeteer,* 17 July 1774; [Thomas Bradbury Chadler], *A Friendly Address to All Reasonable Americans* . . . (New York, 1774), pp. 4, 25, 27; [Issac Hunt], *The Political Family* . . . (Philadelphia, 1775), pp. 17–19, 24; [Anon.], *Civil Prudency* . . . (Norwich, Conn., 1776), pp. 10, 16–17; Galloway, *A Candid Examination,* p. 1; [James Chalmers], *Plain Truth* . . . , in Merrill Jensen, ed., *Tracts of the American Revolution, 1763–1776* (Indianapolis, Ind., 1967), p. 458; Douglass Adair and John A. Schutz, eds., *Peter Oliver's Origin and Progress of the American Rebellion* (Stanford, Calif., 1961), p. 50; [Charles Inglis], *The True Interest of America Impartially Stated* . . . (Philadelphia, 1776), p. 23.

Many Loyalists were unwilling to deprecate war. Jonathan Boucher, the fiery Anglican pastor, alleged that conflict resulted in "much permanent good," and he pointed to the colonial domain, which had been enlarged repeatedly by Britain's military prowess. He even attributed the supposedly virtuous character of the Americans to the severity of combat, claiming that the colonists manifested a degree of "taste for the social arts, a spirit of manly sentiment, of industry, and of integrity" that were rarely displayed among the peoples of the "more peaceable nations." Other Loyalist pamphleteers argued that more tranquil states tended to exhibit "idleness, treachery, and cowardice . . . as the predominant features of national character." Holland was often cited as an example of a state that had witnessed war so infrequently it had become infused with a "pacific lethargy" that rendered it constantly "on the brink of becoming a province to France."[68]

The Tories timidly anticipated that imperial rupture would result in a new round of international warfare. Many warned that European monarchies would regard an independent United States as dangerous to their vital security. American republicanism, the anticolonialism implicit in an independence movement, and, finally, the restless expansionist tendencies that had always characterized American behavior were certain, in the Tories' estimation, to make Europeans anxious for the survival of their remaining New World outposts. Moreover, Europe was likely to fear that a renewed round of warfare would accompany American independence. Hostilities might occur when the United States sought new markets outside the British Empire; new trade alignments might lead to alterations in the balance of power which, in turn, could produce another world war. Any European power that initiated a free trade policy with America, for example, was likely to be attacked by its rivals. Therefore, instead of ushering in the new order for mankind which the radicals so confidently predicted, commerce, without the protective cloak of Britain, would provoke a new round of warfare.[69]

Like Hamilton and other radicals, the Loyalists grieved over the probability that an independent America might be encircled once again by foreign powers. At the very least, Britain was likely to possess Canada, Florida, and the transmontane West, not to mention the Atlantic gateway, following the war. Even

68. Boucher, *A View*, pp. 8–9n, 29, 43; Chalmers, *Plain Truth*, in Jensen, *Tracts*, pp. 455, 457–58; *Pennsylvania Packet* (Philadelphia), 2 January 1775.

69. [James McPherson], *The Rights of Great Britain Asserted* . . . (London, 1776), pp. 83–84; Chalmers, *Plain Truth*, in Jensen, *Tracts*, pp. 461–67; *True Interest*, pp. 23–24. The Loyalists were beside themselves with anxiety at the prospect of the colonists receiving foreign aid. They believed French and Spanish intervention in the Revolutionary war was merely a pretext for territorial aggrandizement. Many Tories predicted that the war would terminate in a stalemate, with the European powers and Britain negotiating a settlement that would partition America among the European belligerents. See, John E. Ferling, "The American Revolution and American Security: Whig and Loyalist Views,"*The Historian* 60 (May 1978), pp. 492–507.

worse, Britain might have to return some of these territories to Roman Catholic France and Spain. Unlike the radicals, however, the Tories believed that a war-weary United States would either be easy prey for foreign adventurers or be reduced to a "state of slavery." Moreover, the new nation would be unable to expand to its "natural" frontiers and would be denied access to foreign commerce and the Newfoundland fisheries.[70]

If French and Spanish foreign assistance was necessary to attain independence, many Loyalists believed the United States would be compelled to conclude formal treaties with these powers in order to maintain its newly won independent status. But foreign alliances tended to be two-way affairs: if a foreign power was obligated to assist a beleaguered United States, this country also would be forced to aid the imperiled ally. The Loyalists concluded, therefore, that if foreign aid was inevitable, an alliance with the Protestant sovereign in Britain was preferable to one with a Catholic monarch in France or Spain.[71]

The best hope for peace, the Loyalists insisted, was for America to maintain its ties with Britain. The Anglo-American victory during the French and Indian War had swung the balance of power to the forces of the British Empire. For the first time since Louis XIV had opened the modern age of warfare a century earlier, one power bloc had achieved unparalleled sway over its rivals. If America and Britain remained united, another European war was unlikely for generations. The Loyalists dreamed that an Anglo-American union could grow even stronger and more secure. In its commercial endeavors Anglo-America would be strong "beyond all possibility of competition." Militarily, Anglo-America would not only possess North America up to the Mississippi River, but it could acquire dominion over much of South America, becoming the "*richest* and most *powerful*, and consequently the safest" of empires, the "admiration and envy of mankind."[72]

Thus, both the radicals and the Loyalists hoped that America could escape unwanted wars, but both, unwittingly, anticipated that America would act in the same greedy, self-aggrandizing manner which they believed to be habitual

70. For an extended discussion of the colonial fear of encirclement, see Max Savelle, *The Origins of American Diplomacy* (New York, 1967), pp. 512–19. See also, [Daniel Leonard], *The Present State of the Province of Massachusetts Bay* . . . (New York, 1775), pp. 6–11, 81–82; Chalmers, *Plain Truth*, in Jensen, ed., *Tracts*, pp. 459–60; [Charles Inglis], *The Letters of Papinian* . . . (New York, 1779), p. 123; *Pa. Evening Post*, 21 February 1778; Boucher, *Reminiscences*, p. 135; *Virginia Gazette*, 27 April 1776.

71. Inglis, *True Interest*, p. 45; *N.Y. Gazette*, 14 June, 19 July, 2 August, and 8 November 1779; Hunt, *Political Family*, pp. 15–17.

72. Chalmers, *Plain Truth*, in Jensen, *Tracts*, p. 466, 474; Inglis, *True Interest*, pp. 35, 48–49, 68; Douglas Adair and John A. Schutz, eds., *Peter Oliver's Origin* (Stanford, Calif., 1961), p. 148; William A. Benton, *Whig-Loyalism* (Rutherford, N.J., 1969), p. 168; Inglis, *Letters of Papinian*, pp. 70–71, 86, 110; Boucher, *A View*, pp. 8–11, 13, 15–17, 21, 28, 32; [Joseph Galloway], *Cool Thoughts on the Consequences to Great Britain of American Independence* . . . (London, 1780), pp. 5–7, 12–4, 33, 52.

among the decadent Europeans. Both shared similar dreams of expansion. And both factions realized these aspirations could be attained only through the muscle provided by a professional army.

Despite recurrent uses of overblown rhetoric, national and state officials generally appeared to act in a reasonably restrained manner toward the neutral and Loyalist population during the War for Independence. The colonies were at war for fourteen months before Congress defined treason. Those persons, it rather moderately proclaimed, "who shall levy war against any of the . . . colonies . . . or be adherent to the King of Great Britain" or who shall render "aid and comfort" to the colonists' enemies were to be deemed "guilty of treason." After independence was proclaimed, each state passed legislation based on this congressional resolve, although, like Virginia, many states defined certain acts that were "injurious to the Independence of America" as "inferior in malignity to treason." New York and South Carolina, for example, declared such acts as inciting disorders and giving intelligence to the foe felonies, not treasonous offenses. For the most part, when states moved against a suspect, every effort was made to dispense justice with probity and exacting care. As a result, most states did not execute a single citizen for treason, and those that did often resorted to such a punishment only when the culprit had actually accepted and acted under British commissions.[73] Of course, many Tories escaped the gallows by fleeing into exile.

Nevertheless, passions aroused by war resulted in the victimization of many civilians. Among the first victims of the rebellion were the peace sects. As in earlier conflicts, tolerance toward pacifists rapidly abated. Problems arose for the Quakers even before hostilities commenced. Although the Friends generally had opposed British taxation policies in the 1760s, the sect balked at the politics of resistance favored by the Continental Congress in 1774. When war erupted the following year, the Friends sought to remain neutral. Both the Friends and smaller pacifist sects were willing to aid civilian victims of the war, but they excoriated cooperation with either the British or the rebel military forces. Most peace sects threatened to disown any member who took a loyalty oath to either belligerent government, served with the armed forces, engaged in business dealings with either army, or payed taxes to a wartime government. Some Quakers even questioned the use of currency issued by a government at war. Neither the Congress nor Pennsylvania, where most members of pacifist sects lived, required military service of conscientious objectors, but persecution and some public harassment nevertheless occurred. For instance, Thomas Paine, perhaps the most influential pamphleteer in the colonies, turned his sights on the Friends during the dark days of 1776. Paine accused the Quakers of Toryism.

73. Bradley Chapin, *The American Law of Treason* (Seattle, 1964), pp. 33–37, 39, 41, 46, 59–60, 62.

The most severe instances of mistreatment occurred in the South, but persecution was more widespread in New England, especially in Massachusetts. Pacifists were jailed and flogged for various offenses, and Pennsylvania executed two Friends for serving General Howe. The most common punishments suffered by the pacifists, however, were economic. Fines for some acts eventually ranged up to £1,000. Pacifist dissenters were also liable to the distraint of their property, and ultimately pacifist estates valued at over £100,000 were seized by the Revolutionary governments.[74]

Nor was it very safe to be an avowed, or even a suspected, Tory in the rebellious colonies. On the whole, the constituted governments acted judiciously and leniently toward the Loyalists. Professor Jackson T. Main has correctly suggested that no "people fighting for survival" could have acted "with more restraint against internal enemies" than did the Revolutionary governments. Of course, many Tories suffered heavily for the beliefs. Some were executed, some were jailed, and thousands fled into exile. Although the most widespread state-inflicted punishment was property confiscation, the majority of states moved only with great reluctance to seize property. In Pennsylvania, one recent study has indicated, only "one-tenth of 1 percent of the land in the state was taken from five one-hundredths of 1 percent of the people."[75]

If the constituted authorities normally acted with restraint, the same cannot be said of the citizenry in general. Both Whigs and Tories waged the war with an intensity and ferocity unfamiliar to eighteenth-century Europeans, although their behavior was characteristic of the traditional norms of American warfare and even of the colonial political milieu. Both sides willingly used Indian allies and winked at the atrocities they committed. And both Loyalists and Whigs resorted to a style of partisan warfare long since abandoned in western Europe. A "lawless set of banditta," composed of both popular and Tory partisans, was "constantly in action between the lines of the two armies committing every kind of crime," according to one amazed soldier. These guerrilla forces occasionally murdered political foes and often "waylaid and fired upon [enemy troops] from thickets and stony eminences." Principally, however, they plundered civilians. The Tory raiders came to be known as "cow-boys" because of their cattle-rustling proclivities.[76]

The most systematic partisan violence probably occurred in the South Carolina back country. Nearly two-thirds of the military encounters recorded in that state were waged between such forces, and four thousand people were killed or

74. Brock, *Pacifism in the U.S.*, pp. 183–329; Adair Archer, "The Quaker's Attitude towards the Revolution," *WMQ*, 2d Ser., 1 (July 1921), pp. 167–82; Rufus M. Jones et al., *The Quakers in the American Colonies* (London, 1911).

75. Jackson Turner Main, *The Sovereign States, 1775–1783* (New York, 1973), pp. 269–317; Anne M. Ousterhout, "Pennsylvania Land Confiscations During the American Revolution," *PMHB* 102 (July 1978), p. 342.

76. *Diary of Samuel Richards*, pp. 77–79; *Memoir of Talmadge*, pp. 31, 39.

wounded in a two-year period in these engagements. Some of the worst bar-
barities witnessed during the Revolution likewise occurred in this area. Prisoners
were stripped and hanged, sometimes from gallows so low that the victim's feet
touched the ground, producing death by slow strangulation. The death agony
in such instances produced what one witness termed a "number of indecent
jokes." At Orangeburgh, thirteen prisoners in irons were shot one by one, and
one of the guards who saw the murders remarked that he had never seen "a son
of a bitch bleed so much in his life" as had one of the victims. Later, seven
prisoners at Fort Walton allegedly were killed in the same manner and, in the
"Bloody Scout" incident of November 1781, a force of three hundred Tories
captured thirty revolutionaries, twenty-eight of whom were hacked to pieces by
the sword-wielding troops. Some partisan commanders even hired killers to
murder prisoners against whom they had "conceived a picque." Other prisoners,
many ill or wounded men and women, were forced to make long marches and
to engage in what amounted to slave-labor details; some were tortured with
multiple stabbings, others by flogging, being hung by the thumbs, or being
subjected to thumbscrew devices.

When Loyalist and patriot forces clashed on the battlefield, despicable behavior was commonplace. Legends developed about the reprehensible conduct
of the Tory leader, Colonel Banastre Tarleton, who allegedly was unwilling or
unable to prevent the atrocities committed by his victorious troops. But the
revolutionaries responded in kind at King's Mountain, where 157 Tories perished
and seven hundred were captured. Only 130 of the King's Mountain prisoners
ever reached the prison camp at Hillsborough, however, many being executed
or dying of exhaustion during the long forced march that followed the battle.[77]

Although governmental conduct was often lenient, there were insufficient
restraints to moderate the conduct of the general population. Every schoolboy
is familiar with incidents of tarring and feathering, and few would be surprised
to read of a mob of popular partisans who threw "Hog's Dung in [the Loyalist's]
Face, and rammed some of it down his Throat."[78] However, the day-to-day
agony, uncertainty, and anguish of civilian dissenters is less well remembered.

Less well remembered, too, is the experience of one well-known Tory, J.
Hector St. John de Crevecoeur. Born in France and educated in England, Crev-
coeur emigrated to Canada where he served under General Montcalm in the
French and Indian War. After a period of western exploration, Crevecoeur moved
to New York, and in 1765 became a British citizen. He settled on the frontier
in Orange County, where he gradually penned a panegyric to America, published
collectively in 1783 as *Letters from an American Farmer*. These "letters" are

---

77. The foregoing treatment of partisan warfare is based on *South Carolina Royal Gazette* (Charleston), 9 February, 16 February, 17 April, and 24 April 1782; Brown, *Strain of Violence*, pp. 71–81;
Calhoon, *Loyalists*, pp. 492–96.

78. Adair and Schutz, *Peter Oliver's Origin*, p. 157.

best remembered today for their description of early American life, their praises of the new country, and their characterization of "this new man, the American." But Crevecoeur's later essays, written during the Revolution, when he chose to remain loyal to the Crown, depicted America in far less idyllic terms. These essays are not as well known, but they contain graphic descriptions of the horrors of that struggle.

During the War for Independence, Crevecoeur heard "the groans of thousands of families now ruined and desolated." He witnessed the torture of colonists by colonists, seeing men hung by their toes and thumbs, seeing men slowly strangled, then revived and strangled again. He characterized the American families as "demons of war," as "ruffians," "monsters left to the wild impulses of the wildest nature. Could the lions of Africa be transported here and let loose, they would no doubt kill us in order to prey upon our carcasses; but their appetites would not require so many victims." In the struggle for survival, Crevecoeur knew he would be reduced to the level of his enemies. "I will revert to a state approaching nearer to that of nature, unincumbered either with voluminous laws, or contradictory codes." But he was merely "a feller of trees, a cultivator of land," and he desperately longed for peace. America had lost its charm for Crevecoeur. "I wish for a change of place," he lamented. "Oh, could I remove my plantation" to Canada. "Could I but carry my family along with me, I would . . . in order to enjoy the peace and innocence of that country. . . . Our happiness was our portion; now it is gone from us." "My fate is determined," he added, "but I have not determined it."

Living on the frontier, Crevecoeur's experiences paralleled those of Mary Rowlandson a century earlier in western Massachusetts. But in Crevecoeur's case, colonists were inciting the Indians to make remorseless raids on colonists. "We never sit down either to dinner or supper, but the least noise immediately spreads a general alarm. . . . The very appetite is gone; we eat just enough to keep us alive." At night he was plagued by nightmares, and "sometimes I start awake, as if the great hour of danger was come." When the dogs barked or some unaccustomed sound was heard, his wife, in tears, led the children to the basement shelter while Crevecoeur and his servants took up posts at the windows. "We remain thus sometimes for whole hours, our hearts and our minds racked by the most anxious suspense; what a dreadful situation, a thousand times worse than that of a soldier engaged in the midst of the most severe conflict!"

In 1780 Crevecoeur fled into exile. He returned three years later to find his house destroyed and his property reduced to a primitive wilderness.[79]

79. Hector St. John de Crevecoeur, *Letters from an American Farmer* (Philadelphia, 1792), pp. 270–71, 273–74, 278, 283–84, 289–91, 299; H. L. Bourdin et al., eds., H. St. John Crevecoeur, *Sketches of Eighteenth Century America* (New York, 1925), pp. 183, 185–87; Julia Mitchell, *St. Jean de Crevecoeur* (New York, 1916), pp. 215–20.

Crevecoeur's unhappy experience appears contrary to the "official" treatment of Loyalists prescribed by the constituted governments, but his agony was similar to that of many Tories caught up in the maelstrom of Revolution. His problems stemmed largely from the "unofficial" activities of mobs of neighboring Whigs. Pauline Maier has demonstrated that popular uprisings, mob actions, were deeply rooted in the colonial experience. Since the seventeenth century, sporadic incidents of mob violence had occurred to protect local interests when the legitimate authorities failed to act. Often local officials openly supported the mob, and occasionally they even participated in the uprising. In general, according to Professor Maier, this extralegal activity was given a "certain presumptive acceptability" as a curative force in society so long as it remained moderate or purposeful. Whether it involved food riots, violence to punish outlaws or to secure land titles, or even uprisings to raze a city's red light district, the tradition of resorting to popular insurgence when institutional redress failed was well established by the time of the American Revolution. In the protest against Britain, therefore, a duly constituted body might act "responsibly," secure in the knowledge that mob activity would accomplish what the legitimate authorities found unpalatable. Often the American magistrates were reluctant to openly sanction immoderate measures, fearing that their actions might alienate the neutral population or invite British reprisal. Thus, as Maier observed, although the Massachusetts Provincial Congress in 1774 cautioned the citizenry against assailing former British supporters in that colony's government, it knew that the very act of stigmatizing royal supporters would incite reprisals; the following year the South Carolina Assembly encouraged mob activity by declaring that those who "condemn measures universally received . . . must abide the consequences . . . of Popular Fury."[80] In the case of Crevecoeur and countless other British partisans, the popular fury visited upon them was characteristic of not only American political behavior but of the eternal trauma of civilians living in a climate overheated by the passions of war.

Some scholars have attributed Britain's defeat in the Revolution, in part, to its failure to sufficiently utilize the tactics of terrorism. Piers Mackesy, the respected British military historian, for instance, suggested that the British army "behaved with a moderation which may have been to its detriment." Many Loyalists made the same charge, and, in fact, no faction labored more diligently to alter Britain's martial policies. Britain's reluctance, or inability, to pursue a more truculent strategy, to adopt a posture of studied malignity, was incomprehensible to these Americans. The Tory pamphleteers repeatedly questioned British personnel, carping at the lack of "able and spirited Officers" within the British command, wondering if any had the fortitude to wage an aggressive war

80. Pauline Maier, *From Resistance to Revolution* (New York, 1972), pp. 4–5, 8–9, 11, 21, 23–24, 32, 278–79, 284, 286.

against the colonists. They even hinted darkly at conspiracies, intimating the existence of cabals of generals and politicians who connived secretly for an American victory.[81]

Joseph Galloway, the former speaker of the Pennsylvania Assembly and Franklin's former political partner, and after 1778 a Loyalist exile in London, was the most prolific of the Tory essayists on the conduct of the war. He watched with disbelief as British armies first refused to attack, then, upon finally taking the field, failed to take advantage of innumerable opportunities. "Force, however great, is useless unless exerted, and victory is Vain unless pursued," he lectured. But what Galloway and other Tories—Americans who were conditioned in the American method of war—most wanted was for England to resort to terrorism. Even the German mercenaries were too temperate for Galloway's taste. He advocated the formation of Loyalist regiments that might wage a partisan war, and he urged the ministry to unleash the Indians along the frontier so that the colonists' food supplies might be eradicated and, in conjunction with a naval blockade, the rebels might be starved into submission. He urged the British generalship to disabuse itself of the "romantic sentiments" of chivalric conduct. When Burgoyne publicly demured, Galloway advised the general that his lofty ideals had "not paid the texture of your mind any great compliment." Terrorism was "a settled & established rule of conduct" in America's wars, and it must be employed if Britain was to win the war. In America, Galloway maintained, the British military officer must come to see himself as a "soldier-executioner." Galloway prepared plans for the capture of the entire Congress and numerous state officials, he urged the destruction of strategic rebel properties by guerrilla forces, and he beseeched the British High Command to bring the war home to the American civilian population with a merciless vigor.[82]

The British never authorized the full range of Loyalist suggestions, but ultimately they did sanction the use of partisan forces. In two brilliant essays John Shy has recently sought to call to the attention of scholars the importance of the savage partisan warfare waged during the rebellion, particularly in the South. It is his contention that by 1778 Britain's hope for crushing the uprising hinged on the pacification of the southern colonies. The British army would seize a region, turn it over to Loyalist militia, and move on to repeat the activity elsewhere. However, the policy failed. Popular guerrilla and militia units arose to fight, and, in most instances, to outfight, the Tories. It was a nasty, particularly American kind of war, with, in Shy's estimation, "little difference between Loyalist and rebels in terms of organization, tactics, or the use of terror." When

81. Piers Mackesy, "British Strategy in the War of American Independence," *The Yale Review* 52 (1963), p. 546; Mary Beth Norton, *The British-Americans* (Boston, 1972), p. 156; William Nelson, *The American Tory* (New York, 1961), pp. 134–44; Ferling, *Loyalist Mind*, pp. 49–64.
82. Ferling, *Loyalist Mind*, pp. 50, 52–53.

the policy of pacification collapsed, General Cornwallis returned, "almost with a sigh of relief, to more conventional operations." He ultimately maneuvered his army to Yorktown.[83]

Wherever the British encountered the Americans, whether friends or enemy colonists, they were aghast at the New Worlders' wanton behavior. Some officers arrived in the provinces full of spirit, certain from their experience in previous wars that "the native American is an effiminate thing, very unfit for . . . war." Most, like Captain James Murray, changed their mind and decided that war with the Americans was "a barbarous business in a barbarous country." From the first day of hostilities, when militia from Lexington and Concord repeatedly ambushed British regulars from behind barns and fences, the redcoats denounced the colonists as "cruel and designing," "the most absolute cowards on the face of the earth," "concealed villians" who made "cowardly disposition . . . to murder us all." Four years after the conflict erupted, the British remained horror-struck at the "Americans . . . treachery & low-lived cruelty," and they continued to denigrate colonial soldiers for "shooting single horsemen from behind trees" and committing acts of "violence that a lawless banditti" would hesitate to perpetrate. An exasperated Philadelphia Tory even remarked that "my countrymen . . . seem to possess a more than savage barbarity." General Clinton even thought the American Loyalists who assisted his army incapable of refraining from committing "indiscriminate depredations."[84]

Throughout the war General Washington was under some pressure to conduct operations in a manner similar to the southern partisans. But, despite British impressions, American armies, like their British counterparts, balked at the tactics of savagery. Professor Shy has suggested that Washington rejected a strategy of "ambush, reprisal, counter reprisal," in part, for fear such tactics might "throw power to a junta—a committee of public safety" headed by someone other than himself. Moreover, Washington, a refined elitist who aped the English gentry, wished, in Shy's estimation, for his army "to be seen as cultivated, honorable, respectable men, not as savages leading other savages in a howling wilderness." Professor Russell Weigley, on the other hand, has argued, as have others, that Washington pursued a conventional strategy, for he thought it essential that the army be preserved for "symbolic purposes: to represent the continuity, stability, and indeed dignity of the Revolutionary cause. . . ." At any rate, Washington and his foreign advisors trained the Continental army according to the "European Plan" of war. There were those among

---

83. Shy, *A People Armed,* pp. 202–14; John Shy, "British Strategy for Pacifying the Southern Colonies," in Jeffrey J. Crow and Larry E. Tise, eds., *Southern Experience* (Chapel Hill, N.C., 1978), pp. 155–71.

84. Robson, *American Revolution,* pp. 124, 127; *N.Y. Royal Gazette,* 3 June 1778; Smith, *A New Age,* vol. I, p. 490; Higginbotham, *American War of Independence,* p. 63; Fisher "Diary of Trifling Occurrences," *PHMB* 82, pp. 430, 440, 454; Shy, "British Strategy," in Crow and Tise, *Southern Experience,* p. 168.

the rebels who, like Galloway on the other side, favored the formal use of terrorism and advised that the war be made into a "popular war of mass resistance." John Adams did not go that far, but he often bemoaned the generals' "timorous, defensive" behavior, and he called for acts of revenge against the British troops. One who did advise such a tactical approach was General Charles Lee, and he perhaps reached this conclusion because, as a foreigner, he saw Americans better than they saw themselves. Raised in England, a veteran of American wars as an officer in the British army, and an adventurer who fought with a Russian army against the Turks in Moldavia, Lee emigrated to the colonies in 1773. He likened American warfare, at least war with the Indians, to the partisan strife he had witnessed in eastern Europe. He regarded the tactics of ambush, deceit, and terrorism employed by the colonists at Lexington and Concord as the normal, intuitive reaction of men long accustomed to this means of warfare. He believed the tactics of "harassing and impeding can alone Suceed." To remain hidebound to the "European Plan" of Formational Arrangement, and Exercise of the Infantry" was to risk making the Continental army an "Ackward Figure" to be "laugh'd at as a bad Army by their Enemy" and "defeated in every Recontre which depends on manoeuvres."[85]

The American command discounted Lee's advice and instead directed the war according to the conventional wisdom of the day. Generally, Washington pursued a defensive strategy, a "War of Posts," he called it, in which he avoided "a general Action, or put anything to the Risque, unless compelled to by a necessity." The general did not always relish such a strategy. He longed to be free to act, to "stand and fight," to "take the offensive whenever and wherever possible," as historian Dave Richard Palmer has observed. On one occasion Washington even intimated that he might have resorted to more violent and destructive measures (in this instance he was speaking of the "mistake" of not having burned New York upon its abandonment by the Continental army in 1776) had his hands not been tied by a pusillanimous Congress.[86]

Washington, however, was not inflexible. According to a recent biographer, he had learned too much from "the kind of action he had seen the Indians carry off in the wilderness." He would fight in the winter months, whereas the Europeans were less likely to be dislodged from their warm quarters. He adopted

85. John Shy, "American Society and Its War for Independence," in Don Higginbotham, ed., *Reconsiderations on the Revolutionary War: Selected Essays* (Westport, Conn., 1978), p. 78; Russell Weigley, "American Strategy: A Call for a Critical Strategic History," in ibid., p. 40; Shy, *A People Armed*, pp. 155–61; Butterfield, *Adams D&A*, vol. II, p. 265; John Adams to Abigail Adams, 2 June 1777, in Butterfield, *Adams FC*, vol. II, p. 253; "Plan of an Army, Etc.," Lee to Washington, 13 April 1778, in *Lee Papers*, NYHS, *Coll.*, *1871–1874*, 4 vols. (New York, 1872–75), vol. II, pp. 382–89; John Alden, *General Charles Lee: Traitor or Patriot?* (Baton Rouge, La., 1951), pp. 1–48, 190–91.

86. Weigley, "American Strategy," in Higginbotham, *Reconsiderations*, p. 50; Dave Richard Palmer, *Way of the Fox*, (Westport, Conn., 1975), pp. 109, 113, 116, 125, 143, 146.

the Indian technique of surprise, of raiding parties that darted amongst the enemy creating disruption, only to depart before a superior force could arrive. And he perhaps understood the correlation between military activities and civilian opinion better than any European commander of his day.[87] What's more, regardless of the commander's wishes, the war in the backcountry continued to be waged in the manner to which this primitive country's warriors were accustomed.

In a sense, the British who surrendered at Yorktown were the victims of the American experience of war, an experience that crystallized in the Revolution. In his final general order to his troops, General Washington suggested that the American military achievements during the rebellion were "little short of a standing miracle." Although their victory was due in part to much good fortune, it was not a miraculous triumph. The colonists had fought with a tenacity and ferocity that reflected their heritage.

The revolutionary generation had come of age in a society far more warlike than is usually conceded. They were the descendants of a people who had experienced what the Connecticut General Court a century earlier had referred to as a "deepe and piersing" past of conflict, who survived what a major in the Connecticut militia called "wilderness work." Increase Mather spoke of the colonists as living by the "Sword of the Wilderness." Their experience of war—of an unremitting struggle for their very survival in the forbidding, primitive continent—had molded and shaped the colonists in such a way that many redcoats would have been prompted to agree with the British lieutenant who, after a clash with the colonists, exclaimed in his diary: "You can hardly suppose how quietly all these Yankees take any distresses, so much so that they appear to have lost all sort of feeling."[88]

87. Flexner, *Washington*, p. 544.

88. Peter Carroll, *Puritanism and the Wilderness* (New York, 1969), pp. 203, 208; Elizabeth Cometti, ed., *The American Journal of John Enys* (Syracuse, N.Y., 1976), p. 29.

Conclusion

The object of this study, as stated in the Introduction, has been to examine how the early American settlers, collectively and individually, experienced warfare, how their encounters shaped the nature of colonial conflicts, and how the colonists viewed warfare.

From the moment the first English statesmen plotted the colonization of America, they also prepared for war with the Indians of America and with the other Europeans who likewise coveted the virgin continent. What resulted was an armed invasion of America.

Soon war was endemic to the colonists. In most colonies, conflict with the native Americans lasted for the initial three generations or more of settlement. Strains between the English and other Europeans in America developed early and; within fifty years of settlement, reached proportions of full-scale war, first with the Dutch, later with France and Spain. In such an atmosphere, the English dispatched professional soldiers to many of the colonies to secure a beachhead. Colonists arrived anticipating hostilities, and, in fact, in many instances immigrants were permitted to enter the colonies only if sufficiently armed for battle. Most male settlers were forced into trainbands. Villages were constructed with an eye to defensive requirements, and a sizable portion of the public revenue was sunk into the erection of military fortifications. The executive leadership appointed for the colonies in London increasingly was drawn from among men with professional military training. The colonies seldom acted jointly, except when military exigency dictated concerted conduct. Likewise, the parent state remained aloof and distant, generally intervening substantively only when extreme conditions seemed to require martial meddling.

While Europe's wars grew less ferocious, or at least had less drastic impact on the civilian population, American wars tended to become more feral. The wars that occurred, although not unlike some contemporary European conflicts (the English suppression of the Irish, for instance), often were total wars in which colonists and Indians killed in order to maintain their very existence as a people, or grappled with others for the survival of the culture with which they identified. But even when Europeans fought one another in America, supported, of course, by their colonial allies, the warfare tended to be Americanized. The environment and the geography, the problem of procuring supplies, the difficulty of controlling unwilling soldiers thousands of miles from home, and especially the utilization of Indian allies affected strategy and tactics and altered the nature of warfare customarily known to Europeans.

When the colonists encountered Indians in battle—and of all the varieties of warfare, this type most directly affected the settlers—the results bore even less resemblance to the wars that plagued Europe. The appurtenances and strategies of European conflict gave way to an American style of war, a style more suitable to a wilderness environment and the stakes for which the conflicts were being fought. War might be waged throughout the year, often uninterrupted by the conventions that dotted European legal codes. Women and children soon were regarded as fair game. No statutory conventions existed to protect the unlucky captives. No quarter was given in battle to the foe. Moreover, the colonists adopted the terrorist tactics of their native foes, and soon Englishmen too wielded the torch and the tomahawk. The colonists also devised tactical innovations, such as the use of canines and the poisoning of their rivals' supplies. Struggle with the natives frequently amounted to genocide.

A common denominator in all these wars was that the American civilian population, native and immigrant, was affected by war in ways that European civilians after the middle of the seventeenth century could only imagine. In every war the civilians were hounded by officialdom, colonial and imperial, to serve in the armed forces. Unprofessional officers often led poorly trained and frequently ill-equipped troops, sometimes from trainband contingents and some-times conscriptees, into these raw encounters. The volatility of the mixture can easily be imagined. Not only were such troops capable of the most unprincipled conduct, but they were themselves frequently victims, through disease and de-privation, of their own inexperience. Armies preparing to mount invasions en-camped among the civilians, siphoning off their food, fuel, livestock, spare jobs, and women. In their wake, these armies often left rampant inflation and epidemic diseases, not to mention a legacy of bitterness that stuck with many civilians. Civilians, even the allies, trapped in the path of armies fared even worse. People and materials were the spoils of men brutalized by war. Civilians in enemy territory usually experienced even worse treatment, for the policies directed against them, including molestation, confiscation of property, uprooting of entire populations, slavery, even genocide through starvation, were approved by governmental authorities and administered by those who were filled with an implacable hatred bred by war.

The action of war is frequently depersonalized in historical accounts. But individual men make wars, and individual soldiers fight them. Those who fought in the wars of early America were beset almost routinely with untrained leaders and woeful support systems. Colonial soldiers, often facing either a better trained, professional European soldier, or a native American skilled in the combat of the wilderness, were hurled together under the command of men who cus-tomarily achieved their status through social class rather than merit. The inad-equacies that resulted too often were exacerbated by the leadership's attempts to flaunt the officers' anachronistic code of chivalry that prevailed even at the end of the era, or to use their exalted military positions to procure civilian benefits for their (or, in reality, their troops') allegedly heroic endeavors. Their expedient gestures were not always the best course. Moreover, too often governments were neither on a sound war-footing nor required to fully answer to a deferential, or even indifferent, citizenry for their errors. They blundered about, time and again permitting their ill-equipped troops to suffer every misery that nature could deal. It was symptomatic of the age that those privileged few at the apex of society urged, defended, and directed wars, but seldom fought in them. Perhaps they suffered psychic pains for their indulgences; perhaps they simply profited from the bloodletting.

This is not to argue that the privileged were solely responsible for the wars that occurred. Often the decision for war was made in London; but even the wars for which the colonists must bear responsibility cannot be dismissed as the work of an elite cabal. Most wars were consented to, perhaps even championed, by most colonists. They, too, were the product and expression of their violent environment. And their actions were the manifestation of the era's prevailing ethic, devised and promulgated by those at the top of the society, and deferentially accepted by those at the bottom.

The earliest colonists transported the sixteenth- and seventeenth-century European views of war to wilderness America. Shaped in an environment of ghastly and persistent continental warfare, these ideas took root and ultimately were shaped to suit the aims of the aggressive, expansionist settlers. Indeed, the ideas largely remained locked in, frozen in the colonists' minds. Hence, like the Europeans of the early seventeenth century, the colonists persisted in legitimizing certain kinds of warfare: to defend one's property; to acquire undeveloped terrain; to regain territory; to redress wrongs. Not only was war seen as an inevitable occurrence, it was viewed in such a manner that every conflict could be made to seem demonstrably justifiable. And, just as no thoroughgoing movement in opposition to war had the remotest chance of gaining the machinery of any state in seventeenth-century Europe, so too the pacifists and antiwar spokesmen in the provinces remained unorganized or pitifully few. Indeed, articulate Americans and Europeans were virtually one in their belief that while the fury of war might be curtailed or mitigated, it was an inevitability that conflict would occur.

In the eyes of the colonial elite it was more important to ensure that the colonists were prepared for inevitable warfare than to debate the legitimacy of war for survival. An ethos that upheld the good, courageous, citizen-soldier evolved. Discipline, valor, training, zeal for liberty, and Christianity came to be seen as the prime virtues, and cowardice the principal vice in soldiers. The ethic was hammered home by both secular and clerical leaders, and it was embraced with relish by a submissive populace, many of whom inhabited areas that could never be secured adequately from enemy depredation.

One might expect that the colonists' attitudes toward war would have changed considerably after the middle of the eighteenth century. At the same moment that the frontier, with its attendant threat of violence, was pushed further west and made more remote to an ever larger percentage of the settlers, the nature of European warfare and of the European attitude toward war was perceptably altered. Wars in Europe occurred with less frequency and had a less severe impact on the majority of the civilian population than when the colonization of America commenced. Important intellectual changes accompanied the new style of warfare. Enlightened writers denounced war and the institutions that promulgated conflicts, as well as the alleged virtues essential to the warrior caste.

But the altered concept of European warfare produced by the Englightenment did not take root in America. The recurrent warfare of the provinces, conducted with a spirited ferocity that was on the wane elsewhere in the Western world, froze the old concepts of war and imprinted them on each successive generation of colonists. By the mid-eighteenth century, articulate colonists persisted in legitimizing their wars in the same way that their predecessors had justified their belligerent conduct generations earlier. A society had materialized that equated military exploits with heroism and strived to inculcate its young with the martial virtues of those it saw as heroes. Its people, marked by a violence that influenced its culture and artifacts, longed to exercise greater control over its destiny.

As with so many other aspects of colonial society, its people drew, perhaps unconsciously, on this heritage as the relationship with Great Britain deteriorated in the 1760s to 1770s. America's violent past did not provoke the tensions with the parent state; yet, its martial heritage did not serve to alleviate the steady erosion of the partnership. What John Adams termed the "martial Spirit" of the age rendered most colonists ready, even anxious, to challenge the parent state by 1775. Most colonists were convinced of their inviolability. They were equally certain that the war would cleanse and purify them, leaving them ready to govern their independent interests in a most virtuous manner. Like many European philosophies, the colonists equated war with the institutions, particularly with monarchical government, which persisted on the continent, but the Revolution was not an antiwar movement. The articulate rebels did not propose separation from Britain in order to end war. Instead, they promised only that independence would bring an end to unwanted wars. Many colonists already had developed a concept of American security and expansionism apart from Great Britain, a vision that could be fulfilled only by military endeavors. For most colonists, molded in the savage turmoil of frontier provinces, such a prospect was more liberating than frightening.

In short, war recurred with sufficient frequency and impact on the people and institutions of the age that it played a seminal role in shaping the history of these primitive, remote provinces. One can think of any number of ways in which warfare shaped the lives of the colonists. For some, it brought prosperity—land, trade, resources. For others, however, war led to economic ruin. War helped accelerate technological breakthroughs, but it also gave birth to, and exacerbated, racial, cultural, and religious prejudices. War helped foster American nationalistic sentiments while it simultaneously completely eradicated some native

American nations. War and the presence of armies changed and molded the mores of the civilian population. War left a pall of violence hanging over the landscape. This violent mode of behavior competed with the more exemplary qualities of the people for a place in the national character. War caused men to rethink their institutions, to consider new types of government. It may have induced the crystallization of more egalitarian sentiments in the Revolutionary age. A string of successful wars may have convinced Americans of their invincibility. Perhaps Americans felt cleansed, purged, and more virtuous and worthy because of their experience with war.

The colonial years indicate that war can be as revolutionary as a revolution itself. War can transform a society, sending it careening in unimagined directions. At the same moment, the very act of bloodletting can act unconsciously to prepare and equip people for still more bellicose behavior in the future.

This was early America's experience of war. The irony, indeed the very revolutionary nature of the experience, was that a people who anticipated war; experienced war with great frequency; waged wars in a barbaric manner more akin to the remote past than to contemporary Europe; continued to view war and warriors more consistently with the darker days of antiquity than with the sentiments of the Englightenment Age, would, in the end, produce through warfare an independent society regarded by progressive contemporaries as a model for enlightened people everywhere.

Bibliography

PRIMARY SOURCES

Printed Sources

Abbott, Hull. *Jehovah's Character as a Man of War, Illustrated and Applied. A Sermon Preached at the Desire of the Honourable Artillery Company in Boston* (Boston, 1735).

Adair, James. *The History of the American Indians, particularly those nations adjoining to the Mississippi, East and West Florida, South and North Carolina, and Virginia* (London, 1775).

Adair, Douglas and Schutz, John A., eds. *Peter Oliver's Origin and Progress of the American Revolution* (Stanford, Calif.: Stanford Univ. Press, 1961).

Adams, Amos. *The Expedience and Utility of War, in the Present State of things, considered: A Discourse Before, and at the Desire of the Ancient and Honourable Artillery-Company* (Boston, 1759).

Adams, Charles Francis. *Familiar Letters of John Adams and his Wife Abigail Adams* (Boston, 1876).

———. *The Works of John Adams, Second President of the United States: With a Life of the Author.* 10 vols. (Boston, 1850–1856).

Adams, Zabdiel. *The Grounds of Confidence and Success in War, represented* (Boston, 1755).

Adye, Stephen Payne. *A Treatise on the Courts Martial* (New York, 1769).

Albion, R. G. and Dodson, L., eds. *Journal of Philip Vickers Fithian, 1775–1776* (Princeton, N.J.: Princeton Univ. Press, 1924).

Allaire, Anthony. *Diary of Lieut. Anthony Allaire* (New York: Arno Press, 1968).

Allen, Ethan. *A Narrative of Col. Ethan Allen's Captivity, from the time of his being taken by the British to the time of his exchange* (Walpole, N.H., 1807).

Allen, James. "Diary of James Allen, Esq., of Philadelphia, Counsellor-at-Law, 1770–1778." *PMHB* 9, Nos. 3–4 (1885), pp. 176–96, 278–96, 424–41.

Anderson, Enoch. *Personal Recollections of Captain Enoch Anderson.* Historical Society of Delaware, *Papers,* XVI (Wilmington, 1896).

Angell, Israel. *Diary of Colonel Israel Angell, Commanding the Second Rhode Island Continental Regiment during the American Revolution* (Providence, R. I., 1899).

Anon. *Civil Prudency, Recommended to the Thirteen United Colonies of North America* (Norwich, Conn., 1776).

Anon. "Itinerary of the Pennsylvania Line from Pennsylvania to South Carolina, 1781–1782." *PMHB* 37, No. 2 (1912) Pp. 273–92.

Anon. *Plan of Exercise, for the Militia of the Province of Massachusetts Bay: Extracted from the Plan of Discipline, for the Norfolk Militia* (Boston, 1768).

Anon. *Remarks on a Late Pamphlet entitled Plain Truth* (Philadelphia, 1776).

Anon. *The Power and Grandeur of Great Britain, founded on the Liberty of the Colonies, and the Mischiefs attending the Taxing them by Act of Parliament Demonstrated* (New York, 1768).

Appleton, Nathaniel. *The Origin of War examin'd and applied, in a Sermon Preached at the Desire of the Honourable Artillery Company in Boston* (Boston, 1733).

Arber, Edward, ed. *Travels and Works of Captain John Smith: President of Virginia and Admiral of New England, 1580–1631.* 2 vols. (Birmingham, Eng., 1884).

Bailyn, Bernard, ed. *Pamphlets of the American Revolution, 1750–1776* (Cambridge, Mass.: Harvard Univ. Press, 1965).

Balderston, Marion and Syrett, David, eds. *The Lost War: Letters from British Officers during the American Revolution* (New York: Horizon Books, 1975).

Baldwin, Thomas, ed. *The Revolutionary Journal of Col. Jeduthan Baldwin, 1775–1778* (Bangor, Me.: Privately printed, 1906).

Beebe, Lewis. "Journal of a Physician on the Expedition Against Canada, 1776." *PMHB* 59 (October 1935) Pp. 321–61.

Benezet, Anthony. *Thoughts on the Nature of War, and its Repugnance to the Christian Life* (Philadelphia, 1766).

Bernard, Thomas. *A Sermon Preached to the Ancient and Honorable Artillery Company in Boston* (Boston, 1758).

Bingham, Hiram. *Five Straws Gathered from Revolutionary Fields* (Cambridge, Mass.: Privately printed, 1901).

Bixby, Samuel. "Diary of Samuel Bixby." MHS, *Proceedings,* 1st Ser., 14 (March 1876) Pp. 258–98.

Black, Jeanette D. and Roelker, William G., eds. *A Rhode Island Chaplain in the Revolution: Letters of Ebenezer David to Nicholas Brown, 1775–1778* (Port Washington, N.Y.: Kennikat, 1972).

Bland, Edward. *The Discovery of New Britaine* (Ann Arbor: University Microfilms, 1966).

Borden, Morton, ed. *The Antifederalist Papers* (East Lansing, Mich.: Michigan State Univ. Press, 1965).

Boucher, Jonathan. *A View of the Causes and Consequences of the American Revolution; in thirteen Discourses, Preached in North America between the Years 1763 and 1775: With an Historical Preface* (London, 1797).

———. *Reminiscences of an American Loyalist, 1778–1789* (Pt. Washington, N.Y.: Kennikat 1971).

Boyd, Julian P., et al., eds. *The Papers of Thomas Jefferson* (Princeton, N.J.: Princeton Univ. Press, 1950   ).

Boyd, William K., ed. *William Byrd's Histories of the Dividing Line betwixt Virginia and North Carolina* (New York: Dover Publications, 1967).

Bradford, William. "Bradford's Verse History of New England," MHS, *Collections,* III (1794), pp. 77–84.

Bricker, Henry. "Orderly Book of the Second Pennsylvania Continental Line, Col. Henry Bricker." *PHMB* 26, Nos. 1–2 (1912) Pp. 22–40.

Bridge, Ebenezer. *A Sermon Preach'd to the Ancient and Honourable Artillery Company in Boston* (Boston, 1752).

Bridge, Thomas. *The Knowledge of God, Securing from Flattery, and Strengthening to the most Noble Exploits* (Boston, 1705).

Burges, Tristam. *War, Necessary, Just and Beneficial: An Oration, pronounced on commencement at Rhode Island College* (Providence, R.I., 1799).

Burgh, James. *Political Disquisitions; or, an Enquiry into Public Errors, Defects, and Abuses* (Philadelphia, 1775).

Burnett, Edmund C., ed. *Letters of Members of the Continental Congress.* 8 vols. (Washington, D.C.: Carnegie Institution of Washington, 1921–1936).

Butterfield, L. H., et al., eds. *Adams Family Correspondence* (Cambridge, Mass.: Harvard Univ. Press, 1963   ).

———. *Letters of Benjamin Rush.* 2 vols. (Princeton, N.J.: Princeton Univ. Press, 1951).

———. *The Diary and Autobiography of John Adams.* 4 vols. (Cambridge, Mass.: Harvard Univ. Press, 1964).

———. *The Earliest Diary of John Adams* (Cambridge, Mass.: Harvard Univ. Press, 1966).

Byles, Mather. *The Glories of the Lord of Hosts, and the Fortitude of the Religious Hero* (Boston, 1740).

Calder, Israel M., ed. *Colonial Captives, Marches and Journeys* (Port Washington, N.Y.: Kennikat, 1967).

Carmichael, John. *A Self-Defensive War Lawful, proved in a Sermon* (Lancaster, Pa., 1775).

Carter, Clarence E., ed. *The Correspondence of General Thomas Gage*. 2 vols. (New Haven: Yale Univ. Press, 1931).

Chalmers, James. *Plain Truth: Addressed to the Inhabitants of America, Containing, Remarks on a Late Pamphlet, entitled Common Sense* [1776]. In Jensen, Merrill, ed. *Tracts of the American Revolution, 1763–1776* (Indianapolis, Ind.: Bobbs, Merrill, 1967).

Chandler, Thomas Bradbury. *A Friendly Address to All Reasonable Americans on the Subject of our Political Confusions: in which the necessary consequences of Violently opposing the King's Troops, and of a General Non-Importation are fairly stated* (New York, 1774).

Chew, Samuel. *The Speech of Samuel Chew, Esq., on the Lawfulness of Defence against an Armed Enemy* (Philadelphia, 1775).

Clark, Peter. *Christian Bravery* (Boston, 1756).

Cogswell, James. *God, the pious Soldier's Strength and Instructor: A Sermon* (Boston, 1757).

Cometti, Elizabeth, ed. *The American Journal of John Enys* (Syracuse, N.Y.: Syracuse Univ. Press, 1976).

Cook, Frederick, ed. *Journals of the Military Expedition of Major General Sullivan against the Six Nations of Indians in 1779* (Auburn, N.Y., 1877).

Cooper, Samuel. *A Sermon Preached to the Ancient and Honourable Artillery Company, in Boston* (Boston, 1751).

Cooper, Thomas and McCord, O. J., eds. *Statutes at Large of South Carolina*. 10 vols. (Columbia, S. C., 1836–1841).

Corner, George, ed. *The Autobiography of Benjamin Rush, His "Travels Through Life" together with his Commonplace Book for 1789–1813* (Princeton N.J.: Princeton Univ. Press, 1948).

Cotton, John. "God's Promise to His Plantation." *Old South Leaflets*. 8 vols. (New York, n.d.) III, No. 53.

Crary, Catherine, ed. *The Price of Loyalty: Tory Writings from the Revolutionary Era* (New York: McGraw-Hill, 1973).

Crevecoeur, Hector St. John de. *Letters from an American Farmer* (Philadelphia, 1792).

————. *Sketches of Eighteenth Century America*. Bourdin, H. L., et al., eds. (New York: A. and C. Boni, 1925).

Cushing, Harry Alonzo, ed. *The Writings of Samuel Adams*. 4 vols. (New York: G. P. Putnam's, 1904).

Dankin, Robert. *Military Collections and Remarks* (New York, 1777).

Davies, Samuel. *The Curse of Cowardice, A Sermon Preached to the Militia of Hanover County in Virginia* (London, 1759).

de Forest, Louis E., ed. *Louisbourg Journals, 1745* (New York: Da Capo Press, 1970).

Dickerson, Oliver M., ed. *Boston Under Military Rule, 1768–1769, as revealed in a Journal of the Times* (New York: Da Capo Press, 1970).

Dickinson, John. *Letters from a Farmer in Pennsylvania to the Inhabitants of the British Colonies* (Philadelphia, 1769).

Douglass, William. *A Summary, Historical and Political, of the British Settlements in North America*. 2 vols. (Boston, 1755).

Drake, Samuel G., ed. *The History of the Indian Wars in New England from the First Settlement to the Termination of the War with King Philip in 1677. From the Original Work by the Rev. William Hubbard*. 2 vols. (Roxbury, Mass., 1865).

Drinker, Mrs. Henry. "Extracts from the Journal of Mrs. Henry Drinker, of Philadelphia, from September 25, 1775, to July 4, 1778." *PMHB* 13, No. 3 (1889) Pp. 294–302.

Dulany, Daniel. *Considerations on the Propriety of Imposing Taxes in the British Colonies, For the Purpose of Raising a Revenue, by Act of Parliament* (Annapolis, Md., 1765).
———. "Military and Political Affairs in the Middle Colonies in 1775." *PMHB* 3, No. 1 (1879) Pp. 11–31.

Dwight, Timothy. *Travels in New England and New York.* Solomon, Barbara, ed. 4 vols. (Cambridge, Mass.: Harvard Univ. Press, 1969).

Elliot, Jonathan, ed. *The Debates in the several State Conventions on the adoption of the Federal Constitution as recommended by the General Convention at Philadelphia in 1787.* 5 vols. (New York, 1888).

Evans, Israel. *A Discourse delivered at Easton to the Officers and Soldiers of the Western Army* (Philadelphia, 1779).

Fausz, J. Frederick and Kukla, Jan, eds. "A Letter of Advice to the Governor of Virginia, 1624." *WMQ,* 3d Ser., 34 (January 1977) Pp. 104–29.

Feltman, William. *The Journals of Lieut. William Feltman, of the First Pennsylvania Regiment, 1781–1782, including the March into Virginia and the Siege of Yorktown* (Philadelphia, 1853).

Fish, Elisha. *The Art of War Lawful, and Necessary for a Christian People, Considered and Enforced* (Boston, 1774).

Fisher, Elijah. *Elijah Fisher's Journal while in the War for Independence and Continued Two Years After He Came Home, 1775–1784* (Augusta, Me., 1880).

Fisher, Sarah. "A Diary of Trifling Occurrences." *PMHB* 82 (October 1958) Pp. 411–65.

Fitzpatrick, John C., ed. *The Writings of George Washington.* 39 vols. (Washington, D.C.: U.S. Govt. Printing Office, 1931–1944).

Foner, Philip S., ed. *The Writings of Thomas Paine.* 2 vols. (New York: The Citadel Press, 1945).

Force, Peter, ed. *American Archives: Fourth Series Containing a Documentary History of the English Colonies in North America, from the King's Message to Parliament, of March 7, 1774, to the Declaration of Independence by the United States.* 6 vols. (Washington, D.C., 1837–1846).
———. *Tracts & Other Papers, Relating Principally to the Origin, Settlement, and Progress of the Colonies in North America to the Year 1776.* 4 vols. (Washington, D.C., 1836).

Ford, Paul L., ed. *Pamphlets on the Constitution of the United States* (Brooklyn, 1888).
———. *The Writings of Thomas Jefferson.* 10 vols. (New York, 1892–1899).

Ford, Worthington C., ed. *Defenses of Philadelphia in 1777* (Brooklyn, 1897).
———. *Journals of the Continental Congress, 1774–1789.* 34 vols. (Washington, D.C.: U.S. Govt. Printing Office, 1904–1937).

Franklin, Benjamin. *The Absolute and Obvious Necessity of Self-Defense* (Philadelphia, 1748).
———. *The Autobiography of Benjamin Franklin and Selections from his Other Writings* (New York: Random House, 1944).

Galloway, Joseph. *Cool Thoughts on the Consequences to Great Britain of American Independence. On the Expence of Great Britain in the Settlement and Defence of the American Colonies. On the Value and Importance of the American Colonies and the West Indies to the British Empire* (London, 1780).
———. *A Candid Examination of the Mutual Claims of Great Britain, and the Colonies: With a Plan of Accomodation, on Constitutional Principles* (New York, 1775).

Gardener, Lion. "Gardener's Pequot Warres." MHS, *Collections,* 3d Ser., 3 (1833) Pp. 131–64.

Gardiner, C. Harvey, ed. *A Study in Dissent: The Warren-Gerry Correspondence, 1776–1792* (Carbondale, Ill.: Southern Illinois Univ. Press, 1966).

Gay, Ebenezer. *Well-accomplished Soldiers, A Glory to their King, and a Defense to their Country* (Boston, 1738).

Gibbs, Henry. *The Right Method of Safety, or the Just Concern of the People of God, to Joyn in a Due Trust in Him* (Boston, 1704).

Gilbert, Humphrey. *Sir Humphrey Gilberte and his enterprise of Colonization in America* (New York: Burt Franklin, 1967).

Gilman, Caroline, ed. *Letters of Eliza Wilkenson, During the Invasion and Possession of Charleston, S.C. by the British in the Revolutionary War* (New York: Da Capo, 1969).

Graham, Gerald S., ed. *The Walker Expedition to Quebec, 1711* (Toronto: Champlain Society, 1953).

Gray, Robert. *A Good Speed to Virginia* [1609] (New York: Walter J. Johnson 1970).

Green, Jacob. *Observations on the Reconciliation of Great-Britain and the Colonies* (New York, 1776).

Grotius, Hugo. *The Law of War and Peace* (Indianapolis: Bobbs, Merrill, 1925).

Hakluyt, Richard. *Divers Voyages Touching the Discoverie of America* (Ann Arbor: University Microfilms, 1966).

Hall, Clayton C., ed. *Narratives of Early Maryland, 1633–1684* (New York: Charles Scribner's, 1910).

Hamer, Jonathan. *The Character and Duties of a Christian Soldier, considered and applied in a Sermon, Preached before the ancient and honorable Company of Artillery* (Boston, 1790).

Hamor, Ralph. *A True Discourse of the Present Estate of Virginia.* Harwell, Richard B., ed. (Richmond: Virginia State Library, 1957).

Hancock, John. *An Oration; delivered March 5, 1774, at the Request of the Inhabitants of the Town of Boston: To Commemorate the Bloody Tragedy of the Fifth of March 1770* (Boston, 1774).

Haven, Jason. *A Sermon Preached to the Ancient and Honorable Artillery Company in Boston* (Boston, 1761).

Heartman, Charles F., ed. *Letters Written by Ebenezer Hartman during the American Revolution* (New York: Charles Scribner's, 1915).

Hopkins, Stephen. *The Rights of Colonies Examined* (Providence, R.I., 1765).

Howard, Simeon. *A Sermon Preached to the Ancient and Honorable Artillery-Company in Boston, New-England, June 6, 1774* (Boston, 1774).

Hubbard, William. *The Happiness of a People in the Wisdome of their Rulers* (Boston, 1676).

———. *The Present State of New England, Being a Narrative of the Troubles with the Indians in New England* (London, 1677).

Hubly, William. *The Soldier caution'd and counsel'd* (Boston, 1747).

Humphreys, David. *The Glory of America; or Peace triumphant over War: A Poem* (Philadelphia, 1783).

Hunt, Isaac. *The Political Family, or a Discourse, pointing out the Reciprocal Advantages which flow from an Uninterrupted Union between Great-Britain and her American Colonies* (Philadelphia, 1775).

Inglis, Charles. *The Letters of Papinian; in which the conduct, Present State and Prospects, of the American Colonies, are Examined* (New York, 1779).

———. *The True Interest of America Impartially Stated, in certain Strictures on a Pamphlet entitled Common Sense* (Philadelphia, 1776).

Jameson, J. Franklin, ed. *Johnson's Wonder-Working Providence, 1628–1651* (New York: Charles Scribner's, 1910).

Jones, David. *Defensive War in a Just Cause Sinless* (Philadelphia, 1755).

Jones, Thomas. *History of New York During the Revolutionary War.* 2 vols. (New York, 1879).

Kennedy, Benjamin, ed. *Muskets, Cannon Balls & Bombs: Nine Narratives of the Siege of Savannah in 1779* (Savannah: The Beehive Press, 1974).

Kenyon, Cecilia M., ed. *The Antifederalists* (Indianapolis: Bobbs, Merrill, 1966).

Kingsbury, Susan Myra, ed. *The Records of the Virginia Company of London.* 4 vols. (Washington, D.C.: U.S. Govt. Printing Office, 1906–1935).

Kirkland, John Thornton. *A Sermon, preached before the Ancient and Honorable Artillery Company in Boston* (Boston, 1795).

Koch, Adrienne, ed. *The American Enlightenment* (New York: George Braziller, 1965).

Labaree, Leonard Woods, ed. *Royal Instructions to British Colonial Governors, 1607–1776.* 2 vols. (New York: Frederick Ungar, 1935).

————, et al., eds. *The Papers of Benjamin Franklin* (New Haven, Conn.: Yale Univ. Press, 1959 —).

Lacey, John. "Memoirs of Brigadier-General John Lacey, of Pennsylvania." *PMHB* 25, Nos. 1–4 (1901) Pp. 1–13, 191–207, 341–54, 495–515; and 26, Nos. 1–2 (1902) Pp. 101–11, 265–70.

Lambert, Richard. *A New System of Military Discipline Founded upon Principle* (Philadelphia, 1776).

Lathrop, John. *A Sermon Preached to the Ancient and Honorable Artillery Company in Boston, New-England, June 6, 1774* (Boston, 1774).

Laurens, John. *The Army Correspondence of Colonel John Laurens in the Years 1777–8* (New York: Arno Press, 1969).

Lawrence, Mason I. and Bumgardner, Georgia B., eds. *Massachusetts Broadsides of the American Revolution* (Amherst, Mass.: University of Massachusetts Press, 1976).

Lee, Andrew. "Sullivan's Expedition to Staten Island in 1777: Extract from the Diary of Captain of Andrew Lee." *PMHB* 3, No. 2 (1879) Pp. 167–73.

Lee, Arthur. *An Appeal to the Justice and Interests of the People of Great-Britain, in the present disputes with America* (New York, 1775).

Lee, Charles. *General Lee's Letter to General Burgoyne, upon his arrival in Boston* (New York, 1775).

————. *Strictures on a Pamphlet entitled a "Friendly Address to All Reasonable Americans on the Subject of our Political Confusions"* (Boston, 1775).

————. *Lee Papers, NYHS, Collections, 1871–1874.* 4 vols. (New York, 1872–1875).

Leonard, Daniel. *The Present State of the Province of Massachusetts Bay in general and the town of Boston in particular* (New York, 1775).

Lesser, Charles, ed. *The Sinews of Independence: Monthly Strength Reports of the Continental Army* (Chicago: University of Chicago Press, 1976).

Lincoln, Charles, ed. *Narratives of the Indian Wars, 1675–1699* (New York: Charles Scribner's, 1913).

————, ed., *The Correspondence of William Shirley.* 2 vols. (New York: Macmillan, 1912).

Linn, William. *A Military Discourse, Delivered in Carlisle* (Philadelphia, 1776).

Livesay, R., ed. *The Prisoners of 1776; a Relic of the Revolution Compiled from the Journal of Charles Herbert* (Boston, 1854).

Livingston, William. *A Review of the Military Operations in North America, from the Commencement of the French Hostilities on the Frontiers of Virginia to the Surrender of Oswego* (London, 1758).

Lockwood, James. *The Worth and Excellence of Civil Freedom and Liberty Illustrated, and Public Spirit and Love of our Country Recommended* (New London, Conn., 1759).

Lyman, Simeon. "Journal of Simeon Lyman of Sharon, Aug. 10 to Dec. 28, 1775." CHS, *Collections* 7 (Hartford, Conn.) Pp. 111–34.

McClenachan, William. *The Christian Warrior. A Sermon preach'd at the French Meeting House in Boston* (Boston, 1745).

McMichael, James. "Diary of Lieutenant James McMichael, of the Pennsylvania Line, 1776–1778." *PMHB* 16, No. 2 (1892) Pp. 129–59.

McPherson, James. *The Rights of Great Britain Asserted against the Claims of America: being an Answer to the Declaration of the General Congress* (London, 1776).

Madison, James, Hamilton, Alexander, and Jay, John. *The Federalist* (New York: Random House, 1941).

"Major French's Journal." CHS, *Collections* 1 (Hartford, 1860) Pp. 187–224.

Mason, John. *A Brief History of the Pequot War.* MHS, *Collections,* 2nd Ser., 8 (1819) Pp. 120–53.

Mather, Cotton. *A Discourse Delivered unto some part of the Forces Engaged in the Just War of New England Against the Northern and Eastern Indians* (Boston, 1689).

———. *Frontiers Well-Defended. An Essay, to Direct the Frontiers of a Countrey Exposed unto the Incursions of a Barbarous Enemy, How to Behave Themselves in their Uneasy Station* (Boston, 1707).

———. *Military Duties, Recommended to an Artillery Company, at Charlestown* (Boston, 1689).

———. *Decennium Luctuosum: An History of Remarkable Occurrences in the Long War, which New England hath had with the Indian Savages, from the Year 1688 to the Year 1698, faithfully Composed and Improved* (Boston, 1698).

———. *Souldiers Counselled and Comforted. A Discourse Delivered unto some part of the Forces engaged in the Just War of New England against the Northern and Eastern Indians* (Boston, 1689).

———. *The Life of Sir William Phips* [1697] (New York, 1929).

———. *Things to be Look'd for. Discourses on the Glorious Characters in the Latter Days* (Cambridge, Mass., 1691).

Mather, Increase. *A Brief History of the Warre with the Indians in New England Together with a Serious Exhortation to the Inhabitants of that Land* (Boston, 1676).

———. *The Day of Trouble is Near. Two Sermons wherin is shewed what reason there is for New England to Expect a Day of Trouble* (Cambridge, Mass., 1674).

Mather, Samuel. *War is Lawful, and Arms are to be proved* (Boston, 1739).

Mayo, Lawrence S., ed. *Thomas Hutchinson, The History of the Colony and Province of Massachusetts-Bay*, 3 vols. (Cambridge, Mass.: Harvard Univ. Press, 1936).

Militia Act; together with the Rules and Regulations for the Militia, The (Boston, 1776).

Military Journals of two Private Soldiers, 1758–1775, with numerous illustrative notes to which is added, A Supplement, The (New York: Da Capo, 1971).

Morgan, John, et al. *Four Dissertations on the Reciprocal Advantages of a Perpetual Union between Great-Britain and her American colonies* (Philadelphia, 1766).

Morton, Robert. "The Diary of Robert Morton." *PMHB* 1, No. 1 (1877) Pp. 1–40.

Moses, Montrose, J., ed. *Representative Plays of American Dramatists.* 3 vols. (New York: B. Blom, 1964).

Newell, Samuel. *Abraham in Arms; or, The first Religious General with his Army engaging in a War for which he had wisely prepared, and by which, not only an eminent Victory was obtained, but a Blessing gained also* (Boston, 1678).

Niles, Samuel. *A Brief and Plain Essay on God's Wonder-working Providence for New-England, In the Reduction of Louisbourg, and Fortresses thereto belonging on Cape-Breton* (New London, Conn., 1747).

Ordinance for Regulating the Militia of New Jersey, passed at a Sitting of the Provincial Congress, held at Trenton, An (Burlington, N.J., 1776).

Osgood, David. *A Sermon preached at the request of the Ancient and Honorable Artillery Company in Boston* (Boston, 1788).

Otis, James. *The Rights of the British Colonies Asserted and Proved* (Boston, 1764).

Pargellis, Stanley, ed. *Military Affairs in North America, 1748–1765: Selected Documents from the Cumberland Papers in Windsor Castle* (New York: Archon, 1969).

Parsons, Joseph. *Religion recommended to the Soldier* (Boston, 1744).

Peabody, Oliver. *An Essay to revive and encourage Military Exercises, Skill and Valour among the Sons of God's People in New England* (Boston, 1732).

Peckham, Howard H. and Brown, Lloyd A., eds. *Revolutionary War Journals of Henry Dearborn, 1775–1783* (Chicago: Caxton Club, 1939).

Pemberton, Ebenezer. *A Sermon preached to the Ancient and Honorable Artillery-Company, In Boston* (Boston, 1756).

Penhallow, Samuel. *The History of the Wars of New England, with the Eastern Indians. Or, a Narrative of their continued Perfidy and Cruelty, from the 10th of August, 1703 to the Peace renewed 13th of July, 1773* (Boston, 1726).

Pennsylvania Archives. 9 Series (Philadelphia and Harrisburg: Pennsylvania Museum Comm., 1852–1935).

Perkins, Nathan. *A Sermon preached to the Soldiers, who went from West Hartford, in Defense of their Country* (Hartford, 1775).

Phillips, Samuel. *Souldiers Counselled and Encouraged, A Sermon Preached at the Request, and in the Audience of the Ancient and Honourable Artillery-Company in Boston* (Boston, 1741).

Phips, Spencer. *A Proclamation for Encouragement to Volunteers to prosecute the War against the Indian Enemy.* Broadside (Boston, 23 August 1745).

Prentice, Thomas. *A Sermon Preached at Charlestown, on a General Thanksgiving for the Reduction of Cape-Breton* (Boston, 1745).

Putnam, David. "Colonel David Putnam's Letter Relative to the Battle of Bunker Hill and General Israel Putnam." CHS, *Collections,* 1 (Hartford, 1860) Pp. 242–57.

Quincy, Josiah. *The Journals of Major Samuel Shaw, the First American Consul at Canton* (Boston, 1847).

Ramsay, David. *An Oration on the Advantages of American Independence: Spoken before a Public Assembly of the Inhabitants of Charlestown in South-Carolina, on the Second Anniversary of the Glorious Era* (Charleston, S.C., 1778).

Randolph, Edward. *Edward Randolph; Including His Letters and Official Papers from the New England, Middle and Southern Colonies in America* (Boston, 1899).

Raynal, Abbe. *The Sentiments of a Foreigner, on the Disputes of Great-Britain with America* (Philadelphia, 1775).

Richards, Samuel. *Diary of Samuel Richards, Captain of Connecticut Line, War of Revolution, 1775–1781* (Philadelphia: Privately Printed, 1909).

Richardson, John. *The Necessity of a well experienced Souldiery, or, a Christian Common Wealth ought to be well Instructed & Experienced in the Military Art* (Cambridge, Mass., 1679).

Robbins, Nathanial. *Jerusalem's Peace Wished. A Sermon Preached to the Ancient and Honorable Artillery Company in Boston* (Boston, 1772).

Roberts, Kenneth, ed. *March to Quebec* (New York: Doubleday, Doran, 1938).

Rolfe, John. *A True Relation of the state of Virginia lefte by Sir Thomas Dale Knight in May last 1616* (Charlottesville, Va.: University of Virginia Press, 1971).

Rowlandson, Mary. *The Sovereignty and Goodness of GOD, Together with the Faithfulness of His Promises Displayed; Being a Narrative of the Captivity and Restauration of Mrs. Mary Rowlandson* (Cambridge, Mass., 1682).

Ruggles, Thomas. *The Usefulness and Expedience of Souldiers as discovered By Reason and Experience, and Countenanced and Supported by the Gospel* (New London, Conn., 1737).

Seymour, William. "Journal of the Southern Expedition, 1780–1783." *PMHB* 7, Nos. 3–4 (1883) Pp. 286–98, 377–94.

Sheer, George, ed. *Private Yankee Doodle* (Boston: Little, Brown, 1962).

Shippen, Joseph. "Military Letters of Captain Joseph Shippen of the Provincial Service, 1756–1758." *PMHB* 36, Nos. 3–4 (1911) Pp. 367–78, 385–463.

Showman, Richard, ed. *The Papers of General Nathanael Greene* (Chapel Hill, N.C.: University of North Carolina Press, 1976 —).

Shute, Daniel. *A Sermon, preached to the Ancient and Honorable Artillery Company in Boston, New England* (Boston, 1767).

Simes, Thomas. *The Military Guide for Young Officers* (Philadelphia, 1776).

Smith, William, *An Oration in Memory of General Montgomery, and of the Officers and Soldiers who Fell with Him before Quebec* (Philadelphia, 1776).

Smyth, Albert H., ed. *The Writings of Benjamin Franklin.* 8 vols. (New York: Macmillan, 1905–1907).

Sparks, Jared, ed. *Correspondence of the American Revolution; being Letters of Eminent Men to George Washington.* 4 vols. (Freeport, N.Y.: Books For Libraries, 1970).

Sterling, Daniel. "American Prisoners of War in New York: A Report by Elias Boudinot." *WMQ*, 3d Ser., 13 (July 1956), Pp. 376–93.

Stevens, Benjamin, ed. *Facsimilies of Manuscripts in European Archives Relating to America, 1773–1783.* 23 vols. (London, 1889–1898).

Stevenson, Roger. *Military Instructions for Officers detached in the field: Containing a Scheme for forming a Corps of a Partisan* (Philadelphia, 1775).

Stillman, Samuel. *A Sermon Preached to the Ancient and Honorable Artillery Company in Boston* (Boston, 1770).

Symonds, William. *Virginia. A Sermon Preached at White-Chappel, In the presence of many, Honorable and Worshipfull, the Adventurers and Planters for Virginia* [1609] (New York, 1968).

Syrett, Harold C. and Cooke, Jacob E., eds. *The Papers of Alexander Hamilton* (New York: Columbia Univ. Press, 1961 —).

Talmadge, Benjamin. *Memoirs of Col. Benjamin Talmadge, Prepared by Himself, at the Request of his Children* (New York, 1858).

Taylor, Robert J., et al., eds. *Papers of John Adams* (Cambridge, Mass.: Harvard Univ. Press, 1977 —).

Tennent, Gilbert. *The late Association for Defense, encouraged, or The Lawfulness of a Defensive War Represented in a Sermon preached at Philadelphia* (Philadelphia, 1748).

Thacher, James. *Military Journal of the American Revolution, from the commencement to the disbanding of the American Army* (Hartford, Conn., 1862).

Tilden, John Bell. "Extracts from the Journal of Lieutenant John Bell Tilden, Second Pennsylvania Line, 1781–1782." *PMHB* 19, Nos. 1–2 (1885) Pp. 51–63, 208–33.

Tilghman, Tench. *Memoir of Lieut. Col. Tench Tilghman, Secretary and Aid to Washington* (Albany, N.Y., 1876).

Turner, Joseph, ed. *The Journal and Order Book of Captain Robert Kirkwood of the Delaware Regiment of the Continental Line* (Port Washington, N.Y.: Kennikat, 1970).

Tyler, Lyon Gardiner, ed. *Narratives of Early Virginia, 1606–1625* (New York: Charles Scribner's, 1907).

Underhill, John. *News from America.* MHS, *Collections*, 3d Ser., 6 (1837) Pp. 3–28.

Vail, R. W. G., ed. *The Revolutionary Diary of Lieut. Obadiah Gore, Jr.* (New York: New York Public Library, 1929).

Van Der Beets, Richard, ed. *Held Captive by Indians: Selected Narratives, 1642–1836* (Knoxville, Tenn.: University of Tennessee Press, 1973).

Vincent, Phillip. *A true Relation of the late Battle fought in New England between the English and the savages.* MHS, *Collections*, 3d Ser., 6 (1837) Pp. 33–43.

Wade, Herbert T. and Lively, Robert A., eds. *This Glorious Cause: The Adventures of Two Company Officers in Washington's Army* (Princeton, N.J.: Princeton Univ. Press, 1958).

Waldo, Albigance. "Valley Forge, 1777–1778: Diary of Surgeon Albigance Waldo, of the Continental Line." *PMHB* 21, No. 3 (1897) Pp. 299–323.

Warren-Adams Letters: Being chiefly a correspondence among John Adams, Samuel Adams, and James Warren. MHS, *Collections*. 2 vols. (Boston, 1925).

Warren, Mercy Otis. *History of the American Revolution. Interspersed with Biographical, Political and Moral Observations* (Boston, 1805).

Waterhouse, Edward. *A Declaration of the State of the Colony and Affairs in Virginia* (London, 1622).

Webster, Samuel. *Rabshakeh's Proposals Considered, in a Sermon, Delivered at Groton* (Boston, 1775).

Wells, Bayze. "Journal of Bayze Wells, of Farmington; May 1775–February 1777, at the Northward and in Canada." CHS, *Collections*, 7 (1899) Pp. 239–96.

Willard, Joseph. *The duty of the good and faithful Soldier, Attempted in a Sermon delivered at Mendon* (Boston, 1781).

Williams, Roger. *The Complete Writings of Roger Williams*. 7 vols. (New York: Russell and Russell, 1963).

Williams, William. *A Sermon Preach'd at the Desire of the Honourable Artillery Company in Boston* (Boston, 1737).

Winthrop, John. *The History of New England from 1630–1649* [1690]. Savage, James, ed. 2 vols. (Boston, 1853).

Wise, Jeremiah. *Rulers the Ministers of God for the Good of the People. A Sermon* (Boston, 1729).

Wolcott, Roger. "Journal of Roger Wolcott at the Siege of Louisbourg, 1745." CHS, *Collections*, 1 (Hartford, 1860) Pp. 131–45.

Wood, William. *Wood's New England Prospect* (Boston, 1865).

Wright, Alfred Hazen, comp. *The Sullivan Expedition of 1779; Contemporary Newspaper Comment and Letters. Studies in History*. Nos. 5–8 (Ithaca, N.Y., 1943).

Young, William. "Journal of Sergeant William Young, Written during the Jersey Campaign in the Winter of 1776–1777." *PMHB* 8, No. 3 (1884) Pp. 255–78.

Newspapers

Boston Gazette
New York Gazetteer
Pennsylvania Evening Post
Pennsylvania Packet
South Carolina Royal Gazette
Virginia Gazette

SECONDARY SOURCES

Books

Adcock, F. E. *The Greek and Macedonian Art of War* (Berkeley, Calif.: University of California Press, 1967).

Alden, John. *General Charles Lee: Traitor or Patriot?* (Baton Rouge, La.: Louisiana State Univ. Press, 1951).

Allmands, C. T., ed. *War, Literature and Politics in the Late Middle Ages* (New York: Harper and Row, 1976).

Anon. *Biographical Sketch of Gen. Joseph Warren, Enhancing the Prominent Events of his Life, and his Boston Massacre Orations of 1772 and 1775* (Boston, 1857).

Ashley, Maurice. *Louis XIV and the Greatness of France* (London: Watson and Viney, 1963).

Axtell, James. *The School upon a Hill: Education and Society in Colonial New England* (New Haven, Conn.: Yale Univ. Press, 1974).

Bailyn, Bernard. *The Ideological Origins of the American Revolution* (Cambridge, Mass.: Harvard Univ. Press, 1967).

Bainton, Roland H. *Christian Attitudes Toward War and Peace* (New York: Abingdon, 1960).

Bakeless, John. *Background to Glory: The Life of George Rogers Clark* (Philadelphia: J. P. Lippincott, 1957).

Baldwin, Alice M. *The New England Clergy and the American Revolution* (New York, Frederick Ungar, 1928).

Ballis, William. *The Legal Position of War: Changes in Its Practice and Theory from Plato to Vattel* (New York: Garland, 1973).

Barbour, Philip L. *The Three Worlds of Captain John Smith* (Boston: Houghton, Mifflin, 1964).

Barnett, Correlli. *Britain and Her Army, 1509–1970* (New York: W. Morrow, 1970).

Behrens, C. B. A. *The Ancien Regime* (London: Harcourt Brace, 1967).

Benton, William A. *Whig-Loyalism: An Aspect of Political Ideology in the American Revolutionary Era* (Rutherford, N.J.: Farleigh Dickinson Univ. Press, 1969).

Bodge, George Madison. *Soldiers in King Philip's War, Being a Critical Account of that War* (Boston: Privately Printed, 1906).

Bolton, Charles K. *The Private Soldier under Washington* (New York: Charles Scribner's, 1902).

Boorstin, Daniel. *The Americans: The Colonial Experience* (New York: Random House, 1958).

Bowman, Allen. *The Morale of the American Revolutionary Army* (Port Washington, N.Y.: Kennikat, 1976).

Bowman, Larry G. *Captive Americans: Prisoners During the American Revolution* (Athens, Ohio: Ohio Univ. Press, 1976).

Breen, Timothy. *The Character of the Good Ruler: A Study of Puritan Political Ideas in New England, 1630–1730* (New Haven, Conn.: Yale Univ. Press, 1970).

Bremmer, Francis J. *The Puritan Experiment: New England Society from Bradford to Edwards* (New York: St. Martin's 1976).

Bridenbaugh, Carl. *Cities in Revolt: Urban Life in America, 1743–1776* (New York: Capricorn, 1955).

——. *Cities in the Wilderness* (New York: Capricorn, 1938).

Brock, Peter. *Pacifism in Europe to 1914* (Princeton, N.J.: Princeton Univ. Press, 1972).

——. *Pacifism in the United States: From the Colonial Era to the First World War* (Princeton, N.J.: Princeton Univ. Press, 1968).

Brodie, Fawn and Bernard. *From Crossbow to H-Bomb* (Bloomington, Ind.: Indiana Univ. Press, 1973).

Brown, Louis K. *A Revolutionary Town* (Canaan, N.H.: Phoenix Publications, 1975).

Brown, Wallace. *The Good Americans: The Loyalists in the American Revolution* (New York: W. Morrow, 1969).

Bush, Martin. *Revolutionary Enigma: A Re-appraisal of General Philip Schuyler of New York* (Port Washington, N.Y.: Kennikat, 1969).

Caldwell, Wallace E. *Hellenic Conceptions of Peace* (New York: Columbia Univ. Press, 1967).

Calhoon, Robert M. *The Loyalists in Revolutionary America, 1760–1781* (New York: Harcourt, Brace, 1973).

Callahan, North. *Henry Knox, General Washington's General* (New York: Holt, Rinehardt and Winston, 1958).

Carroll, Peter. *Puritanism and the Wilderness: The Intellectual Significance of the New England Frontier, 1629–1700* (New York: Columbia Univ. Press, 1969).

Cary, John. *Joseph Warren: Physician, Politician, Patriot* (Urbana, Ill.: Univ. of Illinois Press, 1961).

Chapin, Bradley. *The American Law of Treason: Revolutionary and Early American Origins* (Seattle, Wash.: Univ. of Washington Press, 1964).

Clark, G. N. *War and Society in the Seventeenth Century* (Cambridge, Eng.: Cambridge Univ. Press, 1958).

Cometti, Elizabeth. "Depredations in Virginia during the Revolution." In Rutman, Darrett B., ed. *The Old Dominion: Essays for Thomas Perkins Abernathy* (Charlottesville, Va.: Univ. of Virginia Press, 1964).

——. "The Labor Front During the Revolution." In Ferling, John E., ed. *The American Revolution: The Home Front*. West Georgia College *Studies in the Social Sciences*, XV (Carrollton, Ga.: Thomasson Printers, 1976) Pp. 79–80.

Corkran, David. *The Cherokee Frontier: Conflict and Survival, 1740–1762* (Norman, Okla.: Univ. of Oklahoma Press, 1962).

——. *The Creek Frontier, 1540–1783* (Norman, Okla.: Univ. of Oklahoma Press, 1962).

Corvisier, Andre. *Armies and Societies in Europe, 1494–1789* (Bloomington, Ind.: Indiana Univ. Press, 1979).

Craven, Wesley F. *The Southern Colonies in the Seventeenth Century, 1607–1689* (Baton Rouge, La.: Louisiana State Univ. Press, 1949).

Crow, Jeffrey J. and Tise, Larry E., eds. *The Southern Experience in the American Revolution* (Chapel Hill, N.C.: Univ. of North Carolina Press, 1978).

Cruicksank, C. G. *Elizabeth's Army* (London: Oxford Univ. Press, 1966).

Daniels, Bruce C. "Emerging Urbanization and Increasing Stratification in the Era of the American Revolution." In Ferling, John, ed. *The American Revolution: The Home Front*. West Georgia College, *Studies in the Social Sciences*, XV (Carrollton, Ga.: Thomasson Printers, 1976) Pp. 15–30.

Davidson, Philip. *Propaganda and the American Revolution, 1763–1783* (Chapel Hill, N.C.: Univ. of North Carolina Press, 1941).

Dawson, Harry. *The Assault on Stony Brook* (Morisiana, N.Y., 1863).

Delbrück, Hans. *History of the Art of War, Antiquity* (Westport, Conn.: Greenwood Press, 1975).

De Mond, Robert O. *The Loyalists in North Carolina during the American Revolution* (Durham, N.C.: Duke Univ. Press, 1940).

Dollard, John, et al., eds. *Fear in Battle* (Washington, D.C.: U.S. Govt. Printing Office, 1944).

Dorn, Walter L. *Competition for Empire, 1740–1763* (New York: Harpers, 1940).

Ducross, Louis. *French Society in the Eighteenth Century* (London: G. Bell, 1926).

Duffy, Christopher. *The Army of Frederick the Great* (New York: Hippocrene, 1974).

Dunbar, Louise B. "A Study of Monarchical Tendencies in the United States from 1776–1801." University of Illinois, *Studies in the Social Sciences*, X (Urbana, Ill.: Univ. of Illinois Press, 1922) Pp. 18–48.

Dunn, John. *The Political Thought of John Locke: An Historical Account of the Arguments of the "Two Treatises of Government"* (Cambridge, Eng.: Cambridge Univ. Press, 1969).

Elliot, J. H. *The Old World and the New, 1492–1650* (London: Cambridge Univ. Press, 1970).

Elton, G. R., ed. *The Reformation, 1520–1559*. 2 vols. (Cambridge, Eng.: Cambridge Univ. Press, 1958).

Ferling, John E., ed. *The American Revolution: The Home Front*. West Georgia College, *Studies in the Social Sciences*, XV (Carrollton, Ga.: Thomasson Printers, 1976).

————. *The Loyalist Mind: Joseph Galloway and the American Revolution* (University Park, Pa.: Pennsylvania State Univ. Press, 1977).

Flexner, James T. *George Washington and the American Revolution* (Boston: Little, Brown, 1967).

Flick, Alexander C. *Loyalism in New York during the American Revolution* (New York: Charles Scribner's, 1901).

Foner, Philip S. *Blacks in the American Revolution* (Westport, Conn.: Greenwood Press, 1975).

Fortescue, John W. *The History of the British Army*. 13 vols. (London: Macmillan, 1910–1930).

Frothingham, Richard. *Life and Times of Joseph Warren* (Boston, 1865).

Gay, Peter. *The Enlightenment: An Interpretation. This Science of Freedom*. 2 vols. (New York: Simon and Schuster, 1969).

Gilbert, Felix. *To the Farewell Address: Ideas of Early American Foreign Policy* (Princeton, N.J.: Princeton Univ. Press, 1961).

Ginzberg, Eli, et al. *The Ineffective Soldier: Lessons for Management and the Nation*. 3 vols. (New York: Columbia Univ. Press, 1959).

Gipson, Lawrence Henry. *The Great War for Empire: The Years of Defeat, 1754–1757*. Vol. VII. In *The British Empire Before the American Revolution*. 14 vols. (New York: Alfred A. Knopf, 1958–1968).

Graymont, Barbara. *The Iroquois in the American Revolution* (Syracuse, N.Y.: Syracuse Univ. Press, 1972).

Greven, Philip. *The Protestant Temperment: Patterns of Child-Rearing, Religious Experience, and the Self in Early America* (New York: Alfred A. Knopf, 1977).

Grinker, Roy R. and Spiegel, John P. *War Neurosis* (Philadelphia: Blakiston, 1945).

Gross, Robert. *The Minutemen and Their World* (New York: Hill and Wang, 1976).

Gruber, Ira. *The Howe Brothers and the American Revolution* (New York: W. W. Norton, 1972).

Haffenden, Philip S. *New England in the English Nation, 1689–1713* (Oxford, Eng.: Oxford Univ. Press, 1974).

Hale, J. R. "Armies, Navies, and the Art of War." In Elton, G. R., ed. *The Reformation, 1520–1559*. 2 vols. (Cambridge, Eng.: Cambridge Univ. Press, 1958) Pp. 481–503.

Hamilton, Edward P. *The French and Indian Wars: The Story of Battles and Forts in the Wilderness* (Garden City, N.Y.: Doubleday 1962).

Hamilton, Milton W. *Sir William Johnson: Colonial American, 1715–1763* (Port Washington, N.Y.: Kennikat 1976).

Hammond, Otis G. *Tories of New Hampshire in the War of the Revolution* (Boston, The Gregg Press, 1972).

Hancock, Harold B. *The Delaware Loyalists* (Boston: The Gregg Press, 1972).

Harrell, Isaac C. *Loyalism in Virginia* (Durham, N.C.: Duke Univ. Press, 1926).

Hartz, Louis. *The Liberal Tradition in Amerca* (New York: Harcourt, Brace, 1955).

Hauser, Arnold. *The Social History of Art*. 4 vols. (New York: Alfred A. Knopf, 1952).

Hawke, David. *Benjamin Rush: Revolutionary Gadfly* (Indianapolis, Ind.: Bobbs, Merrill, 1971).

———. *Franklin* (New York: Harper and Row, 1976).

Hazard, Paul. *The European Mind, 1680–1715* (New Haven, Conn: Yale Univ. Press, 1952).

Held, Julius S. and Posner, Donald. *17th and 18th Century Art: Baroque Painting, Sculpture, Architecture* (New York: H. N. Abrams, 1971).

Higginbotham, Don, ed. *Reconsiderations on the Revolutionary War: Selected Essays* (Westport, Conn.: Greenwood Press, 1978).

———. *The War of American Independence: Military Attitudes, Policies, and Practice, 1763–1789* (New York: Macmillan 1971).

Jennings, Francis. *The Invasion of America: Indians, Colonialism and the Cant of Conquest* (Chapel Hill, N.C.: Univ. of North Carolina Press, 1975).

Jensen, Merrill. *The Founding of a Nation: A History of the American Revolution* (New York: Oxford Univ. Press, 1968).

———. *The New Nation: A History of the United States during the Confederation, 1781–1789* (New York: Alfred A. Knopf, 1958).

———. *Tracts of the American Revolution, 1763–1776* (Indianapolis, Ind.: Bobbs, Merrill, 1967).

Jones, Howard Mumford. *Revolution and Romanticism* (Cambridge, Mass.: Harvard Univ. Press, 1974).

Jones, James. *WWII: A Chronicle of Soldiering* (New York: Grossett and Dunlap, 1975).

Jones, Rufus M., et al. *The Quakers in the American Colonies* (London: Russell and Russell, 1911).

Kaplan, Lawrence. *Colonies to Nation: American Diplomacy, 1763–1801* (New York: Macmillan, 1972).

Kay, Marvin L. Michael. "The North Carolina Regulators, 1766–1776: A Class Conflict." In Young, Alfred, ed. *The American Revolution: Explorations in the History of American Radicalism* (DeKalb, Ill.: Northern Illinois Univ. Press, 1976).

Kitchen, Martin. *A Military History of Germany: From the Eighteenth Century to the Present Day* (Bloomington, Ind.: Indiana Univ. Press, 1975).

Knollenberg, Bernhard. *Washington and the Revolution: A Reappraisal* (New York: Macmillan, 1941).

Kohn, Richard. *Eagle and Sword: The Federalists and the Creation of the Military Establishment in America* (New York: The Free Press, 1975).

———. "The Murder of the Militia System in the Aftermath of the American Revolution." In Martin, James K., ed. *The Human Dimensions of Nation Making: Essays on Colonial and Revolutionary America* (Madison, Wisc.: Univ. of Wisconsin Press, 1976) Pp. 304–22.

Kopperman, Paul E. *Braddock at the Monongahela* (Pittsburgh: Univ. of Pittsburgh Press, 1977).

Lanctot, Gustave. *Canada and the American Revolution, 1774–1783* (Cambridge, Mass.: Harvard Univ. Press, 1967).

Leach, Douglas. *Arms for Empire: A Military History of the British Colonies in North America, 1607–1763* (New York: Macmillan, 1973).

———. *Flintlock and Tomahawk: New England in King Philip's War* (New York: W. W. Norton, 1958).

Lefler, Hugh T. and Powell, William S. *Colonial North Carolina: A History* (New York: Charles Scribner's, 1973).

McCartney, Eugene S. *Warfare by Land and Sea: Our Debt to Greece and Rome* (New York: Cooper Square, 1963).

McGowan, George. *The British Occupation of Charleston, 1780–82* (Columbia, S.C.: Univ. of South Carolina Press, 1972).

Mackesy, Piers. *The War for America, 1775–1783* (Cambridge, Mass.: Harvard Univ. Press, 1975).

Main, Jackson Turner. *The Anti-Federalists: Critics of the Constitution, 1781–1788* (Chapel Hill, N.C.: Univ. of North Carolina Press, 1961).

Maier, Pauline. *From Resistance to Revolution: Colonial Radicals and American Opposition to Britain* (New York: Alfred A. Knopf, 1972).

Martin, James Kirby, ed. *The Human Dimensions of Nation Making: Essays on Colonial and Revolutionary America* (Madison, Wisc.: Univ. of Wisconsin Press, 1976).

Marshall, S. L. A. *Men Against Fire: The Problem of Battle Command in Future War* (New York: W. Morrow, 1964).

Matthews, Lois Kemball. *The Expansion of New England: The Spread of New England Settlement and Institutions to the Mississippi River, 1620–1865* (New York: Columbia Univ. Press, 1909).

Meriwether, Robert. *The Expansion of South Carolina, 1729–1765* (Kingsport, Tenn.: Southern Publishers, 1940).

Miller, Perry. *The New England Mind: The Seventeenth Century* (Cambridge, Mass.: Harvard Univ. Press, 1953).

Millis, Walter. *Arms and Men: A Study in American Military History* (New York: G. P. Putnam's, 1956).

Mitchell, Julia. *St. Jean de Crevecoeur* (New York: Columbia Univ. Press, 1916).

Montgomery, Charles F. and Kane, Patricia E. *American Art: 1750–1800, Towards Independence* (New Haven, Conn.: Yale Univ. Press, 1976).

Montross, Lynn. *Rag, Tag and Bobtail: The Story of the Continental Army, 1775–1783* (New York: Harper's, 1952).

———. *War Through the Ages* (New York: Harper and Row, 1960).

Morgan, Edmund S. *Roger Williams: The Church and the State* (New York: Harcourt, Brace, 1967).

———. *The Puritan Dilemma: The Story of John Winthrop* (Boston: Little, Brown, 1958).

Morison, Samuel E. *Builders of the Bay Colony* (Cambridge, Mass: Harvard Univ. Press, 1930).

———. *The European Discovery of America*. 2 vols. (New York: Oxford Univ. Press, 1971–1974).

Morris, Richard B. *Government and Labor in Early America* (New York: Harper and Row, 1946).

Morton, Richard L. *Colonial Virginia*. 2 vols. (Chapel Hill N.C.: Univ. of North Carolina Press, 1960).

Nash, Gary. "Social Change and the Growth of Prerevolutionary Urban Radicalism." In Young, Alfred, ed. *The American Revolution: Explorations in the History of American Radicalism* (DeKalb, Ill.: Northern Illinois Univ. Press, 1976) Pp. 5–36.

Nelson, Paul David. *General Horatio Gates: A Biography* (Baton Rouge, La.: Louisiana State Univ. Press, 1975).

Nelson, William. *The American Tory* (New York: Clarendon Press, 1961).

Norton, Mary Beth. *The British-Americans: The Loyalist Exiles in England, 1774–1789* (Boston: Little, Brown, 1972).

————. " 'What an Alarming Crisis Is This': Southern Women and the American Revolution.'' In Crow, Jeffrey J. and Tise, Larry E., eds. *The Southern Experience in the American Revolution* (Chapel Hill, N.C.: Univ. of North Carolina Press, 1978) Pp. 203–34.

Nye, Russell B. *This Almost Chosen People: Essays in the History of American Ideas* (East Lansing, Mich.: Michigan State Univ. Press, 1966).

Ogg, David. *England in the Reigns of James II and William II* (Oxford, Eng.: Oxford Univ. Press, 1955).

Oman, C. W. C. *The Art of War in the Middle Ages, A.D. 378–1515* (Ithaca, N.Y.: Cornell Univ. Press, 1953).

Palmer, Dave Richard. *The Way of the Fox: American Strategy in the War for America, 1775–1783* (Westport, Conn.: Greenwood Press, 1975).

Pargellis, Stanley M. *Lord Loudon in North America, 1756–1758* (New Haven, Conn.: Yale Univ. Press, 1933).

Parkman, Francis. *Pioneers of France in the New World,* Vol. II. In *The Works of Francis Parkman.* 20 vols. (Boston, 1897–1898).

Parks, George B. *Richard Hakluyt and the English Voyages* (New York: Frederick Ungar, 1961).

Pearce, Roy Harvey. *Savagism and Civilization: A Study of the Indian and the American Mind* (Baltimore: Johns Hopkins Univ. Press, 1953).

Peckham, Howard. *The Colonial Wars, 1689–1762* (Chicago: Univ. of Chicago Press, 1964).

————. *The War for Independence* (Chicago: Univ. of Chicago Press, 1958).

Pocock, J. G. A. *The Machiavellian Moment: Florentine Political Thought and the Atlantic Tradition* (Princeton, N.J.: Princeton Univ. Press, 1975).

Preston, Richard and Wise, Stanley. *Men in Arms: A History of Warfare* (New York: Praeger, 1970).

Pritchett, W. Kendrick. *Ancient Greek Military Practices* (Berkeley, Calif.: Univ. of California Press, 1971).

Proun, David. "Style in American Art, 1750–1800." In Montgomery, Charles F. and Kane, Patricia E., eds. *American Art: 1750–1800, Towards Independence* (New Haven, Conn.: Yale Univ. Press, 1976) Pp. 32–87.

Quarles, Benjamin. *The Negro in the American Revolution* (Chapel Hill, N.C.: Univ. of North Carolina Press, 1961).

Quinn, David Beers. *England and the Discovery of America, 1481–1620* (New York: Alfred A. Knopf, 1974).

Rankin, Hugh. *Francis Marion: The Swamp Fox* (New York: Thomas Crowell, 1973).

Rapp, Theodore. *War in the Modern World* (Durham, N.C.: Duke Univ. Press, 1959).

Robbins, Caroline. *The Eighteenth-Century Commonwealthmen: Studies in the Transmission, Development and Circumstances of English Liberal Thought from the Restoration of Charles II until the War with the Thirteen Colonies* (New York: Atheneum, 1968).

Roberts, Michael. *The Military Revolution, 1560–1660* (Belfast: Bowes, 1956).

Robson, Eric. "The Armed Forces and the Art of War." In Clark, G. N., et al., eds. *The New Cambridge Modern History.* 13 vols. (Cambridge, Eng.: Cambridge Univ. Press, 1969–1970) vol. VII. Pp. 163–89.

Root, Winfred T. *The Relations of Pennsylvania with the British Government* (New York: Burt Franklin, 1912).

Rosenblum, Robert. *Transformations in Late Eighteenth Century Art* (Princeton, N.J.: Princeton Univ. Press, 1967).

Rowe, Constance. *Voltaire and the State* (New York: Octagon Books, 1968).

Rutman, Darrett B., ed. *The Old Dominion: Essays for Thomas Perkins Abernathy* (Charlottesville, Va.: Univ. of Virginia Press, 1964).

Savelle, Max. *The Origins of American Diplomacy: The International History of Anglo-America, 1492–1763* (New York: Macmillan, 1967).

Schonberger, Arno and Soehner, Halden. *The Roccoco Age: Art and Civilization of the Eighteenth Century* (London: McGraw-Hill, 1968).

Schutz, John. *William Shirley: King's Governor of Massachusetts* (Chapel Hill, N.C.: Univ. of North Carolina Press, 1961).

Schwoerer, Lois G. *"No Standing Armies!" The Antiarmy Ideology in Seventeenth-Century England* (Baltimore: Johns Hopkins Univ. Press, 1974).

Seliger, M. *The Liberal Politics of John Locke* (New York: Praeger, 1969).

Sellers, John. "The Common Soldiers in the Revolution." In Underal, Stanley J., ed. *Military History of the American Revolution: Proceedings of the 6th Military History Symposium, USAF Academy* (Washington, D.C.: U.S. Govt Printing Office, 1976).

Shaw, Peter. *The Character of John Adams* (Chapel Hill, N.C.: Univ. of North Carolina Press, 1976).

Sherman, Richard. *Robert Johnson: Proprietary & Royal Governor of South Carolina* (Columbia, S.C.: Univ. of South Carolina Press, 1966).

Shy, John. *A People Numerous and Armed: Reflections on the Military Struggle for American Independence* (New York: Oxford Univ. Press, 1976).

———. "American Society and Its War for Independence." In Higginbotham, Don, ed. *Reconsiderations on the Revolutionary War: Selected Essays* (Westport, Conn.: Greenwood Press, 1978) Pp. 72–82.

———. "British Strategy for Pacifying the Southern Colonies." In Crow, Jeffrey J. and Tise, Larry E., eds. *The Southern Experience in the American Revolution* (Chapel Hill, N.C.: Univ. of North Carolina Press, 1978).

———. *Toward Lexington: The Role of the British Army in the Coming of the American Revolution* (Princeton, N.J.: Princeton Univ. Press, 1965).

Silverman, Kenneth. *A Cultural History of the American Revolution: Painting, Music, Literature and the Theatre in the Colonies and the United States from the Treaty of Paris to the Inauguration of George Washington, 1763–1789* (New York: Thomas Crowell, 1976).

Smith, Page. *A New Age Now Begins*. 2 vols. (New York: McGraw-Hill, 1976).

———. *John Adams*. 2 vols. (New York: Doubleday, 1962).

Souleyman, Elizabeth V. *The Vision of World Peace in Seventeenth and Eighteenth-Century France* (Port Washington, N.Y.: Kennikat, 1965).

Stille, Charles J. *Major-General Charles Anthony Wayne and the Pennsylvania Line in the Continental Army* (Philadelphia, 1893).

Stouffer, Samuel, et al. *The American Soldier*. 2 vols. (Princeton, N.J.: Princeton Univ. Press, 1949).

Stourzh, Gerald. *Alexander Hamilton and the Idea of Republican Government* (Stanford, Calif.: Stanford Univ. Press, 1970).

———. *Benjamin Franklin and American Foreign Policy* (Chicago: Univ. of Chicago Press, 1969).

Talpaler, Morris. *The Sociology of the Bay Colony* (New York: Philosophical Library, 1976).

Thayer, Theodore. *Nathanael Greene: Strategist of the American Revolution* (New York: Twayne, 1960).

Trelease. *Indian Affairs in Colonial New York: The Seventeenth Century* (Port Washington, N.Y.: Kennikat, 1971).

Underal, Stanley J., ed. *Military History of the American Revolution: Proceedings of the 6th Military History Symposium, USAF Academy* (Washington, D.C.: U.S. Govt Printing Office, 1976).

Underhill, Ruth Murray. *Red Man's America: A Brief History of the Indians in the U.S.* (Chicago: Univ. of Chicago Press, 1953).

Vagts, Alfred. *A History of Militarism: Civilian and Military* (New York: The Free Press, 1959).

Vail, M. G. A. "New Techniques and Old Ideals: The Impact of Artillery on War and Chivalry at the End of the Hundred Years War." In Allmands, C. T., ed. *War, Literature and Politics in the late Middle Ages* (New York: Harper and Row, 1976).

Van Alstyne, Richard. *The Rising American Empire* (Oxford, Eng.: Blackwell, 1960).

Van Doren, Carl. *Benjamin Franklin* (New York: Viking, 1938).

Vaughn, Alden. *The New England Frontier: Puritans and Indians, 1620–1675* (Boston: Little, Brown, 1965).

Wallace, Willard M. *Traitorous Hero: The Life and Fortunes of Benedict Arnold* (Freeport, N.Y.: Books For Libraries, 1970).

Waller, G. M. *Samuel Vetch: Colonial Enterpriser* (Chapel Hill, N.C.: Univ. of North Carolina Press, 1960).

Ward, Harry. *The United Colonies of New England, 1643–90* (New York: Vantage, 1961).

————. *Unite or Die: Intercolony Relations, 1690–1763* (Port Washington, N.Y.: Kennikat, 1971).

Washburn, Wilcomb E. *The Governor and the Rebel: A History of Bacon's Rebellion in Virginia* (Chapel Hill, N.C.: Univ. of North Carolina Press, 1957).

————. *The Indians in America* (New York: Harper and Row, 1975).

Watson, G. R. *The Roman Soldier* (Ithaca, N.Y.: Cornell Univ. Press, 1969).

Webster, Graham. *The Roman Imperial Army* (New York: Funk and Wagnalls, 1969).

Weigley, Russell. "American Strategy: A Call for a Critical Strategic History." In Higginbotham, Don, ed. *Reconsiderations on the Revolutionary War: Selected Essays* (Westport, Conn.: Greenwood Press, 1978) Pp. 32–53.

————. *The American Way of War: A History of United States Military Strategy and Policy* (New York: Macmillan, 1973).

————. *Towards an American Army* (New York: Columbia Univ. Press, 1962).

Weinberg, Albert K. *Manifest Destiny: A Study of Nationalist Expansion in American History* (Baltimore, Md.: Johns Hopkins Univ. Press, 1958).

Wells, William. *The Life and Public Services of Samuel Adams*. 3 vols. (Boston, 1865–1868).

Whittemore, Charles P. *A General of the Revolution: John Sullivan of New Hampshire* (New York: Columbia Univ. Press, 1961).

Wign, J. W. "Military Forces and Warfare, 1610–1648." Vol. IV In Clark, G. N., et al., eds. *The New Cambridge Modern History*. 13 vols. (Cambridge, Eng.: Cambridge Univ. Press, 1969–1970).

Williams, Basil. *The Whig Supremacy, 1714–1760* (Oxford, Eng.: Oxford Univ. Press, 1939).

Wills, Garry. *Inventing America: Jefferson's Declaration of Independence* (Garden City, N.Y.: Doubleday 1978).

Wilson, Joan Hoff. "The Illusion of Change: Women and the American Revolution." In Young, Alfred, ed. *The American Revolution: Explorations in the History of American Radicalism* (DeKalb, Ill.: Northern Illinois Univ. Press, 1976) Pp. 38–57.

Wintringham, Tom. *The Story of Weapons and Tactics: From Troy to Stalingrad* (Boston: Houghton, Mifflin, 1943).

Wolf, John. *The Emergence of the Great Powers, 1685–1715* (New York: Harpers, 1951).

Wood, Gordon S. *The Creation of the American Republic, 1776–1789* (Chapel Hill, N.C.: Univ. of North Carolina Press, 1969).

Wright, Louis B., et al. *The Arts in America: The Colonial Period* (New York: Charles Scribner's, 1966).

Young, Alfred, ed. *The American Revolution: Explorations in the History of American Radicalism* (DeKalb, Ill.: Northern Illinois Univ. Press 1976).

Zampaglione, Gerardo. *The Idea of Peace in Antiquity* (South Bend, Ind.: Notre Dame Univ. Press, 1973).

Zook, David H. and Higham, Robin. *A Short History of Warfare* (New York: Twayne, 1966).

Journal Articles

Akers, Charles W. "Religion and the American Revolution: Samuel Cooper and the Brattle Street Church." *WMQ*, 3d Ser., 35 (July 1978) Pp. 477–98.

Archer, Adair. "The Quaker's Attitude towards the Revolution." *WMQ*, 2d Ser., 1 (July 1921) Pp. 167–82.

Axtell, James. "The Scholastic Philosophy of the Wilderness." *WMQ*, 3d Ser. 29 (July 1972) Pp. 335–66.

Bernath, Stuart. "George Washington and the Genesis of American Military Discipline." *Mid-America* 59 (April 1967) Pp. 83–100.

Breen, Timothy H. "English Origins and New World Development: The Case of the Covenanted Militia in Seventeenth-Century Massachusetts." *PP* 57 (November 1972) Pp. 74–96.

———. "Persistent Localism: English Social Change and the Shaping of New England Institutions." *WMQ*, 3d Ser. 32 (January 1975) Pp. 3–28.

Buffinton, Arthur A. "The Puritan View of War." CSM *Publications* 28 (Trans. 1930–1933) Pp. 67–86.

Cometti, Elizabeth. "Women in the American Revolution." *NEQ* 20 (December 1947) Pp. 329–46.

Craven, Wesley Frank. "Indian Policy in Early Virginia." *WMQ*, 3d Ser. 1 (January 1944) Pp. 65–82.

Eccles, W. J. "Frontenac's Military Policies, 1689–1698: A Reassessment." *Canadian Historical Review* 37 (September 1956) Pp. 201–24.

Eisenger, Chester E. "The Puritan's Justification for Taking the Land." *Essex Institute Historical Collections* 84 (April 1948) Pp. 131–43.

Ferling, John E. "The American Revolution and American Security: Whig and Loyalist Views." *The Historian* 60 (May 1978) Pp. 492–507.

Gipson, Lawrence H. "The American Revolution as an Aftermath of the Great War for Empire, 1754–1763." *Political Science Quarterly* 65 (March 1950) Pp. 86–104.

Greene, Jack P. "The South Carolina Quartering Dispute." *South Carolina History Magazine* 60 (October 1959) Pp. 304–19.

Hamilton, Edward P. "Colonial Warfare in North America." MHS, *Proceedings* 80 (1969) Pp. 3–15.

Hale, J. R. "Sixteenth Century Explanations of War and Violence." *PP* 51 (May 1971) Pp. 3–26.

Henretta, James A. "Economic Development and Social Structure in Colonial Boston." *WMQ*, 3d Ser. 22 (January 1965) Pp. 75–92.

Jennings, Francis. "Virgin Land and Savage People." *AQ* 23 (October 1971) Pp. 519–41.

Jorgensen, Paul. "Elizabethan Religious Literature for Time of War." *Huntington Library Quarterly* 37 (November 1973) Pp. 3–21.

Kohn Richard H. "War as Revolution and Social Process." *Reviews in American History* 5 (March 1977) Pp. 56–61.

Kulikoff, Alan. "The Progress of Inequality in Revolutionary Boston." *WMQ*, 3d Ser. 28 (July 1971) Pp. 375–412.

Lanning, John Tate. "The American Colonies in the Preliminaries of the War of Jenkins' Ear." *GHQ* 11 (June 1927) Pp. 129–55.

Leach, Douglas E. "The Military System of Plymouth Colony." *NEQ* 24 (September 1951) Pp. 342–64.

Lofgren, Charles A. "Compulsory Military Service under the Constitution: The Original Understanding." *WMQ*, 3d Ser. 38 (January 1976) Pp. 61–88.

McCoy, Drew R. "Benjamin Franklin's Vision of a Republican Political Economy for America." *WMQ*, 3d Ser. 35 (October 1978) Pp. 605–28.

Mackesy, Piers. "British Strategy in the War of American Independence." *The Yale Review* 52 (1963) Pp. 539–57.

Mahon, John K. "Anglo-American Methods of Indian Warfare, 1676–1794." *MVHR* 45 (September 1958) Pp. 254–75.

Maier, Pauline. "Popular Uprisings and Civil Authority in Eighteenth-Century America." *WMQ,* 3d Ser. 27 (January 1970) Pp. 3–35.

Malone, Patrick. "Changing Military Technology Among the Indians of Southern New England, 1600–1677." *AQ* 25 (March 1973) Pp. 48–63.

Maurer, Maurer. "Military Justice under George Washington." *MA* 27 (Spring 1964) Pp. 3–18.

Morton, Louis. "The Origins of American Military Policy." *MA* 22 (Summer 1958) Pp. 75–82.

Nash, Gerald. "The Image of the Indians in the Southern Colonial Mind." *WMQ,* 3d Ser. 24 (April 1972) Pp. 197–230.

Ousterhout, Anne M. "Pennsylvania Land Confiscations During the Revolution." *PMHB* 102 (July 1978) Pp. 328–43.

Papenfuse, Edward C. and Stiverson, Gregory A. "General Smallwood's Recruits: The Peacetime Career of the Revolutionary War Private." *WMQ,* 3d Ser. 30 (January 1973) Pp. 117–32.

Pargellis, Stanley. "Braddock's Defeat." *AHR* 41 (January 1936) Pp. 253–69.

Powell, William S. "Aftermath of the Massacre: The First Indian War, 1622–1632." *VMHB* 46 (January 1958) Pp. 44–75.

Pugh, Robert. "The Revolutionary Militia in the Southern Campaign, 1780–1781." *WMQ,* 3d Ser. 14 (April 1957) Pp. 154–75.

Radabaugh, Jack S. "The Militia of Colonial Massachusetts." *MA* 28 (Spring 1954) Pp. 1–18.

Russell, Peter E. "Redcoats in the Wilderness: British Officers and Irregular Warfare in Europe and America, 1740 to 1760." *WMQ,* 3d Ser. 35 (October 1978) Pp. 629–52.

Sharp, Morrison. "Leadership and Democracy in the Early New England System of Defense." *AHR* 50 (January 1945) Pp. 224–60.

von Elbe, Joachim. "The Evolution of the Concept of the Just War in International Law." *AJIL* 33 (October 1939) Pp. 665–88.

Wall, Robert E. "Louisbourg, 1745." *NEQ* 37 (March 1964) Pp. 64–83.

Webb, Stephen Saunders. "Army and Empire: English Garrison Government in Britain and America, 1569–1763." *WMQ,* 3d Ser. 34 (January 1977) Pp. 1–31.

Dissertations

Johnson, Warren B. "The Content of American Colonial Newspapers Relative to International Affairs, 1704–1763." (University of Washington, 1962).

Malone, Patrick K. "Indian and English Military Systems in New England in the Seventeenth Century." (Brown University, Rhode Island, 1971).

Royster, Charles. "The Continental Army in the American Mind, 1775–1783." (University of California, Berkeley, 1978).

Rutman, Darrett B. "A Militant New World." (University of Virginia, 1959).

Stuart, Reginald Charles. "Encounter with Mars: Thomas Jefferson's View of War." (University of Florida, 1974).

White, John Todd. "Standing Armies in Time of War: Republican Theory and Military Practice During the American Revolution." (The George Washington University, District of Columbia, 1978).

Index

About the Author

JOHN E. FERLING is associate professor of history at West Georgia College, Carrollton, Georgia. His earlier works include *The Loyalist Mind: Joseph Galloway and the American Revolution* and *The American Revolution: The Home Front*.